MOTIVATION
AND
EMOTION

Motivation
and Emotion

Evolutionary, Physiological,
Developmental,
and Social Perspectives

Denys A. deCatanzaro
McMaster University
Ontario, Canada

Prentice Hall, Upper Saddle River, New Jersey 07458

Library of Congress Cataloging-in-Publication Data

deCatanzaro, Denys.
   Motivation and emotion: evolutionary, physiological,
  developmental & social perspectives / Denys deCatanzaro.
    p. cm.
  Includes bibliographical references and index.
  ISBN 0-13-849159-3
   1. Motivation (Psychology) 2. Emotions. 3. Psychology,
Comparative. I. Title.
BF503.D425 1999
363.7'0071—dc21   98-7523
                                 CIP

Editor-in-Chief: Nancy Roberts
Executive Editor: Bill Webber
Acquisitions Editor: Jennifer Gilliland
Assistant Editor: Anita Castro
Managing Editor: Bonnie Biller
Editorial/Production Supervision: Alison Gnerre
Art Director: Jayne Conte
Cover Photo: Tony Stone Image
Manufacturing Manager: Nick Sklitsis
Manufacturing Buyer: Tricia Kenny
Marketing Manager: Michael Alread

This book was set in 10/12 Palatino by Pub-Set Inc. and printed and bound by
R.R. Donnelly, Harrisburg. The cover was printed by Phoenix.

 © 1999 by Prentice-Hall, Inc.
Simon & Schuster/A Viacom Company
Upper Saddle River, New Jersey 07458

10 9 8 7 6 5 4 3 2 1

ISBN   0-13-849159-3

Prentice-Hall International (UK) Limited, London
Prentice-Hall of Australia Pty. Limited, Sydney
Prentice-Hall Canada Inc., Toronto
Prentice-Hall Hispanoamericana, S.A., Mexico
Prentice-Hall of India Private Limited, New Delhi
Prentice-Hall of Japan, Inc., Tokyo
Simon & Schuster Asia Pte. Ltd., Singapore
Editora Prentice-Hall do Brasil, Ltda., Rio de Janeiro

to
Elspeth,
Graham,
Rachel,
& Tony

CONTENTS

Chapter 3

Genetics, Learning, and Development   41

Chapter 4

General Physiological Perspective   64

Chapter 5

Thirst, Hunger, and Elimination   88

Chapter 9

Anger, Hate, and Aggression   198

Chapter 10

Happiness, Sadness, and Coping Strategies   218

Chapter 11

Love and Attachment   247

Chapter 12

Motivation to Learn   265

Chapter 13

Conflicts Among Motives   280

Chapter 14

Self, Family, and Community   292

PREFACE

What has motivated me to write this book? Surely, it is a summation or synergy of many factors, personal and circumstantial. I would like to think that a large part was a desire to spread information with intrinsic worth for many people, improving self-understanding, understanding of others, and the ability to cope and succeed.

A wealth of information has surged from several scientific disciplines during the latter half of the 20th century. The general public is only beginning to appreciate this knowledge. There has been a need to collect and synthesize data and ideas from diverse disciplines, including general and developmental psychology, evolutionary theory, neuroscience, endocrinology, and cultural anthropology. I felt that this task had not yet been accomplished.

This has been a mammoth undertaking. The scope of this text includes perhaps half of the field of physiological psychology (other parts include perception, motor behavior, and substrata of learning and cognition). It also encompasses modern evolutionary and sociobiological perspectives, as well as some cultural anthropology and developmental psychology. Arguably, all of this is a very large fraction of modern general psychology. No one person can keep abreast of all developments in these fields, and I apologize for any oversights. With the rapidity of current scientific progress in many relevant disciplines, any text of this sort will some day be outdated.

I am convinced that a broad integration of scientific fields is necessary to understand human motivation and emotion. The traditional academic disciplines that we have inherited have artificially compartmentalized knowledge. No one of them neatly encompasses all of the new data that scientists of many stripes have gathered in recent years. I have tried in this book to be eclectic and integrative, without regard to disciplinary boundaries.

If this book can be said to have a bias, it is toward biology, on the understanding that psychology and social organization are a function of biological beings. I believe that the relevance to motivation and emotion of evolutionary, physiological, and ecological approaches should be self-evident as the book unfolds. Nevertheless, one cannot neglect cultural influences, cognitive processes, analyses from sociopsychological levels, and other human concerns. The general strategy of the book is to proceed from fundamentals of biology, as they structure the behavior of all animals toward self-preservation and reproduction, and to move progressively in latter chapters to more uniquely human emotions and higher-order motivational issues.

The ideas and information in this book rest on the painstaking contributions of thousands of scientists, many of whose names are listed in the References. So, I must thank, first and foremost, all those whose work I cite, plus countless others whose research contributed to their ideas.

My wife, Jennifer deCatanzaro, has made substantial contributions to this work. She made critical comments on all parts of the book. She has helped to collect and process literature, particularly some portions of chapters 8, 10, 11, 13, and 14. Initial drafts on the topics of boredom, thrill-seeking, laughter, play, risks of childbirth, and embarrassment were written by her. She has been very supportive and understanding of my obsession with this project, as have our children, to whom I have dedicated this work.

I have been very fortunate to have paid student assistants, each of them exceptionally competent. Urszula Kosecka skillfully produced the hand-drawn elements of the figures in chapters 4, 7, and 8. Miriam Hansen used her superb library skills to help me track down the most recent scientific papers in several areas, especially those in the second half of the book. Neena Prasad provided able assistance for some of this library research, and both she and Miriam helped with proofreading.

I must thank more than one thousand students in Psychology 3M3 (Motivation and Emotion) at McMaster University. In recent years, their feedback has helped me to know this field even better and to improve my communication skills. Several students have made me aware of pertinent areas of research. Some commented on previous drafts, especially of the first seven chapters. Many took this course when we had no textbook, and encouraged me to proceed with this project in order to fill the gap.

I. Eibl-Eibesfeldt, P. Ekman, T. Field, S. Chevalier-Skolnikoff, J. DeFries, K. Lagerspetz, J.E. Steiner, and A. Tellegen have all given generous permission to reproduce their copyrighted material.

I have given much thought to the professors who most influenced me about 20 years ago, as I began my career. Bruce Pappas taught my undergraduate course in Motivation and Emotion, showing me the path to bio-psychology. I often reflect on how much new information has emerged in intervening years. Brock Fenton taught me animal behavior and sociobiology; I always enjoyed his lectures on evolution and critiques of psychologists of that era. Hymie Anisman mentored some of my earliest research, introducing me to neuroscience and neurochemistry and mice, and showed me just how motivated a scientist could be. Boris Gorzalka mentored my Ph.D. research in a kind and supportive manner, and taught me all about hormones and brain chemistry and reproductive behavior. John Pinel taught graduate-level biopsychology with insight and enthusiasm, and encouraged my career in teaching and research.

I must thank several people from Prentice Hall. In particular, I thank Ralph Courtney and Pete Janzow for the invitation to write this book, Bill Webber and Jennifer Gilliland for their encouragement while I completed it, and Alison Gnerre for her superb work as production editor. I also thank Ilene Kalish, Tamsen Adams, Anita Castro, and any others who have contributed but remained nameless to me. You have all been consistently friendly and supportive, and have helped to ensure the high quality of this book. Prentice Hall solicited reviews from several of my peers who teach Motivation and Emotion at other institutions for the initial outline of the book. In addition, four reviewers (including Randy D. Fisher, University of Central Florida; Diane K. Gjerde, Western Washington University; Norman G. Gordon, Eastern Michigan University; and Jaak Panksepp, Bowling Green State University) provided extensive commentaries on an earlier draft of this book. These comments have provided invaluable advice.

Denys A. deCatanzaro

Chapter 1

HISTORY AND OVERVIEW

We all know motivation and emotion subjectively. People report internal sensations that we call feelings, moods, and emotions. Some of these sensations can change from moment to moment, and others may vary over the longer term. They relate to our thoughts and experiences, and they drive us to actions that shape our lives. We can feel hungry and thirsty, cravings for specific foods, or the need to eliminate. These feelings can drive us to cook, seek food, plant crops, and work for money that lets us buy food. We can feel heat, cold, fatigue, or wear on our bodies, driving us to work for comfortable homes. Often we endure work that brings immediate discomfort but ultimately produces benefits that enhance our comfort. We can feel strongly attracted to other individuals or we can dislike them, driving us to seek or avoid relationships, potentially promoting reproduction or aggression. Mere words of praise or criticism from other people can lift or lower our moods and change our actions.

Our emotions and drives are inextricably linked. Motivation generally refers to our impulses to behave to alter or sustain the course of life, by seeking survival, growth, reproduction, social advancement, or changes in finer aspects of our relationship to nature and other people. Emotions usually refer to internal sensations of individuals, generally in association with physiological events that respond to events in life. The distinction is not always clear, because emotions respond to progress in achieving goals and they often motivate action. Both motivation and emotion have profound biological aspects, as well as psychological and social dimensions. Thus, the two topics are best considered together.

The Scope of This Work

This book will discuss human motivation and emotion from a scientific perspective. Surely, we all want to understand drives and feelings in ourselves and other people. I hope to make it clear that a modern scientific approach, when compared to other philosophical perspectives, is the most valid, practical, and in tune with modern common sense.

This text will discuss several scientific perspectives on motivation and emotion, ranging from those that are biological, including evolutionary and physiological, to those that are psychological, social, and cultural. All of these levels of analysis have to be considered to give a complete picture. They have to be integrated and balanced. In my view, these different levels of analysis do not compete with one another, but rather explain different aspects of our drives and emotions.

Most of us are interested primarily in people. However, we can often learn about ourselves by examining other species, especially in this area of science. Even plants and microorganisms are driven to survive and reproduce! We can especially learn by studying other mammals, because many basic features of human motivation reflect neuroendocrine and behavioral adaptations that occurred long before our own species evolved. We will see the roots of some of our emotions and associated body language in other primates. At the same time, human beings are obviously very special among species in intelligence, modes of learning, behavioral flexibility, and culture. We will consider many unique human qualities, directly in our drives and emotions, and indirectly in higher cognitive and cultural processes that often compete with emotions in controlling our actions.

This past century has brought enormous progress in scientific understanding of motivation and emotion, and the last few decades of research have been especially productive. This progress has come from many directions. Evolutionary theory and studies of animal behavior have shown the origins of motivational processes, emotions, and body language. There has also been extensive research into the neural and hormonal substrata of emotions. It is now possible to identify specific neural and biochemical processes that underlie variation in drives and moods. There are also rich new data from psychosocial and cross-cultural studies.

Prescientific Notions

Throughout history, people have attempted to understand themselves. Emotions are associated with strong internal feelings. In many intense emotions, we feel our hearts race and our breathing accelerate. In fear, for example, we may also feel a paralysis or a strong tendency to flee. In elation we may be bouncing with energy and very talkative. Hunger, coldness, sexual arousal, and many other sensations are felt internally. Introspecting, or look-ing within ourselves, directly provides some idea about drives and emotions. Common sense and most philosophical systems have always had much to say about human motivation and emotion.

According to anthropologists, many people in preliterate, prescientific cultures understood their own feelings and others' motivation in terms of *animism*. Animism is the attribution of spirits to humans, other animals, and even plants, natural forces, and abstract concepts (McDougall, 1911; Tylor, 1871). The blanket attribution of animistic belief to all primitive peoples has been criticized, as has the vagueness of the concept (Bohannan, 1963). Never-theless, examples of such beliefs have been reported for many cultures, espe-cially African and Amerindian cultures prior to modern influences, and such beliefs may persist in poorly educated persons in many cultures (Capps, 1976; Douglas, 1975). The vitality of living beings and nature is explained by spirits, whereas objects that do not move are "inanimate." At death, anima-tion withdraws from a body, but vivid memories may remain in survivors, such that they may "see" the spirit of the deceased as "present" without the active body. This is, of course, the common idea of ghosts. Dreams, memory, and sensory reality may be confused. People may not accurately discrimi-nate between internal emotional sensations and external reality. For exam-ple, Roth (1915) reported that Guyana Indians saw spirits in their feelings and dreams, and also in the bush, mountains, water, and sky. The immortal spirits in the body could "change skins," rising after death to the sky.

In ancient Greek mythology, the gods were seen as controlling or at least representing human emotions (Stassinopoulos & Beny, 1983). Ares was the em-bodiment of aggression, war, and strife, but Athena defended and protected in war. Hades was the god of death, also bringing us depression, anxiety, and grief. Hera was jealousy itself: bitter, frustrated, raging, and resentful. Aphrodite was the goddess of beauty and love. Dionysos was the god of music, dance, ecstasy, and wine, liberating the individual from too much rea-son and control. Artemis was the goddess of wild, untrammelled freedom. Zeus, on the other hand, was the personification of order, principle, con-sciousness, and strategy.

Without much knowledge of physiology, emotional sensations such as a fast-beating heart may be misconstrued. When ancient peoples did ascribe thoughts and feelings to physiology rather than spirits, the heart was cited more often than the brain. In the King James version of Genesis (6:4–8), "God saw that the wickedness of man was great and that every imagination of the thoughts of his heart was only evil continually," and "it repenteth the Lord that he had made man on the earth and it grieved him at his heart." These statements ascribe emotions to the deity as well as to humans. In Matthew (15:19,20), we learn that "out of the heart proceed evil thoughts, murders, adulteries, fornications, thefts, false witness, blasphemies; these are the things which defile a man."

Animistic ideas linger in common language today. We are in good spirits when circumstances are fine, or dispirited when circumstances are bad. An excited person is said to be animated. Many people still believe that a spirit leaves the body at death. Cruel people are said to be heartless, while kind people are said to be good-hearted or soft-hearted. If you are mistreated by a hard-hearted person, you may feel heartache or even heartbroken. In Barry Goldwater's 1964 American presidential campaign, the slogan was, "In your heart, you know he's right."

In the past, unusual motivation and emotion was often explained as possession by evil spirits. In Mark (9:17–29), Christ encountered a boy with a "deaf and dumb spirit," which "teareth him: and he foameth, and gnasheth with his teeth, and pineth away" and "hath cast him into the fire, and into the waters, to destroy him." Although the spirit was said to be exorcised, previous attempts by disciples had failed because "This kind can come forth by nothing, but by prayer and fasting." Today, of course, most psychologists would ascribe such deafness, aphasia, and child schizophrenia to sensory, neurological, and developmental abnormalities. Animistic beliefs and practices of exorcism were found in Europe during the Middle Ages and persisted in early North American colonies. Following Exodus (22:18), "Thou shalt not suffer a witch to live," witches were hunted and tortured, especially during the 15th to 17th centuries. At the time, the philosophical and religious systems which prevailed also recognized rationalism and "free will," that a person is free to choose any course of action, and is responsible for actions even if they are unwise or immoral. Thus, burning, drowning, crushing, and the like were inflicted on countless individuals, either to destroy the physical vessel inhabited by devils or to make it totally inhospitable for those devils, and to punish the person for allowing them to enter.

The philosophical view that the human mind is separate from biology has persisted, even to the present day for some people. As science began to show the mechanisms of the body, higher human intelligence and subjective experience were still viewed as distinct from these mechanisms. This view is epitomized in the work of the philosopher Descartes (1596–1650), who tried to reconcile physiology and spirituality through *dualism*. Descartes suggested that human conduct was mediated through complex interactions of mind and body. He argued that passions may arise from mind or body and determine action. He spoke of hunger and sexual desire from the body, and joy and anger from the mind. Nevertheless, he preserved the idea of the mind as a soul that inhabits the physical body. Interestingly, Descartes was so bold as to assert that the pineal, a small gland in the center of the brain, was the seat of the interface of mind and spirit. He argued that its central location and absence of known functions made it the probable site of this interface. Although this notion is hardly supported by modern science, we now know much more about the pineal's functions, which paradoxically may influence our moods, or what people loosely call our "spirits."

One still hears dualistic ideas today, often based on religion, and there are many current ideas about matters that go beyond the scope of science. We will see throughout this text that, as scientific understanding has developed, progressively fewer aspects of our sensations, drives, and emotions are left unexplained by concrete factors of biology and psychological development.

Early Scientific Ideas

To see the origins of scientific inquiry, we actually have to look back to more than 2,000 years ago to ancient Greece, to ideas that subsequently lay dormant until the Renaissance. Socrates (*c.* 470–399 B.C.) taught that virtue was knowledge, placing emphasis on rational argument in the search for definitions. His pupil, Plato (*c.* 428–347 B.C.) founded the Academy in Athens, which has often been described as the first university, wherein astronomy, mathematics, biology, political theory, and philosophy were discussed. Plato was convinced that knowledge was attainable, and that true knowledge must be certain and infallible. Plato suggested that the human soul was divided into three parts: the rational part, the will, and the appetites. Meanwhile, the first psychobiological theory of motivation and emotion was put forward by Hippocrates (*c.* 460–370 B.C.). Hippocrates saw the brain as the organ of human intellect, and he viewed mental illness and very odd behavior as physical pathology of the brain. His descriptions included three general moods: mania, melancholia, and phrenitis or brain illness. He saw these and other moods as the result of balances among four "humors" in the body, those being blood, black bile, yellow bile, and phlegm. For example, a sluggish person was viewed as phlegmatic, a melancholy person dominated by black bile, a volatile or moody person controlled by blood, and an irascible person influenced by yellow bile. Although we can hardly uphold his specific scheme through modern scientific evidence, there is a gist to this perspective that corresponds to the view we will see in this book. Plato's pupil, Aristotle (*c.* 384–322 B.C.), also deserves special credit for sowing the seeds of scientific progress. He developed rules for chains of logic that laid the foundations of the scientific method, and he placed primary emphasis on biology.

Much of the development of modern science can be traced to post-Renaissance European thinkers. Bacon (1561–1626) believed that "nothing is beneath science, nor above it." He insisted that human judgment and human behavior are natural phenomena that can be studied. He felt that the Greek philosophers spent too much time on theory, and too little on observation. Hobbes (1588–1679) took a mechanistic and naturalistic view of human nature. He attempted to lay the foundations of a scientific view of society, by applying principles of physical science to human beings. He proposed a comprehensive theory of human motivation based on the principle of *hedonism*. Essentially, the idea of hedonism is that we behave purely in ways which will bring pleasure or avoid pain. Hobbes extended this to the political realm, arguing that people naturally fear one another, and that competition arises only when one person's desires conflict with those of another. Locke (1632–1704) founded the school of *empiricism*, which today is viewed as being at the essence of science. This emphasizes the importance of concrete information that is readily available to the five senses. All knowledge, in this view, is to be built upon sensory experience that we all share, rather than intuitive speculation. Nevertheless, Locke went beyond his data base to speculate that people were born with a blank state of mind, or *tabula rasa*, and that all knowledge and behavior were built through experience.

Physiology

We now know a great deal about the physiological mechanisms that underlie primary drives and emotions. There has been enormous progress in this realm, especially during the 20th century.

The first studies of animal physiology were probably undertaken by Herophilis of Alexandria (*c.* 300 B.C.), who reportedly vivisected the bodies of criminals. For about 1,900 years thereafter, the science of physiology remained dormant. In the 16th century, Vesalius once again described human anatomy in detail. Modern animal physiology was further stimulated by the discovery of the circulation of the blood by Harvey in 1616. In the 17th century, the development of the microscope led to descriptions of red blood cells and spermatozoa by van Leeuwenhoek, demonstrations of existence of capillaries and descriptions of the histology of major organs by Malpighi, identification of biological cells by Hooke, and descriptions of ovarian follicles by de Graaf. The 18th century saw, among many other achievements, the modern classification of organisms developed by Linnaeus. In the 19th century, Bernard advanced physiology by describing carbohydrate metabolism and the autonomic nervous system, and put forward the notion that the body seeks to maintain internal equilibrium, or *homeostasis*. Among many other noteworthy achievements of that century were descriptions of the nervous system by Bell, Magendie, and Flourens.

Cannon (1915) provided some of the first descriptions of bodily changes during simpler emotions. He described the adrenal gland and adrenaline, acting in conjunction with the sympathetic portion of the *autonomic nervous system*, as active during emergencies and many emotions. He also described some of the mechanisms of hunger (Cannon & Washburn, 1912), although we know today that his explanation was incomplete. Cannon further advanced the concept of homeostatic mechanisms, or mechanisms maintaining equilibrium as described by Bernard. Departures from homeostasis were seen as motivating the organism to action, an idea which persists today with respect to some simpler aspects of motivation.

As discussed below, the latter part of the 20th century has brought an enormous amount of new knowledge, with countless individuals making contributions. Understanding of human physiology has fed the notion of the human body as an adapted mechanism. There has been progressively less of human psychological functioning left that cannot be accounted for by physiology, diminishing the plausibility of explanations involving "spirits."

Evolution

Human naiveté, and indeed our conceit, once viewed earth as the center of the universe and larger than the sun and stars. Human beings viewed themselves as spirits above nature albeit below God. Formal astronomy, as advanced by Copernicus and Galileo, destroyed that view of the universe, while physiology has shown just how much we resemble other animals. Human cells are animal cells as much as are those of a mouse or a cat. The general organization of our internal organs is basically the same as that of any other mammal. We survive and reproduce as do other mammals, and we are driven at the most basic level by the same biological needs. The development of our bodies is determined by DNA just as with other organisms. Indeed, the basic layout of our neural and endocrine systems is very much like those of other mammals.

Humans were placed squarely in nature by the formalization of evolutionary theory by Darwin (1859). He built on the work of other biologists and presented a view that remains at the core of modern biological science. He saw a macroscopic pattern in life, occurring over numerous generations and across species. Individuals within any species show variation in traits. Many of these traits are heritable, capable of being passed from mother and father to son and daughter. Within any generation, only a subset of individuals reproduce. Such differential reproduction can correlate with trait differences, because some traits are more adaptive than others. Accordingly, the frequency of traits within a species can change over generations, conforming to the changing environmental circumstances with which they interact. Separated populations of a species may move in different directions and become separate species.

Darwin (1872) also provided the basis for modern understanding of human emotions. He showed similarities between human emotional body language and that of other mammals. He viewed emotions as evolved rather than learned adaptations. You will see this view preserved and elaborated by modern evidence throughout this book. We will describe the downcast posture of loss, depression, and social subordination, comparing it to the erect posture, smiles, and laughter of happiness and success. We will see the stereotyped facial expressions of surprise, fear, anger, and disgust. Essentially, basic emotions may be viewed as primitive "instincts," adaptations to environmental

and social contingencies that affected our primate forebears and human ancestors. We will argue that simple drives and emotions are crude predispositions to react to life events, shaped by our evolutionary heritage but not
always adaptive in the modern context.

Experimental Psychology, Psychiatry, and Ethology

William James (1890) is viewed as one of the founders of modern experimental psychology. He built on the work of the empiricists, physiologists, and evolutionary theorists to propose a modern psychological science.
He suggested that psychology was far behind the physical sciences, primarily because it is more difficult to view ourselves objectively. He argued that
we must use the most rigorous methods in studying ourselves. This means
an empirical and concrete approach, involving precise definition, measurement, and quantification, and systematic data collection and experimentation. He suggested that we must be skeptical of other people's reports, and
seek replication by independent observers before we confirm any knowledge. He disputed the popular view of humans as motivated by rational intelligence, compared to other animals, which were guided by innate behavior.
Instead, he suggested that people are not as rational as they like to believe,
and in fact may have a richer set of instincts than do other animals. Many of
these instincts, to James, are what we commonly call our emotions. He suggested what has come to be called the James-Lange theory of emotional sensations. This theory essentially states that physiological changes occur during
emotions, and that our subjective experience of these emotions involves
internal sensation of these changes. For example, in many intense emotions,
we feel our hearts race, our breath become shorter, our stomachs tighten, and
our skin tingle.

In another independently developing vein of psychology, using a clinical rather than experimental perspective, Freud (1915) viewed human motivation in terms of instinctual drives. Like James, Freud rejected the notion
that we humans are completely rational, suggesting that rationality is only a
facade and that the true motives of behavior are often subconscious. He said
that instinctual drives cause a continuous production of energy, and that this
energy is in opposition to the stability of the nervous system. Psychic energy,
or libido, was thought to rise until it reached an outlet, like water building
up in an hydraulic system. Freud thought that people learned to attain certain objects or goals that make the discharge of this energy possible. Outlets
of psychic energy through action were thought to be pleasurable. Freud's
work has had substantial impact, but has been criticized by experimental psychologists as being insufficiently empirical, involving hypothetical and un-
measureable ideas. It also was not based on a large data base; instead it was
derived from a small number of case studies.

During the 20th century, an increasing number of researchers addressed human and animal behavior systematically through experimental methods. A major school of thought developed around efforts to unveil the "laws" of learning and motivation, while studying the behavior of animals in controlled laboratory environments. One foundation of this area was Pavlov's (1927) demonstration of conditioned reflexes, which showed that formerly neutral stimuli could come to evoke responses when paired with events that naturally evoke those same reflexes, as ringing a bell could come to elicit salivation in dogs if a bell were previously paired with food. Another foundation was Thorndike's (1911) demonstration that cats would habitually repeat responses that successfully let them escape from a puzzle box. Thorndike suggested that behavior becomes "stamped in" when it is repeatedly followed by a favorable outcome, or "stamped out" if it leads to a negative outcome. These notions are essentially those commonly called reward and punishment.

Subsequent experimental psychologists like Tolman, Guthrie, Hull, and Spence debated concepts of instinct, drive, reward, and incentive while studying the behavior of animals, mostly rats, in puzzles and mazes (see reviews by Bolles, 1967; Nevin & Reynolds, 1973). Hull (1951), in particular developed an extensive theory to explain learning and motivation. Motivation was viewed through the concept of *drive*, which was anchored in the organism's physiological needs. The drive most commonly studied was that induced by several hours of food deprivation. Hull suggested that behavioral changes occur through *reinforcement*, which occurs when an individual organism's response is closely followed in time by a reduction in a drive state, or a reward. Reinforcement was said to cause an increase in frequency of the response that preceded it. According to Hull, a frequently repeated response could form a *habit*, and sometimes habit could become independent of drive.

From this same general school of thought emerged certain radical behaviorists who were especially keen to abandon common-sense language and all of its nonscientific baggage. In trying to follow the best rules of scientific inquiry and empiricism, they reached a point where they rejected many concepts of motivation and emotion that we have since reinstated. The earliest well-known radical behaviorist was Watson (1930), who argued that we must no longer speak of instinct, and that instead we must recognize that all of human behavior is shaped by the environmental contingencies that condition it. Essentially, this was a return to the idea of *tabula rasa*, epitomized in this famous quote (Watson, 1930, p. 104): "Give me a dozen healthy infants, well-formed, and my own specified world to bring them up in and I'll guarantee to take any one at random and train him to become any kind of specialist I might select." Later, in a similar vein, Skinner (1953) argued that motivational and emotional concepts must be discarded in order to purge the discipline of unscientific inferences and imprecise common language. Like Locke and Watson, Skinner attributed virtually all of behavior to shaping by the environment. The central concept to Skinner was reinforcement, the increase in frequency of a response that is followed by a reinforcing stimulus. He argued that we must be strictly descriptive and empirical, dealing only with directly observable stimuli and responses, without looking inside the organism. He argued that we should not speak of "hunger," but instead of food deprivation. According to Skinner, "drive" does not exist; instead, the organism's behavior is controlled by stimuli that consistently precede and follow it. He said that moods and emotions are subjective and introspective notions that would not bear the scrutiny of science. Instead, we must work exclusively with objectively measurable environmental stimuli and concrete responses or behavior. According to Skinner (1953, p. 160), "The emotions are excellent examples of the fictional causes to which we commonly attribute behavior."

Other theorists (e.g., Cofer, 1972; see also Bolles, 1967) argued that we cannot account for human motivation just in terms of reinforcement. Instead, they suggested that intelligent organisms can learn new responses in anticipation of rewards that they have never actually experienced. According to the traditional notion of reinforcement learning, organisms must experience a reward contingent upon their behavior in order for the behavior to increase in frequency. Most of the studies substantiating the notion of reinforcement were conducted with simpler animals like rats and pigeons. *Incentives* are said to operate with more intelligent and sophisticated organisms like ourselves. Intelligent people might perform new responses because they learn, through language, culture, and observation of others, that certain forms of behavior potentially lead to rewards. Accordingly, behavior can be motivated and its frequency can change without any direct experience with rewards and punishers. What is needed is some cognitive representation of the reward or punishers. Numerous experiments by Bandura (1977) have shown how this can occur through imitation, modeling, and social learning. Bandura and his coworkers have repeatedly demonstrated that people's behavior can change merely because they observe other people's behavior. Observation of a response being performed by other people can increase the frequency of the same sort of response in observers.

In their zeal to discard unscientific constructs and build an empirical science of behavior, many learning theorists of the mid-20th century placed concepts of instinct, innate behavior, and emotion in disrepute (see Beach, 1955). However, this narrow view was increasingly challenged by perspectives on behavior from biological sciences, where a quite different view of animal behavior had developed (see Burghardt, 1973). Pure conditioning theories failed to account for many aspects of animal behavior, and were increasingly challenged by researchers trained in biology.

Ethologists, who studied many different animal species in their natural environments, had developed a radically different view of animal behavior. This view did not neglect learning, but emphasized innate species-typical behavioral patterns that had evolved in response to natural selection. Tinbergen (1951) documented how many forms of stereotyped innate behavior were elicited by *sign stimuli*, configurations or events in the environment that have had biological significance to individuals of the species during natural selection. For example, male stickleback fish respond with stereotyped aggressive behavior when they see red markings on other males. These marks are specific to the mating season, and the aggressive behavior can be evoked by crude models with the red marking. Lorenz (1950) spoke of *fixed action patterns (FAPs)*, stereotyped innate behavior patterns that are shaped by natural selection rather than a history of conditioning. Appetitive behavior was said by Lorenz to be a search for a situation in which the FAP could be released, and the performance of the FAP was said to be rewarding. The longer the period of time since the response is elicited, the more readily the response is performed. Like Freud, Lorenz saw an analogy to an accumulation of hydraulic pressure. There could be "vacuum-activities," where the animal would perform the FAP in the absence of any stimulus. Lorenz suggested that the intensity of an act depends on two independent factors, the effectiveness of the stimulus situation and the level of internal motivation.

Even some researchers schooled in Skinnerian principles came to argue that this conventional learning theory was inadequate to account for the motivation of behavior. Breland and Breland (1961) trained animals for advertising and other commercial enterprises, and reported several attempts to train animals using strict principles of conditioning, only to find that unwanted stereotyped or instinctive behavior would intrude. Many other exceptions to conventional "laws" of learning began to emerge from several sources (see the edited volumes of Hinde & Stevenson-Hinde, 1973; Seligman & Hager, 1972, and chapter 3 of this book for more details). For example, Garcia et al. (1966) showed that animals learn to avoid poisons through manners that do not fit the conventional rules of conditioning. Shettleworth (1973) found that grooming behavior in hamsters occurs with a regular frequency regardless of whether it is rewarded. Bolles (1970) found that animals cannot learn arbitrary responses to avoid aversive stimuli like electric shock, but instead are highly predisposed to show responses like fleeing, freezing, or fighting, which Bolles called *species-specific defense reactions*. Thus, during the 1970's many researchers began to suggest that "laws" oversimplify learning, and that some behavior is best explained by natural selection. It came to be understood that biological factors place many constraints on the processes of learning. This gave renewed respectability to concepts of instinct and innate behavior.

Behavioral Genetics, Sociobiology, and Evolutionary Psychology

Another emerging field was aimed at integrating the understanding of genetics and the behavior of humans and other animals. Behavioral genetics had historical roots in the work of Galton (1865), but its modern development is especially attributable to the text of Fuller and Thompson (1960). Individual differences are evident with respect to many traits in animals, both morphological and behavioral. Understanding of genetic inheritance, following the work of Mendel (1866), was more usually applied to morphological features, such as physical size, and shape and color of bodily features. Only recently have we studied genetics in relation to behavior. There is now a wealth of evidence that individual differences in motivational and emotional traits are in part influenced by genetics, and thus are heritable from father and mother to son and daughter. In humans, there is very substantial evidence that aspects of personality, temperament, and intelligence are at least in part heritable. Much of this evidence is well summarized in a volume by Plomin et al. (1990).

A further impetus for conceptual change in the psychology of motivation and emotion came with the publication of Wilson's (1975) book, *Sociobiology*. This volume was a comprehensive review of biologists' studies of social behavior in diverse species, working from simpler species, like colonial aquatic animals and social insects, to more complex organisms, including various social mammals and humans. Most of the book was quite empirical and really just a summary of a vast array of existing research, built on Darwinian and ethological traditions. One of the main issues that has preoccupied researchers in this area is explanation of the balance between selfish and altruistic motivation seen in various aspects of animal behavior. Wilson's book caught the eye of many researchers, including social scientists. Some social scientists reacted with hostility, but others embraced this perspective. Wilson actually said very little about human beings, but where he did, he placed us firmly in the context of other primates and mammals. His review showed the regularities of social behavior patterns as adaptations to ecological demands.

The idea that human emotions and social patterns might have some basis in evolution really was not very radical, because it was clearly present in Darwin's (1872) and James' (1890) work, for example. Part of the adverse reaction from social scientists might be ascribed to the fact that academic structures had traditionally separated social science and science into different streams. Social scientists of that era typically had little training in biology, and developed schemes of understanding without reference to biological sciences. The exception was in some areas of psychology, but as described above, these too had become inbred.

Researchers operating within the sociobiological tradition have collectively proposed a comprehensive theory about the general motivation of organisms. These researchers suggest that natural selection operates upon individual organisms such that they seek to maximize the representation of their genes in future generations. This is the idea of *inclusive fitness maximization*. Organisms individually are said to work to survive to reproductive age, to compete to reproduce, thus maximizing biological fitness, or the representation of their genes in future generations. They are also said to behave nepotistically, that is in ways that promote the reproduction of their kin, who share many of the same genes by common descent. Some of these ideas were particularly advanced by Hamilton (1964), who developed the most commonly cited ideas about how natural selection operates upon traits affecting the welfare of biological relatives.

Today, there has been a resurgence of interest in evolutionary psychology, a term that was once used by James (1890). There is a new fertilization of psychology by ideas from evolutionary biology and ecology, crossing former artificial disciplinary boundaries. We will see throughout this book that most basic human drives and emotions are now viewed as adaptations to ancestral ecology, including social ecology. This perspective applies to hunger, pain, and fear, and limitations to such self-preserving drives. It applies very clearly to reproductive motivation. It helps to explain various strategies of courtship, mating, and nurturance of children. It even helps to explain why some individuals voluntarily forgo reproduction. Many ideas have emerged concerning the relationship of pressures of natural selection to other aspects of motivation and emotion, including jealousy, violence, stress, depression, and suicide.

Neuroscience and Endocrinology

The 20th century has seen an explosion of new data concerning physiological mechanisms underlying motivation and emotion. Modern physiological inquiry is progressing rapidly, uncovering mechanisms behind major motivational and emotional dimensions. Often the evidence is combined with cross-species comparisons, because other mammals share our basic drives and neuroendocrine structures. Physiological perspectives also shed light on evolutionary and developmental issues, because we can identify innate mechanisms at a physiological level.

There are mechanisms in our neural and hormonal systems predisposing toward self-preservation, deeply ingrained in humans and other animals. Thirst, for example, is influenced by the kidney, adrenal gland, and hypothalamus of the brain. Hunger is influenced by numerous factors, including blood glucose levels, activity in the gastrointestinal tract, stress and activity levels, olfactory mechanisms, and the hypothalamus of the brain. Pain perception is structured by sensory nerves throughout the body, which pass information to the thalamus of the brain through the spinal cord, but it can be dramatically altered by experience, context, and hormones. Fear has a substrate in the sympathetic nervous system, the adrenal glands, and the hypothalamus and amygdala of the brain.

There are also physiological mechanisms behind reproductive motivation. Hormonal differences between males and females are found in the patterns of activity of the hypothalamus, the pituitary gland, and the ovaries or testes. The female pattern involves cycling of estrogens and progesterone, whereas the male pattern involves a simpler dynamic of androgens. The hypothalamus contains regions that differ between the two sexes, and these regions are known to play important roles in sexual drives. During pregnancy and nursing, there are dramatic hormonal changes in women that can influence motivation and emotion. Some modern data suggest reasons individuals of either gender vary in sexual orientation and degree of reproductive motivation. Motivational processes change with the life span, from juvenile development through reproductive years and into the postreproductive period. They also change according to circumstances.

We will see how parts of the autonomic nervous system are active during the strong internal sensations we call emotions. The sympathetic portion of the autonomic nervous system fires in emotions like fear, anger, and elation; the parasympathetic portion brings us back to a resting state. The adrenal glands (actually the center or *medulla* portion of these glands) act during intense emotions in conjunction with the sympathetic portion. In long-term stress, other parts of the adrenal glands (the *cortex* or outer portion of each gland) help us to cope with stress by changing brain and body chemistry and metabolism. The chemistry of the body and brain vary with psychological stress. The body can redirect its resources away from vegetative processes, altering our appetites and reproductive drives, favoring instead defensive activities, mental alertness, and muscular energy. It can reverse these processes when circumstances are more relaxed.

The hypothalamus and limbic system of the brain are dynamically involved in hunger, thirst, fear, aggression, and reproductive motivation. These brain structures interface with chemical systems, both as hormonal systems involving the pituitary, adrenals, gonads, pineal, and other glands, and as neurochemical systems in the brain. Chemical dynamics of the blood, cerebrospinal fluid, and many tiny synapses between neurons in the brain alter our motivation and mood. They are responsive to diet, health, and psychological as well as social circumstances. Chemicals like serotonin, melatonin, norepinephrine, and endorphins play roles in our moods and motivational states. There is a stereotyped basis for emotions such as happiness and sadness in neurochemistry and the limbic system of the brain. Such evidence suggests innateness of this emotional dimension, without contradicting the importance of psychosocial circumstances. The brain's chemistry changes in dynamic manners in response to our life experiences.

We have come a long way from the simple stimulus-response psychology that characterized learning theory of the first part of the 20th century, where the organism was simply identified as a black box between stimulus and response. Physiologists have rapidly been filling in the mysteries of the black box. Many of the processes uncovered have given new respectability to concepts of drive, instinct, and emotion. We will see how it is the evolutionarily older hormonal and neural systems that especially relate to motivation and emotion. We humans have these areas in common with other mammals. These older systems are more important for understanding motivation and emotion than is the human cerebral cortex, which we view as the seat of our advanced learning, cognition, and intelligence. Nevertheless, we must carefully consider our unique human intelligence in this book. This is because motivation for intelligent and mature animals can originate from high-order cognitive processes as well as more primitive subcortical impulses. Modern humans are often confronted with conflicts between rational and emotional impulses in driving motivation.

Modern research in neuroscience is progressing very rapidly. Where previously we had only ideas about brain processes, we can now gain images of human neurological functioning in specific areas of the brain in conjunction with psychological events, through technologies such as Positron Emission Tomography (PET) and Magnetic Resonance Imaging (MRI). Histological techniques, employing immunoreactive proteins like *c-fos*, are being developed to label the brain for molecular changes that accompany ongoing behavior in laboratory animals. Genetic engineering with laboratory animals is permitting new insights into genetic substrata of physiology and behavior. Continuing technological advances of this sort mean that descriptions of neurological substrata of drives and emotions, as we are able to characterize at present in this book, will undoubtedly be surpassed by future descriptions.

Cultural Perspectives

One of the weaknesses of 20th century psychology was an excessive focus on culture-specific phenomena, with extensive use of the most convenient subject, the American college student. According to Burghardt (1973, p. 324), "most psychologists have concentrated on only a few types of behavior and have studied a surprisingly limited number of organisms, the most common being the highly domesticated white rat and the white college sophomore." The impact of ethology has been to broaden our focus to include more species and forms of behavior. Cross-cultural psychology, integrating anthropology and psychobiology, together with the globalization of the scientific enterprise, promise to broaden the diversity of subjects that we study.

We must give full recognition to our species' unique intellect. We are a highly social species whose culture is anything but static. Our adaptations have changed substantially during our own lifetimes, and certainly have been rapidly transformed by technological and social changes over the past century. Much of this comes from "cultural evolution," which builds upon the flexibility that comes with our unique learning ability and cognitive intelligence, communicated socially through language and imitation. We often override our primitive emotions on the basis of higher reasoning. This may sometimes put us in conflict with ourselves. If each of us acted on every emotion of fear, anger, or sexual arousal, we might end up in serious trouble. We are actively taught to inhibit many emotional impulses in modern society.

Indeed, in later chapters we will discuss how this may have been essential for civilization, and how our emotions may often be better understood as adaptations to ancestral conditions, which sometimes have a poor fit with modern circumstances.

Not all cultures have exactly the same view of human drives and emotions. Most linguists and bilingual persons are aware that there are many subtle nuances that cannot always be translated. For example, English-speaking people all seem to know what it means to be "bored," and may not necessarily feel "annoyed" when they are bored. However, the French term *ennuyé* can mean bored or annoyed depending on the context. Although terms related to primary drives and emotions like hunger, thirst, fear, anger, joy, or sadness are found in all languages, whole linguistic cultures may have subtly different ways of describing the finer qualities of emotions. New terms, like *stressed-out* or *hung-up*, may arise in the vernacular, describing subtle variations in moods that might not be fully captured by conventional language, although these terms are also surely somewhat vague.

Nevertheless, some of the most interesting data that we will review show that some of the fundamental features of body language and facial expression are constant across cultures, despite these cultural and linguistic nuances. There is evidence that a grimace or grin has largely the same meaning in the United States, Japan, Europe, and even New Guinea. A fearful face can be read with accuracy by different individuals across many cultures. On the other hand, we can identify a number of gestures that are culture-specific. Through careful comparison, we can use cross-cultural data of this sort to address fundamental issues of human nature, gaining greater understanding of the causes of variation in motivation and emotion.

Scientific Methods

Science has progressed by discarding preconceptions from earlier philosophical systems, then rebuilding knowledge employing the strictest methods. There are assumptions in the philosophy of science which can be questioned, such as the heavy emphasis on empiricism. However, empiricism is validated by the fact that it leads to greater consensus than do more subjective alternatives. We rely on observations that can be made visible to any rational observer. People generally agree about concrete, directly observable events, but are much more likely to disagree about abstract and interpretive statements. One can generally reach a complete consensus, for example, about whether the sun is visible, or about the number of people within a defined small room. People are less likely to agree about whether the weather is pleasant, or about whether other people in the room are anxious.

Experience has proven that we can build on concrete observations about which there is consensus. We can produce precise statements about magnitude by careful measurement and quantification. Rather than simply rank-ordering the size of three men by our impressions, we can measure their height and weight and specify size with precision. We can progress to more complex concepts and abstractions provided that we pin these abstractions down to sets of concrete observations. This means *operational definition*, or definition in terms of the concrete steps taken to measure something. For example, *anxiety* is a vague and abstract term. You might relate to this term somewhat differently from the way I do, because my subjective experiences of anxiety probably differ to some extent from yours. Accordingly, we cannot fully communicate by using such terms without more careful definition. However, it might be possible to pin down the idea by some recipe that combines concrete, measurable observations. For example, concrete measures of heart rate, blood pressure, adrenal hormone levels, perspiration, or fidgeting could be used as physiological indices. Concrete measures of verbal statements expressing fear or avoidance of specific events or things, or even verbal expressions related to impending doom, might similarly be defined and measured. We could describe an inventory of anxiety on a basis that could be published and used world-wide, allowing more precise communication and standardization. This is much better than if each observer simply uses his or her own subjective impressions.

Any modern language, such as English, is full of terms that are abstract, vague, and interpretive. This is especially true of the vocabulary applied to human motivation and emotion. When we restrict ourselves to such terms, we can communicate, but there is a large measure of imprecision. Happiness to me and you may mean somewhat different things. My experiences of embarrassment, seen in others or myself, may be similar to yours but not entirely the same, or perhaps you are one of those people who has no subjective experience with this emotion. I cannot directly feel what you feel as pain, or anguish, or joy, or remorse. I can hear your statements about these feelings, and try to relate them to my own feelings. We can vaguely communicate on this basis, but this is inadequate for science.

You will see everyday words regarding primary and universal drives and emotions used as chapter and section headings in this book, because I believe that there is a gist in most of these terms that can be scientifically validated. We will see evidence that there are definable reactions in people that relate to most everyday emotional terms. Nevertheless, beyond the most general of topic headings, use of such everyday terms will be abandoned as we discuss details, in favor of precise concrete descriptions with a higher order of scientific communication value.

Modern science has progressed with structured methods of inquiry involving the development of hypotheses, which are then tested through systematic observation and carefully controlled experimentation. Any hypothesis survives or falls on the basis of concrete data. The publication of data is critical, because it allows for scrutiny by others around the world. A scientist should be able, through careful description of methods and measures, to provide a clear recipe for others to make the same observations. Skeptical treatment of sensational new findings is appropriate and constructive. Published data can survive or perish under the scrutiny of other researchers who attempt replication. The history of science is littered with theories and conceptualizations that have subsequently been abandoned or refined. There is no unchallengeable authority in science, and international scrutiny has revealed imperfections in the postulations of many of the greatest names, from Aristotle to Freud. This is in contrast to the prescientific spread of information, which often depended on the method of prophesy. The words of seemingly wiser leaders, from Confucius to Moses, have gathered followers and often been treated as infallible. Many teachers have pronounced on the root causes of the universe and made statements about how people should be motivated, and which emotions and behaviors are appropriate. No matter what we as individuals today might think about their teachings, the methods differ from those of science. In scientific approaches, we cannot accept information just because it is given by a prominent spokesperson, and any theory rises or falls on the basis of factual evidence.

The true measure of science's value comes from overwhelming evidence that it improves our understanding of nature. It is obvious that the scientific era has brought unprecedented progress in knowledge and technology. I am confident that a careful reading of the subsequent chapters of this book will convince you that scientific perspectives also give us greater insight into human motivation and emotion than do any alternative perspectives.

Let me conclude this introduction by suggesting that the only proper perspective on human motivation and emotion is one which is eclectic, drawing the best information from diverse fields. In looking at the history of ideas, it seems obvious that many obsolete theories were developed on the basis of a very limited scope, without adequate breadth and communication with other fields. While integrating disparate fields, we must scrutinize all data to be sure that the highest scientific standards have been met. It is my intention to attempt an integration of modern scientific perspectives on motivation and emotion, treating the different levels of analysis as congruous and complementary.

Chapter 2

THE EVOLUTION OF MOTIVATION AND EMOTION

Let us consider the broadest perspective that we can take. An evolutionary perspective gives a general theory of the nature of motivation, and it also suggests how specific emotions serve such motivation. The idea of evolution is not new, and it did not begin with Charles Darwin. Probably very few people would dispute that life on earth has changed and progressed, for better or worse, over time. Nevertheless, until Darwin described the mechanism of natural selection, intergenerational change and species development were not properly understood.

We have always been confined in our view of nature, if only because our lifespans are short. It is impossible to observe the processes of life as they change over thousands or millions of years. Western conceptualization of human behavior has also been distracted by the competing idea of relatively instant creation, taken for example from literal interpretation of the biblical stories of Genesis. Nevertheless, the notion that humans are related to other life, and indeed that all of life might be of common origin, also came before Darwin (see Eiseley, 1958). Darwin's work formalized our understanding of biological evolution, by describing the mechanism of natural selection. This provided a conceptualization of life that is widely accepted in the scientific community as a central tenet of biology.

Grand explanations of the whole nature of life (and the universe) may be proven highly pretentious in the long run. No one really knows the whole story, and we still need research. There are competing ideas about the origins of life, about whether evolution has occurred gradually or in leaps and bounds, and about many of the details. Nevertheless, the general mechanism of evolutionary change described by Darwin has survived in scientific thought for almost a century and a half. Today we know much more than ever about the development of life on earth, and about how evolution has shaped human nature.

Darwin described a process of gradual change in the characteristics of species. Individuals differ in heritable traits and only a subset of each generation reproduces. Species differentiate because various barriers discourage interbreeding; the characteristics of subpopulations begin to differ in response to drift and ecological distinctness. Adaptations, in terms of physiological features and behavior, evolve over generations in conformation with features of the natural environment. Darwin did not know about genetics, but instead worked from a rough sense that traits are heritable. Today, we know much more about genetics, from the pioneering work of Mendel through modern molecular and population genetics. This has complemented our understanding of natural selection by explaining the mechanism of inheritance.

Evolution is Evident in Common Observations

Individual humans obviously differ from one another with respect to many traits. It is also fairly obvious that there is resemblance within families. Among close relatives we still see many individual differences, but some characteristics tend to be found in common. Many traits are passed from mother and father to son and daughter, albeit imperfectly because each individual is a unique recombination of genes. Variation among individuals and "family" resemblance are also commonly observed in domesticated species. Indeed, modern genetics has produced a large amount of formal evidence that variation and heritability are general rules within plant and animal species.

All living things tend to reproduce in numbers that exceed those necessary for mere replacement of existing numbers. For the population to remain constant, each two parents would produce two offspring. In many insects there is an extreme departure from this; a single pair can produce thousands of eggs. If numbers were unchecked by other factors, the earth would be quickly coated in houseflies. A pair of house mice can produce far more offspring than necessary for replacement. A healthy female can have litters of 6 to 12 pups and can produce over ten litters in a lifetime. Accordingly, mice also have the potential for exponential population growth. We humans are much more conservative in our reproduction, especially in modern times. However, in the absence of birth control, a healthy couple can often produce as many as 6 to 10 children.

Nevertheless, in most circumstances and species, population numbers are stable or cyclical. Not all offspring can survive to reproductive age. The majority of houseflies and mice succumb to predation, disease, starvation, or harsh elements in their environments. Only a small subset survives and finds the resources of food and shelter necessary to reproduce. Indeed, within any species, some individuals reproduce more than do others. In humans, this is an obvious fact, with some persons having large numbers of children while others have none. Part of this variance in reproductive success within any species, including humans, is due to competition for limited resources of food and shelter.

Some of the genetic traits that vary among individuals have a bearing upon whether individuals reproduce. Examples of probable results of selection abound in nature. Flies that are alert to looming objects and poised to flee quickly are less likely to be swatted by human hands or horses' tails than are their slower cousins. Indeed, any potential prey that effectively hides or escapes may live to see another day, while the slow and conspicuous will perish. Faster and more cunning predators more readily catch the prey. Humans with greater intelligence may more effectively master their challenging environments. Thus, not all individuals make it to reproductive age, or have the strength and resources to reproduce if they do reach adulthood, partly depending on their individual characteristics.

The real key to natural selection is reproduction. Any heritable trait which fosters reproduction potentially makes copies of itself for future generations. Survival is a necessary condition for this, but it is not sufficient. Reproduction also requires a willing mate, food resources for fertility and nursing of young, and good nesting sites to protect young from harsh elements.

Trait frequency within a species can change over generations, especially when there are transitions in environmental pressures. The essence of natural selection is *differential reproduction*. Imagine a population of moths with individual genetic differences, one of which affects the degree of attraction to electric lightbulbs. Suppose that humans introduce a new, very hot lightbulb for outdoor use. This suddenly sets up a new selective pressure. If any moth which flies into the light dies, moths that are not attracted to this light suddenly have an advantage. Hot-light-avoiding moths are more likely to survive, and thus more likely to reproduce. The frequency of flying into lights in the next generation is probably going to be reduced. After a number of generations, any genes that support flying into hot lights could be weeded out of the population. There will have been a transformation in the motivation of this species. Phototropism will be out, and fear of hot lights will be in, simply for reasons of genetics and natural selection.

Within most species there is competition for mates. This adds another dimension to evolution that we call *sexual selection*. Mate choices of one sex help to determine which members of the other sex reproduce, influencing which traits get passed on to future generations. Those judged as attractive by members of the opposite sex have an advantage in reproduction. "Attractiveness" may in part reflect good health, adaptive characteristics to confer on young, and possession of resources such as food and nesting sites. But sexual selection can also lead to somewhat arbitrary outcomes. Many sexually dimorphic traits, or those that differ between the sexes within a species, have resulted from generations of sexual selection. Numerous examples are known in nature, for example male peacock feathers, red spots on a male red-winged blackbird, and antlers of many large male herbivores. In people, consider men's beards and the relative absence of facial hair on women, and the average sex differences in adult voice pitch. There is no obvious adaptive reason why these traits would need to differ between men and women. Rather, over many generations, men must have selected to mate with women with less facial hair and higher-pitched voices, while women chose men with more facial hair and lower voices.

Insofar as observable characteristics of organisms (their *phenotypes*) have some basis in the genetic constitution of organisms (their *genotypes*), these characteristics are heritable. Certainly not all traits are heritable, and most phenotypes reflect both genetics and environment. Purely learned traits, acquired by experience during individual development, are not strictly related to genes, and their frequency over generations does not depend upon natural selection. Natural selection will occur when phenotypes have a genetic basis as well as an influence over survival and reproduction.

Accordingly, our question is this: Do motivational and emotional traits have enough of a genetic substrate to be influenced by natural selection? As we shall see in future chapters, the answer is clearly yes, with some qualifications. In chapter 3, we focus directly on this issue, discussing scientific perspectives on heritability of motivation and emotion. These perspectives indicate several qualities of interaction between genetic and environmental characteristics during individual development.

EVOLUTION OF MOTIVATION

Imperatives of Survival and Reproduction

There are two general themes of motivation that apply to all of life, including plants and microorganisms as much as animals. Due to the fundamental characteristics of natural selection, all organisms strive to survive and reproduce. The logic is actually very simple, and it shows how Darwinian evolution is natural and inevitable.

Basically, any organism has to have means of perpetuating itself. Otherwise, it will soon perish. Consider, hypothetically, primitive organisms with various individual differences in behavior. Suppose that some of these organisms are programmed to seek nutrition and avoid harm, while others neglect these fundamental tasks and behave more randomly. Surely, those that seek food and avoid danger will outlast those that do not. With time, the life that lives will be the life that effectively tries to live. Survival motivation is directly favored by natural selection, because anything else tends to eliminate itself.

The story is more complicated, because organisms are not eternally self-perpetuating. For complex reasons that may relate to wear and tear, random death, and competition with other organisms, eternal life has not evolved. Instead, the problem of long-term survival has been addressed by reproduction. Individual organisms decay, have accidents, succumb to predation, and die. Immortal organisms would probably not compete effectively. Reproducing, recombining, selected organisms may produce newer and better models of life, which might then feed upon the once eternal life or take away its food or nesting sources. The issue of death affects motivation and emotion in several ways (see chapters 8, 10, and 13).

Reproduction provides a way of overcoming mortality. Organisms leave copies of their genetic material, fresh and vital and ready to carry on. Sexually reproducing organisms leave novel recombinations of their genes in their offspring. These recombinations may do less well than their parents, but they may also do better. Genetic variability provides protection against changing environments and competition from other organisms.

Only the most successful subset of each generation, that which survives and reproduces, passes on genetic material to the next generation of the species. Those that strive to reproduce, being physiologically and behaviorally oriented to produce healthy offspring, are far more likely to leave offspring than are those that neglect this motivation or behave randomly. Reproduction is the very essence of natural selection, because it determines the genetic composition of the next generation. There are thus strong and direct selective pressures favoring (1) survival at least until reproductive age and (2) reproduction itself. This affects any organism, plants as much as animals, humans as much as other animals. It explains the very foundations of motivation.

All organisms have mechanisms of self-preservation and reproduction that pervade their motivation. We need only to look at ourselves. Human hunger and thirst are strong drives that keep us nourished and alive (see chapter 5). We seek food and water in many ways, from simple hunting and gathering, to agriculture, to work for money exchanged with others for food. We also avoid events that threaten survival. Bodily harm causes us pain; we fear and avoid this pain if we anticipate it (see chapter 6). We avoid disease and try to cure it when it occurs. We seek comfort, shelter from adverse temperatures and other discomforts that threaten our physical welfare. All of these motivations are clearly self-preserving. Reproductive motivation is also obviously evident in humans, as in other animals and plants (see chapter 7). Most mature individuals seek affiliation with the opposite sex. They may be gratified by sexual activity, provided appropriate circumstances. Prior to modern birth control, this usually led to pregnancy. When infants are born, they are usually nurtured and protected (see chapter 11).

Natural selection operates directly on these motivational dimensions. Organisms that fail to survive and reproduce will not pass on their heritable characteristics. Organisms that do strive to survive and reproduce pass on any heritable characteristics that give them those motivations. Thus natural selection bears a very direct relationship to the most fundamental characteristics of motivation. It strongly favors survival and reproduction. There are exceptions, instances where organisms do not seek survival or reproduction. There are circumstantial limits to these fundamental drives, where it is advantageous to die or to avoid reproduction, as we discuss in later chapters (see chapters 6, 7, 8, and 10). For now, however, let us note that the general trend is toward heritable mechanisms yielding a strong motivation to stay alive and produce offspring.

Competition

Many organisms have devised means of meeting the basic challenges of self-preservation and reproduction. The number of habitable niches is, however, limited. Food sources and good property for nesting sites are limited. Given that most species overreproduce, there is usually not enough to go around. Accordingly, there is competition, both within any single species and among species. Competition sets the stage for certain complex social emotions, such as those affecting reproductive strategies and aggressive behavior (see chapter 9).

Some species overreproduce in astounding dimensions, while others are much more conservative, responding to ecological pressures that have been characterized as r- and K-selection (MacArthur & Wilson, 1967). At one extreme, r-selectionists produce enormous numbers of offspring but typically invest very little in each of them. Many insects, fish, and some mammals like mice and rats produce far more offspring than are necessary to replace the parents. This may act as compensation for predation, which takes a heavy toll on many species. A minority of individuals in each generation may escape predation and other calamities, however, and reproduce. This can result in a rapid rate of natural selection, which can lead to evolutionary change if there is a consistent direction to the selection. At the other extreme, K-selectionists still overreproduce but invest heavily in a smaller number of offspring in each generation. We humans are among the species that epitomize this strategy. Each of our children receives a great deal of care. Indeed, we take this to an extreme in nature, with each child requiring nurturance and being dependent on the parents for about 15 years historically, and even longer in modern times.

Different strategies reflect different ecologies, but very few individuals escape competition. The competition among species takes many forms, including direct competition for food sources and shelter, parasitism, and predation. Accordingly, organisms evolve mechanisms to try to outcompete, evade predation, or hunt effectively. There are variations among species in the characteristics of their motivational dispositions to forage, hunt, or evade other species. Competition within species is also common, and it takes forms that are species-characteristic. Territoriality and dominance hierarchies involve partitioning of resources of food, nesting sites, and mates, and around these issues evolve motivational and emotional dispositions influencing aggression, defense, and social dominance.

Selfishness and Altruism

We generally think of natural selection as operating through differential reproduction of individuals. There has been an enormous discussion among evolutionary biologists about the units upon which natural selection operates, from species to group to individual to gene. It has long been recognized in this debate that this issue has substantial bearing on our understanding of "selfishness" and "altruism" in the motivation of animal behavior. Recently, there has been some consensus that the most important consideration, apart from an individual's own reproductive success, is his or her relationship to kin, and the impact over numerous generations of the interactions of kin.

Selfish behavior can be understood as protection of one's own prospects of survival and reproduction as opposed to those of competing individuals. However, the social structure within a species and the dynamics of genetic relationship can set the stage for more socially oriented motivation. Relatives share genetic material and reproductive interests. They share interests in replication of their common genetic material.

Genetic relationship can be quantified through the *coefficient of relatedness*, which is the degree of gene-sharing among pairs of relatives (see Table 2-1). This considers genetic material that varies among individuals in the population (excluding the many genes that are fixed and common to all members of the species). We can quantify the degree of genetic similarity of kin on the basis of common descent in recent generations. The coefficient of relatedness considers that each parent contributes half of a child's chromosomes. Normal people have 46 chromosomes, in 23 pairs, one member of each pair from each parent. A parent passes only 23 chromosomes to each sex cell (sperm/egg), a novel recombination of genetic material from his or her full set of chromosomes. At fertilization, each of these chromosomes then matches with an equivalent, newly recombined chromosome from the other parent. Thus, there is the potential for numerous unique combinations in the offspring.

Mutual genetic interest is the basis of much of social motivation. Parental behavior obviously serves to propagate the parents' genes. Parental behavior is widespread in nature, but varies among species in adaptation to particular ecological demands (see Clutton-Brock, 1991). Parents raising offspring effectively pass on any genetic attributes that support such parenting

TABLE 2-1. *The Coefficient of Relatedness* (**r**)**,** defining the degree of genetic commonality among kin (as defined by Galton, 1889; Hamilton, 1964; Wright, 1922). All values, except those given for identical twins and parent-child, are average values and can vary among particular pairs.

Relationship	*r*
Identical twins	1.0
Parent-child	0.5
Siblings	0.5
Half-siblings	0.25
Grandparent-child	0.25
Uncle/Aunt–Nephew/Niece	0.25
First cousins	0.125
Second cousins	0.0625

behavior. Parents neglecting their offspring risk passing on nothing. Similarly, close genetic relationship sets the stage for family-oriented helping behavior. Kind grandparents, aunts, and uncles serve their own genetic interests. *Nepotism*, or behavior favoring kin, is well-known in all human cultures, and it is also found in many other species.

Hamilton (1964) explained the evolutionary process known as *kin selection*. A gene may be favored by natural selection if it causes the bearer to confer benefits on copies of the gene in others who share it by common descent. Even an individual who does not reproduce can influence the replication of her or his genes by facilitating the reproduction of others who share those genes. In theory, "altruistic" behavior benefiting relatives can evolve, insofar as the gain in reproductive success in the beneficiaries outweighs the loss in reproductive success of the altruist. If some expression of a gene causes a loss to an individual bearing it, but a benefit to the replication of the same gene by family members, the benefit may outweigh the loss and the gene may be propagated. This process, acting over many generations, is thought to produce nepotism, and even may allow occasional self-sacrificing behavior oriented toward helping kin.

Consider the motivation of the bee that stings the colony invader, but dies as it is eviscerated by leaving its stinger in the target. It has effectively given its life in defense of its community, which represent it many times over genetically (see Wilson, 1971). The human being who sacrifices his or her life for family in times of warfare may perform a similar feat. Such extreme acts cannot be explained by a concept of every individual selfishly promoting itself; rather, evolutionary explanation may require the idea of kin selection (see chapters 6, 8, and 10 for discussion of soldiering, limits to self-preservation, and suicide).

Inclusive Fitness Maximization: The Ultimate Motivator

A new and exciting general synthesis explaining motivation is emerging among evolutionary psychologists and sociobiologists. This idea elaborates on basic concepts of survival, reproduction, and kinship as we have just discussed, but it also shows a higher principle that explains more subtle dimensions of conduct. Essentially, this theory suggests that individuals have been fashioned by natural selection such that they strive to maximize the representation of their genes in future generations (see general reviews by Barash, 1982; Krebs & Davies, 1991; Slater & Halliday, 1994; and Wilson, 1975).

Natural selection operates through differential reproduction of individuals. However, gene sharing among relatives can mean that direct reproduction is not the only way to bring one's genes into future generations. Given that individuals can indirectly replicate their genes by helping their relatives reproduce, the idea of reproductive success can be enhanced. Hamilton (1964) gave us the idea of *inclusive fitness*, which considers not only the individual's direct reproductive success, but also his or her contribution to the replication of genes via helping kin.

Let us consider inclusive fitness more formally. An individual's fitness, in a strict biological sense, has often been defined as the number of offspring produced. Note carefully that this is not the same meaning as in "physical fitness," which refers to health rather than reproduction, nor is it the same meaning found in the phrase *survival of the fittest* (it is unfortunate that English is so imprecise). Fitness, in the sense of reproductive success, can be measured as the number of offspring that an individual produces. Reproductive success is often measured after two generations, because many poor quality offspring may themselves reproduce less than do fewer high quality offspring. Inclusive fitness is the individual's reproductive success, plus the increment (or decrement) that he or she causes in reproductive success in kin, each weighted by the coefficient of relatedness.

Behavior motivated toward increasing the representation of the individual's genes in future generations should, in principle, have an evolutionary advantage over more random behavior. If there are genes underlying such inclusive fitness-maximizing behavior, they naturally work to pass themselves on to future generations. It is again a matter of logical necessity that evolution would work like this. That which leads to self-replication finds its way to future generations; anything else is more likely to be lost over generations.

The idea, then, is that individuals have been shaped by natural selection such that they generally seek to maximize the representation of their genes in future generations. They strive to maximize or optimize inclusive fitness. This encompasses survival-oriented motivation, reflected in hunger and thirst (see chapter 5), and avoidance of harm like disease or harsh environments (see chapter 6), while also explaining circumstantial exceptions to self-preservation (see chapters 8 and 10). The idea also encompasses reproductive motivation, as reflected in sexual behavior, nurturance of young, and many associated emotions, as well as limits to reproductive motivation (see chapters 7 and 11). It also explains the nature of aggressive behavior (see chapter 9), and subsumes the basis of social behavior oriented toward the welfare of kin and community (see chapter 14). This all-encompassing idea is thought to explain the "motivation" of plants and microorganisms as well as humans and other animals.

As with most generalities, there may be limits to this notion of inclusive fitness maximization. No one would suggest that modern human beings are consciously oriented just toward replicating their genes. For one thing, modern culture has often intervened, teaching individuals other interpretations of human goals. The sociobiologist would counter that we need not be conscious of such striving, we just need to do it.

Each of us shares genes with all other humans due to ancient common ancestry and intermixture in every generation. In fact, chimpanzees and humans share the vast majority of their genes (King & Wilson, 1975). Many genes are fixed and invariable, just as the basic organization of our bodies is much the same in all individuals. What concerns us more is the variation that does occur among individuals within the same species. The coefficient of relatedness discussed above refers only to the proportion of variable genes shared among kin due to recent common descent. Thus, genetic sharing per se is certainly not a sufficient condition for altruism. Instead, there must also be a mechanism of evolution that bears upon genetic relationships, as kin selection does on interactions within families.

Arguably, it is the gene that is "selfish," because natural selection favors genes leading to their own replication (Dawkins, 1978). Many genetic factors conducive to survival, reproduction, and kin solicitude work to replicate themselves. It is not a collective "effort" on the part of our genes to propagate. Rather, competitive genes are differentially propagated over generations; those producing traits conducive to their own replication should prosper over generations. Individuals, who represent specific collections of genes (genotypes), cannot survive over generations in the same aggregates, because sexual reproduction produces novel recombinations.

Inclusive fitness maximization accommodates limits to the value of traits leading to survival, reproduction, and kin-nurturance. Sometimes individuals voluntarily sacrifice themselves or commit suicide (deCatanzaro, 1991b). Survival in nonreproductive and non-nurturant conditions may have little bearing on the replication of the individual's genes, and sometimes survival impedes inclusive fitness or can be spent to promote inclusive fitness. Sometimes individuals avoid reproduction. Reproduction is not always advantageous, especially when resources are insufficient and the prospects of survival of offspring are poor, so optimality may mean postponement of reproduction for a better day (Clutton-Brock, 1991). Sometimes, despite general tendencies to nurture kin, offspring are neglected or murdered; the motivation for this has substantial evolutionary roots, explicable through considerations of inclusive fitness (Blaffer-Hrdy, 1979; Daly & Wilson, 1988).

It is unrealistic to suggest that individuals as we observe them should always be on an optimal course of adaptation. Existing genes are the result of successful reproduction in interaction with ecological circumstances in previous generations, but their fate in current and future generations is another matter. Not all novel recombinations will necessarily function in optimal manners, and mutation and environmental transitions may also undermine optimality. Current genes were selected for their adaptation in the past. Their expression in present generations may not necessarily produce successful adaptation to changing and competitive conditions. For example, faster and keener predators may upscale the requirements for survival among prey, which in turn might evolve improved evasive behavior which increases the demands on the skills of predators. Where there are winners, there must be losers.

We must also be careful not to construct "Just-So Stories" (named after Rudyard Kipling's classic children's stories), weaving complex speculations about the origins of current observations (such as, how the elephant got his trunk). Although behavioral adaptations in animals often conform neatly to obvious ecological pressures, post hoc speculative explanations of long and unobservable evolutionary processes must not take the place of solid scientific data.

Cultural Evolution

Complex mammals have evolved a generalized ability to learn and adapt without genetic change. This is especially obvious for human beings. Our behavioral flexibility, intelligence, language, and culture provide means of individual behavioral change that can allow rapid adaptation. There is now a large literature on the coevolution of genetics and culture in humans (e.g., Alexander, 1979; Barkow et al., 1992; Boyd & Richerson, 1985; Dobzhansky, 1963; Durham, 1991; and Lumsden & Wilson, 1981). See Inset 2-1 for discussion of the unique human situation in nature that modern cultural evolution has engendered.

Learning allows behavioral change without requiring genetic change. Consider the example discussed above of the phototropic moths faced suddenly with hot outdoor electric lights. Hypothetically, if moths were already intelligent and had language, they might change their behavior and evade the danger after a mere word of warning from other moths. Cultural transmission of information would lead directly to altered behavior, producing quick adaptation to the changed environment. Natural selection and genetic change might be circumvented. Moths surely cannot do this, but people can.

Inset 2-1   Cultural evolution and our biological context

Humans have hardly been content to sit still during recent history. Our relationship to nature has been transformed through agriculture, civilization, and revolutions in communication, transportation, and manufacturing technologies. As is well known, the pace of cultural and technological change has been exceptional during the 20th century, transforming our adaptation in remarkable and unprecedented fashions.

According to anthropologists and evolutionary biologists, we are a terrestrial mammal whose normal social organization was the hunting-gathering band, but we have embarked on a course of rapid transition in recent millennia (see Alexander, 1979; Bigelow, 1969; Flannery, 1972). During most of hominid evolution, we lived in low density in cooperative kin-groups, simply hunting and gathering for food. In many respects, such adaptation resembled that found in social carnivores and other social primates like baboons, chimpanzees, and gorillas. The evolution of agriculture, especially during the past 10,000 years, allowed us to settle in larger villages, and our capacity to use tools facilitated this. Language has allowed transmission of information and technology. Cooperative role specialization has permitted more complex social organization and effective exploitation of resources for community development. Competition among groups may have been intense and warfare common, also influenced by weapons technology. Such competition has ultimately favored larger groups with more advanced technology. Civilization, within the past 5,000 years, has meant much higher-density living. This requires intragroup cohesiveness that is unprecedented, and corresponds to the development of more complex systems of political and social order, involving social sanctioning of uncooperative or insubordinate behavior. Written language and travel technology have increased the rate of global information exchange.

The 20th century has dramatically hastened the pace of this journey of a species into an uncharted (albeit more sophisticated and intelligent) relationship to nature. Transportation technology has allowed most people to travel well beyond the natural limits of our physical capacities, and now large numbers travel worldwide by jet. Modern cities have reached enormous, unprecedented proportions, with higher population density than ever before, often with a cosmopolitan intermixture of peoples of diverse genetic and cultural backgrounds. At the same time, family members may now live at great physical distance from one another. In some countries like the United States, extended family contacts are certainly reduced and even nuclear family ties have been eroded. People may often find themselves in a sea of unfamiliar faces. Political organization is at the highest levels in history, often at the national and international levels. Occupational skills are now very diverse and complex. There is less and less simple unskilled work. We are surrounded by technologies, like cars and planes, chemicals and drugs, tools and even guns for which we have no evolutionary preparation.

This is a far cry from the hunting-gathering village, where an individual might have lived his whole life among kin and other familiar persons, with a much simpler and more predictable relationship to nature. It has often been suggested that we have placed ourselves out of biological context, because our genetic adaptation lags far behind cultural change. While modern life has many comforts and is surely more stimulating than old-fashioned ways, some people may not be prepared to cope effectively. It has often been suggested that our emotions are vestiges of hunting-gathering days. Since there could not have possibly been enough time for evolved emotional predispositions to catch up with rapid cultural and technological change, we may need to look to stable ancestral conditions to understand the evolutionary roots of human emotions.

Many behavioral characteristics of humans and other complex mammals show flexibility that could not conceivably be understood in terms of genetics and evolution. The frequency of use of the English language in the population, as opposed to use of Latin or Spanish for example, certainly has no strong basis in genetics and is better understood in terms of learning. Young children from diverse regions of the world readily learn the language of any culture in which they are totally immersed. This does not mean that inheritance is irrelevant to the general nature of language development (cf. Chomsky, 1972). The interactions of genes and culture found in behavior can have a number of forms and qualities. For any trait in question, we might ask about the extent to which genetics and inheritance, as opposed to learning and culture, contribute to the trait. We deal with the research addressing the relative contributions of nature and nurture in detail in chapter 3, and we show the relevance of neuroscience in chapter 4.

EVOLUTION OF EMOTIONS

Darwin (1872) conducted some pioneering work concerning emotions. He considered emotions in terms of concrete and stereotyped facial expressions and bodily postures, rather than less accessible internal sensations (see Figure 2-1). He saw evidence of emotions in other animals, especially large mammals, as well as people, consistent with his belief in the continuity among species. Assuming human evolution, it followed that our closest relatives, the primates, would be similar to human ancestors and provide clues to the origins of our facial expressions and gestures. He also began studies of

Figure 2-1   Illustrations from Darwin (1872). Darwin's captions read: *Top row*: Left, Dog in a humble and affectionate frame of mind. Right, Same dog approaching another dog with hostile intentions (both drawn by Riviere). *Bottom row*: Left, Dog caressing his master (drawn by A. May). Right, Cat terrified at a dog (drawn by Wood).

emotional expressions in children, arguing that their expressions were more intense and less formed by experience. He also advocated comparisons of emotional expressions across cultures, suggesting that culturally invariant forms would be due to inheritance more than learning. Although he recognized a limited role of learning, he argued that emotions were instinctive behavior patterns selected by pressures of natural selection, generally orienting behavior toward adaptation.

According to Ekman (1973), Darwin's perspective was somewhat neglected and criticized scientifically for about 100 years. The early 20th century saw a shift toward environmental interpretations of human behavior (see chapter 1). Darwin's reasoning was criticized as anthropomorphic, because he described animal emotions through projections of terms usually reserved for humans, like *affection, fear,* and *love.* He also relied heavily on anecdotal methods or case histories, without the more precise research designs used in modern work. Nevertheless, modern evidence has increasingly supported the idea that emotions are evolved crude dispositions to react to environmental events, explained better by pressures of natural selection than learning.

There is a wealth of modern evidence that supports the gist of Darwin's theory of emotions, as we discuss throughout this book. The evidence comes from many sources, including cross-cultural and cross-species comparisons in facial expressions, expressions of emotions during child development, behavioral-genetic studies, and substrata in neural and endocrine systems of human and animal emotions.

Substantial evidence shows that human facial expression related to basic emotions is universal across cultures. Much of this work has been conducted by Ekman and associates (e.g., Ekman, 1973; Ekman et al., 1987). Essentially, this method involves showing standardized pictures of human faces displaying specific emotions to subjects from diverse nations of the world, then measuring the percentage of instances in which they identify the emotion in specific terms (see Table 2-2). The agreement among diverse cultures about the meaning of specific facial expressions is truly impressive. These data have been

TABLE 2-2.   *The Percentage of Subjects in Each Culture Who Correctly Identified the Predicted Emotion.*

Nation	Happiness	Surprise	Sadness	Fear	Disgust	Anger
Estonia	90	94	86	91	71	67
Germany	93	87	83	86	61	71
Greece	93	91	80	74	77	77
Hong Kong	92	91	91	84	65	73
Italy	97	92	81	82	89	72
Japan	90	94	87	65	60	67
Scotland	98	88	86	86	79	84
Sumatra	69	78	91	70	70	70
Turkey	87	90	76	76	74	79
United States	95	92	92	84	86	81

SOURCE: Ekman et al., 1987, p. 714. Copyright © 1987 by the American Psychological Association. Reprinted with permission of the author and the publisher.

Figure 2-2 Facial expressions of *Macaca arctoides* according to intensity and emotion. Reading left to right (anger axis) and top to bottom (fear axis), the expressions are: (a) Neutral face, (b) "Stare"; mild, confident threat, (c) "Round-mouthed stare"; intense, confident threat, (d) Slight "grimace"; slight fear (e) No name; a mild fear-anger blend, (f) "Open-mouthed stare"; moderately confident, intense threat, (g) Extreme "grimace"; extreme fear, (h) Mild "bare-teeth stare"; extreme fear, blended with anger, (i) "Bare-teeth stare"; intense fear-anger blend. Drawings by Eric Stoelting. Figure and expression names from Chevalier-Skolnikoff (1973).

interpreted as indicating that much of our most basic facial expression is not learned. This general finding of broad cross-cultural agreement about the meaning of basic facial expressions has been replicated many times (see also Eibl-Eibesfeldt, 1989; Izard, 1971; 1991; Poyatos, 1988). There has been some debate about the meaning of these data (cf. Ekman, 1994; Izard, 1994; Russell, 1994), and there are certainly cultural differences in some aspects of emotions and many features of body language (Mesquita & Frijda, 1992), but there is now strong evidence that expression of the most basic emotions (including fear, anger, disgust, happiness, sadness, and surprise) is common to all cultures.

Although it might be argued that international communication could have led to some standardization of facial language via cultural means, the evidence suggests otherwise. Consider especially the data of Ekman and Friesen (1971). These researchers examined subjects from the Fore linguistic group of the highlands of New Guinea, at a point when many of the subjects had had little exposure to outside cultural influences. They were preliterate, had seen no movies, spoke only their local language, and had never visited a Western settlement or government town. When shown photographs of American faces expressing happiness, sadness, anger, disgust, and fear, the vast majority of both children and adults associated them with labels that correspond to those of Western cultures. Similarly, American subjects interpret faces posed by individuals from the Fore of New Guinea much as do the Fore themselves. Primitive body language may thus transcend linguistic and cultural barriers.

A second line of evidence concerning the "innateness" of basic dimensions of facial expression comes from studies of infants and children (see Camras et al., 1991; Charlesworth & Kreutzer, 1973; Kellerman, 1983; Plutchik, 1983). Cross-cultural consistency in labelling of facial expressions according to emotions has set the stage for significant advances in this area, including standardized terminology and methodology. Infants show clear indications of grimacing and smiling very early in life. Indeed, the first behavior that they display is a stereotyped combination of respiration, vocalization, facial contortion, and autonomic nervous system discharge that we call crying. Fear reactions are evident in the startle response, and once locomotion has begun, infants will avoid visual cliffs, darkness, and solitariness. Congenitally blind infants show many facial expressions that are similar to those of sighted individuals; smiling in particular is evident in blind infants despite an obvious inability to learn such an expression by imitating what they see in others (Freedman, 1964; 1979). We will discuss developmental evidence throughout this book in relation to specific motivational and emotional processes.

Facial expressions among our social primate relatives do bear some resemblance to those of humans, while containing many distinct and species-

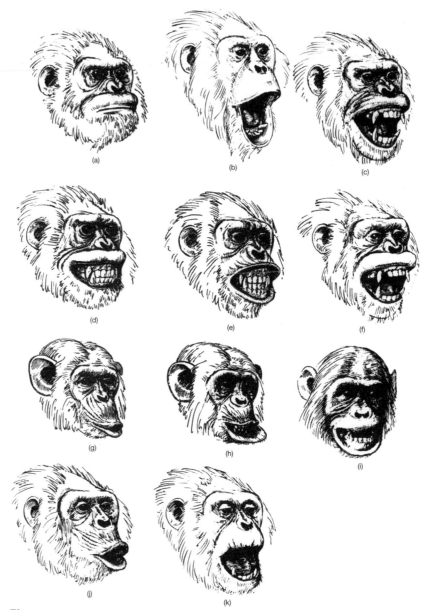

Figure 2-3 Some facial expressions of chimpanzees: (a) "Glare"; anger, (b) "Waa bark"; anger, (c) "Scream calls"; fear-anger, (d) "Silent bared-teeth"; type 1, submission, (e) "Silent bared-teeth"; type 2, fear-affection, (f) "Silent bared-teeth"; type 3, affection, (g) "Pout face"; desiring-frustration (?), (h) "Whimper face"; frustration-sadness (?), (i) "Cry face"; frustration-sadness, type 2, (j) "Hoot face"; excitement-affection (?), (k) "Play face"; playfulness. Drawings by Eric Stoelting. Figure and expression names from Chevalier-Skolnikoff (1973).

specific features. Chevalier-Skolnikoff (1973) compared facial expressions of lemurs (a relatively primitive primate), macaques (a more complex Old World monkey), chimpanzees (our great ape relative), and humans. Comparison of facial expression among species, in conjunction with its social-behavioral context, reveals strong similarities between corresponding emotional expressions for threat, fear, and affection. She concluded that the form, as well as the circumstances of expression, show continuity among nonhuman primates, and that Darwin's central hypothesis of similarity of human facial expressions to those of nonhuman primates has been confirmed. See Figures 2-2 and 2-3 for a sample of primate expressions. Not only are there similarities in perceived forms of facial expression, there are also commonalities in the musculature and neurophysiological substrata. More primitive vertebrates (fish, reptiles, and amphibians) lack musculature in the face for much more than opening and closing the eyes, nose, and mouth, with few if any muscular connections to the skin. Mammals have two muscle layers, including a more superficial layer with extensive connections to the skin (Huber, 1931). Among the primates, facial mobility is most prominent among those that live in societies, such as the Old World monkeys and apes, in conjunction with increased communication, vocalization, and visual skills that permit such expressions to be read (Andrew, 1963; 1965). Facial expression, concomitant vocalization, and bodily postures are critical for communication in social nonhuman primates (Altmann, 1968), and obviously in humans, elaboration of vocalization is the foundation of our language.

Accordingly, the origins of basic human facial expressions and emotions are deep in primate and even general mammalian evolution. That does not mean that the rich diversity of human gestures is all explained by instinct and evolution. It would be unreasonable to claim that learning is irrelevant to facial expressions and gestures. There is a voluntary aspect to facial expression and gesture as well, as any actor or actress must exploit to perform effectively. There are also many features of gesture that are learned and culture-specific (e.g. Schneller, 1988; Sparhawk, 1981). Nevertheless, the data discussed above support the assertion that emotional expressions represent primitive adaptations that shape motivation and communicate with other members of the species. Facial expressions and bodily postures can constitute primitive language that influences the behavior of others. It is very familiar to all of us, but we may not always be fully conscious of it and its social impact. Nonverbal language provides a wealth of information to our kin and community. It can display our own drive states and alter the motivation of others. Primitive body language may function to remotivate others, as for example a mother will attend to her baby expressing distress, or a friend may seek to comfort someone who is visibly upset. We elaborate upon this throughout this book, but for now, let images speak (see Figures 2-4 to 2-6, pp. 38–40).

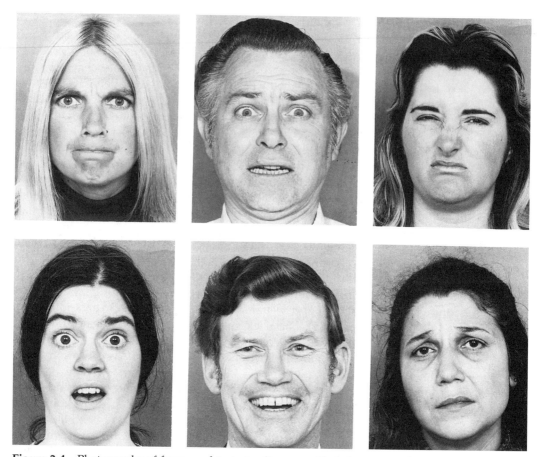

Figure 2-4 Photographs of faces used to test culture-specific judgements of emotions by Ekman. Emotions depicted in the top row, left to right: anger, fear, disgust; in the bottom row, left to right; surprise, happiness, sadness.

Unmasking the Face by Paul Ekman & Wallace V. Friesen, 1975, copyright © Paul Ekman 1975.

Very forceful modern evidence comes from scientific study of neuroendocrine processes that underlie motivation and emotion. In chapter 4 and beyond, we will discuss evidence that emotions involve specific processes in the peripheral and central nervous systems, and neurochemical and hormonal states. Many emotions involve relatively fixed neural and neurochemical substrata that are stereotyped across individuals. For example,

Figure 2-5 Video frames of attempts to pose emotions by subjects from the Fore of New Guinea. The instructions for the top left photograph were "your friend has come and you are happy"; for the top right "your child has died"; for the bottom left "you are angry and about to fight"; and for the bottom right "you see a dead pig that has been lying there for a long time."

Paul Ekman, "Universals and Cultural Differences in Facial Expressions of Emotion," in J. Cole (ed.), *Nebraska Symposium on Motivation, 1971*. Lincoln, NB: University of Nebraska Press, 1972. Pp. 207–83. Reprinted with permission.

there is the ability of modern drugs to instigate states of euphoria (happiness) and dysphoria (sadness) artificially, even when there is no objective reason or environmental event to elicit the emotion. Together with other evidence, this implicates specific neurochemical systems in happiness and sadness. Such physiological evidence bolsters the claim that basic emotions involve inborn predispositions.

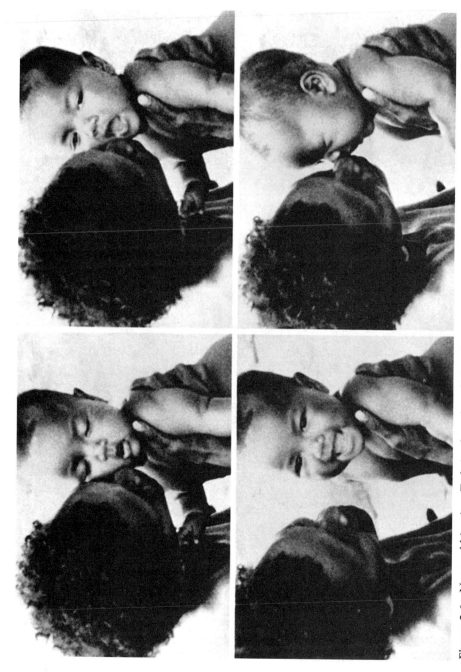

Figure 2-6 Nose-rubbing in a Trobriand mother elicits a happy expression on the child's part (play face), which in turn creates joy for the mother.

From: Eibl-Eibesfeldt, Irenäus. *Human Ethology* (New York: Aldine de Gruyter) Copyright © 1989, Irenäus Eibl-Eibesfeldt. Reprinted with permission.

Chapter 3

GENETICS, LEARNING, AND DEVELOPMENT

The purpose of this chapter is to delve more deeply into the roles of nature and nurture in motivation and emotion. This will shed light on the relevance of evolution and culture, and their interactions.

Nature-nurture arguments have always been at the core of psychology as a discipline, something of a hornet's nest perhaps. The modern pat answer is that all behavior is due to both nature and nurture. This is true in a sense; the concrete actions of any individual are necessarily a product of some kind of interaction of inborn characteristics and experiences during development. Categorical thinking, classifying any behavior as instinctive or learned, is certainly simplistic. Whether characteristics are innate or learned is rarely black and white, but this does not dismiss the issue. A more sophisticated modern perspective examines various forms of interaction among inheritance and environmental influence. What varies is the quality of the interaction. A wealth of evidence addresses the mechanics of innate and learned behavior. Such evidence comes from both field studies and experimental laboratory studies of nonhuman mammals and humans, including systematic attempts to examine the genetic contribution to behavior.

INNATE VERSUS LEARNED BEHAVIOR

Genetic change via evolution occurs over generations, not within an individual's lifetime. Evolution occurs as the characteristics of species conform to changes in their natural ecology, because the best-adapted subset of each generation reproduces. Although this is effective for long-term adaptation, it is inefficient for complex, rapidly changing, or unpredictable environments. Accordingly, organisms have evolved mechanisms for adjusting their behavior within their lifetimes to deal with changing circumstances. These are mechanisms of learning, which allow efficient adjustment and development of behavior that is finely adapted. We humans can do this to a remarkable extent.

Simpler organisms rely more upon relatively fixed, stereotyped behavior. Invertebrates and more primitive vertebrates (fish, amphibians, reptiles) have simpler nervous systems (see chapter 4) that do not permit complex learning and high-order information processing. In birds and small mammals like mice and rats, stereotyped behavior is clearly present, but there are also basic learning mechanisms that allow adaptation to variable environments.

Complex mammals have developed greater flexibility of behavior, allowing them to profit from experience and alter their behavior to adapt more finely to changing environments. Large mammals, higher in the food chain and often predatory, have the most complex nervous systems in nature. They also have the most flexible behavioral repertoires. They are more K-selectionist (see chapter 2), investing heavily in fewer young. Part of that investment is training. Young lion cubs, for example, are actively instructed by their parents in the arts of predation that suit their local circumstances (Schaller, 1972). Larger social primates like macaques, baboons, chimpanzees, and gorillas, live in groups in which there is substantial exchange of information about the environment (e.g., Marler, 1965). This does not mean, however, that relatively fixed and stereotypical behavior is absent in complex mammals.

Learning mechanisms are a sort of shortcut to evolution, because they allow individuals to adapt quickly without genetic change. Animals that can alter their behavior, during their lifetimes when the demands of their environments change, have an advantage over those whose behavior is more rigid. Accordingly, natural selection has produced learning mechanisms and flexibility, especially in birds and mammals. In changing and demanding environments, animals that learn quickly will probably leave more progeny than those that cannot. Imagine two raccoons faced with human innovation in garbage container lids. One raccoon is restricted to instinctive behavior, approaching food by smell, then manipulating in simple stereotyped manners. If the lid requires a special twist to open, a second raccoon with better learning ability might employ trial and error, remembering and repeating whatever succeeds. The first raccoon could perish, while the second is well fed and reproduces.

In conceptualizing instinctive and learned behavior, an analogy is often made to computer hardware and software. The hardware is like innate structure, fixed by physical production, constraining functions of the device. The software is like learning: programmable, flexible, and variable. This analogy does not entirely convey the complexity actually seen in animals. Animal "hardware" is not completely fixed; it changes with growth, nutrition, endocrine changes, maturation, and senescence. Genetic expression can be contingent on the phase of development and environment, as in hormonal adaptations related to reproduction, stress, and aging. Animal "software" may interact in more complex ways with the hardware. Computers may be motivated, when the programmer gives them a specific task, but no one would call them emotional.

Species-Characteristic Stereotyped Behavior

Simple, innate, involuntary responses are clearly present in animals, including humans, in the form of *reflexes*. Physiologically, reflexes involve simple inborn stimulus-response relationships. Among many others in humans are suckling in babies, the knee-jerk, the eyeblink, and withdrawal of the hand from a hot surface. We see numerous reflexes in other animals. Other mammals also withdraw their feet from hot surfaces. In many mammals, startling is elicited by sudden noises, involving a postural change and perking of eyes and ears toward the source. Most reflexes are clearly oriented toward survival, readily explained by natural selection.

Reflexes can come in complex sets. If a cat is held upside down, about one foot (32 cm) above the ground (over a very soft surface, please, at your own risk), then let go, a remarkable feat of adaptation occurs. Most cats can completely right themselves on the way down, landing safely on all four feet. This set of reflexes has very obvious survival value.

More complex sets of coordinated motor movements, responding to specific stimuli, are well known in animal behavior. In plain English, we refer to these as *instincts*. In chapter 1, the ethologists' idea of a *fixed action pattern (FAP)* was introduced. FAPs are described as fairly complex forms of instinctive behavior. They are usually explained as products of natural selection rather than learning.

For example, grooming behavior in many species fits the definition of FAP. Many readers will have observed such behavior in domestic cats, which routinely lick most of their bodies, and when they cannot directly reach a body part, lick a forepaw and rub the area with it. For many species, grooming occurs without much learning. Shettleworth (1973) compared the responsiveness of various forms of behavior in hamsters to conditioning procedures involving reinforcement (see below). Although arbitrary responses would easily change in frequency depending upon whether or not rewards were contingent on the behavior, grooming occurred with a regular frequency regardless of whether it was rewarded.

Another example is nest-building in rats, which will occur even when animals are completely deprived of the opportunity to learn this behavior. Eibl-Eibesfeldt (1961) raised rats without any objects to manipulate, even without their own tails, and later mated them and gave them nest-building material in their home cages. The mother rats constructed nests for their young in a normal fashion and showed normal behavior of bringing pups to the nest.

There is also neurophysiological evidence that supports the idea that some forms of behavior, particular those related to primary emotions, have an unconditioned basis. Hess (1954) was the first to perform comprehensive studies of the effect of electrical brain stimulation on behavior. He was able to elicit coordinated movement sequences that were the same as natural behavior patterns, simply by stimulating specific regions of the cat brain. One of the most reliable patterns elicited was a "rage" sequence, involving hissing and teeth-baring. He could also elicit a sequence normally seen in sleep, involving a search for an appropriate place, circular movements that normally pat down materials on the floor, curling up, closing of eyes, and going to sleep. We discuss much more evidence of this sort in future chapters in relation to specific emotional behavior and regions of the brain.

Moltz (1965) cited four properties often associated with FAPs: stereotypy, independence from immediate external control, spontaneity, and independence from learning. *Stereotypy* refers to a fairly fixed nature of the response. FAPs are said to recur within individuals in the same essential pattern, and to be relatively invariable among members of the same species. This does not preclude subtle differences over time within individuals, or among individuals, or among subpopulations of the same species. *Independence from immediate external control* means that there may not always be stimuli in the environment that provoke the behavior. This feature is less common, because there is usually a stimulus configuration that provokes the behavior (called a *sign stimulus* or *releasing stimulus*). Most FAPs depend to some degree on background sensory stimulation and feedback. *Spontaneity* refers to the fact that an animal responds not only because of immediate stimuli, but also because of internal factors such as maturation and hormonal levels. *Independence from individual learning* refers to the fact that many instinctive behavior patterns can be shown to occur without any opportunity to learn them.

Lorenz (1950) described *vacuum activities*, FAPs occurring without any stimulus, and also suggested that the longer the time since the performance of an FAP, the less stimulation needed to provoke it. For example, domestic cats may perform a sequence of stalking prey, even when no prey object is present. Male turkeys isolated in soundproof chambers, without any stimulation, continue to gobble in a stereotyped manner at regular intervals (Schleidt, 1965).

The concept of FAP has been criticized by some researchers, because not all instinctive behavior patterns are fixed (see Burghardt, 1973). Variations do occur among individuals and subspecies, and experience can alter the form of behavior in some instances. One alternative suggestion has been *modal action pattern* (Barlow, 1968). This removes attention from fixedness, while retaining the more valuable aspects of the concept. In any event, it is probably unwise to think categorically about innate forms of behavior. As with other aspects of nature, there is a wealth of variation and complexity in animal behavior, and individual patterns of behavior in different species may have unique qualities.

Simple Learning Mechanisms

A fundamental learning process found in most animals is *classical conditioning*. Pavlov (1927) showed that, through this process, the stimuli that elicit reflexes may be altered. An *unconditioned stimulus (US)* is any stimulus that naturally elicits an *unconditioned response (UR)*, part of the species' innate behavioral repertoire. If we pair a neutral stimulus (perceptible but without a natural influence on behavior) with a specific US, the once neutral stimulus may become a *conditioned stimulus (CS)* able to elicit a *conditioned response (CR)* on its own. In one classic experiment, Pavlov altered the stimuli evoking dogs' salivation (UR), which naturally occurs in response to the sight and odor of food (US). Ringing a bell in the presence of dogs normally has no influence on salivation. Pavlov repeatedly rang a bell just before presenting food. Eventually, the bell elicited salivation when presented alone without food. The bell became a CS eliciting a CR that resembled the UR.

Classical conditioning has been demonstrated in some of the simplest organisms as well as in diverse processes in complex organisms like large mammals. For example, conditioning can alter the stimuli controlling the human eyeblink and heart rate. Numerous other reflexes in animals can be conditioned to occur in the presence of formerly neutral stimuli following similar procedures, although the CR can take forms that differ from those of the UR (Terrace, 1973).

Emotional responses are typically evoked by specific stimuli. Through classical conditioning, they may often be conditioned to be produced by stimuli that originally did not elicit them. *Conditioned emotional responses* are evident in experimental studies of nonhuman mammals. This has particularly been established for fear or avoidance responses. If a neutral stimulus is turned on, then followed a few minutes later by a brief electric shock, merely presenting the neutral stimulus alone can later suppress rats' food-seeking behavior, even though there has never been a relationship between the stimulus and food presentation (Estes & Skinner, 1941; Hunt & Brady, 1955). Human emotional responses may also be classically conditioned. This is especially established for anxiety responses. Formerly neutral stimuli can come to evoke fear and anxiety through traumatic single-trial conditioning (Wolpe, 1958) or exposure to a series of subtraumatic events (Eysenck, 1960; see also chapters 6 and 12).

Another form of learning, found especially in animals with more complex nervous systems like birds and mammals, is *instrumental* or *operant conditioning*. The idea is that the consequences of ongoing behavior shape future behavior. Thorndike (1911) showed that cats would habitually repeat responses that successfully let them escape from a puzzle box. Thorndike suggested that behavior became "stamped in" when it was repeatedly followed by a favorable outcome, or "stamped out" if it led to a negative outcome. These notions are essentially those commonly called reward and punishment. Hull (1951), Skinner (1938), and many others have developed knowledge of this process. Responses which are followed by a favorable outcome are *reinforced*, or increase in frequency.

Numerous experiments have shown that laboratory animals can be taught responses not previously in their repertoires by operant conditioning (see Nevin & Reynolds, 1973). Rats will learn arbitrary responses like barpressing if food delivery is made contingent on the behavior. Once such responses have been established, they will recur as long as they are reinforced with food on at least some occasions. Intermittent reinforcement, where a response is only rewarded after some of its occurrences, can sustain many simple responses. If a response is consistently not reinforced for some time, it will ultimately decrease in frequency and cease occurring, or *extinguish*. Responses can also be increased in frequency if they cause the offset of an aversive stimulus, for example if they terminate a shock, a process called *negative reinforcement*. On the other hand, responses which are followed by aversive events may decrease in frequency, a process known as *punishment*. There is a wealth of evidence that behavior of many mammals and birds changes during development according to these basic processes. Instrumental learning is obviously of great value in adaptation, because it provides flexibility, unlike stereotypical "instinct" or FAPs. We will discuss mechanisms of learning in later chapters, because they are a critical part of motivation.

Relatively complex chains of responses can be formed through operant conditioning. Circus animals, from bears to elephants to killer whales, are often trained to perform sequences of maneuvers in interaction with the stimuli provided by trainers. Responses become conditioned in the context of cues. These cues provide *stimulus control*. Specific stimuli evoke specific responses, which in turn lead to new stimuli, which in turn set the stage for another response, which in turn leads to a stimulus change, and so forth. Finally, one response leads to a reward, such as the fish thrown to the seal after its performance is complete. Such chains of responses are evident in humans each time that we tie our shoes or make our beds.

Stimuli can acquire power to reinforce or punish, even though they once were neutral. Many of the stimuli that motivate organisms, like food and water for hungry and thirsty animals, have their power over behavior for biological reasons. These stimuli have been called *primary reinforcers*. It is possible to make stimuli that were once neutral in their influences on behavior, come to influence behavior. This phenomenon has been called *conditioned reinforcement*. This has clearly been demonstrated with laboratory animals (see Dinsmoor, 1983). A rat will normally not work to hear a tone or see a light flash. However, if the tone or light is repeatedly paired with the presentation of food, it may later be used on its own to motivate behavior. With people, money and school grades have many of the properties of conditioned reinforcers (see chapter 12).

Operantly conditioned chains of responses can resemble innate stereotypical behavior (or FAPs). A sign stimulus, or a stimulus eliciting an FAP due to innate processes, may resemble discriminative cues involved in stimulus control of an operant response. Instrumental behavior (operantly conditioned responses) may become stereotypical if repeatedly reinforced. Complex interactions of innate processes and learning have been described in other instances. A classic example is the development of species-typical song patterns in sparrows, which depend both upon membership in the species and cultural transmission of dialect from male models of the same species during a critical period of development (Marler & Tamura, 1964).

There are limits to animal learning that derive from biological constraints. Breland and Breland (1961) trained animals for advertising and commercial enterprises. They reported several attempts to train animals using strict principles of conditioning, only to find that unwanted stereotyped behavior would intrude. Such "misbehavior" seemed insensitive to the laws of learning. For example, a raccoon was being trained to deposit coins into a piggy bank. The first problem arose when the raccoon had a tendency to rub the coin, a response that was never reinforced. He tended to dip it into the container then pull it out, and when given two coins, he would rub them together, behavior which persisted despite nonreinforcement. Later, the Brelands similarly tried to condition a pig to deposit a dollar in a bank. Initially, the pig would eagerly deposit one dollar in the bank, then go back for another and deposit it. But with repeated practice, the behavior became slower and slower. Despite no reinforcement, the pig would drop the dollar and rub its snout in the ground, or root, then throw the dollar in the air, then root again. The Brelands argued that these and other instances of misbehavior, despite rigorous applications of standard methods of conditioning, represented "a clear and utter failure of conditioning theory." Instead, they suggested that the natural behavior of raccoons includes rubbing and washing behavior associated with their natural food-gathering procedures, and that rooting in the ground is a natural food-gathering behavior in pigs.

Many other exceptions to conventional "laws" of learning began to emerge from several sources (see Hinde & Stevenson-Hinde, 1973; Seligman & Hager, 1972). For example, Garcia et al. (1966) showed that animals' learning to avoid poisons does not fit conventional rules of conditioning. Whereas most conditioning is found when stimuli and responses are closely associated in time, animals will subsequently avoid foods even when their sickness comes hours after consumption. Bolles (1970) found that animals cannot just learn any pattern in response to aversive stimuli like electric shock. Instead, they are predisposed to show responses like fleeing, freezing, or fighting, which Bolles called *species-specific defense reactions*. He found that it was impossible to condition responses like bar-pressing to escape or avoid an aversive stimulus because such responses are incompatible with unconditioned responses like fleeing or freezing.

Complex Learning, Cognition, and Culture

A wealth of evidence suggests that human behavior is generally responsive to principles of operant conditioning (see the large literature on behavior modification, for example, Craighead et al., 1981). However, we cannot properly account for human motivation just in terms of reinforcement and punishment. Intelligent organisms can learn new responses in anticipation of rewards that they have never actually experienced. In simple operant conditioning, changes in the frequency of behavior require contingent consequences. Humans may often learn without direct experience with contingencies of reinforcement and punishment, through *incentives* and *disincentives*. These concepts imply some cognitive representation of potential rewards and punishers, not previously experienced. We learn through language, culture, and observation that certain forms of behavior can lead to various consequences. Insight and intelligence can allow us to perform new responses in anticipation of such potential consequences.

A number of higher mammals have the capacity to learn through observation, without the actual performance of responses. For example, Menzel (1973) demonstrated that chimpanzees can rapidly learn the location of food in a large field simply by observing the baiting of the locations. In people, numerous experiments by Bandura (1977) and others have demonstrated that individuals' behavior can change merely because they observe others' behavior. Through *vicarious learning*, behavior can be motivated and its frequency can change without any direct experience with rewards and punishers. Other common terms for related phenomena are imitation, modelling, and social learning. Bandura and his coworkers have shown that observation of a response being performed by other people can increase the frequency of the same sort of response in observers.

Humans are renowned for their intelligence, language, and culture. Although members of some other species can solve complex problems, and many have some simple language and culture, we rightfully recognize that our capacities in these domains are quantitatively unique. We do not just learn by random trial, error, and reinforcement. We transmit information through language and observation of others. We actively instruct our children to cope with modern realities that differ very substantially from those of our primitive ancestors. Modern history is replete with technological and social change that rely on culture. We have devised many new technologies and forms of behavior, such as intercontinental air travel or computer programming.

Consciousness of our flexibility and culture might give us the conceit that we, as rational human beings, are radically different from other organisms. We might even be tempted to embrace the notion that other animals rely on instinct, while humans are rational, born a *tabula rasa* with all knowledge deriving from experience, in line with some of the historical philosophies discussed in chapter 1. It is true that cognition, insight, and high-order cortical direction of behavior are characteristic of the intelligent and rational adult human. Nevertheless, evidence throughout this book will show that people still have primitive emotional impulses that derive from ancestral conditions, in some instances deeply rooted in mammalian and indeed vertebrate evolution. Especially in modern times, cognitive processes, in the context of social pressures, may suppress and redirect emotional impulses. We will return to these issues in later chapters, although many high-orders aspects of human motivation are complex and beyond the scope of this book, being addressed by several disciplines in social sciences and humanities.

BEHAVIORAL-GENETIC PERSPECTIVES

Researchers in the subdiscipline of behavior genetics have conducted systematic studies designed to discern whether particular forms of behavior have inherited substrata. With nonhuman animals, it is possible to conduct comprehensive studies based on artificial selection and interbreeding of genetic strains (or breeds within a species). With humans, we must employ more observational methods, examining the natural correlation of behavioral features and the degree of genetic relationship.

Animal Studies

Motivational and emotional traits have long been subject to artificial selection in domestic animals such as dogs, horses, sheep, and cattle (see Inset 3-1). Cumulative experience in this area suggests that there is a substantial genetic contribution to complex behavior. This general conclusion is strengthened by numerous demonstrations of selection for particular traits in systematic modern laboratory experiments. Many of these formal studies employ rats and mice because their short generation spans facilitate selective breeding. In European house mice (*Mus musculus*), a species bred extensively for laboratory use, we now have thousands of strains (or breeds), varying in behavior as well as physical qualities.

Some motivational traits follow simple Mendelian rules for single genes. Mice that exhibit unusual dances have long been collected. Among several distinct forms is one mutant, the Nijmegen waltzer (van Abeelen & van der Kroon, 1967), which runs in tight circles and shakes its head. In a cross of

Inset 3-1 Selection for motivation and emotion in domestic animals

Over thousands of years, people have developed tremendous diversity in domesticated species of animals and plants, without formal knowledge of biology. Darwin (1868) noted that manmade variety and form provide strong evidence of traits' heritability and responsiveness to differential reproduction. This is obvious for physical traits (e.g., improved yields of corn, multiple forms of roses, diversity of form in dogs). More interesting to us are selected traits that directly concern motivation and emotion.

Dog breeds, all from one species (wolves), have been deliberately selected for motivational and emotional traits. People have selected both peaceful manners and aggressive defense. Spaniels are reputed to be people-oriented, loving, gentle, and loyal. Pitbulls are now banned in many jurisdictions due to a reputation for unprovoked vicious attacks. Humans needing defense have bred watchdogs; the proper breeds are well known. It might be challenging to achieve the same performance from some cute pet dogs (look on the trains or in the restaurants of France) that some people treat with solicitude that others reserve for their babies. You may teach stick-retrieving with varying success to a Doberman or a Chihuahua, but this game happens most easily with a Labrador retriever. A sheep farmer would probably not choose a pit bull or a Pomeranian, but might own a collie for assistance with shepherding or a sheep dog because of both deceptive appearance and willingness to live with and defend herbivores. Greyhounds, bloodhounds, or German shepherds have remarkable abilities to trace scents.

Why suit the purposes of a master from another species? Any skilled animal trainer uses rewards and possibly punishment. However, historic experience and systematic data (see Scott & Fuller, 1965) suggest that dog breeds differ in aptitude for specific chores as a function of genetics in interaction with training.

Horses have similarly been bred for motivation and emotion. A wild stallion would surely be very reluctant to pull a plow through a farmer's field for hours on end, but Clydesdales have both muscular ability and inclination. Many horses startle and bolt with sudden loud noise, making them unsuitable for children to ride, but artificial human selection has produced "bomb-proofness" in ponies. Similarly, a Clydesdale would be a poor choice for racing, but thoroughbreds are thoroughly bred to be suitable. Consider the obedience and motivation required for successful performance in Olympic dressage or cross-country courses. Would a farm-horse or a wild stallion ever be trainable for such tasks? Training is critical, but common sense and experience indicate that genetics are also crucial. The sperm of horses with highly specialized skills is very expensive.

We also bred domestic cats for docile behavior in human presence, probably without systematic methods until modern times, simply by feeding and sheltering those that are inoffensive. Some domestic cats have lost the capacity to hunt, and instead rub human legs and meow when hungry, and many toilet train with remarkable efficiency. Cattle and sheep have made motivational and emotional adaptations to human demands. They are surely more docile than their wild ancestors, and more capable of adapting to confined spaces and handling.

Selection of domestic mammals by people acting collectively over generations suggests a partial genetic basis of animal emotions and shows the power of differential reproduction. By analogy, pressures of nature over millions of years, ranging from physical environmental conditions to competition from other organisms, are widely believed to have produced the general character of motivation and emotion in humans and other mammals.

---

waltzing and nonwaltzing mice, all 254 offspring failed to waltz. When members of this new generation were bred with one another, the resulting generation consisted of 124 nonwaltzing and 47 waltzing mice. These data suggest a single recessive gene. Chromosomes come in pairs, one from each parent, and traits are generally controlled by the combination of corresponding *alleles*, or genetic loci on the two chromosomes. The only mice that will waltz are those with the waltzing allele on both chromosomes (i.e., homozygous). When these mice are crossed with normal mice with the normal gene on both chromosomes, all of the resulting mice have one waltzing allele and one normal one (i.e., heterozygous). This does not result in waltzing, because the normal gene dominates the mutant gene. However, when these hybrid mice are bred with each other, about one quarter should be homozygous for the waltzing gene.

More often, traits are influenced by multiple genes, whose expression may be modulated by experience during development. Stereotyped aggressive behavior is quite conspicuous in house mice. This highly studied behavior (see Brain & Benton, 1983) occurs in many but not all strains, although individuals vary. It is found predominantly in males, usually directed toward other males. Females are much more tolerant of one another, and normally will only fight in defense of themselves or their young. Aggressive behavior in mice is very stereotyped, with predictable patterns, including boxing stances, tail rattling, and flank and hindquarters biting, that could be called FAPs. It is easy to demonstrate that this behavior is not learned. A male mouse can be raised without any experience with or observation of this behavior, without any reinforcement or other form of training. In adulthood, it will show the full expression of this behavior within minutes of intrusion of another male into the cage, so it is inconceivable that this relatively complex behavior could be learned.

Lagerspetz (1964) conducted an experiment artificially selecting for and against aggressive behavior in mice. It was possible to produce two substrains within a small number of generations, one of which was more aggressive than the other (see Figure 3-1). The principle is straightforward. From the parent

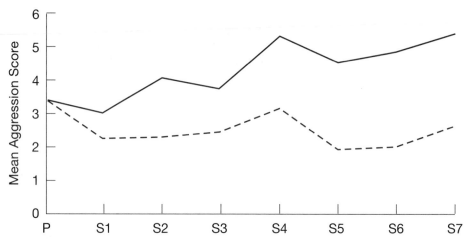

Figure 3-1   Data from Lagerspetz (1964) showing the aggression scores of male mice, selectively bred for seven generations for either nonaggressiveness or aggressiveness. On the X-axis, P refers to measures of the initial (parent) generation, then S1 through S7 refer to measures from successive generations after differential breeding for aggressiveness.

Data used with permission of the author.

strain, males were measured in standardized aggression tests, then two sub-sets were chosen for breeding, those most and least aggressive. Females, which showed little spontaneous aggression, were chosen for breeding based on their brothers' behavior. Male offspring were then tested, and the subset of the aggressive line that was most aggressive was again chosen to breed the next generation, while the least aggressive subset of the nonaggressive line was separately selected for breeding. This procedure was repeated for seven generations and resulted in two distinct substrains. Ebert and Hyde (1976) selected for aggressiveness in wild female mice. Unlike most other females of this species, about 25 percent of their sample of wild females normally fight when presented with an intruder after several days of isolation. After selective breeding of those showing and those not showing such a response, within four generations there was a clear differentiation of lines that were high and low in aggressiveness. There are several other studies indicating that different strains of laboratory mice differ in degree of aggressiveness, and that crosses of these strains behave as one would predict if aggressiveness had a major genetic substrate (Maxson et al., 1983). Nevertheless, aggressiveness in male mice is also dependent upon experience, as mediated by social dominance and neuroendocrine factors (see chapter 9). For example, male mice that are repeatedly victorious tend to become more aggressive, and those that are repeatedly injured or defeated subsequently avoid other males and stop initiating attacks (Brain & Benton, 1983; deCatanzaro & Ngan, 1983; Leshner, 1983).

Artificial genetic selection has also been applied to exploratory and "emotional" behavior in laboratory mice and rats. This behavior is tested in an open field, which is simply a large platform of fixed dimensions, usually unfamiliar to the animal. When released into this field, some mice and rats are more venturous than others, exploring the surface, while others are more timid, tending to freeze and defecate. Defecation has often been viewed as a sign of emotionality or "fearfulness" because it correlates with less exploration and is reflexively associated with emotional arousal (see chapter 6). Broadhurst (1975, 1976) developed two separate genetic strains of rats by inbreeding on the basis of these two stereotyped forms of response, which respectively show low and high defecation scores in the open-field test. In another study (DeFries et al., 1978), 30 generations of mice were selected for open-field behavior, with more than 14,000 mice being tested over 10 years. Three lines of mice were selected: high activity, low activity, and a randomly bred control. After 30 generations of selective breeding, the low-active lines showed almost no activity in the open field, whereas the high-active lines had still not reached an asymptote, showing more than 30 times the activity of the low lines. Although selection was conducted simply on the basis of exploration, the defecation scores of the low lines were about seven times those of the high lines, suggesting that activity and defecation are affected by the same genes (see Figure 3-2).

There are many other demonstrations that motivational and emotional characteristics respond to differential breeding in laboratory animals. For example, fruit flies have been bred for courtship and mating speed (Manning, 1961). Chickens have been bred for male aggressiveness and mating behavior (Cook et al., 1972; Siegel, 1972). Rats have been bred for high and low performance in avoiding an aversive stimulus in a shuttle box (Bignami, 1965). Mice have been selected for traits such as degree of alcohol preference (Lindzey et al., 1971) and nest building (Bult & Lynch, 1996).

Human Studies

We cannot, for practical, ethical, and legal reasons, study controlled selective breeding in humans! Nevertheless, more indirect methods suggest that aspects of human motivation and emotion are heritable. This enterprise has historical roots in the work of Darwin's cousin, Galton (1865), who set out to examine the inheritance of intellectual abilities and other traits. Galton looked at familial concordance, or how traits run in families. He initiated the study of identical and nonidentical twins as a means of separating genetic and environmental components. Modern behavioral genetics has enriched his procedures and turned its attention to numerous human attributes (see Plomin et al., 1990).

In theory, identical (monozygotic, or MZ) twins are genetic replicates of one another, sharing all genes. On the other hand, nonidentical (dizygotic, or DZ) twins are no more similar than are any other siblings. Like other broth-

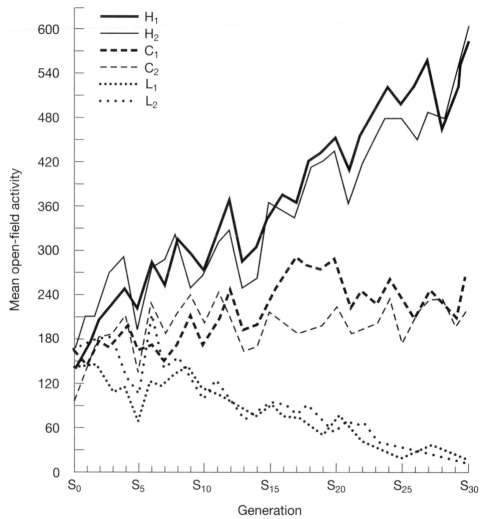

Figure 3-2   When mice are placed in novel space that they can explore, they tend either (1) to move about and investigate or (2) to freeze and defecate. Mice have been selected for low or high activity in this new arena then bred, or they have been randomly bred. When the offspring of the different genetic lines are measured, activity levels in the open field in mice show consistency with their parents' behavior, in accordance with differential selection. Six lines of mice were selected: two for high open-field activity (H_1 and H_2), two for low open-field activity (L_1 and L_2), and two randomly mated to serve as controls (C_1 and C_2).

Figure from DeFries, J. et al. (1978). Copyright © 1978, Plenum Publishing Corporation. Reprinted with permission.

ers and sisters (see chapter 2), DZ twins share about 50 percent of the genes that are variable within the population, whereas MZ twins share 100 percent. Accordingly, assuming that parents (and other environmental factors) do not treat MZ and DZ twins in radically different manners, greater similarity of

MZ twins may indicate a genetic substrate. Thus, behavior geneticists often compare the concordance rate of specific traits in MZ and DZ twins, or the proportion of pairs where a trait is the same. When concordance is greater in MZ twins than in DZ twins, it suggests a role of genetics in the trait under study. The absolute degree of concordance is also of interest. Low levels of concordance for both MZ and DZ twins might be taken to suggest that environmental factors play a significant role in the behavior. Surely, if a trait differs substantially between twins, especially MZ twins, the trait must be flexible and subject to developmental influences.

There are limits to these comparisons that hamper clear inferences. Twins may not represent the general population. For example, the average gestational age at birth is slightly less than for singletons, and twins must compete for resources at many phases of development, from the prenatal environment to mother's milk to parents' attention and financial resources. It may not be safe to assume that MZ twins are treated as are DZ twins; for example, many of us have seen identical twins dressed identically. MZ twins are always of the same sex, and DZ twins can come in any combination, so sex must be controlled in such studies. Nevertheless, we cannot discount the value of data from these methods, when appropriately qualified.

Another important method involves study of adoptees, whether singletons or twins, comparing their traits to those of biological and adoptive parents. In theory, the correlation with the biological family should be greater if a trait has a genetic basis. Correlation with the adoptive family should be greater if a trait has an environmental basis. The child's genetics are provided by the biological parents, while the environment is provided by the adoptive family. Thus, we should be able to separate influences of nature and nurture and get some idea about heritability. This method also requires some careful controls, and it has inferential limitations. The age of adoption is critical. Unless a child is placed for adoption right at birth, there are concerns about environmental influences from the biological parents and about disruptions in emotional bonding. Environmental factors can also mistakenly end up on the genetic side of the equation if there are relevant influences of the prenatal environment. For example, the biological mother's nutritional habits, use of drugs, and even her emotions during pregnancy may influence the child's development. Another concern is differences in socioeconomic status of those who tend to place children for adoption and those who tend to adopt; it is well known that poor, young, unmarried mothers most often place children for adoption, while older and wealthier childless couples most often adopt. Each of these problems should be considered carefully in interpreting any adoption study. Such studies can be invaluable provided that they are carefully conducted and appropriately qualified.

A substantial amount of evidence shows that human individual differences in personality characteristics, many of which are related to motivational and emotional traits, have a partial basis in genetics. For example, personality traits related to emotions of dysphoria and depression have a partial basis in genetics (see chapter 10). No one would suggest that environmental factors, such as major stressors, are not important in the capacity to become depressed. However, different individuals respond differently to the same sorts of life-history events, and some are prone to react with depression while others soldier on with a cheerful disposition despite major stressors. Several large-sample studies indicate that the capacity to become depressed, including the quality of depression, whether unipolar, bipolar, or suicidal, shows high familial concordance (see Lester, 1986; Nurnberger & Gershon, 1981; Rice et al., 1987; Rosenthal, 1970). Similarly, there is evidence for some degree of familial concordance for traits such as anxiety (Slater & Shields, 1969) and schizophrenia (Gottesman & Shields, 1982; Kety, 1976; 1987), although these conditions are complex and experience is certainly important.

Another extensively studied personality trait is the dimension of "extraversion" versus "introversion," which many personality theorists argue is a fundamental characteristic related to sociability, impulsiveness, and liveliness. One can debate whether this characteristic is stable over development or constant across situations, or whether the concept is the most appropriate way to construe individual differences. In any event, studies aimed at addressing this characteristic have provided data suggesting a substantial genetic contribution to the factors that they measure. Generally, DZ twin concordance rates are less than half those of MZ twins (Henderson, 1982; Lykken, 1982). Genetic factors are also implicated in this personality dimension by a study of twins reared together or separately after adoption (Pederson et al., 1988).

One of the most interesting recent studies has taken place at the University of Minnesota. Tellegen et al. (1988) recruited 44 pairs of MZ twins who had been reared in separate families from shortly after birth. These researchers also examined samples of MZ and DZ twins reared together. This study thus combined twin and adoption methods, yielding a very powerful technique. One might expect that there would be substantial differences between MZ twins who had been reared in separate families, simply due to a lifetime of different experiences. Table 3-1 gives some of the correlations for MZ twins reared apart, for personality factors. Remember that a correlation of 1.0 indicates a perfect relationship, a correlation of 0 indicates no relationship, and a negative correlation indicates an inverse relationship. The values obtained by the researchers suggest very similar personality characteristics within the pairs who share genetics but not upbringing. The correlations are often as high as those found for MZ twins reared together. The researchers concluded that there was remarkable similarity between the MZ pairs reared apart, and thus that genetics makes a very substantial contribution to personality.

INTERACTIONS DURING DEVELOPMENT

To summarize so far, the evidence from behavioral genetics bolsters the evolutionary perspective on motivation and emotion described in chapter 2. In nonhuman mammals, some relatively innate behavior remains despite a

TABLE 3-1. *Intraclass Correlations for 11 Primary Scales and 3 Higher Order Scales for the Multidimensional Personality Questionnaire for Four Kinship Groups.* Note: MZA = monozygotic twin pairs reared apart (n=44), DZA = dizygotic twin pairs reared apart (n=27), MZT = monozygotic twin pairs reared together (n=217), and DZT = dizygotic twin pairs reared together (n=114).

Scale	MZA	DZA	MZT	DZT
Primary				
Well-being	.48	.18	.58	.23
Social potency	.56	.27	.65	.08
Achievement	.36	.07	.51	.13
Social closeness	.29	.30	.57	.24
Stress reaction	.61	.27	.52	.24
Alienation	.48	.18	.55	.38
Aggression	.46	.06	.43	.14
Control	.50	.03	.41	−.06
Harm avoidance	.49	.24	.55	.17
Traditionalism	.53	.39	.50	.47
Absorption	.61	.21	.49	.41
Higher order				
Positive emotionality	.34	−.07	.63	.18
Negative emotionality	.61	.29	.54	.41
Constraint	.57	.04	.58	.25

From: Tellegen, A. et al. (1988). Copyright © 1988, American Psychological Association. Reprinted with permission.

capacity to learn, and selective breeding can influence the frequency of motivational and emotional traits. Human individual differences related to motivation and emotion are also partly mediated by genetics, suggesting again the relevance of evolution. In the author's opinion, it is inappropriate to try to quantify precisely the heritability of any particular human trait involving motivation and emotion. Rather, there are many complicated interactions influencing the motivation and emotion of any individual at any point. Inherited predispositions, expressed contingent on maturation and the environment, interact with various modalities of learning and culture. As one more perspective, let us consider human development.

Infants are born with a large number of reflexes, or automatic physical responses triggered involuntarily by specific stimuli (see Hofer, 1981). Many of these reflexes remain in adulthood, such as the knee-jerk, breathing, shivering, the automatic eyeblink when a puff of air hits the eye, or the involuntary narrowing of the pupil in a bright light. Many others are only prominent in newborns. Among these are rooting, where an infant touched on the cheek will turn toward the stimulus and search for something to suck on; sucking, as adapted to the mother's breast; the Moro or startle reflex, wherein an infant throws his or her arms outward and arches the back in response to a sudden noise or physical shock; the Babinsky reflex, which is found when the bottom of the foot is stroked and the baby splays his or her toes then curls them in; the palmar grasp, wherein a baby will curl fingers around an object; and stepping, where a baby will show walkinglike movements of the feet when held upright just above the ground.

Humans are also not lacking in more complex behavior that might be classified as stereotypical and innate. Infancy in particular provides evidence of this. Consider crying. Virtually all human infants cry almost immediately at birth. Such behavior involves stereotyped vocalization, coordinated respiration, postural changes, and facial expression. In later life, in all children and many adults, this behavior is elicited by emotional circumstances, most of which are stressful or aversive. In the newborn, it is inconceivable that there is any opportunity to learn this behavior. Does it not take a very fine actor to mimic this convincingly, and are there not many times when it occurs despite volition to suppress it? Contrary to an operant conditioning model, which would suggest that babies cry because they are reinforced, babies that receive greater attention for crying actually cry less than those whose crying is ignored (Ainsworth, 1972; Aldrich et al., 1946).

Infant motivation obviously includes attempts to stimulate caring behavior from the mother and other caretakers. Crying tends to evoke attention from adults, who in turn look after the infant's needs, from nursing to diaper changing and comforting. Such behavior probably has very deep roots in evolution. Acute distress is evident upon isolation from mother in infant rats (Hofer & Shair, 1978), cats (Seitz, 1959), dogs (Scott, 1962), monkeys (Seay et al., 1962), and humans (Bowlby, 1969; 1973). In most mammals, newborn young vocalize in response to the mother's withdrawal, stimulate her return through such crying, and generally cease crying upon being comforted. Where there is locomotor ability, nursing young will show clear proximity seeking behavior and rooting for the nipple.

In addition to fear of separation from mother, many children show fear of strangers, as observed in facial expression, vocalization (crying), and activation of motor behavior oriented toward the mother or caretaker. Fear of maternal separation and fear of strangers are often characterized as peaking at about 8 months of age, although there are individual differences and experts debate this age profile (Ainsworth et al., 1978; Buechler & Izard, 1983). Fear during normal preschool years is oriented toward many other objects, commonly including darkness, aloneness, animals, and imaginary creatures (Jersild & Holmes, 1935). This is increasingly verbalized and may in many preschoolers assume phobic dimensions. Nightmares are normal and common in children. With increasing age, normal and common fears become elaborated to include many different stimuli, including social situations. In chapter 6, we discuss some very common fears (e.g., heights, darkness, deep waters, snakes, and spiders) that arguably have an innate basis prepared by evolution. Nevertheless, fears such as that of snakes illustrate interactions of learning with innate predispositions; fear of snakes is rapidly acquired by young monkeys that observe adults behaving fearfully toward snakes, but not by monkeys that observe adults behaving fearfully toward rabbits (Cook & Mineka, 1989; see chapter 6).

Consider also laughing, smiling, and grimacing. As mentioned in chapter 2, basic dimensions of facial expression emerge early in infant development (Camras et al., 1991; Charlesworth & Kreutzer, 1973). Smiling can be seen very early in development in blind as well as sighted infants, particularly in response to attention from caregivers (Fraiberg, 1974; Freedman, 1964; 1974), although the subsequent development of the behavior may be distinct in blind children because they lack feedback from the caregivers' facial expressions (Fraiberg, 1974). In normal infants, not only do such socially oriented facial expressions develop early, but there is also a tendency to be interested by and react to the facial expressions of others. In the first five days of life, there is evidence of selective attention of infants to facelike stimuli as opposed to stimuli with similar features that are scrambled (Fantz, 1963). In another study, four month old infants showed equivalent fixation times to regular faces and faces with scrambled features, but in response to the former they also smiled and had significant decreases in heart rate (Kagan et al., 1966). Neonates can discriminate among adult facial expressions and imitate them selectively (Field et al., 1982; see Figure 3-3). As discussed in later chapters, eye gazing and recognition of facial expression are critical elements of social nonverbal communication, and they are characteristic of interactions between infant and mother.

Upon weaning, basic human functions such as those involved in feeding reflect both innate processes and learning. Chewing and swallowing are not taught, and the will to eat or not to eat, as any parent knows, emerges spontaneously from the child much more than from outside encouragement. Simple emotions of attraction to good odors and disgust at the presence of foul odors are evident in very young infants, reflected in facial expression and attraction or withdrawal from substances (Rosenstein & Oster, 1988; Steiner, 1973). On the other hand, parents may be able to encourage their children to eat foods that they initially might avoid. Also, toddlers commonly mouth inedible substances (behavior known as "pica") and are actively discouraged from doing so, and they have to be supervised and directed in feeding (Wicks-Nelson & Israel, 1997). Toileting is also well known to be an interaction of innate expression and active training of timing, location, control, and hygiene.

Children show a broad range of temperamental differences, many of which persist through development (Thomas & Chess, 1977), concordant with behavioral genetic data discussed above. While some young children are more cheerful and placid, others present their parents with occasional tantrums, apparent full-blown fits of rage. Many of us have seen toddlers stubbornly refusing to move in the supermarket, engaged in a seemingly uncontrollable bout of vocalization, perhaps even hammering the floor with legs and fists, and apparently totally resistant to their mothers' vain attempts to reason with them. There are substantial individual differences among infants in excitability and emotional lability, or the tendency to move quickly among emotional

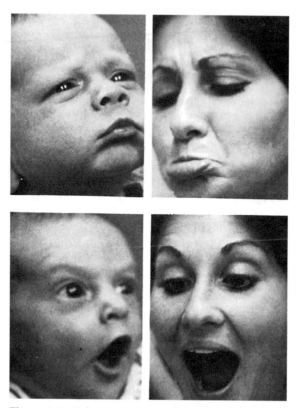

Figure 3-3 Infants may respond to adult facial features by mimicking them. In this case, a model is demonstrating an emotion via facial expression and vocalization, and the infant is mimicking it.

Figure from: Field, T.M. et al. (1982). *Science, 218,* 179–181. Copyright © 1982, American Association for the Advancement of Science. Reprinted with permission.

states. Differences in lability may exist broadly among ethnic groups, as shown by Freedman (1974; 1979), who has observed and tested American infants of Chinese, Japanese, Navaho, and European ancestry. Those of European background were most active and irritable and the hardest to console. Both the Chinese and Navaho infants were relatively placid, whereas Japanese infants responded vigorously but were easier to quiet than European infants.

Motivational and emotional development occurs in a complex web of interactions with family, peers, community, and environment. According to Harlow and Mears (1983), the emergence of the emotions of love, fear, and anger among socially reared primates, both human and nonhuman, customarily follows the same sequence. Nevertheless, an individual's emotional development is shaped by the nature of familial bonding and peer bonding, which in turn interact with the prominence of emotions of fear and rage. Numerous findings from psychological science suggest that emotional adjustment in life is profoundly influenced by the quality of bonding to mother, family, and

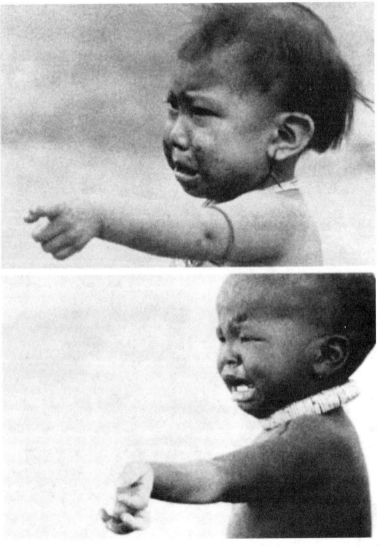

Figure 3-4 Those who are attacked appeal to others for help. *Top*: Small Yanomami boy appeals for help by pointing to the wrong-doer. *Bottom*: Himba boy appeals for help by displaying injured hand.

From: Eibl-Eibesfeldt, Irenäus. *Human Ethology* (New York: Aldine de Gruyter) Copyright © 1989, Irenäus Eibl-Eibesfeldt. Reprinted with permission.

peers (e.g., Bowlby, 1969; 1973; Harlow, 1958; 1965; Harlow & Harlow, 1969; Hofer, 1983; Wicks-Nelson & Israel, 1997). Such studies indicate that early prolonged separation from mother, and to a lesser extent social isolation from peers, can have dramatic influences on affective behavior and social bonding.

In complex mammals, especially carnivores and primates, we see active play and learning during development (Ewer, 1968). In all human cultures,

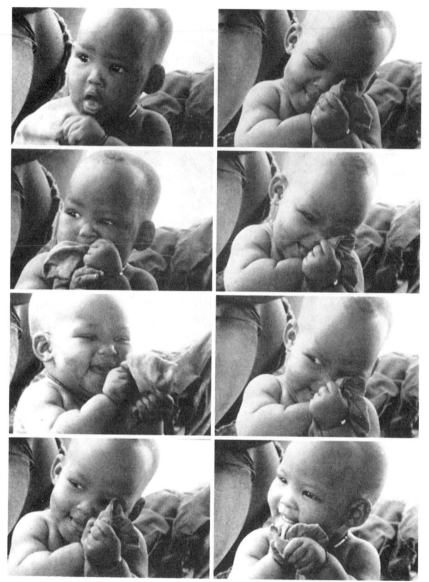

Figure 3-5   The ambivalence between approach and withdrawal expressed in the behavior of a G/wi Bushman (central Kalihari) infant.

From: Eibl-Eibesfeldt, Irenäus. *Human Ethology* (New York: Aldine de Gruyter). Copyright © 1989, Irenäus Eibl-Eibesfeldt. Reprinted with permission.

children obviously seek to play, often with peers, and some of our play patterns resemble those of other primates. Among the functions of play may be the socialization of emotional responses (Buck, 1983). In social primates, play may provide experience with affective behavior. Elements of adult social behavior can appear during play, including sexual posturing, aggressive and threat gestures, and submissive behavior (Harlow, 1971).

Humans educate children in many fashions that may mold motivation and emotion. People actively use rewards and incentives, punishers and disincentives to influence the behavior of others, especially their developing children. They also provide models that can be imitated. During development, there may also be extensive suppression, redirection, and conditioning of emotional responses, such as affection, fear, and aggression. Emotions are very prominent in childhood, indeed in infancy, and they may be progressively moderated by more rational behavior with age. For example, children generally become less fearful with age (King et al., 1989; Lapouse & Monk, 1959). It is well known that crying frequency usually diminishes with age, and tantrum behavior generally subsides in middle childhood. Indeed, it is probably safe to say that the hallmark of human "maturity" is more cognitive direction and less emotional direction of behavior.

Thus, while we can provide ample evidence for innate bases for basic emotions, including individual differences in temperament, the expression of emotion is modulated by experience (Buck, 1983). In an 18- to 22-year follow-up of infants whose temperamental patterns had been studied, statistical correlations showed significant relationships between "difficult-easy" temperament at 3 to 5 years of age and early adult "difficult-easy" temperament and adjustment (Thomas & Chess, 1982); however, the researchers emphasized the importance of qualitative analyses of idiosyncratic developmental factors.

Despite an innate and culturally universal basis for facial expression, people can exert some voluntary control, as when they smile for the camera. Facial and other gestures can be enriched through social learning (Ekman & Friesen, 1981). Our basic emotions may be predisposed by inheritance, but their specific expression is brought out by life circumstances and modulated by culture.

Maturation alone can produce profound motivational and emotional change. At puberty, drives and emotions emerge surrounding courtship, mating and bonding. Postreproductive years again bring transitions. In later chapters we will explore influences of diverse factors, including stress, health, nutrition, social status, and successes and failures. For example, dynamics of the adrenal gland, dependent on stress, influence brain chemistry and emotions. Within normal experience, adult life can bring confidence, competence, and dominance, or frustration, helplessness, and depression. Situations shape emotional tone and redirect motivation. Even aging varies in rate and quality according to emotional experience (e.g., Appel et al. 1983; Dembroski et al., 1983; Solomon & Amkraut, 1983).

To conclude, human development is a complex unfolding of basic drives and emotions, altered and elaborated by experience. Evidence given here bolsters the evolutionary perspective described in chapter 2. Nevertheless, from prenatal development onward, environmental variables build upon inherent structure and mold emotion and motivation.

Chapter 4

GENERAL PHYSIOLOGICAL PERSPECTIVE

This chapter completes our introduction, before we look at specific motivational and emotional systems. It also reinforces the general theme, developed in earlier chapters, that basic motivational and emotional processes are "instinctive," that is, that they involve ancient, highly ingrained mechanisms that are better explained by natural selection than by learning. There are physiological structures and biochemical systems that underlie motivation and emotion. These are principally found in hormonal systems and areas of the nervous system below the surface of the brain.

The material in this chapter is supported by the work of a large number of neuroscientists, endocrinologists, and physiological psychologists. In recognition of the general introductory nature of this material, and to keep the discussion readable, I do not provide specific references for most points. Instead, I suggest some general readings in neuroanatomy, neurochemistry, endocrinology, and relations to behavior (Banich, 1997; Bear et al., 1996; Brown, 1994; Carlson, 1994; Cooper et al., 1991; Dodd & Role, 1991; Kalat, 1995; Kandel, 1991a; 1991b; Kandel et al., 1991; Kelly & Dodd, 1991; Kupfermann, 1991a; 1991b; Pinel, 1997; Role & Kelly, 1991; Rosenzweig et al., 1996; Schwartz, 1991; Willard, 1993).

OVERALL STRUCTURE
AND EVOLUTION

Structure of the Human Nervous System

At first sight from the external surface, there are at least three brains in our heads (the left cerebral cortex, the right cerebral cortex, and the cerebellum). Actually there are many other structures as well, hidden under the elaborate folds of the cortex. Such subsurface structures are of especial interest to us in the study of motivation and emotion. We are also especially interested in brain chemistry, affected by nutrition and hormones in the blood, and including some localized chemical events in the brain.

There are two general divisions of the nervous system, although in reality they are completely interconnected. The *central nervous system (CNS)* includes the brain and spinal cord (see Figure 4-1). The *peripheral nervous system* includes numerous nerves in the body outside the CNS. Let us begin our general description by considering peripheral nerves, rising gradually to structures higher in the central nervous system.

There are many nerves throughout the body, connecting muscles, sensory systems, and almost every major organ to the CNS. There are also small clusters of nerve cells called *ganglia* found outside the CNS. Most peripheral nerves connect to the spinal cord, although 12 pairs of nerves, the cranial nerves, connect to the base of the brain at the top of the spinal cord, the brainstem. Some peripheral nerves bring sensory information to the CNS (afferent nerves), while others conduct information from the CNS to the muscles and organs (efferent nerves).

Some simple sensory information is processed directly in the spinal cord, relaying back to muscles and organs. Other information is transmitted up the spinal cord to various regions of the brain. There are also descending tracts within the spinal cord that bring information down from higher brain structures through the spinal cord to the muscles and organs.

Just above the spinal cord is the *hindbrain*. This contains two regions of the brainstem, the *medulla oblongata* and the *pons*. Also in the hindbrain is the *cerebellum*. The medulla oblongata (which we will simply call the medulla) contains some nuclei that regulate vital functions, such as the heartbeat and respiration. The pons contains several nuclei related to the cranial nerves, simple sensory processing, and general activation of the individual. The cerebellum, connected to the pons, is a fascinating organ, a little brain that performs remarkable nonconscious integration of sensory and motor information, allowing complex coordination, but it may not be especially relevant to motivation and emotion.

The *midbrain* is the region of the brainstem above the hindbrain, containing the tectum and tegmentum. The tectum is involved in auditory and

CENTRAL NERVOUS SYSTEM

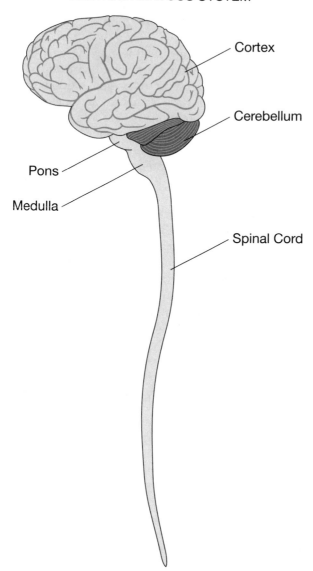

Cortex

Cerebellum

Pons

Medulla

Spinal Cord

Figure 4-1   A view of the human central nervous system from the left side, showing the left cerebral cortex, the cerebellum, the brainstem (pons and medulla), and the spinal cord. Many of the most interesting structures are hidden under the folds of the cerebral cortex.

visual information and probably plays no substantial role in motivation and emotion. The tegmentum contains nuclei controlling eye movements, and it is involved in one of the body's motor systems.

The *forebrain* contains many of the regions that interest us most in the study of motivation and emotion. Above the midbrain is the *thalamus*. The majority of neural input that goes to higher areas of the cerebral cortex is received via projections from specific regions of the thalamus. There are several nuclei in the thalamus. Many of these nuclei receive sensory information and relay it to the cortex. Other thalamic nuclei project to motor and other nonsensory regions of the cortex. Below the thalamus at the base of the brain is the *hypothalamus*, just above the *pituitary gland* (see Figure 4-2). The hypothalamus is a relatively small structure, but in terms of motivation and emotion, there may be no structure that is more important (see below).

The forebrain also contains the *basal ganglia, limbic system*, and *cerebral cortex*. The basal ganglia consist of the caudate nucleus and putamen, which are primarily concerned with motor control. The limbic system includes the hippocampus, amygdala, septum, anterior thalamus, and mammillary body, as well as the hypothalamus and parts of the cortex. The limbic system is critically involved in many aspects of motivation and emotion (see below). This brings us finally to the region that usually is discussed most in psychology, and of which we as humans are most proud, the cerebral cortex. There are actually two of them, left and right, connected by a band of fibers known as the corpus collosum. The role of the cortex in motivation and emotion is very complex, just as is the relationship between rational thought and emotion.

Evolution Reflected in Structure

The oldest form of communication within the bodies of organisms, in evolutionary terms, involves chemicals rather than nerves. Hormones are found in plants as well as animals, coordinating the organism's response to maturation and environmental changes. Hormones send messages to cellular targets through blood circulation, controlling such matters as growth, reproduction, and responses to stress. Nervous systems, on the other hand, conduct information via electrical impulses, allowing much more rapid responses to the environment. Nerves interact closely with hormonal processes, and they also require chemical messengers among different neurons.

The earliest vertebrates, like primitive fish, had very simple nervous systems consisting of peripheral nerves leading from the body's organs and skin to a small central nervous system. The central nervous system was mainly the spinal cord, with a slight enlargement at the anterior end, the basis of a brain.

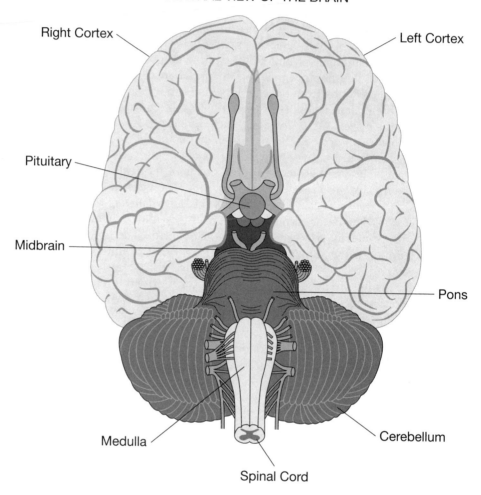

VENTRAL VIEW OF THE BRAIN

Right Cortex

Left Cortex

Pituitary

Midbrain

Pons

Medulla

Cerebellum

Spinal Cord

Figure 4-2   A view of the human brain from the ventral (lower-front) surface.

Nerves to and from the spinal cord formed simple adaptive reflexes controlling the organs' activities and linking sensory and motor responses.

Modern vertebrates have a definite brain, consisting of brainstem (hindbrain and midbrain) and forebrain sections. The hindbrain processes reflexive
behavior. More anterior portions of the brainstem process vital functions, such
as daily rhythms, feeding, and reproduction. These regions are also associated
with simpler species-characteristic behavior. Apart from tactile responses, olfaction (the chemical sense of smell) is the oldest sense in vertebrates. The forebrain is linked to incoming olfactory information and general arousal, sending

activating impulses to lower brain regions. Where other sensory systems have developed, these also link to the forebrain. The forebrain processes sensory information and allows behavioral adaptation to incoming dangers, food sources, and other environmental changes.

Such organization describes the general nervous structure of fish, amphibians, and reptiles, whose nervous systems are meager above the brainstem. Birds and mammals both have enlarged forebrains, but have evolved in somewhat different directions. There is enriched sensory input, especially in visual and auditory modalities. In this text, we are most concerned with mammals. The human brain is very much a mammalian brain, and our basic drives and emotions are shared with other mammals (see Figure 4-3).

In many primitive mammals, such as rodents, olfaction is a very strong sense, as is clearly reflected in prominent olfactory bulbs. Evolutionarily older forebrain regions include the limbic system, which is closely related to arousal and emotions. A region deep within the forebrain, the hypothalamus, has substantial control over motivational functions, including sleep, reproduction, feeding, and drinking. The cortex or brain surface in simpler mammals is smooth, without clear regional differentiation of functions.

As the forebrain became enlarged in more complex mammals, new cortex (neocortex) sprouted out laterally from older cortex (paleocortex). This rendered the paleocortex and the associated limbic system to form a ring around the brainstem. In many carnivores and primates, there is increased input of visual and auditory modalities. In Old World monkeys, apes, and human beings, the areas for processing other sensory modes, particularly visual stimuli, are highly developed. These higher primates have specialized areas in the cortex related to the senses, and also regions of cortex that integrate information from various senses (see Figure 4-4). A greater capacity to store information allows the organism to profit from past experiences. Specialized areas of the cortex are also involved in motor responses, more "voluntary" than those controlled by the lower brain. Higher-order processing of information permits coordination of sensory input, stored information, and motor responses.

The brains of advanced mammals reveal a conservation of more primitive structures, with newer structures built above the old. Simpler, stereotyped behavior may involve impulses passing up and down from spinal cord reflexes to hindbrain regions to lower regions of the forebrain, and some simple conditioning may occur at that level. However, substantial behavioral change and complex learning may require neocortical input. Higher mammals owe their more advanced abilities to the neocortex. We humans can ascribe our intelligence, flexibility, language, cognition, and culture to our elaborately folded neocortex. At the same time, lower and evolutionarily older structures have been conserved in us. Older forebrain structures are still most relevant to motivation and emotion.

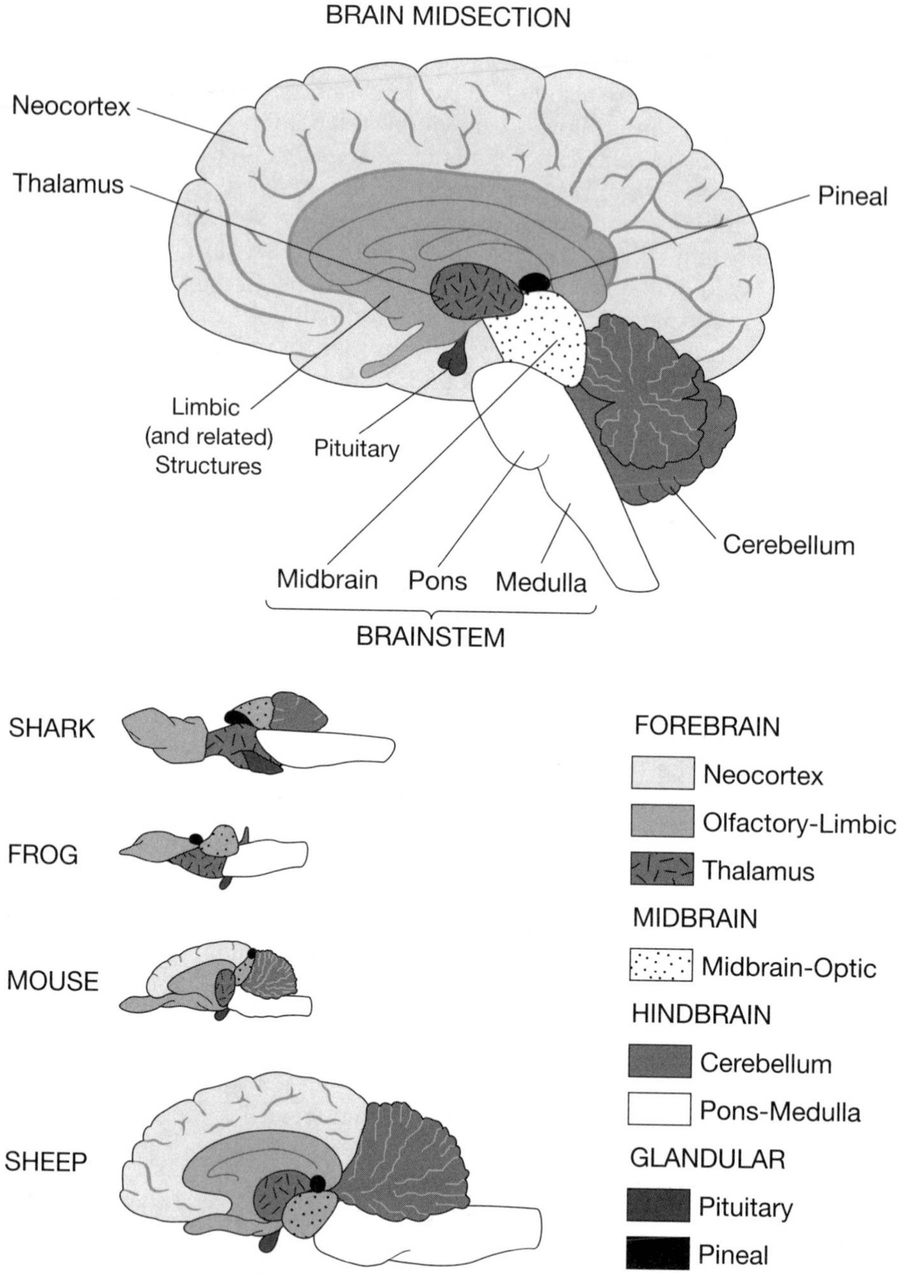

Figure 4-3 A midsection of the human brain. The perspective is just off the mid-saggital plane, i.e., taking a slice slightly right of the center line from back to front between the cerebral hemispheres. Limbic structures are simplified for conceptual reasons. Nervous systems of some other species are given to show the evolution of brain structures. Note that correspondence of structures from simpler vertebrates to higher mammals is only approximate.

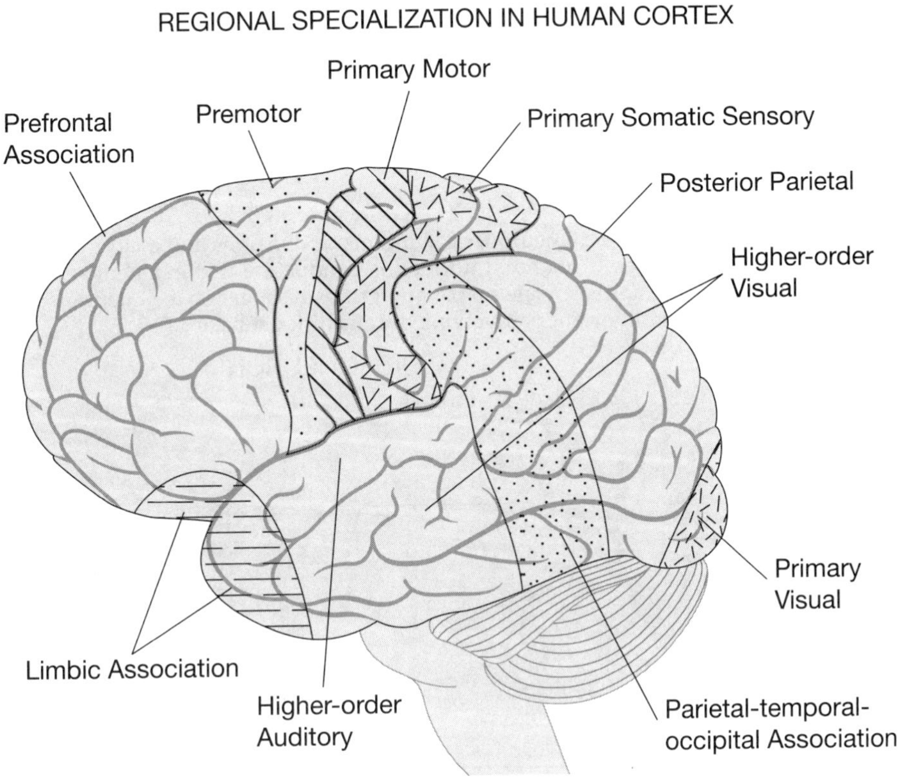

REGIONAL SPECIALIZATION IN HUMAN CORTEX

Figure 4-4 The human left cerebral cortex, showing regional specialization related to higher functions.

Cells of the Nervous System

Looking microscopically, there are two major classes of cell in the CNS, *neurons* and *glial cells*. Neurons are nerve cells that conduct information via electrical impulses. Glial cells act as support, providing structure, controlling nutrition, and removing waste. The peripheral nervous system has three types of cells: neurons, satellite cells, and Schwann cells.

Glial cells, which take several forms, are actually more numerous than neurons. These cells surround the neurons and hold them in place. They transport substances for the nourishment of neurons, bringing them in from the capillaries of the circulatory system. They also export waste from the neurons to venous outflow, and destroy carcasses of dead neurons. They insulate neurons from one another, such that electrical messages are not mingled. In the peripheral nervous system, satellite cells serve the structural and metabolic functions of glial cells, while Schwann cells produce myelin, which coats the axons of many nerves and speeds the rate of information transmission, and they can guide growth, death, and recovery from injury of peripheral nerves.

Neurons directly perform the information transmission in the nervous system (see Figure 4-5). They come in many shapes and varieties, according to various specialized roles. There are usually four structures in each neuron: (1) the soma, or cell body, which contains the nucleus; (2) the dendrites, which

Figure 4-5   A typical neuron, showing major divisions and a close-up of a synapse with a postsynaptic neuron. Information conduction within a neuron occurs via an electrical impulse, while information transmission between neurons occurs via chemical communication, involving a transmitter substance.

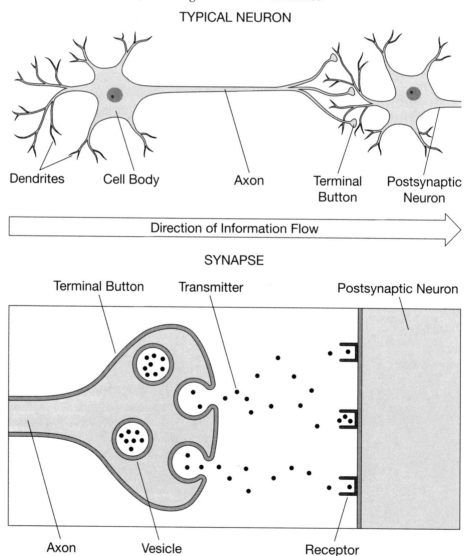

TYPICAL NEURON

Dendrites   Cell Body   Axon   Terminal   Postsynaptic
                                               Button   Neuron

Direction of Information Flow

SYNAPSE

Terminal Button   Transmitter   Postsynaptic Neuron

Axon   Vesicle   Receptor

are like trees that sprout out, in some cases with many branches, from the soma; (3) the axon, which is a long, slender tube that carries electrical information away from the soma toward other neurons; and (4) the terminal buttons, which terminate the axons, after they have branched a number of times, and release chemical substances that communicate with other neurons.

Information transmission within a neuron occurs as an electrical impulse conducted from dendrite to terminal button, principally along the axon. The electrical potential within a neuron is formed by the location of positive and negative ions in the fluids on either side of a permeable cell membrane. A rapid reversal of the electrical potential of membrane, due to changes in membrane permeability to Na+ and K+, carries an electrical message down the axon. This is the *action potential*, which within a few milliseconds carries messages to the terminal buttons of the axon, which then may release chemicals affecting other neurons.

Neurons communicate with other neurons chemically by means of synapses. A synapse is the junction of the terminal button of the presynaptic neuron with the somatic or dendritic membrane of the postsynaptic neuron. One-way chemical transmission occurs across this gap. The axon terminal button of a presynaptic neuron releases a transmitter substance, which in turn alters the probability of electrical firing (an action potential) in the postsynaptic neuron.

For most of our purposes in understanding motivation and emotion, events at the cellular level will not directly concern us. However, chemical neurotransmission, events at the synapse, are of substantial interest to understanding motivation and emotion.

STRUCTURES MOST RELEVANT TO MOTIVATION AND EMOTION

The Autonomic Nervous System

The autonomic nervous system (see Figure 4-6) is a major part of the peripheral nervous system that innervates all major organs of the body and some glands. Autonomic reflexes are active in most emotions, contributing to subjective emotional sensations. The responses of this system are "involuntary," usually not controlled by conscious processes, and they regulate "vegetative" processes controlling smooth muscle, cardiac muscle, and glands. Smooth muscle is found in the skin associated with hair follicles, in blood vessels, in the eye where it controls pupil size and accommodation of the lens, and in the wall and sphincters of the gut, gall bladder, and urinary bladder. There are three major divisions of the autonomic nervous system. The *sympathetic* and *parasympathetic* divisions may be most important for our understanding of motivation and emotion, because they respectively control flight/fight and rest/digest functions in a reciprocal fashion relating closely

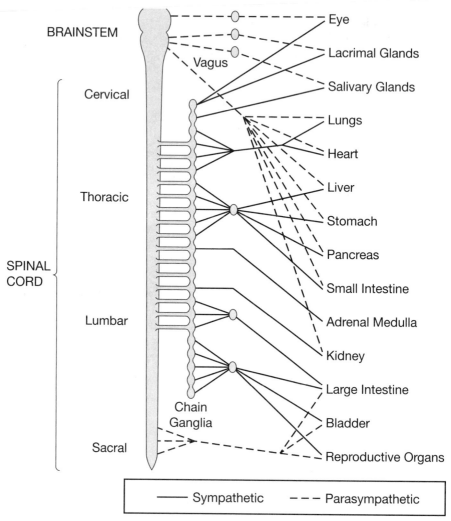

Figure 4-6   A schematic representation of the autonomic nervous system, showing the sympathetic (solid lines) and parasympathetic (dashed lines) divisions and the major organs innervated.

to excitement and relaxation. The third or enteric division, mostly gastrointestinal, is less relevant to our purposes.

The sympathetic portion is rapidly activated during arousal, stress, and many emotions. It promotes catabolic processes, those expending energy from stored reserves. It causes increased blood flow to skeletal muscles, secretion of epinephrine (adrenaline) from the adrenal glands (see below), and reduction of blood flow to the digestive organs. Cell bodies of sympathetic neurons are located in the thoracic and lumbar regions of the spinal cord. The fibers exit the spinal cord then pass into spinal sympathetic ganglia. These ganglia are connected to neighboring ganglia above and below, forming the *sympathetic chain*, a column of nervous tissue parallel to the spinal cord. All sympathetic motor fibers enter the sympathetic chain ganglia but not all synapse there. Some travel to other sympathetic ganglia among the internal organs, then synapse on postganglionic neurons, which in turn send axons to target organs such as the intestines, stomach, and kidney. Of those synapsing at the chain ganglia, many travel directly to targets like the heart, bronchi, large blood vessels, and sites in the head. Others synapsing at the chain ganglia travel to the skin, sweat glands, and hair follicles via the spinal nerves. Neurotransmission at the ganglionic sympathetic synapses involves the substance acetylcholine, whereas terminals at the target organs involve the substance norepinephrine (see discussion on neurochemistry below). Firing of the sympathetic system stimulates a number of reflexes that any person will experience during excitement of one sort or another: increased heart rate, increased respiration rate, perspiration, pupil dilation, and piloerection or goose bumps.

The parasympathetic portion of the autonomic nervous system also innervates most major organs of the body, stimulating reflexes that reverse the functions set off by the sympathetic portion. It is associated with recovery from acute excitement and restorative functions, generally favoring vegetative processes such as digestion. It supports anabolic functions, those which increase the body's storage of energy. It branches from cranial and sacral areas of the spinal cord, in the head or neck and at the base of the spine on either side of the sympathetic regions. One of the cranial nerves, the vagus nerve, serves autonomic functions in the thoracic and abdominal cavities. Parasympathetic ganglia are located in the immediate vicinity of their target organs, with short postganglionic fibers. Neurotransmission at both the ganglionic synapses and the terminals of postganglionic neurons of the parasympathetic portion involve acetylcholine.

The Reticular Activating System

The reticular formation is a large brainstem structure consisting of numerous nuclei and a diffuse network of neurons with a complex net of connections. The reticular formation occupies the central core of the brainstem, from the lower border of the medulla oblongata through the pons to the upper border of the midbrain, projecting to cortex, thalamus, and spinal cord. It is like a web of neurons, too complex to present as a picture. It receives sensory information via various pathways. It plays a role in what we commonly call "arousal," in sleep and wakefulness, and possibly in selective attention.

Peripheral Endocrine Systems

Hormones are chemicals distributed by the bloodstream, and many play major roles in motivation and emotion. There are a few major classes of hormone. *Steroid* hormones are lightweight molecules with a basic 17-carbon structure, with other chemical appendages depending on the form. Steroids are normally produced from dietary cholesterol. They readily pass to all parts of the body, including the brain and the fetus during pregnancy. They are generally fat soluble, having actions over the longer term, and are excreted from the body by actions of the liver and kidney. *Protein* hormones may be *peptides*, sequences of amino acids linked by peptide bonds, or *monoamines*, based on a single amino acid, often water soluble and more rapid in action and excretion. Protein hormones often do not pass through what is known as the blood-brain barrier, a collection of factors controlling membrane permeability and enzymatic actions that prevent or facilitate specific chemical transport. Specific hormones interact with only a subset of the body's cells, which have receptors. Steroids actually enter the cells and bind with specific receptors, while protein hormones act on receptors on the cell membrane.

The two *adrenal glands* of mammals are found just above each kidney (toward the animal's head). These remarkable and complex glands are essential for life. They influence vital functions related to carbohydrate, fat, protein, and mineral metabolism. More importantly for our purposes, they play major roles in emotional sensations such as fear, anger, and elation, and motivational dimensions related to stress, reproduction, and aggression.

Each adrenal gland is actually a compound of two glands (see Figure 4-7). The inner core, or *adrenal medulla*, is an overgrown ganglion of the sympathetic portion of the autonomic nervous system. The outer capsule layer of the adrenal gland, or *adrenal cortex*, is a steroid-secreting organ that has many metabolic influences.

The adrenal medulla (not to be confused with the medulla oblongata) secretes monoamines called catecholamines, epinephrine (adrenaline) and norepinephrine (noradrenaline), directly into the bloodstream. As described below, catecholamines are also produced in synapses as transmitter substances of the central and sympathetic nervous systems. The release of catecholamines by the adrenal medulla is rapid, occurring in conjunction with sympathetic nervous system firing. Adrenal catecholamines reach targets largely outside the brain, where they enhance reflexes of the sympathetic nervous system. Once again, we are all familiar with the subjective sensations caused by sympathetic-adrenal-medullary response: increased heart rate and blood pressure, increased respiration rate, and perspiration, in the seconds or few minutes of the classic flight-or-fight reaction. This reaction may be especially associated with fear and nervousness, but it also accompanies other sudden emotional arousal such as anger or exhilaration.

ADRENAL GLAND

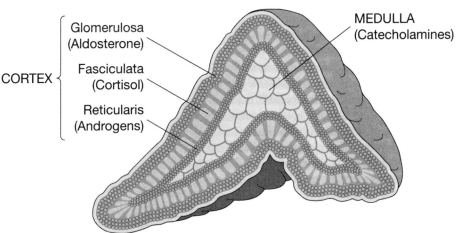

Glomerulosa
(Aldosterone)

Fasciculata
(Cortisol)

CORTEX

Reticularis
(Androgens)

MEDULLA
(Catecholamines)

Figure 4-7 The human adrenal gland. There are two adrenal glands in the body, just above either kidney. The gland is actually a complex of two glands: The center, or adrenal medulla, secretes catecholamines into the blood in conjunction with activity of the sympathetic nervous system, while the external surface, or adrenal cortex, secretes various steroid hormones.

The adrenal cortex, on the other hand, affects processes taking place over hours, weeks, and months. Unlike the adrenal medulla, it has no nervous input, or innervation. Rather, it is controlled by peptides from the pituitary (see below), in particular ACTH. There are many different steroids secreted by the mammalian adrenal cortex. These include aldosterone, a large steroid implicated in mineral metabolism and thirst. There are also glucocorticoids (e.g., cortisol, corticosterone), which have many metabolic functions, influencing carbohydrate, protein, and lipid metabolism. Glucocorticoid release is quite reliably associated with long-term psychological stress. The adrenal cortex also can produce what we normally think of as *sex steroids*, including progesterone and a host of low-weight steroids, androgens and estrogens (e.g., testosterone, 17β-estradiol, androstenedione, DHEA).

The *gonads* (*testes* in males, *ovaries* in females) also secrete sex steroids. In mature males, the testes secrete androgens and estrogens, most notably testosterone, sustaining masculine physiology and behavior. The production of testosterone and other androgens is under control of the pituitary and hypothalamus. Both male sexual and aggressive behavior are influenced by androgens in many mammals. Castration generally diminishes male sexual motivation and may alter aggressiveness, although this depends on species, age, and experience. In mature females, estrogens and progesterone are released in a cycle, the estrous cycle for most mammals and the menstrual cycle for higher primates including humans. Ovarian activity occurs in conjunction with activities of the anterior pituitary gland and hypothalamus (see below). Generally, with some variance among species, estrogen rises in the preovulatory phase of the cycle, there is a surge in the pituitary peptide LH at mid-cycle, followed by ovulation and progesterone release, which falls toward the end of the cycle unless there has been fertilization. Pregnancy involves sustained high progesterone levels and cessation of hormonal cycling.

There are receptors for specific steroids in peripheral organs and regions of the central nervous system. Various steroids bind at sites in the limbic system of the brain, and are implicated in many facets of motivation and emotion. As we shall discuss, there are reciprocal interactions of the adrenal cortex and the gonads, underlying major motivational shifts related to stress, reproduction, aggression, and social dominance.

The Hypothalamus and Pituitary

This brings us to what must be the most important structures for motivation and emotion. The hypothalamus and pituitary, found centrally at the base of the brain, form a gateway between neural and endocrine systems, and they have an intimate relationship. The pituitary is often called the "master gland," because it controls many of the other endocrine functions in the body (some of which we have just described). The hypothalamus, below the thalamus, is composed of multiple nuclei, many of which are pictured in Figure 4-8.

The pituitary has two major sections, anterior and posterior. The anterior pituitary secretes several peptide hormones, some of which directly influence other glands, including the adrenals, gonads, and thyroid gland. The posterior pituitary is composed of neural projections from the hypothalamus. The major hormones released by the pituitary and their primary functions are summarized in Table 4-1.

The anterior pituitary is glandular tissue that is not directly innervated. However, it is affected chemically by a fine blood capillary network, into which neurons of the hypothalamus release small quantities of peptide hormones. In turn, the anterior pituitary releases its own peptides into general circulation. Most of these pituitary peptides cannot reach much of the brain, but instead their primary targets are elsewhere in the body. Peripheral glands, like the adrenals, ovaries, testes, and thyroid, pick up these peptides and change their function in response, in turn secreting their own hormones, like cortisol or testosterone. Steroids from the adrenals and gonads have receptors at the hypothalamus and pituitary, which keep subsequent pituitary hormone release in equilibrium. For example, CRF from the hypothalamus stimulates pituitary ACTH release, which stimulates adrenal cortisol release, but cortisol receipt at the hypothalamus and pituitary dampens subsequent ACTH output.

HYPOTHALAMUS AND PITUITARY

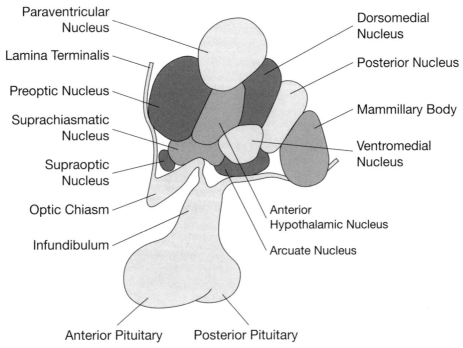

Figure 4-8 The hypothalamus and pituitary gland. This region is a major interface of the neural and endocrine systems, and it is probably the most important structure for motivation and emotion.

At the base of the medial section of the hypothalamus and around the third ventricle (see below) are many small neurons secreting substances (releasing factors) that are passed via local circulation to the anterior pituitary. The hypothalamus also has large neurosecretory neurons in the paraventricular and supraoptic nuclei that project directly to the posterior pituitary, secreting the hormones oxytocin and vasopressin into general circulation. Parts of the hypothalamus also link to the autonomic nervous system.

In the hypothalamus, primary drives of hunger, thirst, temperature regulation, and reproduction all have some basis, and the emotions of fear and aggression in mammals are also partly represented here, in connection with other limbic system structures, as we discuss in detail in later chapters. The hypothalamus undergoes structural and biochemical change in response to behavioral demands, as do other glands like the adrenals and gonads. Hypothalamic cells that regulate pituitary and peripheral glands are themselves influenced by hormones from those glands.

TABLE 4-1.   *Relevant Major Hormones Released by the Pituitary Gland, Sites of Action, Primary Functions, and Hypothalamic Factors Providing Control*

Hormone	Target	General functions	Hypothalamic control
Anterior pituitary			
ACTH	adrenal cortex	stress	CRF
endorphins	diverse	stress, pain	CRF, MSH
LH	*female:* ovaries	ovulation, progesterone	GnRH
	male: testes	testosterone	GnRH
FSH	ovaries	stimulating follicle development	GnRH
Prolactin	mammary glands	lactation, maternal behavior	PRF (+) dopamine (−)
Growth hormone	diverse	growth	GRH
TSH	thyroid	thyroid hormone production	TRH
Posterior pituitary			
Oxytocin	mammary glands, uterus	birth, lactation, sexual behavior	direct
Vasopressin	kidneys, blood vessels	water resorption, vasoconstriction	direct

The Ventricular System

The circulatory system is not the only medium for chemicals to reach cells and cell-systems in the brain. The ventricular system (see Figure 4-9) is an ancient system, found in all vertebrates, that contains cerebrospinal fluid. It acts as a cushion at the center of the CNS, but it also acts as a medium for chemical transport among clusters of neurons. The hypothalamus is built around it, as are other structures of the limbic system and brainstem. It also extends through the central canal through the spinal cord. The cerebrospinal fluid of the third and lateral ventricles interfaces with limbic structures, allowing the potential for chemical communication among the structures.

Cerebrospinal fluid bathes many of the regions of the brain that are critical for human emotions, and its chemistry is dynamic. There are many neurosecretory cells in the hypothalamus, synthesizing and secreting peptide hormones. Individual neurons often secrete more than one peptide, and many of these neurons are adjacent to the ventricular system. These peptides may end up in local circulation or in cerebrospinal fluid. Some pituitary hormones also find their way into cerebrospinal fluid. The chemical dynamics in the ventricular system thus may assume importance as a potential mediator of mood. Chemical flow among neurons, via circulation or cerebrospinal fluid, has a bearing on electrical firing and chemical secretion of other neurons. Thus, there is rich chemical communication among neuromodulating chemicals in these regions, which we may fairly suspect can underlie aspects of our moment-to-moment changes in subjective moods.

VENTRICULAR SYSTEM

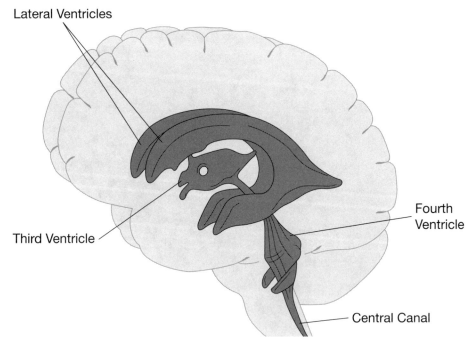

Figure 4-9 The ventricular system of the brain. This ancient system, found in all vertebrates, contains cerebrospinal fluid. It also extends through the central canal through the spinal cord.

The Limbic System

The limbic system is a complex part of the forebrain that is critical for many emotions (see Figure 4-10). Papez (1937) presented a theory of emotions of higher mammals in terms of the roles of the cortex, limbic system, and hypothalamus. He argued that emotions influence consciousness, and hence the cortex, and in turn higher cognitive functions influence emotions. Thus, emotional substrata must communicate directly with higher cortical functions. He described a circuit from the mammillary body, through anterior thalamic nuclei to the paleocortex, through the hippocampus, returning back via the fornix to the mammillary body. Modern research has confirmed this outline and has elaborated knowledge of the circuitry of this system. The limbic system consists of the hypothalamus and interconnecting limbic structures including the septum, amygdalas, hippocampus, and some adjacent areas of the cortex. This is essentially much of the older forebrain, other than the neocortex.

LIMBIC SYSTEM

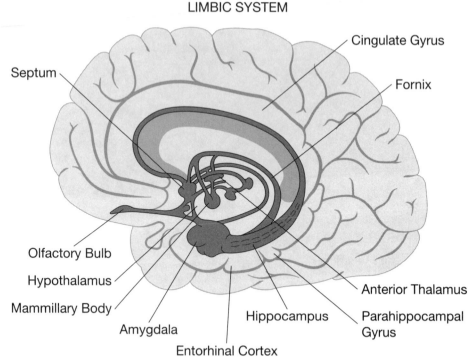

Figure 4-10 The human limbic system. This region, found below the surface in the older areas of the forebrain, is critically involved in many emotions.

The hypothalamus is well-connected to limbic structures, and it is often considered as a part of the limbic system. At the posterior end of the hypothalamus are the mammillary bodies, which give rise to the mammillothalamic tract, which passes through the anterior thalamus to the cingulate gyrus, an evolutionarily old area of cortex (paleocortex) tucked away under the midline folds of neocortex. The bilateral hippocampal formations are horn-shaped structures. Each receives input via the perforant path from the entorhinal cortex, the adjacent region of paleocortex, which is in turn linked to other association areas of the cortex. This provides a link between the neocortex and the limbic system. The hippocampus sends information via the subiculum, an area of cortex with reciprocal connections to many areas of the brain. An important bundle of fibers, the fornix, forms a loop connecting the hippocampus to the anterior thalamus, mammillary bodies, and hypothalamus. The two amygdalas are each composed of many nuclei that are reciprocally connected to the hypothalamus, hippocampal formation, neocortex, and thalamus. Each receives much information from the olfactory system. The main projections from the amygdala are to the hypothalamus. Lesions and electrical stimulation of the amygdalas produce influences on the autonomic nervous system, changes in socio-emotional response, and feeding (as we will discuss). The septum is in the anterior end of the older limbic forebrain, lodged between the two lateral ventricles.

Although we are giving less attention to neocortex than other regions of the brain, we cannot ignore it completely. Higher-order cognition is influenced by emotions, while emotions and motivation are influenced by higher-order reasoning. There are substantial interconnections of the neocortex and limbic system that subserve these interactions.

Synaptic Transmitter Substances

Chemical transmission at the junctions of neurons may be as important as the electrical transmission in the cells themselves in determining whether the neural path sends a message. A transmitter substance is released into the synapse by the presynaptic neuron, then can be received by the postsynaptic neuron. The probability of electrical firing in the postsynaptic neuron may be altered, positively (facilitatory effect) or negatively (inhibitory effect), by receipt of the transmitter substance by receptors (see Figure 4-5). In general, these chemicals are synthesized within the presynaptic neuron, stored in vesicle pools from which they may be released, and vulnerable to enzymes within the cell and inside the synapse that metabolize them, breaking them down to inert chemicals that are taken away by the circulatory system. Most of these transmitter substances are based upon amino acids, the molecules that are constituents of the proteins of all cells.

Acetylcholine has been long established as a neurotransmitter. It is the only low-molecular-weight transmitter substance that does not derive from an amino acid. Instead, it comes from dietary choline delivered to neurons through the bloodstream, and local reaction with acetyl CoA. Acetylcholine is the transmitter used by motor neurons of the spinal cord, all nerve-skeletal muscle junctions in vertebrates, for all preganglionic neurons in the autonomic nervous system, and also the postganglionic synapses of the parasympathetic nervous system. It is also used in many synapses in the brain, especially basal forebrain nuclei (basal ganglia and septum) with widespread projections to cortical regions and some olfactory-limbic sites, and in brainstem nuclei with diverse projections to spinal cord, cranial nerve nuclei, thalamus, basal ganglia, and cerebellum. There are two major classes of receptor for acetylcholine, muscarinic and nicotinic.

The catecholamines dopamine, norepinephrine, and epinephrine also act as neurotransmitters. We already spoke of hormonal functions of catecholamines from the adrenal gland, but here we are concerned with more minute amounts released by individual neurons. Catecholamines are synthesized from the amino acid tyrosine (see Figure 4-11). Their rate of production is especially limited by the enzyme tyrosine hydroxylase. This enzyme is

BIOSYNTHESIS OF CATECHOLAMINES

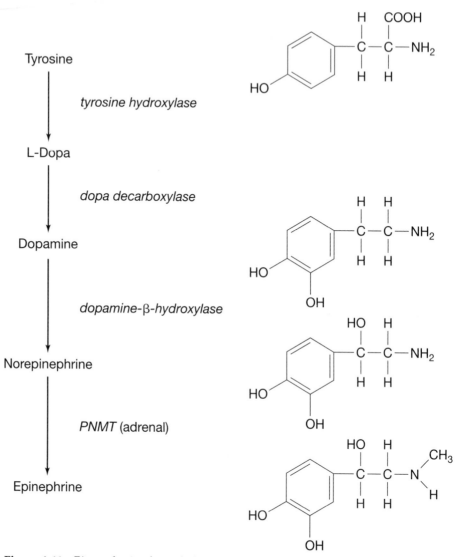

Figure 4-11   Biosynthesis of catecholamines. Catecholamines are neurotransmitter substances in the brain. Two of them, epinephrine (adrenaline) and norepinephrine (noradrenaline), are also hormones released into the bloodstream by the adrenal glands. Norepinephrine is also a transmitter substance in the sympathetic nervous system.

present in every cell secreting catecholamines. The major enzymes that break down catecholamines are monoamine oxidase (MAO) and COMT.

Dopamine is found in scores of thousands of synapses, especially in subcortical structures. There are short neurons in the retina and olfactory bulb using this neurotransmitter. Some dopaminergic neurons project from the arcuate and periventricular nuclei of the hypothalamus to the pituitary, within other regions of the hypothalamus and to the septum. Long-length dopaminergic systems link midbrain regions with the basal ganglia, various limbic system structures (septum, amygdala), and paleocortex (cingulate gyrus, entorhinal cortex, prefrontal cortex). Dopaminergic systems are implicated in motor behavior, arousal and selective attention, concentration, and possibly reinforcement mechanisms, as we will see in later chapters.

Norepinephrine is involved in a much smaller number of neurons. Norepinephrine is used especially by nerve cells whose cell bodies are located in the brainstem nucleus known as the locus ceruleus. Although these cells are few, they project diffusely to diverse regions of the cortex, limbic system, cerebellum, and spinal cord. Peripherally, norepinephrine is also the transmitter of the postganglionic neurons of the sympathetic nervous system, and a hormone released from the adrenal gland. As we discuss in later chapters, there is evidence of a role of norepinephrine as a substrate of aspects of arousal and mood, and it may provide a basis for the action of some psychotropic drugs.

Epinephrine has usually been viewed as simply an adrenal medullary hormone, but recent evidence has also shown that it exists in the brain as a neurotransmitter, in periventricular regions and various hypothalamic nuclei, in the brainstem, and in sympathetic regions of the spinal cord.

Indoleamines are another major class of monoamines acting as neurotransmitters. These substances derive from the amino acid tryptophan (see Figure 4-12). Various indoleamines are widely distributed in animals and plants. The best known of the indoleamines are serotonin and melatonin. Melatonin is a product of the pineal gland, discussed below.

Serotonin (also known as 5-HT) is found in many cells that are not neurons. In the brain, serotonin is a transmitter substance, involving more neurons than the catecholamines combined. The cell bodies of serotonergic neurons are found in and around the raphe nuclei of the brainstem. The projections of these cells are widely distributed throughout the brain and spinal cord (like those of the locus ceruleus are for norepinephrine). One of the most important sets of projections passes from the brainstem through what is called the medial forebrain bundle to limbic system structures and other regions of cortex. The rate-limiting enzyme in the production of serotonin is tryptophan hydroxylase. Serotonin can be metabolized by MAO. The pharmacodynamics of serotonin are fairly well known, and provide evidence that these neurons play a very important role in human mood states.

There are several other transmitters, amino acids or derivatives, whose role in emotions and motivation, if any, is less established. *GABA*, gamma-aminobutyric acid, is derived from glutamate, and is believed to be a major inhibitory transmitter that is abundant in the CNS. GABA is anatomically associated with acetylcholine, dopamine, and serotonin, and a role of subsets of GABAergic neurons is under investigation in many conditions, the most relevant of which is anxiety, but the data are not yet conclusive. Glutamate is

BIOSYNTHESIS OF INDOLEAMINES

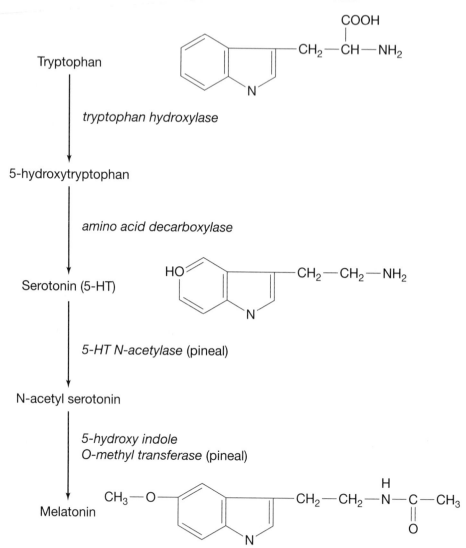

Figure 4-12   Biosynthesis of indoleamines. Serotonin is a neurotransmitter substance in the brain. Melatonin is a hormone released by the pineal gland.

believed to operate as an excitatory transmitter in the brain, glycine is widespread in mammalian tissues and believed to be a transmitter, and other substances like aspartate have been proposed as transmitters, but relevance to our subject matter is not established.

The Pineal Gland

The pineal gland is central in the brain, adjacent to the third ventricle, and it releases indoleamines, especially melatonin (see Figures 4-3 and 4-12). The pineal is glandular rather than nervous tissue, sitting near cerebrospinal fluid, innervated by an ancient branch of the autonomic nervous system. Melatonin acts as a hormone, rather than a neurotransmitter. Melatonin is synthesized via the same biosynthetic pathway as is serotonin, taken two enzymatic steps further. Melatonin and other indoleamines are secreted into the bloodstream, largely in response to the cycle of light and darkness. These same hormones also enter the cerebrospinal fluid, directly or indirectly. The best-known functions of melatonin are in regulating daily (circadian) rhythms, through actions on the suprachiasmatic nucleus of the hypothalamus. It is critical for biological rhythms, and reproductive rhythms in particular may be affected. Seasonal breeding cycles in some mammals may be controlled by melatonin, because they change with circannual light cycles north or south of the tropics. Something to do with the pineal response may also play a role in human mood, because there is emerging evidence that human affect can relate to seasonal day-length.

Chemical Interactions

Peptide activity is widely associated with monoaminergic and GABA-ergic neurons. These may often act as neuromodulators, altering the probability of firing of subsets of neurons. Pituitary and hypothalamic peptides are often found in other regions of the brain and cerebrospinal fluid. As discussed above, steroid hormones from the adrenal glands and gonads also reach the brain, and their receptors are especially found in the limbic system. Such chemical modulation may affect the functions of specific groups of cells, and potentially this provides a substrate for some of our mood variations.

Nutrition affects our blood chemistry, in that amino acid availability can be critical for synaptic transmission. Numerous peptide hormones and enzymes depend upon diet, as do cholesterol-dependent steroids, or choline-dependent acetylcholine transmission. The common subjective impression that diet influences mood is thus given ample scientific substance. Nevertheless, chemical availability in the brain depends not only on nutrient availability, but also on membrane properties, fat or water solubility, differential regional blood flow, and active membrane transport mechanisms, both inhibitory and facilitatory.

This chapter has given only a brief overview of processes that are quite complex. Readers are encouraged to consult textbooks as cited above and to take courses in neuroscience and physiological psychology.

Chapter 5

THIRST, HUNGER, AND ELIMINATION

Drives related to seeking nutrients and eliminating waste are obviously critical for survival, and thus highly favored by natural selection. Subjectively, we all know that thirst, hunger, and the need to eliminate can provide strong internal sensations, urgencies that quickly rise to the top of our priorities. Thirst and hunger are experienced even though many of us live in affluent times where, if anything, we are overfed.

THIRST

Water constitutes the better part of our bodies, about two-thirds of our total mass, dependent on age and amount of body fat. Without clean fresh water to drink, we would die within a day or two. The subjective experience of thirst can provide strong internal sensations. No matter what else is on our agenda, except perhaps immediate physical danger, if we are truly water deprived nothing will be psychologically more important than satisfying this need.

Although many of us need merely turn on the tap or open the refrigerator to relieve thirst, there are dry parts of the world where fresh water is scarce. In Saharan Africa, some people spend hours every day walking to water sources and carrying it back to their families and livestock. There are urban areas in southern Asia where drinking water is highly polluted and a source of diseases such as cholera. Countless battles have been fought in times of war over sources of fresh water. Massive amounts of money and labor have been spent in southern California to make the desert habitable. Water deprivation is a strong motivator in any animal species.

In any organism, there is a constant cycle of water intake and excretion. In humans, this daily exchange is approximately two or three liters of water per day, considerably more in hot weather due to perspiration. The largest amount of water is lost via the kidneys' production of urine, with smaller amounts in feces. Water is also lost through respiration and perspiration. Of course, this is balanced by drinking.

Water balance in the body clearly fits the traditional motivational idea of *homeostasis*. You recall from chapter 1 that homeostatic drives are those which serve to restore balance in physiological state in some manner. When there is a disturbance in the balance, as in water deprivation, a drive state arises, and the organism behaves in an appropriate manner until equilibrium is reestablished. The amount of water that an organism consumes tends to closely match that required to restore normal balance. Adolph (1939) reported that the amount of water that dehydrated dogs would drink, as a percent of body weight, was the same as the deficit in body weight induced by dehydration.

Extracellular Thirst and Cellular Thirst

Physiologically, there are two forms of thirst, which have separate but interrelated mechanisms. During water deprivation, we first lose the fluids that are stored outside of the cells in our bodies. This also leads to depletion of the water inside the body's cells, especially under more extreme thirst. About two-thirds of the water in our bodies is inside of cells (intracellular), and about one-third is outside (extracellular). Of that which is outside of cells, about one-third, or a tenth of the total in our bodies, is in blood vessels.

When an animal is water-deprived, it retains salt while excreting water through respiration, perspiration, urination, and defecation. Extracellular fluid begins to lose water, and thus is reduced in volume. The reduction in water lowers blood pressure. Salt, which is carefully balanced with water in the body, increases in concentration in extracellular fluid. The increased salt concentration outside of the cells begins to draw water through the cell membranes, through osmotic pressure, because salt and water physically seek to balance with each other inside and outside the cells.

Thirst due to extracellular fluid loss is set off by the drop in blood pressure. There are blood pressure receptors (baroreceptors) in the heart and kidneys. As blood flow decreases in the kidneys, blood pressure receptors cause release of a substance called renin from kidney cells. Renin is an enzyme that converts angiotensinogen in the blood to angiotensinI, which in turn is converted to angiotensinII. Angiotensin is a hormone. It causes vasoconstriction, compensating for water loss, and also acts on adrenal glands to release aldosterone, a steroid promoting reabsorption of sodium in kidneys to prevent excess loss in urine. Furthermore, angiotensin's actions can cause the hypothalamus and posterior pituitary to increase production of vasopressin (also known as anti-diuretic hormone). Vasopressin in turn signals to the kidneys to increase water reabsorption.

Intravenous angiotensin given to rats stimulates drinking behavior (Fitzsimons & Simons, 1969). So does angiotensin injection directly into the brain, probably via actions in structures around the third ventricle of the brain (Epstein et al., 1970; Johnson & Cunningham, 1987).

Cellular thirst (also called sodium or osmometric thirst) occurs as intracellular fluids are lost. Although initial water loss is extracellular, increases in extracellular sodium leads to osmotic force that draws water out of cells to balance sodium concentrations in and out. This produces cellular dehydration, actual shrinkage of the cells due to loss of water. In a classic experiment, Gilman (1937) injected hypertonic saline solutions, which have higher sodium chloride (salt) content than is normal in body fluids, into dogs' bloodstreams. This reliably caused the dogs to drink. Although osmoreceptors are found in several parts of the body, the evidence suggests that those critical for thirst and drinking are found in the brain (see review by Grossman, 1990). Introduction of hypertonic saline solutions directly into the hypothalamus can induce drinking behavior (Malmo & Mundl, 1975). Several distinct regions of the hypothalamus have been suggested as sites of osmoreceptors (e.g., Hatton, 1976; Johnson & Buggy, 1978).

The lateral hypothalamus in some manner plays a prominent role in thirst. Bilateral lesions of this region (which means damaged tissue on both sides of the hypothalamus) can produce a near-total failure to drink (Blass & Epstein, 1971), as well as appetite failures as discussed below. Similarly, the electrical stimulation of this area can produce drinking behavior in rats and goats (Andersson, 1955; Mogenson et al., 1971). This drinking induced by electrical stimulation has been described as compulsive, and may include substances that are normally aversive, such as concentrated salt solutions or urine.

Other areas of the limbic system play a role in thirst, the nature of which is not fully determined. For example, lesions of some parts of the septum can produce a condition of hyperdipsia, where the animal drinks excessively and compulsively (Harvey & Hunt, 1965).

Prandial Drinking

In people, fluid intake is usually associated with meals. The same is true in rats and many other species. This is called prandial drinking. Food absorption will normally upset the balance between salt and water in the body, because some fluids must enter the digestive tract to aid the process, and because there are salts in the food. Thus, it is necessary to drink to maintain balance. The interesting thing about this is that animals drink in anticipation of this need, before enough time has passed for thirst mechanisms to set in. LeMagnen and Tallon (1966) showed that rats ingest an amount of water that is closely correlated with the osmotic demand of their meal.

Cessation of Drinking

Why do animals stop drinking after starting? This is a more complicated issue than you might imagine. It is clear that it is not simply the absence or offset of signals that initiate drinking, because drinking stops before cellular and extracellular fluids are restored. Although it may be rather hard to drink too much water, as excesses are simply excreted, even water can be toxic if overingested, and mechanisms have evolved to prevent this.

Among mammals, the answer may vary depending on the species. Dogs tend to drink a lot of water very rapidly, rats drink slowly and mostly with meals, while we humans are capable of both patterns, depending on the individual and the degree of thirst. After 24 hours of water deprivation, dogs will drink enough water within 2 or 3 minutes to compensate for the loss. Humans, on the other hand, consume only about 75 percent of the deficit within 5 to 10 minutes of water availability, then continue to sip additional amounts for 30 to 45 minutes (Rolls et al., 1980). In either case, drinking terminates before there is sufficient time for reestablishment of normal levels of cellular and extracellular fluids.

Nervous feedback from the throat and stomach are believed to be responsible for cessation of drinking (see review by Grossman, 1990). Dogs still terminate drinking, albeit after a much larger quantity, when an esophageal fistula (or tube into the esophagus) is implanted to let water out before it reaches the stomach (Towbin, 1949). However, when rats have water infused directly into the stomach, they reduce their oral intake of water by as much as 90 percent (Kissileff, 1973), with results varying depending on the method of infusion.

Early studies showed that gastric distention (using a balloon) inhibits drinking in dogs (e.g., Adolph, 1950), but these studies have been criticized. More recently, Maddison et al. (1977; 1980) implanted gastric and duodenal cannulae in rhesus monkeys, meaning that tubes were placed directly into the digestive system. They found that if water was not allowed to accumulate in the stomach or duodenum, the animals continued to drink excessively. Although the presence of water in the duodenum had significant satiating effects, a comparable amount of isotonic saline did not. Therefore, it is not just distention, but osmotic imbalance and absorption of water from the duodenum which appears to activate a satiety mechanism. This is still not understood. Liver osmoreceptors have been suggested to play a role.

HUNGER AND SATIETY

Motivation, from Starvation to Satiation

Food is obviously a major motivator of behavior. In any species, foraging and consumption of food are critical activities, often involving more time and energy investment than any other behavior. In laboratory animal experiments, food deprivation is the most common variable used to motivate behavior, and animals readily acquire and maintain responses that are reinforced with food. Human history is replete with diverse strategies to obtain food, including conflicts among individuals and cultures. Over the better part of human evolution, food hunting and gathering were the most important and time-consuming activities. Agriculture and domestication of animals revolutionized strategies, but food acquisition still consumed the better part of human effort. Until the 20th century, most people gained a living through agriculture. Despite modern role specializations, a large portion of the economy revolves around food, and individuals spend significant portions of their time and money acquiring and preparing food. Food consumption is usually a source of pleasure, and social celebration in many cultures is centered on food.

Probably through most of human history, and indeed through animal evolution, food shortage was a common event and a limitation to activities and population growth. Existing physiological homeostatic mechanisms evolved in that context. Many of them are ancient, showing similarity across mammals due to conservation through evolution. Today many people have other eating-related problems, surely novel in evolutionary terms in their dimensions, such as overeating, obesity, insufficient physical activity to counterbalance caloric intake, anorexia nervosa, and chemically altered diets.

During times of famine, human motivation can be substantially altered. The historical record shows that food shortage motivates migration and aggression, in humans as well as other species. Migration is the easiest behavior change to document, but there is little doubt that some people become agitated and aggressive when food deprived. For example, Valunjkar (1966) compared migration patterns in two villages of India, matched for social and caste structure, one with chronic food shortage and the other with more abundant food supplies. In the famine-afflicted village, almost half of the families had members that migrated, primarily to find new sources of work, whereas in the other village, fewer than one quarter did, and most did so in normal activities to graze their animals. Kachhawaha (1992) studied the influences of localized famine in Rajasthan, India in 1936 to 1938, reporting that over 600,000 persons migrated from the worst-affected regions in 1938 alone. Police in the region reported an increase in criminal activities, and there was political unrest. Mariam (1986) studied rural famine in Ethiopia from 1958 to 1977. He estimated that over 2 million people migrated during this period in one small area of Ethiopia alone, and that many also died, usually in the process of migrating. Although migration carries risk, such risk may be outweighed by the potential benefit of finding other territory with better food sources.

Circumstances in developed countries have produced unprecedented abundance and diversity of food choices. Manufacturing technologies have given us artificial food additives, refined foods, and high quantities of substances like salt and sugar that appeal to our natural appetites. In conjunction with more sedentary lifestyles and reduced physical exercise, this has led to unprecedented levels of obesity in the population. For many people, natural mechanisms may not be producing optimal adaptation in these circumstances (see Inset 2-1).

Feasting, Fasting, and General Metabolism

Feeding clearly has many homeostatic properties. Much scientific effort has been devoted to uncovering the physiological signals that determine the onset of *hunger*, motivating food-seeking and consumption, and those that produce *satiety*, which causes termination of a meal. The factors that control hunger and satiety are not just opposite sides of the same coin. The control of feeding behavior is one of the most complicated issues in this text. There are multiple factors that influence appetite and satiety, both physiological and psychological. Several interacting (and possibly redundant) physiological systems have evolved to control feeding behavior.

Metabolically, the body can be viewed as having two phases, an absorptive phase and a fasting phase. Broadly, we know that these phases of metabolism are under the influence of gut content, blood sugar, hormones from the pancreas, and activities of the autonomic nervous system. During meal intake, insulin is released from the pancreas, promoting energy absorption by the body's cells. Energy is converted to forms in which it can be stored, including adipose. Absorption of energy is facilitated by the parasympathetic nervous system and rest. Between meals, when the individual is active, release of glucagon from the pancreas causes a release of stored energy, converting reserves to blood glucose. Maintenance of fasting is facilitated by activity of the sympathetic nervous system and the adrenal glands.

People usually do not eat and may not experience hunger while they are exercising and physically active. The body is in a mode of burning up stored reserves, activated by adrenal activity and the sympathetic nervous system, in conjunction with glucagon from the pancreas. On the other hand, while relaxed and resting, at least in the short term, appetite may be stronger. The body's metabolism is then in a mode of absorption of calories, under the influence of autonomic reflexes that are pro-digestive, while the pancreas secretes insulin which helps to bring energy into the body's cells.

Brain Mechanisms

The brain must be involved in the regulation of feeding, as it controls motivation of food-seeking behavior. The hypothalamus in particular has important input into the control of feeding behavior. Early research focused on two specific areas. Hetherington and Ranson (1942) reported that lesioning of the ventromedial hypothalamus (VMH) results in a syndrome of overeating and chronic obesity in rats. Anand and Brobeck (1951) reported that bilateral lesioning of the lateral hypothalamus (LH) resulted in a failure to eat. Electrical stimulation of the same regions can produce the opposite effect: VMH stimulation can suppress feeding, while LH stimulation can induce it. These regions were once thought to be "control centers" of satiety and hunger, but we now know that this is simplistic.

Some neurons in the lateral hypothalamus (LH) play a significant role in feeding as well as drinking (Bernardis & Bellinger, 1996). It has been known for some time that bilateral LH lesions lead to aphagia, a failure to eat. Initially following such lesions, rats will eat and drink nothing, and they may starve to death if not force-fed. Progressively with time, they will eat only dry food if water is available. With more time, they will eat only highly palatable foods. They will only drink prandially, that is in the context of food intake. The LH is thus involved in both feeding and drinking. Catecholaminergic and serotonergic transmitter systems have been implicated in the LH undereating syndrome.

VMH lesions produce very marked eating in rats. Hyperphagia lasts for about 4–12 weeks after the lesioning, during which the animal becomes obese. After that, weight may stabilize, and the motivation for food may change. The obese animal may be unwilling to work hard for food, unlike food-deprived rats, and it may choose a shock to the foot rather than food when forced to make a choice. It tends to become finicky, eating highly palatable foods and rejecting those which might, by the human as well as the rat, be viewed as less tasty. This may depend upon body weight, however, because VMH-lesioned rats may be no more finicky than normal rats if their body weights are first equalized by controlled diets (Ferguson & Keesey, 1975).

Many other brain regions play roles in feeding (Wyrwicka, 1988). The VMH's inhibitory role may be attributable to processes passing through it, and this area is not unique in its response to lesions and stimulation. Septal lesions can produce transitory overeating, and lesions of the amygdalas can produce prolonged overeating and obesity of comparable magnitude to that induced by VMH lesions. Lesions in the rostral hypothalamus and preoptic area in cats can produce complete aphagia for several days. Electrical stimulation of many regions of the brain apart from the LH can induce feeding behavior, including the rostral hypothalamus and preoptic area, the mammillary bodies, the midbrain, the middle and posterior pons, the cerebellum, and the medulla. Stimulation of parts of the amygdala and elsewhere can disrupt feeding.

Recent evidence indicates that a local peptide neurotransmitter in the arcuate nucleus of the hypothalamus, called neuropeptide Y (NPY), plays an important role in the regulation of energy balance, and that this peptide interacts with a circulating peptide hormone known as leptin (Figlewicz et al., 1996; Rohner-Jeanrenaud et al., 1996; Tomaszuk et al., 1996; White & Martin, 1997). NPY is chemically related to pancreatic peptides. NPY synthesis is associated with negative energy balance, insulin deficiency, and fasting. Artificial injection of NPY into sites of its neuron terminals in the hypothalamus is associated with food-seeking behavior. Some evidence suggests that overactivity of NPY may be implicated in obesity in laboratory animals. Insulin levels increase in rats infused with NPY as opposed to saline. Leptin may be released from adipose tissue (body fat stores). Leptin then may modulate NPY activity, forming a sort of homeostatic feedback loop.

Glucostatic Mechanisms

It has long been argued that blood sugar levels are critical for perceptions of hunger (Mayer, 1953). Glucose is the main currency of energy in the body. Many other nutrients are metabolized to glucose, which is then transported to the body's cells. It has been suggested that availability and utilization of glucose is responsible for the strength of desire to eat.

An involvement of blood glucose levels in appetite is now widely accepted. Increased hunger and ingestion occur when sugar availability to cells is diminished. One line of evidence comes from the dynamics of insulin and blood glucose. Insulin injections, which decrease blood glucose, lead to excessive eating in normal animals (MacKay et al., 1940). However, in untreated diabetes mellitus, where the pancreas fails to secrete insulin, blood glucose levels are high but affected persons report increased hunger. This paradox is now explained by the fact that glucose is unable to enter cells due to the absence of insulin, and that glucose must enter cells somewhere in the body to produce satiety. The drug 2-deoxy-D-glucose competes with glucose for receptors in cells, thereby lowering glucose uptake and utilization. Administration of this drug leads to an increase in animals' food consumption (Smith & Epstein, 1969).

There has been concerted effort in many laboratories to identify glucose receptors in the brain to explain the role of blood sugar in appetite. Blood glucose levels are associated with electrical activity in areas of the hypothalamus linked to feeding and satiety (Anand et al., 1962). However, the evidence is actually much stronger for the existence of receptors in the liver. Injections of glucose into the hepatic portal vein, which leads from the intestines to the liver, can produce longlasting suppression of appetite in dogs, but similar injections of glucose into the jugular vein near the brain does not affect food intake (Russek, 1963). Niijima (1969) found that low glucose levels cause electrical activity in neurons leading from the liver to the brain. Schmitt (1973) found that infusions of glucose into the hepatic portal vein caused electrical changes in the hypothalamus. Thus, the liver contains receptors sensing glucose concentrations in the blood, relaying this information via nervous connection to the hypothalamus. The liver experiences profound meal-related changes in metabolism, and it may also send signals to the brain in consequence to other specific metabolic changes induced by meals, although the most conclusive evidence exists for glucose sensors (Langhans, 1996).

Some studies have shown that ongoing changes in blood glucose levels are directly related to meal initiation. This was first shown by Louis-Sylvestre and LeMagnen (1980), who reported that a fall in blood glucose was correlated with meal initiation in rats. Campfield et al. (1985) similarly examined blood glucose concentrations, continuously monitored by computer in freely behaving rats, and found that natural transient declines in blood glucose levels tend to precede meal initiation. More recently, these findings have been extended to human beings. Both the perception of hunger and meal requests were preceded by spontaneous, brief, transient declines in blood glucose levels that were continuously monitored in human subjects (Campfield et al., 1996).

Lipostatic Factors

There is an old idea that animals adjust their food intake in the long term to maintain a "set point" in body weight. Accordingly, fat or adipose stores are maintained in homeostasis about some normal point. Eating is said to occur when stored fats fall below a certain level, and to be diminished when fat deposits rise above that level.

Some evidence appears to support this idea. After being force-fed for days, animals subsequently reduce their food intake if allowed to feed freely; but after being food deprived, animals increase their intake until they regain a normal weight (Cohn & Joseph, 1962; Hoebel & Teitelbaum, 1966; Steffens, 1975). Evidence from VMH-lesioned and LH-lesioned rats, described above, has often been interpreted as supporting this theory. The suggestion has been that the animals' natural set point is altered by such surgery (Keesey & Powley, 1975; Nisbett, 1972), and that the hypothalamus might be naturally sensitive to varying concentrations of metabolites from fat reserves.

The idea, then, is that hunger is controlled over the longer term in a homeostatic fashion by the amount of fat (adipose tissue) in the body. However, the search for hypothetical "liporeceptors" in several laboratories has failed to turn up any concrete evidence of such receptors, as would surely be necessary if fat levels were a critical determinant of appetite and satiety. Currently, most researchers appear to view lipostatic factors as secondary and not entirely proven, possibly important in long-term regulation but not implicated in short-term regulation of appetite and satiety. However, a mechanism of adipose tissue feedback to the hypothalamus may exist in actions of the peptide leptin, which may modulate NPY as discussed above (see Rohner-Jeanrenaud et al., 1996).

An individual's adipose level clearly is influenced by genetics, partly through individual differences in metabolic rate and activity levels. Adipose stores also interact with a host of developmental variables. One important factor may be the mother's choice to breast or bottle feed her infant (see Inset 5-1). Rates of obesity are much higher in modern times, especially in North America, than in previous history, suggesting that the factors responsible may be independent of genetics. An individual's adipose levels are also clearly dynamic, being affected by habits, circumstantial demands, and conscious control of diet and exercise. Common sense suggests that people with occupations demanding high levels of physical exertion, like many farmers or frame carpenters, are less troubled by excess adipose than are those with sedentary occupations, like word-processors or computer programmers. It also well known that habits of exercise and leisure influence body fat, metabolism, and physical fitness. Chronic obesity can become self-perpetuating, if one becomes so heavy that running is impossible and even walking causes pain in the joints.

An individual's body-fat level is also influenced by the composition of his or her diet. High fat diets tend to promote greater weight gain than do high carbohydrate diets in both rats and humans, due to higher caloric intake of the high-fat diet, or to more efficient metabolism of fat calories. Warwick (1996) has suggested that high-fat diets promote hyperphagia because their post-ingestive effects include less satiety per calorie, leading to greater calorie intake.

Peripheral Satiety Factors

The gastrointestinal tract obviously plays important roles in hunger and satiety. One early effort to uncover these mechanisms was that of Cannon and Washburn (1912). They reported something that is subjectively familiar to many people, that stomach pangs are associated with an empty stomach. A subject swallowed a balloon attached to a tube, which could be partly inflated to allow the experimenter to measure stomach contractions. There were more stomach contractions when the subject reported that he was very hungry.

An empty stomach is certainly correlated with hunger, and a full stomach with satiety, but we now know that many other factors are involved in the regulation of feeding. According to a review by Smith (1996), the information produced by food stimuli is carried from oral and post-ingestive fibers to networks in the brain that control eating. Information comes from an extensive receptive field extending from the tip of the tongue to the end of the small intestine.

Inset 5-1　Breast versus bottle feeding

Mammalian infants have evolved to be nurtured directly by their mothers. Human mothers in many cultures nurse each infant for up to 2 to 4 years. Other mothers in modern times have opted to alter this practice by bottle-feeding babies, using artificial formulas. Often, such formulas have been based on cow's milk, which differs in chemical composition from human milk, although modern infant formulas are chemically improved.

A nursing mother provides milk to her child in harmony with the child's demand for milk. Often the child must work to obtain milk. On the other hand, a bottle provides milk for little effort in quantities that may exceed the child's requirements. Evidence indicates that artificial feeding may upset natural nutritional regulation, and that this may have lifelong consequences for the child's adipose tissues. Shukla et al. (1972) studied overweight infants, finding a low incidence of breast-feeding and a high incidence of early weaning. Brook et al. (1972) suggested that there is a sensitive period in development of infants' fat cells, from the prenatal age of 30 weeks gestation to about 1 year of age, during which the fat cell number is determined for life. Adebonojo (1975) studied human adipose cells in tissue culture, relating this to the age of the donor, and found that the fat cells of infants tended to multiply much more than did those of older children. Faust et al. (1980) manipulated nutrition during early development in rats, and found that early nutrition has a sustained influence on fat mass and fat cell number. Together, these data suggest that overfeeding in infancy may have a permanent influence on the number of fat cells, and that diet and exercise in later life may influence the size of fat cells but not alter their number. It may thus be that some bottle-fed infants overfeed, that their fat cell number becomes excessive for life, and that this leads to greater proneness to obesity throughout life.

Breast-feeding may have many other benefits relative to bottle feeding. Some recent evidence suggests that human intelligence may be affected. Lucas et al. (1992) found that premature babies who were fed breast-milk performed substantially better on tests of intelligence in later childhood than did those who were formula-fed. This is not easily investigated, and the data cannot be viewed as conclusive, because children are not randomly assigned to conditions of breast-milk versus formula feeding. However, when socioeconomic and other factors were statistically controlled in this study, the trends in favor of natural feeding remained. One possibility is that optimal neurological development is dependent upon nutrients, particularly long-chain fatty acids, that may be uniquely available in mother's milk.

Some factors must be involved before food enters the stomach. A classic experiment involves fitting animals such that food that they ingest comes right out of their bodies without reaching the stomach, that is with a fistula that evacuates food from the esophagus (Janowitz & Grossman, 1949). Such animals will not eat indefinitely, as one might imagine. Instead, the animal eats a meal that is larger than normal, and then stops eating. However, with repeated experience, rats will begin to eat more and more in such a "sham feeding" situation (Mook et al., 1983). Indeed, the evidence suggests that satiety in feeding may be partly conditioned by experience. Weingarten and Kulikovsky (1989) have shown that increased consumption with repeated trials in sham-fed rats reflects a learning-based phenomenon, as rats learn to associate a food's sensory properties with its postingestive properties.

When liquid food is injected directly into the stomachs of rats, they will subsequently eat less than they would otherwise (Berkun et al., 1952), suggesting that there are satiety factors in the stomach and possibly lower in the gastrointestinal tract.

There has been much attention to the possibility that hormones from the gut might mediate some aspects of satiety. In particular, the peptide cholecystokinin (CCK) has been extensively investigated as a possible gut satiety hormone. When food arrives in the intestines, CCK is released into the bloodstream. When CCK is injected into the body, it can inhibit feeding behavior and sham-feeding behavior (where food is evacuated before it reaches the stomach) (Smith & Gibbs, 1994). Such effects of injected CCK on feeding behavior might be due to any of several factors. It could be that the hormone truly is a satiety hormone, and that these injections reflect a real physiological process. On the other hand, it could be some nonspecific action of the hormone, for example the possibility that it makes the animal feel sick.

Many of the signals of peripheral satiety may communicate with the brain via the vagus nerve. The vagus nerve is a major parasympathetic influence on digestion, the pancreas, and many other autonomic functions (see Figure 4-6). Severing this nerve may prevent the obesity produced by VMH lesions (Powley & Opsahl, 1974). Following meals, liver glucose sensors send signals of satiety to the brain via the vagus nerve (Niijima, 1969; Schmitt, 1973). Schwartz and Moran (1996) studied the role of vagal afferent signals critical to the negative feedback control of food intake in the rat, identifying several distinct populations of fibers and showing that nutrients in one gastrointestinal compartment can affect neural signals from another.

There also are roles of the pancreatic hormones, insulin and glucagon, in the regulation of feeding. Glucagon is associated with post-meal satiety (Geary, 1990). Glucagon administration at the beginning of meals reduces the meal size in both humans and animals. The effect of glucagon upon satiety may be partly mediated by the liver (Langhans, 1996). Insulin, acting within the brain, appears to decrease food intake (Woods et al., 1996). Exogenous insulin appears to have the same effect, probably acting through the same brain control mechanisms.

Other Physiological Factors

High body temperature has long been thought to inhibit feeding (Brobeck, 1948). Eating can cause a slight rise in body temperature, and deprivation a decline, and many people find that appetite decreases during hot weather. Warming the hypothalamus in goats can decrease ingestion if the temperature change is great, but this requires temperatures that exceed those that are natural, and will not occur within a normal temperature range (Andersson & Larsson, 1961; Grossman & Rechtschaffen, 1967). Body temperature could be relevant to appetite in extreme conditions.

People who are ill experience malaise, fatigue, and disinterest for usual activities, including feeding and drinking. This may be the result of the depressive effects of interleukin on food intake, possibly acting at the VMH (Kent et al., 1996). Substances involved in immunological responses may have a bearing on appetite; suppression of appetite is associated with both natural release and artificial administration of various biochemicals associated with inflammatory processes and illness (Weingarten, 1996).

Common sense suggests that appetite and satiety are nutrient-specific. We will explore that issue below. Some formal evidence suggests that macronutrients, including proteins, carbohydrates, and fats, may have different influences on satiety mechanisms, but more research is needed (Reid & Hetherington, 1997; Warwick, 1996).

Odor

Food odors can stimulate our appetites and entice us to eat when our attention has been elsewhere, even sometimes when we are satiated. Many dieters know the temptations suddenly induced by the whiff of cookies in the oven, or of meat broiling with fat vaporizing as it drips. It is reputed that some fast-food restaurants deliberately pump food odors into the urban air in order to entice people to enter and buy. Food odors can stimulate salivation and gastric secretions. Odors of foods that one likes and habitually eats may cause greater responses. One study found that in French subjects, the sight and smell of a normal French breakfast produced pancreatic secretions that were four times greater than those induced by beefsteak (Sarles et al., 1968). Patients who must be tube fed (which delivers food directly to the stomach) report little desire for food delivery unless they can sense the food through taste or smell (Bykov & Gantt, 1957).

The sense of smell is a primitive sense, directly involved in orienting many foraging animals toward natural food sources. The olfactory bulbs have many direct links to the limbic system and hence to our emotions (see chapter 4). We are rarely neutral in our emotional responses to odors. We like and are enticed by many odors, and we dislike and are repulsed by many others.

Psychological Factors

Numerous psychological factors have an impact on feeding. Many people are accustomed to eating at certain times of day, suggesting a role of conditioning. Merely knowing that it is noon, for example, sets off the routine of going to eat lunch. Most of us subjectively know how the odor of cooking food can distract us from other motivations and stimulate the desire to eat. Most people, after eating a filling meal, can have their appetite aroused once again by the sight of, oh, say, something like chocolate brownies, lemon meringue pie, pistachio nuts, butter tarts, white chocolate. . . . If your mouth is watering right now, then mere words may suffice. Of course, such words might also provoke disgust for some people, especially if sated with sweets, as in the expression "sickly sweet" (see below).

Food itself can stimulate physiological mechanisms associated with hunger and eating. In Pavlov's (1927) classic experiments with dogs, food elicited salivation in the absence of any conditioning. This response to the mere sight and odor of food, as well other internal secretions, are well known in many species, including people.

Social factors, as well as palatability and habit, can have an important influence over feeding. Feeding is constrained and initiated by social events in almost all cultures. Holidays are often feasts, celebrated in public, and many families and communities gather around food. There are experiments that show that the presence of other people can facilitate feeding; for example, Berry et al. (1985) found that people ate more ice cream when there were more flavors available, and even more still when they were in groups rather than alone.

Feeding is a rewarding process (see Berridge, 1996), one that may directly interact with structures and neurochemical systems in the brain that subserve pleasure and reinforcement. Our intake may often depend more upon the odors and tastes of available food than its nutritional value. This is true even in rats; those given a very palatable diet containing a variety of "junk foods" eat more than those merely offered a bland but fully nutritious diet of "rat chow" (Sclafani, 1976). When rats were offered a variety of common human foods, such as milk chocolate, chocolate chip cookies, cheese, peanut butter, and salami, they became obese compared to rats maintained on normal rat food. Surely, this tells us something about the widespread incidence of excessive weight in humans today.

Schachter (1971) made the rather famous suggestion that people who are obese are more under the control of external factors, such as sight and odor of food, than internal factors, such as low blood sugar and an empty stomach. He suggested that they were like VMH-lesioned rats, finicky and less susceptible to the internal satiety signals that terminate feeding in normal rats and people. He provided some experimental evidence supporting this claim. Obese humans may be more finicky. When offered a milkshake given a bitter taste, they drank less than did people of normal weight. When the milkshake had its normal taste, they drank more of it. They ate fewer nuts than did people of normal weight when the nuts had shells, but more if they had no shells. After a meal of equal size, obese people munched more crackers than did normal-weight people. However, when food-deprived, normal-weight subjects munched more crackers than did obese subjects. However, Rodin (1981) reviewed subsequent studies in this vein, concluding that obese people are not necessarily more responsive to external cues. Many people of average weight, as well as those who are obese, regulate their eating through external cues.

Conscious processes, from higher functions in the cerebral cortex, may affect feeding. It is well known that many people try to exert conscious control over diet. Today, there is an enormous amount of cultural information about feeding, impinging on an individual's knowledge and intelligent decision-making. Naturally, when confronted with delectable food while trying to reduce weight, this sets the stage for internal conflict between higher cognition and more primitive physiological impulses (see chapter 13).

SPECIFIC APPETITES

Sweet Tooth

It is obvious that many people like sweet foods. Most of us subjectively see this in ourselves, almost any parent knows that children crave and are rewarded by candy, and a quick perusal of corner store counters proves that sweets are used widely as snacks. Although the refinement of sugar is a fairly modern development, the preference for sweets is found in many cultures and surely predates the availability of refined sugars (Jerome, 1977; Pfaffmann, 1977).

A preference for sweet foods is evident even in newborn babies. Indeed, it is the practice in many cultures, including those of South and Central America, Polynesia, and South and South-East Asia to give sweet solutions to neonates (Jerome, 1977), in recognition of infant preference for such solutions and the belief that this improves the prospects for survival. Human newborns choose to ingest sugar solutions instead of water, and even show a preference for sucrose solutions over infant formulas (Desor et al., 1977). This preference for sweet solutions persists over development well into adulthood. Interestingly, people only like mildly sweet solutions, and may reject solutions in which the concentration of sugars is very high, although there are substantial individual differences in the level of sweetness preferred.

The tongue can directly sense only a few tastes, and sweetness is one of them. The existence of specific sweet sensors directly at this level provides further evidence that the response to sweetness is innate.

Many other species share this preference for sweet foods (Pfaffmann, 1977). The preference for sweet foods among dogs, horses, mice, rats, and other domesticated mammals is well known. In laboratory experiments, rats and squirrel monkeys will work for solutions containing sucrose, glucose, fructose, or lactose. It has also been widely observed that skunks, raccoons, and bears will selectively raid human garbage containing sweet foods. A sweet tooth may not generalize to all vertebrates, or even all mammals, but many vertebrates will accept sweet foods. Certainly, as any picnicker knows, insects like ants, bees, and wasps are also strongly drawn to sweet foods.

Steiner (1973; 1977) has conducted some fascinating work that relates the facial expressions of newborn babies to food-related chemical stimuli (see Figure 5-1). In the very first hours of extrauterine life, human infants show facial expressions that are stereotyped and communicative. Sweet, sour, and bitter stimuli elicit responses that are distinct, differing from one another and from that produced by a control substance, distilled water. According to Steiner (1977, pp. 174–175): "The sweet stimulus led to a marked relaxation of the face, resembling an expression of 'satisfaction.' This expression is often accompanied by a slight smile and was almost always followed by an eager licking of the upper lip, and suckling movements. . . . The sour stimulus leads to a lip-pursing, in a fashion known as the 'Darwin's pursing of the lips,' may be either continuous or repetitive. This is often accompanied or followed by a wrinkling of the nose and blinking of the eyes."

Thus, there are signs of pleasure and withdrawal from taste stimuli in the first few days of life. This surely suggests that affective responses to basic tastes, and indeed facial expressions associated with them, are innate. Some of the most remarkable data collected by Steiner are from the cases of newborns that were anencephalic, that is lacking forebrain structures, severe malformations due to microcephaly or hydrocephaly. Such neonates showed facial responses much as did normal neonates. This suggests that the gustofacial responses to tastes are very primitive, mediated by brainstem mechanisms.

Sodium Appetite

The fact that people crave salty foods, if not subjectively obvious, is readily seen by looking at the salt contents of "junk foods" that are widely consumed. Like the response to sweetness, the response to saltiness begins right at the tongue.

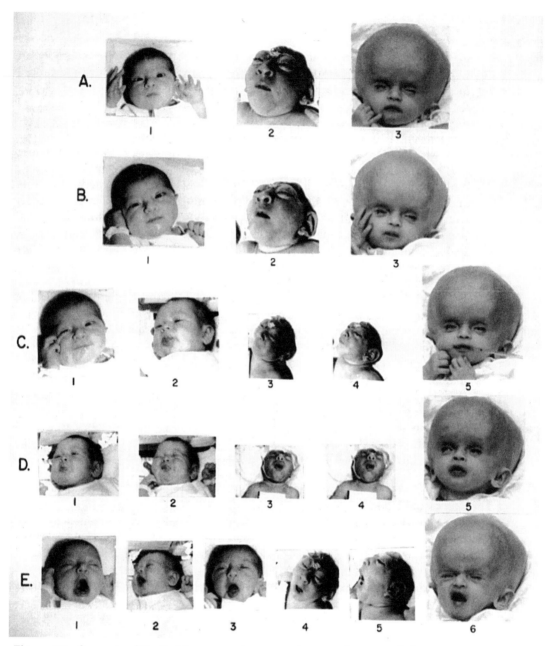

Figure 5-1 Synopsis of the facial response to tastants in normal, anencephalic, and hydroanencephalic neonates. A) Resting face (without stimulation). 1 = normal, 2 = anencephalus, 3 = hydroanencephalus. B) Control face (distilled water). 1 = normal, 2 = anencephalus, 3 = hydroanencephalus. C) Sweet-response (sucrose). 1,2 = normal, 3,4 = anencephalus, 5, = hydroanencephalus. D) Sour-response (citric acid). 1,2 = normal, 3,4 = anencephalus, 5 = hydroanencephalus. E) Bitter-response (quinine sulphate). 1,2,3 = normal, 4,5 = anencephalus, 6 = hydroanencephalus.

From: Steiner, J. E. (1977). Copyright © 1977, J. E. Steiner. Reprinted with permission.

Many other mammals also have innate appetites for salt. Cattle, like many other herbivores, may not get sufficient quantities of salt in their diets, and will travel extensively to salt licks. Carnivores, on the other hand, tend to have abundant sodium in their diets, while omnivores occupy an intermediate position (see Denton, 1982; Grossman, 1990). Laboratory rats, just like many humans, will preferentially eat salty foods even when they have no physiological need for salt.

As discussed above with respect to thirst, salt is delicately balanced in the body with water, such that a drive state of thirst is set up when the balance is upset. Salt (NaCl), or the constituent sodium ion (Na+) plays an important role in maintaining blood volume, regulation of fluid levels in intracellular and extracellular compartments, and in the metabolism of the cells themselves, including neurons. The salinity of our blood is normally just like that of sea water (about 0.9 percent).

Sodium is continually lost from the body through perspiration, urination, salivation, and defecation. When there is a fall in sodium levels in the blood, the renin-angiotensin cascade described above for thirst is set off, and aldosterone is released from the adrenal glands. Aldosterone reduces the excretion of sodium in urine, saliva, and perspiration. Aldosterone's importance is shown by the effects of removal of the two adrenal glands. Adrenalectomized rats will increase their consumption of salt (Nachman, 1962), and constant substitution of saline for water will increase the longevity after adrenalectomy (deCatanzaro & Gorzalka, 1980).

Under acute or chronic sodium deprivation, laboratory rats will drink very salty solutions that they otherwise might reject. Sodium deprivation can motivate a variety of forms of behavior that are rewarded with salt (Krieckhaus & Wolf, 1968). The taste of salt is important in the reduction of salt appetite, because loading the stomach with salt, without allowing the animal to taste it, may not always reduce this appetite. It is widely believed, on the basis of all of this evidence, that the appetite for salt, sodium in particular, is innate (see review by Grossman, 1990).

Other Innate Appetites?

There are, of course, many nutrients that are essential for good health. These include the 20 amino acids that are constituents of proteins, certain essential fatty acids, and a host of vitamins and minerals. One might imagine that there would be specific appetites that make us seek these nutrients, and that these might be built into individuals just as are the sweet tooth and sodium appetite. However, it is not at all clear that there are innate appetites beyond sweet and salty.

There is little doubt, on an obvious subjective level, that people have many strong desires for specific foods. Anecdotally, indeed notoriously, specific food cravings are associated with pregnancy, a phase in development where the specific nutritional requirements for growth may be at their greatest. Specific cravings for food often emerge spontaneously, such as a sudden craving for Chinese food or chocolate. But how could people of, for example, European ancestry have evolved a specific appetite for Chinese spices or beans originally found only in West Africa, when these substances have only been widely available in Western culture in modern generations? One would be hard-pressed to explain such cravings via natural selection alone.

Dietary selection is critical for good health. Some animals, like koalas or giant pandas, eat very few foods. They and other herbivores have special gustatory and intestinal adaptations to extract nutrition from a limited and specific number of sources. Carnivores, such as domestic cats, also have simpler concerns than we do, because meat alone provides a diversity of nutrients that are close in structure to their physiological requirements; basically predators build one animal out of the material of others. Omnivores, like humans, have the challenge of balancing their diets by selecting and apportioning their food intake so as to optimize health. With a lot of choice of food, it is important to have mechanisms to make sure that the right foods are selected, in the right balance for optimal health.

So, are there many other specific innate appetites? Food cravings raise interesting questions. One could speculate that cravings in pregnancy, for example, have an adaptive value in nourishing the growing fetus, and that natural selection has thus had some direct bearing. We do not have all the answers, but nature may have solved the matter without strong fixed drives like those for salt and sugar. Absolute proof of fixed innate appetites, beyond those for sweet and salty, is hard to provide. Although we can readily taste sweetness and saltiness, we cannot taste many specific essential nutrients in the same manner, and our response to odors is quite complex, as we shall explore below. Nature may have solved the problem in another way. There may be special mechanisms of learning involved. We may be predisposed by natural selection to learn rapidly which foods make us sick and which foods make us healthy.

Poison Avoidance

We clearly learn to avoid substances that have made us sick. Many people know this phenomenon all too well on a subjective basis, having had bad episodes with tequila, shellfish, cheap wine, or whatever. Subsequent to an association of sickness with specific foods, a strong aversion can develop. This may or may not always be truly adaptive. We might avoid good wine just because we once drank bad wine. Merely thinking about the food may conjure up memories of illness, and it may be next to impossible to overcome such aversion in future, even when socially constrained at a polite dinner party. The mechanism itself is surely adaptive, given that many people have specific food allergies, and poisons abound in organic substances. It is usually better to be safe than sorry when it comes to potential poisons.

Rats are omnivores, much as we are. Garcia et al. (1955; 1966) have shown that rats rapidly learn to associate a novel taste stimulus with sickness. This is true even when the sickness bears no causal relationship to the taste. Radiation or an injection of lithium chloride can cause a rat to be sick. The rat does not vomit, but its movement slows and it looks about as a sick human would. If radiation or the injection is associated with a novel taste, such as saccharin, rats subsequently avoid foods that taste of saccharin. The rats learn an association of the taste and illness, usually just with one experience.

Garcia has found that rats will learn to avoid novel food flavors even if the illness occurs with a delay of over an hour between the taste sensation and the illness. Only taste stimuli, and not auditory or visual stimuli, can be conditioned to be associated with sickness with such long delays. These properties of conditioned taste aversions initially caused worry and confusion to learning theorists, because most other forms of conditioning in animals required an immediate association of response and consequences. It makes sense, however, that special learning processes would evolve for avoidance of poisons, given the fundamental importance of nutritious eating and the dangers of poisons for any animal. There may be unique learning mechanisms related to food.

One defense against poisons comes from a phenomenon known as *dietary neophobia*. Animals tend to avoid substances that they have not previously eaten. In humans, once eating of solid foods is well established, many parents see this in their children, who generally eat very bland foods and are fearful of new foods with complex tastes. Dietary neophobia is also seen experimentally in laboratory animals (Rozin & Kalat, 1971).

Nevertheless, the motivation to avoid poisons probably interacts with or is overridden by food deprivation. Mariam (1986), who studied rural famine in Ethiopia from 1958 to 1977, observed that during starvation, people will eat substances that they know can be poison, such as grain infected by ergot and a type of pea, *Lathyres sativus*, which is known to paralyze the nervous system.

Acquired Specific Appetites

Rozin (1989; see also Rozin and Kalat, 1971) provides an excellent review of how specific food avoidance and preference are acquired. He suggests that conditioned aversions and conditioned preferences could explain why animals learn to consume diets that are healthy, providing the necessary nutrients. The idea is essentially that we learn to avoid foods that give us discomfort, and to seek foods that make us feel healthy and give us a sense of well-being.

There is much experimental evidence that supports this. For example, Rozin (1968) manipulated levels of vitamin B1 (thiamine) in food given to rats. There is no evidence that rats can taste or smell thiamine, and no evidence that they innately seek it without learning experience. Initially, when the rats' diet was made deficient in this vitamin, they ate food normally. However, with time, the rats began to eat less food and to suffer from the vitamin deficiency. They eventually started to spill the food, as they are inclined to do with poison food. When given another diet with ample thiamine, they quickly switched to the new diet and avoided the old one, showing no dietary neophobia.

Rozin has also reported that rats will quickly return to an old diet that provides full nutrition if they are vitamin deprived with a second diet. If given a healthy diet A, then switched to a new diet B that is short of an essential nutrient, they will choose diet A when given a free choice between A and B. Furthermore, if they are deprived of an essential nutrient, they will develop a conditioned preference for a novel diet if they are injected with the nutrient in conjunction with the taste of the novel diet.

Galef (1977; 1985) has shown that the patterns of feeding in rats are transmitted from adults to weanling pups. Rat pups tend to imitate the dietary preferences of adults in their vicinity. The pups learn which foods are safe and which are not through a number of cues, including factors in mother's milk, adult presence near specific foods, and residual chemical cues such a those on the adult's breath. On this basis, one could say that even rats have "culture," passed from generation to generation, when it comes to food.

Up to about two years of age, the human infant tends to put almost anything into its mouth, a phenomenon known as pica (Wicks-Nelson & Israel, 1997). This phenomenon is clearly affected by learning, because normal children with adequate parenting learn, for example, not to put soap in their mouths, while those with mental deficiencies or neglected by their parents may continue to show pica at later ages. Much early learning concerns what not to eat (see Birch, 1989). When previously neutral foods are followed by malaise such as vomiting, cramps, or respiratory distress, a conditioned taste aversion is formed. This can occur after a single negative experience, and even if the person knows that the specific food did not cause the problem. Parental modeling, food offering, and feedback on eating behavior are surely also very important in the molding of an individual's appetite. There are huge variations in food preferences among different cultures and individuals within cultures.

Birch (1989) has concluded that, for young children, repeated exposure is the most important factor in the development of liking for novel foods. Of course, the food to which the child is exposed is determined by family and cultural habits and rules. Rozin argues that the best predictor of human food preference is culture or ethnic group, and that social forces are the most powerful in determining food preference, particularly the perception by a child that an object is valued by respected others. Systematic studies on the role of social influence on children's food preference by Birch support this idea.

Rozin (1989) has also suggested that humans are unique in developing strong likes for innately unpalatable substances such as irritant spices, coffee, tobacco, and other bitter or strong substances. Chili pepper is strongly liked in many cultures, and Rozin has shown that initial dislike for the burn it produces becomes a like at 5 to 8 years of age. This is mainly accomplished through social pressure and imitation of adults.

Addictions as Acquired Appetites

Food chemistry is very complex, because organic substances are rich in biochemical diversity. The line between foods and drugs is not always as clear as the modern popular media portray it to be. Many if not most drugs are chemically derived from plants, and so are many of our foods. Simple food substances like cheese, wine, chocolate, nutmeg, licorice, bananas, and tea contain many organic substances that are known to have psychotropic properties. They alter brain chemistry, and could, if refined, be classified as drugs.

Addictions are complex phenomena that set up acquired motivation, influenced by psychological, social, and biochemical factors (see Peele, 1985). As is well known, addiction to certain substances like heroin and nicotine can set up strong motivational states, often to the point that they override more adaptive motivational systems. It is common knowledge that such drugs afflict their users with major compulsions that can be life-threatening. These are artificial motivational states that involve infusing the body with chemicals, and thus they can be construed as acquired appetites.

Consider first that, in evolutionary terms, refined drugs are a novelty. Some of the most powerful addictive substances, like heroin and crack cocaine are produced by unnatural chemical processes that involve modern technologies. Milder substances like cannabis, peyote, and opium have long histories, because they are directly derived from unprocessed plants. Many of the most dangerous substances are refined chemicals that are not naturally available. Human interaction with unnatural chemicals is not something for which natural selection has prepared us, so it should not be surprising if maladaptive behavior occurs in their presence (see discussion of evolutionary lag in Inset 2-1).

Alcohol (ethanol) can be classified as both food and drug. It is biochemically close to sugar, and metabolically in low doses it is simply converted to food energy. In higher doses it suppresses cellular metabolism in the central nervous system, and it is well known that it can disinhibit emotions and social inhibitions in many people. This effect may well be due to the fact that higher cortical functions inhibit more primitive lower forebrain functions, a relationship of cognition and emotion which we discuss in chapter 13. There can be no doubt that alcohol consumption can be habit-forming for many people.

Many drugs for which humans acquire appetites operate directly on neurotransmitters and other natural biochemical systems (see Cooper et al., 1991). As we discuss in later chapters, there is strong evidence that these chemical systems are directly involved in our emotions. Heroin and other opiates interact with receptors for endorphins and enkephalins, which are natural substances implicated in dulling pain (see chapters 4 and 6). Nicotine interacts with the subset of acetylcholine receptors known as nicotinic receptors, which are found in autonomic ganglia, parasympathetic reflexes, and parts of the central nervous system. When tobacco smokers say that smoking relaxes and stimulates them, it may be due to some of the autonomic reflexes associated with the parasympathetic nervous system. Cocaine stimulates catecholaminergic synapses. Many other drugs that people use recreationally induce artificial euphoria, via actions on monoamines like serotonin and norepinephrine. As we discuss in chapter 10, these monoamines are directly implicated in natural emotions of happiness and sadness.

Thus, many drugs for which people have appetites alter moods by meddling with natural biochemical systems that are directly involved in our emotions and drives. The reward associated with their initial use accordingly may derive directly from the pain reduction, euphoria, or relaxation that is artificially induced as these drugs tap into the natural mechanisms that underlie emotions. With repeated use, there is physiological adaptation as biochemical adjustments are made to the presence of these substances. Such tolerance is partly related to increased efficacy of excretory mechanisms, through enzymes in the liver, brain, and elsewhere. As the drugs are excreted more efficiently, a greater quantity must be consumed to get the same results on emotions.

Nevertheless, there is a major role of learning mechanisms and cognition in the acquisition and maintenance of addictive behavior (see Marlatt & Donovan, 1981; Peele, 1985). Among such factors are imitation and social inducement, reinforcement mechanisms, and cognitive expectations associated with the particular drug. To come under the biochemical influence of a specific drug like nicotine, cocaine, or heroin, one must first try the substance. Only a subset of people do so, due to exposure, modeling, cognitive expectations, and peer pressure.

Once a drug is tried, the individual has some exposure to its emotional influences. Drug self-administration, after initial experimentation, may be repeated as the individual experiences consequences of pain alleviation, relaxation, euphoria, and so forth set off by the drug. Subsequently, use may become habitual due to the reinforcement properties of these chemically induced mood and motivational changes. This idea is similar to the model of acquired specific food appetites discussed above, where the gustatory consequences of previous food choices influence subsequent food choice.

In the longer term, drug dependence may develop because the body has adjusted to the drug physiologically, and the absence of the drug sets up aversive states, leading to discomfort, craving, and withdrawal symptoms. This produces a deviation from an acquired homeostatic state, leading to motivation to correct this state.

There can be little doubt that conditioning plays a major role in drug tolerance and addiction. When the body is exposed to a substance like morphine repeatedly within a particular situation, cues in that situation acquire control over physiological reflexes and behavior associated with the drug (see MacRae et al., 1987; Siegel et al., 1987). Those cues, when presented in the absence of the drug, can actually elicit a response that is opposite to that induced by the drug, a conditioned anticipatory response. For example, if rats have repeatedly been given morphine (which reduces pain sensitivity) in a specific stimulus context, when later placed in that context without the drug they are actually hypersensitive to pain.

The appetite for specific drugs may be strongly influenced by ongoing social and housing conditions. This was clearly shown in experiments by Alexander, Beyerstein, Hadaway, and Coambs (Alexander et al., 1981; Hadaway et al., 1979). These researchers compared the voluntary morphine intake of rats housed either individually in sterile environments or in colonies in larger and more stimulating environments. Rats are a very social species, and social isolation can be stressful. Traditional individual laboratory cages provide almost no stimulation or opportunity for activity. In contrast, these researchers set up what they called Rat Park, an enriched environment with much more space, social contact, and objects to manipulate. In both conditions, a morphine solution was constantly available next to the animals' normal water bottles, and consumption of morphine was automatically monitored. The results clearly showed that rats in isolation in unstimulating environments consumed much more morphine than did rats in Rat Park. Subsequent studies by these researchers have shown that a combination of space and social stimulation was responsible for the effects.

It may be no coincidence that alcohol use increases during stress, that euphoria-inducing and pain-killing drugs are used by those in poverty and desperation, and that nicotine is used especially by those who are tense. Artificial appetites for specific chemical substances may be acquired because of their biochemical effects upon emotions and drives, which provide artificial rewarding properties, in interaction with social and conditioning processes.

These appetites involve very short-term gratification (see chapters 12 and 13). As is well known, the effect of chronic use of several substances can in the long run be maladaptive. This is not always due to the direct activities of the drug; for example, it is the smoke rather than the nicotine that makes smoking cause respiratory disease, and some of the unhealthy influences of heroin are attributable to associated lifestyle and hygiene problems rather than the drug per se.

Self-administration of specific chemicals takes many forms, from conscious and unconscious control of nutrition, to herbal and medical treatments, to drug experimentation and addiction. The lines are not always clear, and more research is needed in many instances. There are many drug- and nutrition-specific qualities that go beyond the scope of this text.

Modern Consequences of Dietary Predilections

According to Galef (1996, p. 70), "Our hedonic responses to gustatory stimulation and our associated motivations to seek out certain flavors may have been useful in some ancestral environment, presumably one in which sugars, fat and salt were hard to come by and special motivations to seek such substances were of adaptive value. However, when our motivational system, evolved to cope with an environment in which calorically dense materials and sodium were relatively scarce, interacts with the superabundance provided by commercial agriculture, our hedonic responses tend to produce injurious levels of intake of the sweet, the salty, and the greasy."

Consider, for example, the evolution of the sweet tooth. In conditions prevailing over mammalian evolution, where a few substances such as fruits and honey carried a sweet taste, this dietary predilection would be advantageous. At least in consumption of natural organic foods, sweets provide metabolically cheap energy, rapidly raising blood sugar levels while requiring little digestive effort. However, with modern technologies of refining sugar, there are many concerns about dental problems, dietary imbalance, obesity, and diabetes.

The issue of drug consumption just discussed raises the same issues. Many foods contain mild psychotropic substances. The fact that people value spices, which can contain diverse biochemicals with potential pharmacological properties, was certainly evident in the age of exploration. Seafarers like Columbus and Magellan took enormous risks to gain such spices, or at least to gain riches that might come from their sale. Organic substances like opium and coca leaves, which have long histories of consumption in some cultures, have mild influences when compared to heroin and crack cocaine, derived through modern chemical procedures. In chapter 2 (see Inset 2-1) we discuss the lag between modern technological culture and biological adaptation; there may be no better illustration than this.

ELIMINATION AND DISGUST

Now let us turn our attention briefly to the other end of the matter. Obviously, needs associated with elimination bring on very strong biological drives. As anyone knows, such motivation is associated with immediate physical discomfort, relieved immediately by voiding the system as required. Excretory mechanisms are found in one form or another in any organism, because metabolism produces waste products that must be removed from the body. Excretion is not limited to these two processes. We also discard waste through respiration, perspiration, and vomiting.

Urination and Defecation

The needs to urinate and defecate are of course very primitive drives found in all mammals, where the two processes are separated (there is only one process in many other vertebrates). Like other primary drives, these needs can rise above all other motives, to the top of the individual's priority hierarchy when the bladder is full or the bowels are ready.

Unlike mechanisms of nourishment, elimination processes have not been studied intensively from a psychobiological perspective. This is certainly not because they are unimportant as drive states; rather, it is more likely that the naturally disgusting nature of these topics makes them less enticing to researchers.

Much of the instigation of urination and defecation comes simply from physical pressures of a full bladder and/or bowels. Autonomic reflexes control elimination to a degree. The urinary bladder is under influence of sympathetic and parasympathetic nerves, and can accordingly be affected by drugs influencing the transmitter substances norepinephrine and acetylcholine. Urine flow is influenced by actions of the hormone vasopressin.

Involuntary urination and defecation are known to occur in relationship to intense stress and emotion. This is seen readily in laboratory rodents. Students in laboratories of psychobiology quickly discover that the first response of mice and rats to human handling is to deliver urine and feces to the handler. This response has actually been used as an index of "emotionality" in rats allowed to explore an open field (Broadhurst, 1975). Involuntary voiding is also recorded in humans as a response to extreme stress. This is especially evident in young children. It has also been recorded in soldiers under battle conditions.

As any parent (or dog owner) knows, infants do not naturally exert control over these bodily functions, and much learning and parental guidance surrounds elimination (see, for example, Wicks-Nelson & Israel, 1997). Children normally gain bowel control before they gain full bladder control. Daytime bladder control is often achieved before nighttime bladder control. A substantial proportion of children have occasional problems maintaining full control, as do the elderly. Although many factors are involved in enuresis and encopresis, respectively failure to control urination and defecation, among such factors are training routines and psychological stress.

Vomiting

The body also has innate mechanisms for eliminating toxins from the upper gastrointestinal tract. As is well known, vomiting may be brought on by illness or by food poisoning, or by psychological factors. Vomiting is associated with strong release of vasopressin from the posterior pituitary gland. It may also involve a region of the brain known as the area postrema, which is more open than other areas of the brain to chemicals in the blood, which is to say that it is less protected by blood-brain barrier mechanisms than are other brain regions (Ganong, 1973).

Vomiting is very common and normal in infants. It is also found in many older children, and emotional distress is prominent among the many causes (Wicks-Nelson & Israel, 1997). It may simply be brought on by conflict, emotional excitement, and changes in routine, as well as other factors like illness and motion.

Disgust

Disgust in a literal sense means expulsion from the gustatory tract. We also sometimes use the term in a figurative sense, referring to people's undesirable behavior or certain situations as disgusting.

Disgust is widely viewed as a universal and primary emotion. It is associated with stereotyped facial expressions (see chapter 2) that are generally read the same way across cultures. As discussed above, Steiner (1977) identified innate disgust reactions in large samples of newborn infants in response to a bitter taste placed on the tongue (see Figure 5-1). His description of the stereotyped reaction to the bitter stimulus was as follows: "Stimulation with the bitter fluid leads to a typical arch form opening of the mouth with the upper lip elevated, the mouth angles depressed, and the tongue protruded in a flat position. . . . It was often followed by spitting or even preparatory movements of vomiting" (Steiner, 1977, p. 175).

It is not difficult to understand why such an innate reaction to foul tastes would evolve. Surely it is highly adaptive for people and other animals to expel unhealthy food from the mouth.

We spoke above of how odors could please and entice us. Subjectively, most people also are aware that many other odors disgust and repel us. Most people feel repulsed by odors associated with illness, death, elimination, certain toxic bacteria, and some forms of organic decomposition. These smells utterly disgust many people. The limbic system of the brain is directly linked to the olfactory bulbs (see chapter 4). The relationship of odor and emotion is profound and ancient. Indeed, olfactory mechanisms evolved very early, and are major factors in orienting the behavior of vertebrates of many species. Although we as humans may have weaker senses of smell than do many other mammals such as dogs and cats, we have retained a strong emotional reaction to odor. We tend to like or dislike many odors; less commonly are we indifferent to them.

Sensitivity to odor has clear adaptive value. The stench of death is notorious for repulsing people. Decomposing bodies contain many bacteria, some of which are likely to induce illness in living people. There are chemicals, putrescine and cadaverine, that are known to be associated with these odors. Even rats will promptly bury dead and decomposing rats, and will bury items covered in the chemical stimuli associated with death (Pinel et al., 1981). The feces of many animals, especially humans and other carnivores, can elicit disgust.

It is extremely unhealthy to linger around dead bodies, excrement, and deadly bacteria. Many animals, including domestic cats and many dogs, have instincts surrounding their own feces, to keep them away from food and shelter and often to bury them. This is not universal among mammals, because rats, mice, and rabbits are known to eat their own feces. However, especially among carnivores, whose feces most people find very foul, there is a strong adaptive value associated with feces avoidance. Accordingly, instincts related to avoidance of feces and other excreta would not be hard to explain in an evolutionary context. Animals that avoid toxic and bacterial matter should have been far more likely to survive and reproduce than those that fail to do so.

On the other hand, Rozin (1989) argues that the acquisition of disgust for items such as feces or decay are neither innate nor conditioned, but conveyed by parents to children. It is certainly true that some infants handle and even smear their own feces, and that parents in many cases have to instruct their children on basic hygienic practices. There may very well be substantial individual differences in this dimension of conduct, as observed in humans as well as domestic animals such as dogs and cats. There are reasons to believe that both inheritance and training are critical for human hygiene.

Chapter 6

PAIN, FEAR, AND COMFORT

Perils abound on a daily basis in the lives of all animals, including humans in modern times. There are physical dangers of hostile environments, too hot or cold or dry or stormy. There are precipices and swift waters. There are predators, disease organisms, and competitors that would gladly kill to take away one's resources. Although we modern humans have worked to increase comfort and security and reduce disease and danger, removing ourselves from most traditional jungle hazards, we have created many others in the process: cars, planes, guns, nuclear warheads, drugs, and toxic chemicals, for example.

Self-preservation is a fundamental dimension of motivation, as explained by evolutionary contingencies in chapter 2 and illustrated by appetitive behavior in chapter 5. Self-preservation has clear adaptive value in almost all circumstances, with some limits, however, as we explore in chapters 8 and 10.

A simple way to cope with danger is to stay away from it insofar as possible, and when it is encountered, to run and hide. This is more or less what most organisms do, as is easily explained by natural selection. Such defensive behavior may be *escape* behavior, which means that the individual experiences some aversive stimulus and then acts to get away from it. It may otherwise be *avoidance* behavior, which occurs without any contact with the aversive stimulus because the individual anticipates and evades it.

Pain and fear drive us to avoid and escape physical danger. Our perceptual and motor skills are highly adapted to help us detect, avoid, and flee perils. Nevertheless, opportunity may be lost and energy wasted if organisms avoid, flee, and hide too much. Gaining access to food sources and mates often requires a risk of danger. Arguably, one takes a risk merely by getting out of bed in the morning, but nothing would be gained if we failed to do so.

PAIN

Motivation by Pain

Although pain can be highly unpleasant, and is usually viewed as undesirable, it is generally adaptive because of the ways in which it motivates us. Pain performs at least two roles in motivation. First, it is a disincentive for potentially self-damaging behavior. Second, it can slow our behavior to force us to rest and recover, once damage has been taken.

There are several manners in which pain drives us to escape from and avoid potentially damaging situations. In the simplest cases, this occurs as reflex action. If you place your hand on a hot stove burner, you will rapidly remove it without conscious deliberation, because there are simple reflexes between the pain sensation and the motor response of limb withdrawal.

In a somewhat more complex vein, pain is linked to inhibitory mechanisms. Many forms of punishment involve contingent painful stimulation. The application of electrical shock contingent upon a rat's behavior can cause a subsequent decrease in the frequency of the behavior that produced the shock. Whether or not we approve, many parents apply painful stimulation contingent on their children's behavior, in order to reduce its frequency, whenever they dole out a spanking for naughtiness. The processes of conditioning involving aversive stimuli are formally known as *punishment* and *negative reinforcement*. Punishment involves the application of a painful stimulus contingent upon a response in order to decrease its frequency. Negative reinforcement involves the removal of an aversive stimulus contingent on a response in order to increase the frequency of the response. For example, after discovering that immersing the hand in cold water or covering it in a particular salve relieves a painful burn, it may be more likely that one will repeat the successful response in future instances of receiving burns.

The ways in which pain motivates avoidance and escape are numerous and mundane, and affect human behavior routinely. You may decide not to go outside on a winter's day, or not to dive into the lake to swim during summer, because the air or water is too cold. Some people avoid trips to the dentist because they do not like the pain. A pair of shoes or skates may never be worn because they hurt the feet. You may get out of your seat to stretch, or leave work early if you can, because your back is aching from leaning over your desk. You may avoid exercising, even though you have been told many times that it is good for your health, because it brings momentary discomfort. On the other hand, in the face of the inevitable joint pain that aging can bring, you may learn and habitually perform complex sets of exercises that diminish and prevent such pain.

Cognitive processes may cause us not to engage in particular forms of behavior because of the anticipation of pain. This is one of the fundamental ways in which pain and fear are linked. Fear is very often fear of pain, pain that has actually not yet been experienced. The anticipation of pain may cause a person to fear, for example, walking onto a battlefield or being trapped in a burning house.

A second and distinct manner in which pain motivates us applies to recovery from injury. If one has sustained major injury, it is generally adaptive to cease usual activities and rest. Rest allows the body to channel its resources, physiologically, to the site of injury. Metabolically, it can be maladaptive to continue working and moving about when there is a wound to heal. As is common knowledge and standard medical practice, bed rest is advised following many injuries. It is usually better to stay off the broken leg until it has healed, and it will surely hurt if you try to do otherwise. Chronic pain can thus remotivate someone who might be tempted to forge on despite injury, to reset priorities and delay work until sufficient healing has occurred. Immediate acute pain may punish the efforts of an injured person who tries to rise from bed too soon.

Psychological Variability in Pain

One of the most remarkable facts about pain is that psychological variables can make a tremendous difference in its severity. Some people with massive injuries report little pain, and many people with trivial injuries have their attention consumed by pain. This is true despite the fact that there is "hard-wiring" of pain in the body as described below, innate neural mechanisms that should conduct information about injury to the brain. This conundrum has been the major focus of scientific interest in pain, motivating researchers to explore both physiological and psychological mechanisms.

Pain is not always adaptive, and in stress and shock we may not feel it, despite major injury. Imagine yourself in the middle of a battlefield, caught in no-man's land between two enemy front lines. If you suddenly suffer an injury, say a shattered leg, you can either writhe in pain or drag yourself to safety. Immobilizing pain in such circumstances could be maladaptive, if it made you stay in a dangerous spot and be hit again and killed. Better to ignore the injury and move to safety. Similarly, if your car has run off the road and overturned, and you are badly hurt but conscious, and you smell and hear gasoline dripping from the tank, optimally you should not be distracted by intense pain and instead focus on freeing yourself from the vehicle. Speculation about such scenarios has helped researchers to explain some of the curious variability in pain perception. Pain usually accompanies injury, but sometimes pain can be counterproductive despite severe injury.

Although most of us cringe at the thought of severe battlefield injuries, imagining that they must produce excruciating pain, the actual subjective outcome may often be less painful than anticipated. In case-reports from battlefields, severely wounded soldiers often say that they have felt very little pain (Beecher, 1956). Similarly, victims of sports injuries often report that they do not feel much pain, especially while they are focused on playing (Wall, 1979). Also, although cancer can devastate a person's body, Greenwald et al. (1987) found only a weak association between pain intensity and stage of cancer.

On the other hand, pain is often reported in the absence of any obvious tissue damage, especially in psychiatric patients (Chaturvedi, 1987). Clearly, the perception of pain is influenced by many factors besides the strength of the pain stimulus or extent of tissue damage. Two people with comparable injuries may show different psychological reactions to them. Pain perception clearly has some subjective qualities.

This is one of the major problems with the study of pain. Essentially, there is no real way to assess objectively the extent to which individuals experience pain. It almost always depends upon the individual's self-report. The manner in which pain impinges upon a person's attention may depend very much upon the context. Moreover, the perception and the tolerance of pain are two different factors; one may experience the pain, but whether one can stand it without taking action to escape is another matter. There are enormous individual differences in pain tolerance, and tolerance may also depend upon the context.

Many women report intense pain during childbirth, yet this can be a time of extreme joy. The excitement of seeing a new child may overcome the psychological focus on pain. Some women demand anesthetics for childbirth; others endure it without drugs. A small minority may actually view pain as a disincentive for bearing children, but many repeat the experience quite willingly. The very existence of pain in the context of bearing young is a curious phenomenon from an evolutionary perspective. Why feel pain in the process of increasing biological fitness? Physiologically, however, pain makes sense because of tissue damage during childbirth.

Attempts have been made to define some of the variables contributing to pain perception by administering standardized painful stimuli to groups of subjects and measuring their responses. Some studies have found ethnic and cultural differences in pain perception (Morse & Morse, 1988; Bates et al., 1993), but there are too many differences in attitudes, beliefs, and psychological states to provide a clear picture. Other studies have found, for example, that women rate noxious heat stimuli as more intense than do men (Feine et al., 1991). Although people who are depressed may complain more than others of internal pain, depressed psychiatric patients may show lower sensitivity to external painful stimuli than do controls (Lautenbacher et al., 1994). Pain sensitivity may decline with age and experience with painful stimuli; for example, women who have undergone childbirth may be more tolerant of pain than are women who have not had children (Hapidou & deCatanzaro, 1992).

One idea that may help to account for much of the data is the adaptations level hypothesis. According to this hypothesis, people may subjectively judge the intensity of new pain experiences in the context of previous experiences with pain (Rollman, 1979). Thus, a standard aversive stimulus might be viewed as very painful by someone who has previously experienced little pain, while the same standard stimulus is perceived as only mildly painful by someone who has previously suffered extremely painful injuries.

In some historical cultures, pain tolerance has been actively trained and encouraged. In military cultures, such as ancient Sparta in Greece, tolerance of pain was highly valued. Ascetic practices, involving denial of pleasure and tolerance of pain, have been associated with many of the world's religions. Sometimes this has gone to extremes, as with the flagellants of 13th century Europe who would run through the streets of a town lashing themselves while exhorting others to do likewise. The flagellant movement was revived during the Black Plague of the 14th century, when adherents traveled in organized bands, vowing to abstain from all pleasures and to endure tortures and whippings in memory of the sufferings of Christ. During the 7th to 12th centuries, members of an Islamic sect called Sufism similarly followed ascetic practices, teaching that abstinence, patience, and poverty led to knowledge of God, and deliberately wearing clothes made of very coarse cloth.

Neural Structures and Pain

Despite the enormous variability in pain perception due to psychological variables, pain has an innate physiological basis. See the text edited by Wall et al. (1994) or the works of Fields (1987) or Jessell and Kelly (1991) for thorough reviews of the physiology of pain. Essentially, there are free nerve endings acting as receptors in the periphery of the body, which send messages to the spinal cord, where they synapse on tracts leading primarily to the midbrain and thalamus, reaching conscious attention in the brain.

Receptors for pain (*nociceptors*) are not complex specific receptors that filter information. Rather, most nociceptors are just free nerve endings. Nociceptors may respond to mechanical damage, thermal stimuli (heat and cold), and various chemical stimuli set off by tissue damage. These free nerve endings are found in various locations including the skin, the sheath surrounding muscles, the internal organs, the membranes around bones, the cornea of eye, and the pulp of teeth. Nociceptors are not distributed evenly in the body; for example, there are virtually none in the brain.

There are two types of nerve fibers that transmit peripheral pain information. These two types of fibers are associated with different subjective sensations of pain. *Aδ-fibers* are thick fibers associated with thermal and mechanical nociceptors. These fibers are covered in myelin. Myelin is a fatty substance that coats some neural axons and dramatically increases the speed of information transmission. Thus, Aδ-fibers conduct information very quickly. They are believed to mediate sharp, pricking pain sensations. *C-fibers* are thin fibers that conduct information more slowly, because these fibers are not covered in myelin. C-fibers are associated with nociceptors that are activated by a variety of mechanical, chemical, heat, and cold stimuli. C-fibers are believed to be responsible for dull, ongoing, aching pain sensations.

Subjectively, this differentiation of two sorts of pain makes sense to many people. Sharp, acute pain is felt as an immediate and intense response to sudden injury, like a hammer hitting a finger or a stubbed toe. This immediate sharp pain may give way to ongoing aching pain. Slow aching pain may be felt for a matter of days from, for example, a burn, a wound, a sore muscle, or a compressed vertebral disc.

Pain fibers enter the spinal cord at the dorsal horns (toward the back on either side), where they synapse. The postsynaptic neurons then ascend toward the brain via one of a number of different tracts. Three of the most important pain tracts in humans are the spinothalamic tract, the spinoreticular tract, and the spinomesencephalic tract. In plainer English, these tracts lead through the spinal cord respectively to the thalamus, the reticular system of the brainstem, and the midbrain (see chapter 4). There are also two other pain pathways which head through the spinal cord to nuclei in the cervical region of the spinal cord and the medulla oblongata. Those reaching spinocervical nuclei send projections to the midbrain and thalamus.

So, essentially, pain messages reach structures in the brain that are associated with general arousal, including the reticular formation of the brainstem and midbrain, and associated with selective attention, in which the thalamus is often suggested to play a role.

The thalamus is a critical region of the brain for primary receipt and processing of various sorts of sensory information, including pain. The spinothalamic tract is the most prominent and well-studied tract for pain. The medial and lateral thalamus receive information from this tract. The spinoreticular tract also indirectly reaches the thalamus, with projections from the reticular formation to the medial thalamus. The thalamus relays this information to many regions of the cortex, including limbic cortex and somatosensory cortex. Presumably, this is where and how pain links to emotional responses and consciousness. Lesions to the spinothalamic tract can result in marked reduction in pain sensation. Electrical stimulation of this tract can produce pain sensation. Certain specific thalamic lesions can block pain perception, whereas other thalamic lesions can leave the perception of pain, but the subject may feel indifferent to the pain, saying they do not care. On the other hand, electrical stimulation of the thalamus does not produce pain.

The spinomesencephalic tract arrives at the midbrain, as do some projections from spinocervical passages. Here, it links to the midbrain reticular formation and a region around the ventricular system known as the periaqueductal gray (PAG). The PAG in turn links to the hypothalamus, with connections sending information in both directions, and hence contacts the limbic system.

Events in the spinal cord have been postulated to help explain why pain perception can depend on other stimulation, including psychological events. This is the classic gate control theory. Recall that incoming pain-related neurons synapse at the dorsal horn of the spinal cord. There are other neurons in this region that are called interneurons, which synapse on the postsynaptic neurons that send relays to the thalamus and midbrain. These interneurons may act in an inhibitory fashion, preventing transmission of information to the brain. Accordingly, relaying of pain messages to the brain may not be automatic after pain messages arrive at the spinal cord, but may also depend on inhibitory actions of other neurons at the spinal cord. This mechanism, proposed by Melzack and Wall (1965), has led to advances in clinical treatment of pain, but is no longer believed to be the exclusive mechanism through which pain perception is modulated.

Brain mechanisms can modulate pain perception. Direct electrical stimulation of the brain can produce analgesia. This is particularly true of the regions of the brain surrounding the third and fourth ventricles, or the PAG. Electrical stimulation of these regions can produce profound analgesia in both human clinical patients and experimental animals. Such stimulation does not reduce the response to other tactile stimulation, it just reduces the sensation of pain.

There are pathways that descend from the brain to the spinal cord that are involved in these analgesic effects of central stimulation. Electrical brain stimulation as just described has been found to affect nociceptive neurons in the dorsal horn of the spinal cord. Thus, events in the brain, particularly in regions around the ventricles in the brainstem, can feed information down the spinal cord to suppress pain perception.

Chemical Modulation of Pain

Much of the psychological variation in pain perception may be related to neurochemical changes. In particular, during psychological stress, chemicals are released that may dull sensitivity to pain.

It has long been known that opioid drugs can reduce pain sensitivity. Morphine, heroin, and other derivatives of the opium poppy can alleviate pain. There is a long history of morphine use for this purpose; it has been given to injured soldiers in wartime and is still commonly used in hospitals today. In nature, however, it is hard to imagine how the human body would have evolved to interact with chemicals from the opium poppy. The identification of specific receptors for opioids aroused curiosity about what naturally interacts with such receptors. This led ultimately to the identification of endorphins.

If rats are given low doses of opiates directly into specific regions of the brain, there is powerful loss of reaction to painful stimulation. Thus, it is believed that these drugs produce analgesia by stimulating brain mechanisms rather than mechanisms in the periphery of the body. The sites at which central nervous system morphine administration is most effective are the same sites in which electrical stimulation effectively produces analgesia, the PAG around the third and fourth ventricles and the cerebral aqueduct. Thus, opiates may disrupt pain perception by activating descending pain-modulating pathways.

Breakthroughs came in the 1970's that led to understanding of the natural chemical basis of pain modulation. It was found that opioids exert their effects by binding to specific receptors, and that the brain contains natural peptides that act like opioid drugs. We have learned that there are two classes of natural chemicals found in the brain. There are small peptides known as *enkephalins*, which consist of sequences of just five amino acids. There are also larger peptides, *endorphins*, including β-endorphin and dynorphin.

The enkephalins (leu-enkephalin and met-enkephalin) and dynorphin are found in the PAG and the dorsal horn of the spinal cord, just where we know they could be most relevant to pain inhibition. β-endorphin is distributed differently. β-endorphin is actually a hormone produced by the anterior pituitary gland and parts of the hypothalamus projecting to the vicinity of the ventricular system (see chapter 4). β-endorphin has a common chemical precursor with ACTH, and these substances may be released in conjunction during stress.

There are at least three classes of receptors for endorphins and enkephalins, mu, delta, and kappa. Enkephalins act at mu and delta receptors, while dynorphin acts at kappa receptors. These receptors are widely distributed in the central nervous system, and enkephalins and endorphins may be distributed via the ventricular system to reach these receptors, producing other actions as well as those upon pain perception. Mu receptors in particular may be involved in pain reduction. Morphine has potent actions on mu receptors, which are found in PAG and the dorsal horn of the spinal cord.

It is now widely believed, therefore, that descending neural pathways, endorphins, and enkephalins may limit pain, especially under psychological stress. This pain limiting mechanism may be highly adaptive in helping animals to cope with dangerous situations where action is demanded, and where the inhibition and withdrawal that pain tend to elicit might be maladaptive. So, recent evidence has helped us explain the enormous psychological variability that is seen in pain perception, and to tell us why severe injury does not always produce the agony that many people might anticipate. A summary of the known physiological mechanisms of pain perception is given in Figure 6-1.

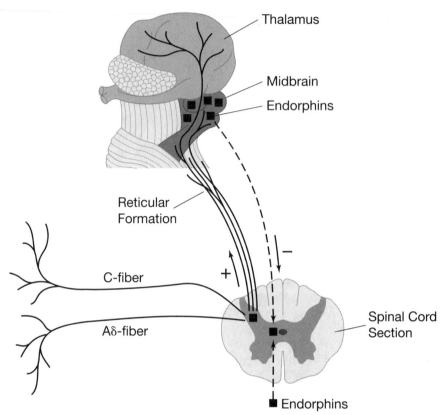

MECHANISMS OF PAIN PERCEPTION

Figure 6-1 Basic neural pathways related to the perception and inhibition of pain. Subcortical brain regions are shown, as is a slice through the spinal cord (not to scale). The major paths for input of pain information, which ascend from the spinal cord to the brain, are shown. Descending paths are associated with chemical actions of endorphins and enkephalins and can inhibit pain perception.

THERMOREGULATION

Let us turn our attention briefly to another form of motivation, partly related to pain but with its own features. This is our drive to seek comfort in reaction to excess heat and cold.

The environments in which most animals live involve considerable temperature fluctuations from day to day and across seasons. Yet warmblooded mammals have evolved to maintain relatively constant internal body temperatures. Consider the challenges to polar bears, who thrive through most of the year in very low temperatures, but also have no difficulty coping in mid-July when mild temperatures briefly arrive, or to bison ("buffalo") of the Great Plains, who cope with both very cold winters and very hot summers. Of course, we humans have adapted ourselves to a wide range of conditions, from the Inuit in the Arctic to the Bedouins of the Sahara.

We are considering thermoregulation here because excessive heat and cold can produce pain and constitute a threat to survival. The human body cells are normally at about 37–38°C; a body-core temperature over 44°C is lethal, as is usually that below 25°C. Excessive heat and cold can also produce pain. The pain may be localized, as when we touch a hot stove or immerse our feet in cold water. Some of the body's receptors for heat and cold are shared with those for other forms of pain. Extreme heat and cold may also be more diffuse, affecting much of the body and for longer periods of time.

There are two mechanisms through which animals adapt to temperature variations: autonomic responses and behavioral responses. Autonomic responses include reflexes such as shivering and panting. Behavioral responses are diverse.

Autonomic Responses

We have reflexes to control bodily temperature, and the hypothalamus plays a significant role in controlling these reflexes (see Arancibia et al., 1996; Mogenson, 1977). Most evidence suggests that the hypothalamus and preoptic regions contain temperature-sensitive neurons, and that the hypothalamus integrates this direct information with input from thermal receptors in the skin. Thermoregulatory responses are controlled by the release of pituitary hormones which regulate energy metabolism and heat production. Under cold conditions, secretions of thyroid hormones increase. There is increased discharge of the sympathetic nervous system, shivering and piloerection occur, and blood vessels constrict to reduce heat loss. In high temperature conditions, the rate of metabolic activity decreases, blood vessels dilate to transfer heat to the surface of the body, and sweat production and evaporation increase, triggering thirst and panting.

Behavioral Responses

Like thirst, thermoregulation fits the classic definition of a homeostatic drive. A drive state is set up when there is a deviation from normal balance, that is when we are too hot or too cold. This impels action, which terminates when we reestablish a normal state. Obviously, humans do this. When outside in cold winter weather with inadequate clothing, we feel cold and impelled to act to rectify the situation. In the hot summer sun, especially when overdressed, we similarly feel discomfort and may act to evade the heat. Subjectively, these drive states can be very strong, pervading our consciousness and rising quickly to the top of our priorities when the discomfort is severe. After all, it is quite possible to die of excessive heat or cold.

The hypothalamus may also be involved in the activation of behavioral responses for thermoregulation, and in the integration of these responses with the autonomic responses described above. Alternatively, Mogenson suggests that autonomic and behavioral responses are separate, and are initiated by separate thermal signals, and have different neural substrata. Behavioral responses are more likely to be triggered by thermal discomfort sensed in the skin, and to involve cerebral cortex and limbic structures as well as the hypothalamus.

The actions that we take encompass many things, from adjusting our clothing, to turning up or down our thermostats, to opening and closing our windows, to seeking shade or going indoors, to diving into a cool lake or pool, to chopping wood and kindling a fire, to spending money on clothing, furnaces, air conditioners, and insulation. In pioneer days of North America, keeping warm through winter was a major endeavor that for many could determine survival. As naked animals, we have always had much work to do to regulate our temperatures.

Other animals similarly show predictable responses to excess heat or cold (Bligh, 1973). Many animals seek shade or go into burrows when the temperature is too high, while others may enter a lake or stream. Elephants will use their trunks to spray water over the surfaces of their bodies. Where animals are in groups, for example young littermates, they tend to huddle together to conserve heat when the temperature is cold. Animals also tend to adjust their activity levels, slowing down when too hot because activity tends to increase body temperature.

FEAR

Fear is an ancient and primitive emotion. Some researchers have preferred to abandon the term, because it implies an internal subjective state, and instead speak of defensive behavior. Recently, Boissy (1996) has argued that the concepts of "fear" and "fearfulness" should be restored, because there are consistent individual differences in these traits, and physiological measures validate ideas about internal states.

Whatever terms we choose, real or perceived aversive stimuli act as powerful motivators of behavior. Whereas pain is a response to actual damage, fear is usually used to refer to anticipation and avoidance of damage that might occur. Many (but not all) of the things that we fear would cause pain if we experienced them. Fear may be said to relate more to avoidance behavior, whereas we generally seek to escape from pain.

Most organisms do all that they can to orient themselves away from perceptible dangers. Very often, this involves locomotion, running away from the threat. Even many simple invertebrates, like ants or spiders, will flee dangers, as any child quickly discovers if he or she tries to toy with these animals (one wishes that houseflies and mosquitoes would fear us more). Among mammals, fearful responses can be observed in any species, but are probably most prominent among animals that are subject to predation, especially herbivores like rabbits, deer, sheep, and antelopes. Sheep and rabbits will run from almost any strange stimulus, but it may be much more challenging to produce this behavior in lions and tigers, carnivores at the top of the food chain.

Fear is highly adaptive, provided that it is oriented toward objective rather than imaginary dangers. It keeps us from interacting with potentially dangerous elements. Death is merely a moment away for any living organism. One bad decision is all that it takes. One does not get a first chance, let alone a second chance, with the abundant dangers in the natural world.

Unconditioned Fears

Gray (1979) classified fear-producing stimuli into five categories. There are dangers that derive from the species' evolutionary history, stimuli that are frightening simply because they are salient and novel, stimuli that an animal learns are dangerous, stimuli that are frightening because they are very intense, and various stimuli that arise due to social interactions. As such, the stimuli that provoke fear do so through interactions of innate and experiential factors.

An innate basis of some fear responses has long been suspected (see Boissy, 1996; Gray, 1987; Rachman, 1978; Rachman & Seligman, 1976; Seligman, 1971; Valentine, 1930). Many researchers contend that certain fears are too common to be attributable to experience alone, and may instead be prepared by evolutionary heritage. These include fear of snakes, heights, deep unknown waters, spiders, large predatory animals, separation, darkness (for diurnal species), and aloneness (for social species). In each case, prepared avoidance behavior would have clear adaptive value, because all of these stimuli are frequent and recurrent dangers to individuals of many mammalian species.

In humans, these fears are related to primitive jungle conditions more than the modern urban environment. Seligman (1971) argued that many human phobias were "prepared" by evolution more than conditioned by experience. Such phobias generally surround a limited and nonarbitrary set of stimuli, whereas conditioning could occur with an unlimited number of stimuli. Phobias are much more resistant to extinction through conditioning procedures or via cognitive reasoning than would be predicted by learning models.

Mineka and coworkers have conducted some very thorough studies of the acquisition of snake fear in rhesus monkeys (Cook & Mineka, 1989; Mineka et al., 1984; Mineka & Cook, 1986). These experiments demonstrate that fear of snakes is certainly influenced by observational or social learning, but also has properties suggestive of evolutionary preparedness. Young monkeys whose parents showed fear of snakes did not show this fear. However, the monkeys did rapidly acquire an intense and persistent fear of snakes if they observed their parents behaving fearfully in the presence of real, toy, and model snakes. This fear acquisition was very rapid, and once established, the fear was very strong and persistent. In one set of experiments, these researchers videotaped model monkeys behaving fearfully, splicing the film so that it appeared that the fearful behavior was either a reaction to "fear-relevant stimuli," such as toy snakes and toy crocodiles, or to "fear-irrelevant stimuli," such as flowers and toy rabbits. Observer monkeys rapidly acquired a strong fear to the fear-relevant stimuli, but not to the fear-irrelevant stimuli. These data suggest that fear is not equally associated with any arbitrarily chosen stimuli, but rather will most readily be associated with stimuli presenting significant hazards in the species' evolutionary history.

Fear of snakes has obvious survival value, given the abundance of poisonous snakes, especially in ancestral environments. Some readers may have seen these reactions while wriggling a vacuum cleaner hose in front of a cat. Many cats will arch their backs, hiss, show piloerection, and extend their claws and swipe at this innocuous stimulus.

Almost any terrestrial animal, when confronted with a precipice, will avoid walking over it. This inhibition of obviously maladaptive behavior occurs without any aversive experience with cliffs. Gibson and Walk (1960) conducted experiments with human babies who were just able to crawl, at about six months of age. Infants will show natural avoidance of cliffs the first time that they are encountered. When mothers cajoled their infants to crawl onto a raised platform, they readily did so. However, when the mothers similarly tried to entice the infants to crawl onto a glass platform of the same height, they refused to do so.

Fear of heights is common in people of all ages, but it is by no means universal and it can be counterconditioned. Many people report strong subjective sensations of fear, for example, when they are on apartment balconies. Certainly not everyone feels this sensation to the same extent, and experience can modify this fear as one repeatedly experiences safety on such balconies. Some people are also able to bring themselves to parachute from airplanes or to bungee-jump. They may feel fear nonetheless, and gain a sense of exhilaration (see chapter 8). What is remarkable is how well some individuals can override their innate fears, presumably by using their higher cognitive powers to reassure themselves that an act is actually safe, when at a primitive perceptual level it seems totally lethal.

While many of us have had aversive experiences with modern matters like cars and electrical outlets, few of us have had aversive experiences with snakes. Nevertheless, snake fear is probably much more common than fear of cars or electrical outlets. Death could be just a step away on an urban sidewalk, but few people fear walking on an urban sidewalk. Many modern fears may be more easily explained by ancestral environments, and not yet be in tune with objective modern dangers.

It is easy to see why pressures of natural selection would produce primitive specific fears. Many common natural dangers do not provide an opportunity to learn. Presumably, primitive mammalian ancestors who failed to avoid cliffs, serpents, predators, and other common dangers often died before reproducing. At some point, mutations causing innate recognition and avoidance of such stimuli must have arisen, conferring strong advantages on those bearing these genes. Over generations, individuals with such natural fears survived and reproduced, while those lacking such fears perished.

What may be truly remarkable is how little fear we show toward objective dangers in modern circumstances. Consider the many maladaptive acts that some people perform in the presence of novel technological innovations like guns, drugs, and cars. There has simply not been enough time for evolution to prepare us to behave in fully adaptive manners in their presence. Once again, we must consider the lag between biological and cultural evolution (see Inset 2-1).

Fear may be so highly prepared by nature that it can occur in some persons in the absence of any objective danger. The human clinical literature describes many instances of "panic attacks," bouts of utter terror that occur without any obvious reason, generally beginning in people in their late twenties (Kandel, 1991c). Such panic attacks involve brief, recurrent, unexpected, and spontaneous episodes involving intense overactivity of the sympathetic nervous system. Classic signs of arousal of this system are seen in increased heart rate, shortness of breath, dizziness, trembling, and a cognitive sense of impending death or of going crazy. Of course, such cognition can hardly help, and may aggravate the situation, especially if the person fails to realize that what really is happening is just a reflex action prepared long ago by evolution to confront actual dangers.

Innate Reactions to Danger

As mentioned in chapter 3, Bolles (1970) has extensively reviewed the literature on experiments in which laboratory animals have been trained to escape and avoid aversive stimuli like electric shock. He has argued that what animals do in these circumstances is not flexible. They are unable to acquire many particular responses even when the best "laws" of learning are applied. It is very easy to teach a rat to flee from danger, but it is quite hard to teach it to press a bar to escape danger. Rats, like many other mammals, are predisposed to show specific responses like fleeing, freezing, or fighting, which Bolles called *species-specific defense reactions*.

Running away obviously works for many dangers. As is well known, herbivores that are set upon by predators commonly flee. It may not always work, if the predator gives chase, but it certainly increases the probability of survival. When a female baboon is chased by a dominant male, she "typically runs away screeching continuously . . . and she may defecate and urinate as she goes" (Hall & DeVore, 1965, p.101). On the other hand, sometimes running away can make an animal more conspicuous to a predator. Under some circumstances, it may be better to freeze so that your movement does not catch attention. Like a deer startled in the headlights of a car, many prey may take this gamble. Of course, a car is not a natural stimulus, and the deer's response can be maladaptive in this context. But in natural forest circumstances, freezing may reduce visibility to predators, such as people, who rely on vision to detect their prey. Immobility is a well-documented mammalian reaction to frightening stimuli (e.g., Boissy & Bouissou, 1995). Fighting may also be a last resort for cornered prey (see chapter 9); there is nothing to lose in bravely putting up a last battle and a small possibility that this will deter the predator.

There are other innate species-specific defensive reactions. For example, rats have been reported to bury objects that are potentially harmful to them, including devices delivering electric shock (Pinel & Treit, 1978), noxious food (Wilkie et al., 1979), and dead conspecifics (Pinel et al., 1981). Another example (see chapter 5), just mentioned for baboons, is the tendency of many mammals to urinate and defecate in conjunction with extreme fear. It has often been suggested that this helps make prey unpalatable to predators. Many social animals like herbivores also cry out during exposure to frightening stimuli (e.g., Boissy & Bouissou, 1995), as also in the baboon example above. Perspiration, especially in the hands (forepaws) and feet (hindpaws) may improve the ability of animals to grip surfaces while running or climbing during flight (Adelman et al., 1975), and it may also cause the skin surface to be more resistant to injury (Wilcott, 1966).

Archer (1979) suggested that the effects of fear-producing stimuli upon behavior tend to vary with the emotional intensity of the fear reaction. When the fear intensity is low, the animal's normal activity, such as feeding, may actually be enhanced. Intermediate levels of fear may lead to a conflict between normal activity (such as feeding, exploratory behavior, sexual activity, or aggression). When the fear is intense, behavior tends to be disturbed or totally inhibited. If no direct reaction to the feared stimulus is possible, there may be displacement activities. For example, pigs were observed to develop compulsive nibbling on a chain when feeding was associated with painful stimulation (Dantzer & Mormède, 1981).

Disruption of normal adaptive functioning is clearly reported in the human clinical literature concerning fear and anxiety. This disruption may take several forms (Paul & Bernstein, 1973). Complex responses may break down, as in performance anxiety surrounding public speaking, test-taking, or interactions with the opposite sex. There may also be avoidance of normal adaptive functioning in order to prevent inappropriate anxiety reactions, such as quitting school to avoid test anxiety, breaking off a relationship to avoid sexual anxiety, or avoiding hikes in the woods to avoid snake or bear phobia. Maladaptive behavior may also be learned and maintained to alleviate or avoid inappropriate responses, such as compulsions, obsessions, or amnesia to avoid contact with or perception of the feared stimuli.

Conditioned Fears

Although some fears may be innate, there is nonetheless flexibility in fearful behavior. Many fears may be acquired, and they may also be desensitized. There may be special learning mechanisms involved, because avoidance behavior shows properties of acquisition and retention that are quite unlike those seen with other forms of conditioning.

Animal experiments demonstrate unique properties of conditioning with aversive stimuli (see reviews by Bolles, 1970; Fantino, 1973). If the required response is part of the species' natural defensive repertoire, such as running away to a safe place, one-trial learning is often seen. On the other hand, as mentioned above, responses that are not part of that repertoire may be learned very slowly if at all. One illustration of the role of the species' natural repertoire comes from studies by Fantino et al. (1966), who found that if rats must learn to bar press to avoid electric shock, this response will be greatly facilitated if the rats are first required to run to the bar.

Avoidance responses, once learned, can be extremely persistent. Animals may continue to run away from cues, like a flashing light that was once associated with electric shock, for thousands of trials, even after the shock has been completely turned off. Of course, the animal may never learn that shock no longer accompanies the cue, because they never stay around to find out. It has often been remarked that human phobias are like this as well. Natural selection may have erred on the side of caution, so to speak, selecting animals to be prone to avoidance even if this means that some show maladaptive phobias (that is, "Better to be safe than sorry"). If you are lucky enough to survive a first encounter with a dangerous stimulus, you may not be so lucky next time.

Human fear can also be rapidly conditioned. Traumatic single events have been known to produce such fears. Wolpe (1958) described a case of a woman who went to the dentist and went into convulsions after he accidentally injected a local anesthetic into a vein rather than the surrounding tissue. Although the women recovered completely, the next day she went to an appointment at the hairdresser. When she sat in the hairdresser's chair, she immediately had a severe anxiety attack. Wolpe interpreted this as being due to classical conditioning, with the hairdresser's chair provoking a conditioned response because of similarity to the dentist's chair. There are cases of individuals who have become extremely phobic about cars after surviving a serious car accident (Cornelius, 1996).

A series of subtraumatic events can also produce conditioned fear in humans (see Eysenck, 1960). For example, a mailman who delivers door to door may be repeatedly threatened by dogs, but never actually bitten. Nevertheless, with repeated experiences, fear of vicious dogs may increasingly interfere with the mailman's ability to perform his job.

Phobias are, of course, a long-studied concern in human clinical psychology. Treatment is given for persistent specific fears that are irrational because objective danger is insignificant. It is often assumed that phobic avoidance behavior is maintained because affected people do not encounter the objects that they avoid, hence never learning that these objects are actually quite safe. So, for example, the person with a phobia about water never learns to swim because he does not confront the fear and acquire skills. There are several reportedly quite successful therapies for phobias based on counterconditioning (see Redd et al., 1979). Wolpe's (1958) method of systematic desensitization, for example, involves progressively associating deep physiological relaxation with increasingly intense exposure to the feared stimulus. Relaxation comes to be associated with the once-feared stimulus, following principles of classical conditioning. Other methods involve direct experience with the once-feared object, either gently through participation with the object, in conjunction with demonstration by a model, or sometimes abruptly where the individual is suddenly flooded with an intense exposure to the feared stimulus (which does not always work!).

Fears are common in young children, and there is a long-established developmental course to childhood fears. As mentioned in chapter 3, acute distress is evident in toddlers upon isolation from mother (Bowlby, 1969; 1973). In addition, many young children show fear of strangers, as observed in facial expression, vocalization (crying), and activation of motor behavior oriented toward the mother or caretaker. Fear of maternal separation and fear of strangers are often characterized as peaking at about 8 months of age, although there are individual differences and experts debate this age profile (Ainsworth et al., 1978; Buechler & Izard, 1983). Common fears during normal preschool years are oriented toward many other objects, commonly including darkness, aloneness, animals, and imaginary creatures (Jersild & Holmes, 1935). This is increasingly verbalized and may in many preschoolers assume phobic dimensions. Nightmares are normal and common in children and adults. Although one cannot predict any individual's behavior on the basis of gender alone, girls may on average be more fearful than boys, a trend that is evident in measures during infancy (Kagan, 1971). With increasing age, normal and common fears become elaborated to include many different stimuli, including more objective dangers such as cars, illness, and social situations. Generally fearfulness decreases in frequency with age (Ollendick et al., 1989).

Higher perceptual and thought processes can clearly direct emotions like fear (see also chapter 8). We may not just reflexively respond to the presence of a venomous snake. Your response would surely be very different if you saw a snake under the sheets of your bed as opposed to one behind glass at the zoo. A mother may not feel fear simply because her child is out of sight; the reaction would be radically different if she knew that she had left the infant with a baby-sitter than if she inexplicably found the child missing.

The Physiology of Fear

Firing of the sympathetic nervous system and release of catecholamines from the adrenal medulla generally accompany fear (see chapters 4 and 8). These commonly set off reflexes producing increased cardiorespiratory functioning and perspiration. More extreme reflexes are seen during intense fear, and include freezing, piloerection, and spontaneous elimination. Activity of the adrenal medulla and the sympathetic nervous system reliably accompanies fear and defensive behavior, but they are also found in many other emotions.

There are also numerous changes in brain chemistry associated with aversive stimuli. Among these are changes in the dynamics of the catecholamine neurotransmitters, norepinephrine and dopamine (see review by Anisman, 1975). Several lines of evidence indicate that aversive stimuli produce short-term elevations in the release and synthesis of catecholamine transmitter substances in subcortical brain regions.

It is possible to stimulate portions of the hypothalamus electrically and obtain classic signs of fear, or at least of sympathetic nervous system arousal. Clemente and Chase (1973) reported that stimulation of the dorsal hypothalamus will produce flight behavior, accompanied by rapid breathing, pupil dilation, and urination and defecation. This effect has been observed in a number of mammalian species. In some cases, the same stimuli may produce attack responses as well as flight responses, which makes sense insofar as the best defense may often be to stand and fight (see chapter 9).

Electrical stimulation of the dorsal PAG or the medial hypothalamus will transform a normally calm and placid animal into one that is highly defensive, stimulating the classic emergency reaction. Sandner et al. (1993) applied different types of electrical and chemical stimulation to these two brain regions in freely moving rats. They monitored subsequent behavior and brain activity, using immunoreactive measures of the protein c-*fos*, a technique that allows labeling of the brain for molecular changes that accompany ongoing behavior. Regardless of the type of stimulation, they identified a stereotyped set of structures that were active during fearful responses, including the amygdala, the hypothalamus, the PAG, and other structures.

The amygdala plays an important role in defensive and fearful responses. We must remember that the two amygdalas (on each side in the temporal region, see chapter 4) are actually quite complex organs, each composed of several nuclei. Egger and Flynn (1963) studied the effects of electrical stimulation of specific regions of the amygdala in cats. Stimulation of certain regions of the lateral area caused defensive behavior, whereas stimulation of other regions inhibited such behavior. Several locations in the lateral amygdala are associated with alerting and attentiveness responses (Ursin & Kaada, 1960), which we might fairly presume help the individual to be prepared for potential dangers.

Administration of CRF to animals or people can cause a number of physiological effects similar to those produced by stressful stimuli, which is consistent with the role of this peptide in the hypothalamic-pituitary-adrenocortical axis (Schulkin et al., 1994). Evidence suggests dynamics of local sources of CRF in the amygdala. Lee et al. (1994) indicated that corticosterone activates CRF in the central nucleus of the amygdala, causing the potentiation of the CRF-enhanced startle responses. Corodimas et al. (1994) reported that the central nucleus of the amygdala in rats plays a crucial role in the learning and expression of conditioned fear reactions. This may be regulated by corticosterone, which was found to potentiate freezing responses to an auditory cue.

Recent work with humans has confirmed an important role of the amygdala in fear responses, and the functioning of this structure may have a bearing on certain forms of psychopathology (Schulkin et al., 1994). The amygdala not only plays a role in fear itself, but it also is important in the reading of fearful facial expressions in other people. People with lesions to the amygdala (conducted, for example, to treat severe epilepsy) are reported to show selective deficits in the recognition of fearful facial expressions in other people (Adolphs et al., 1994). There is also a case of impairment of conditioning of autonomic responses to visual and auditory stimuli in such a patient (Bechara et al., 1995). Another study (Morris et al., 1996) used positron-emission tomography (PET) scans to examine neurological activity in specific regions of the brain in normal humans in conjunction with exposure to happy and fearful facial expressions. It was found that there was neurological activity in the left amygdala during exposure to fearful facial expressions. Activity in the amygdala increased with increasing degrees of fearfulness in the expressions, but there was little such activity in conjunction with happy facial expressions, indeed less and less with increased happiness in the facial expressions.

As well as CRF, other brain peptides may underlie fear responses. In particular, fragments of cholecystokinin (CCK) may play a role in human panic attacks (Bradwejn, 1993). As discussed in chapter 5, CCK is a family of peptides that exists in the mammalian gastrointestinal tract. More recent evidence suggests that CCK fragments exist in the brain, acting as neuromodulators, often in association with dopamine neural networks. When it was injected into the brain of volunteers, a specific 4-amino-acid CCK molecule (CCK$_4$) induced classic signs of sympathetic nervous system arousal and subjective sensations of apprehension and fear. This was true in both patients with panic disorders and in healthy human volunteers. Patients equated the induced attacks to their spontaneous attacks. Healthy volunteers did not know whether they were injected with CCK$_4$ or a placebo, and did not show any such reaction to the placebo.

Hormonal systems beyond those related directly to stress may have a bearing upon fear and defensive responses. In particular, gonadal steroids may have an influence. In herbivores, like humans, there is a sex difference in the frequency of fearful behavior, which is normally somewhat more prominent in females than in males. When they were injected with testosterone, female cattle (Boissy & Bouissou, 1994) and sheep (Vandenheede & Bouissou, 1993) exhibited fewer fear responses in standardized tests than did those that received control injections.

Body Language and Fear

To this day, there is probably no more vivid description of the face of human fear than that given by Darwin (see also Figure 6-2). Here is just an excerpt (Darwin, 1872, pp. 305–309):

> Fear is often preceded by astonishment, and is so far akin to it, that both lead to the senses of sight and hearing being instantly aroused. In both cases the eyes and mouth are widely opened, and the eyebrows raised. The frightened man at first stands like a statue motionless and breathless, or crouches down as if instinctively to escape observation. . . . The heart beats quickly and violently, so that it palpitates or knocks against the ribs. . . . The skin instantly becomes pale, as during incipient faintness. . . . That the skin is much affected under the sense of great fear, we see in the marvelous and inexplicable manner in which perspiration immediately exudes from it. This exudation is all the more remarkable, as the surface is then cold, and hence the term a cold sweat. . . . The hairs also on the skin stand erect; and the superficial muscles shiver. In connection with the disturbed action of the heart, the breathing is hurried. The salivary glands act imperfectly; the mouth becomes dry, and is often opened and shut. I have also noticed that under slight fear there is a strong tendency to yawn. One of the best-marked symptoms is the trembling of all the muscles of the body; and this is often first seen in the lips. . . . As fear increases into the agony of terror, we behold, as under all violent emotions, diversified results. The heart beats wildly, or may fail to act, and faintness ensue; there is a death-like pallor; the breathing is laboured; the wings of the nostrils are widely dilated. . . . the uncovered and protruding eyeballs are fixed on the object of terror; or they may roll restlessly from side to side. . . . The pupils are said to be enormously dilated. All of the muscles of the body may become rigid, or may be thrown into convulsive movements.

As is discussed in chapters 2 and 3, there is substantial evidence that facial expressions associated with fear are read very similarly across cultures. Of course, the modeled photographed faces in human cross-cultural studies provide merely a glimpse of the sequence that Darwin described, which can probably also not be truly reproduced by even the most talented actor. Only in real life misfortunes could one observe the massive autonomic arousal and bodily contortions such as Darwin described.

Figure 6-2 The face of terror.
From Darwin, 1872.

The human voice also reacts to fear. In extremely frightening situations, there may be a natural tendency to call out loudly, shriek if you will, as Darwin also noted. This may have very deep evolutionary roots, because many other animals will cry out, shriek, or squeal in times of immediate danger. In more mild states of fear, spoken language may be influenced. In particular, fear tends to be associated with elevation in the average voice pitch and more variability in voice pitch (see reviews by Kappas et al., 1991; Scherer, 1986).

Through simple sympathetic nervous system reflexes, there may be dryness in the mouth and larynx, accelerated breathing rate, and muscle tremor.

Social Transmission and Pheromones

In social species, fear may often be provoked or learned vicariously. Many people have observed how flocks of birds or herbivores rapidly spread an alarm and collectively flee. The motion or crying out of one member can cause a whole group to fly or run from even the slightest disturbance.

Social animals may sometimes "spread the word" about a potential danger, so that individuals that have no direct experience or observation of the danger show avoidance. Washburn and Hamburg (1965) describe a case in which a parasitologist shot two members of a baboon troop from a car. Up until that point, members of this troop could easily be approached by car. However, even eight months later, the troop avoided cars and could no longer be approached in that manner. Members of the troop that had not observed the shootings behaved the same way as those that had.

There can be little doubt that social transmission, including imitation and vicarious learning, are major modes of spreading fear in humans. It has been demonstrated that people acquire some fears simply by observing others showing fearful behavior associated with specific stimuli (Bandura, 1969; 1977). Accordingly, fears may be passed from mother to child. For that matter, fears can be transmitted widely throughout a culture, as we have witnessed in the spread on information about AIDS and "Mad-Cow" disease.

A few studies with nonhuman mammals have shown that there may be odors produced specifically during frightening events. These odors may elicit avoidance responses in conspecifics. Mice will avoid territories in which other mice have experienced aversive stimuli (Carr et al., 1970; Jones & Nowell, 1974). A comparable odor-based aversion, transmitted by the urine of a stressed conspecific, has been observed in cattle by Boissy (personal communication).

A First Look at Anxiety

We look more deeply at anxiety in chapter 8, in relationship to arousal and stress, and in chapter 13 when we talk about conflicts among drives and emotions. *Anxiety* and *fear* are often used interchangeably, but anxiety can be less concrete than simple fear. Anxiety has a major cognitive component. It can involve intense and prolonged thought about actual or potential experiences, or it can be more diffuse, related to many things and nothing in particular. Like many abstract concepts, "anxiety" has been used in many contexts by different people, not always meaning the same thing.

Given the number of dangers in the world, and the need to plan action and develop strategies, a bit of worry can surely be quite productive. If cognition that we label *worry* and *anxiety* is constructively oriented toward problem solving and decision making, it is surely highly adaptive. Most often, when this issue is studied in humans, it is studied from a clinical perspective, where it is viewed as problem behavior to be diminished. We must remember that clinical psychology and psychiatry have goals that are less objective than those of other sciences; they are fields that seek to solve problems and alter human behavior, rather than simply to describe and explain it. Although there are undoubtedly cases where anxiety is maladaptive, probably no complex human problem is ever solved without some careful deliberation and even fretting.

Simple fear in mammals involves autonomic nervous system responses. Complex human anxiety often shares the autonomic dimensions, but also involves a cognitive component.

One line of evidence about anxiety comes from the sorts of medication that are commonly used to treat it. The drugs that have been used to treat anxiety are the benzodiazepines and barbiturates (see Cooper et al., 1991). The benzodiazepines are most commonly used today, and valium is the best-known member of this class of drugs. It has been established that these drugs exert their actions at certain GABA receptors, specifically by actions stimulating $GABA_A$ receptors (Tallman & Gallagher, 1985). As discussed in chapter 4, GABA is a major inhibitory neurotransmitter, distributed widely in the central nervous system, including the cortex. GABA is not generally viewed as being directly associated with the sympathetic or parasympathetic nervous systems, although it is in some instances collocated with brain monoamines. It is possible that the actions of GABAergic drugs on anxiety come from the capacity simply to stop higher thought processes.

Courage

There is a wealth of historical documentation of fear and courage in humans, because we have so many times engaged in warfare and other activities that impose serious dangers on members of our species.

Rachman (1978) has collected a wealth of evidence from studies of human performance during war. He recounts how, during World War II in London, mass hysteria was initially predicted when it was clear that bombing of civilian targets was imminent. However, such hysteria generally did not materialize. Instead, although signs of fear were common, in terms of verbal expressions and physiological measures associated with sympathetic nervous system arousal, most people continued to carry on with normal activities and accepted the dangers in a matter-of-fact manner. Cases of psychological breakdown in the face of nightly bombings were limited to a small minority.

Rachman also reviewed studies of air force crews, who faced extraordinary dangers in their sorties in defense of Britain or over hostile territory. They flew with full knowledge that many or most of them would die. Rachman notes that initial fears in this context were related more to performance, such as inability to perform duties properly, but that with experience, such fear subsided and fear of the physical dangers increased. Nevertheless, those who had watched their crew members and peers die, and who had themselves survived crashes and injuries, generally were able to continue to fly and perform their tasks.

Soldiers have often been asked to perform tasks that with certainty will lead to death, yet have been able to motivate themselves to proceed. Rachman reviewed evidence that there are substantial individual differences in human response under these circumstances. Most individuals report fear, often intense, but a few individuals report that they are immune to the emotion. Although fear is widespread and common, and indeed is accepted as normal among soldiers, most are capable of overriding this fear to perform their duties. Military culture has defined cowardice as succumbing to fear in the face of danger, being unable to override it cognitively and exercise self-control. Cowardice of this sort has often been distinguished from true emotional breakdown, such as "shell-shock," which may carry on after the objective danger has passed.

Courage is lauded and highly respected, while cowardice is derided and disrespected, in many contexts in both war and peace. There is thus extensive social control over fearful behavior, adding a second level of motivation affecting such behavior (see chapters 13 and 14). Heroes may receive praise and tangible rewards, if they survive their acts, and their families may experience such socially produced rewards if they do not. There is a highly adaptive component to bravery in warfare, at least if it is motivated by defense of family and community. This is one major limit to the drive for self-preservation. We shall explore these complex issues of altruism, limits to self-preservation, and multiple levels of motivation in later chapters.

When death is imminent and certain, fear may not be expressed as one might imagine. Anecdotally, there are many records of calm behavior in such circumstances. For example, the final recordings of aircraft crew facing certain and inescapable calamity in a number of cases show rather calm comportment (see Barlay, 1990; Forman, 1990). In one case, when a Turkish DC-10 was in an inescapable nose dive toward certain destruction near Paris, the final black-box recording from the crew was of them whistling together a tune from a popular Turkish TV advertisement.

Fear, like pain, may only be adaptive and expressed when it can motivate behavior constructively. Fear has value when it drives the individual to withdraw from an escapable, objective danger. Perhaps when the danger is inescapable, or when there are objective reasons to confront the danger, the emotion is inappropriate and not experienced.

Chapter 7

REPRODUCTION

Due to mortality, organisms must reproduce to carry on over time. The competition surrounding reproduction, with its many failures and fewer successes, defines evolution, which is the differential propagation of genes over generations.

Reproduction is a critical dimension of motivation of any species, plant or animal. Of course, such motivation will occur only if an organism has met the challenges of survival to adulthood. As discussed in chapter 2, natural selection bears very directly and strongly on reproductive motivation. Necessarily, the characteristics that make up a new generation are those which have led to survival and reproduction in previous generations. Individuals who strive to survive and reproduce are those most likely to pass on their genes. Genes that lead to reproductive motivation work directly to make copies of themselves.

REPRODUCTIVE STRATEGIES
AND EVOLUTION

Reproduction is competitive, in any species, certainly including humans. As discussed in chapter 2, there is a constant tendency toward overproduction of numbers in all species. Food resources and optimal nesting sites are limited. It takes time, energy, resources, and some good fortune to raise young. For diverse reasons, from genetics and health to availability of food and shelter, not all individuals have the wherewithal to survive and reproduce. Over generations, the differential success of individuals within species, and the differential success of whole species, make evolution an ongoing process.

There is competition within sexes for access to partners of the opposite sex. This is the process of sexual selection (see chapter 2). By selecting with whom to mate, females partly determine which males reproduce, and males partly determine which females reproduce. This can increase the pace of evolution beyond that due to natural pressures alone. For example, if females select only males that are large and vigorous, the size and physical characteristics of males may change over generations.

General Mammalian Sex Differences

Many of the fundamental facts of human reproductive behavior and physiology are similar to those of other mammals. The basic qualities of mammalian reproduction evolved long before our species existed. We can gain insight into the general features of our reproductive motivation by examining other species, before turning attention to unique human adaptations.

Mammals are biologically structured such that there is asymmetry in the roles of males and females in contributions to reproduction. This has many implications for reproductive strategies and psychology, although the nature of these strategy differences depends upon the species and its social ecology.

Sex cell production is distinct in males and females, and this is related to differences in basic life-history. Females produce a relatively small number of ova, numbering in the tens of thousands in humans. Ova are formed prenatally, but do not mature until after the female reaches puberty. Each month, a few ova may mature and be released in the middle of the menstrual cycle, at ovulation. By menopause, a woman has lost fertility, and even before this, the probabilities progressively increase in mid-adulthood that a woman's ova are defective. Males' sex cells, sperm, are much smaller and far more abundant. Sperm are constantly formed during adulthood. Their formation is ongoing and takes a few months, and billions are almost constantly mature and available to ejaculate. Although male sperm production can decline with age, many males remain fertile into old age, with no discrete loss of fertility as at female menopause.

In mammals, females bear much more of the burden of reproduction than do males. Their bodies gestate the young, requiring a major investment of physiological resources. As the fetus grows, there is a need for greater nutrition and rest, which requires major psychological and behavioral changes. Birth is a risky process (see chapter 13). This is well known in humans, where substantial numbers of women once suffered life-threatening complications of pregnancy or died during childbirth, and some do so even with modern medical care (see Llewellyn-Jones, 1974). The physical and psychological burden does not end at childbirth. Nursing of young draws more resources from the mother's body. Beyond just nursing, there are numerous physical and psychological demands of child care in complex mammals like humans.

Males, by simple biology, are less compelled to invest in the whole process. Indeed, in many mammals, male investment is complete at the end of mating. Essentially, the male is able to leave after inseminating the female. For the female, a long and demanding process has just begun. Thus, there is a marked difference between the sexes in the risks associated with mating.

Males and females also differ in confidence about parenthood (see Daly & Wilson, 1983). Females know with certainty that their offspring carry their genes. On the other hand, male psychology hinges on paternity confidence. If it is clear that a male has sired young, his investment is justified from the perspective of inclusive fitness maximization (see chapter 2). On the other hand, it would be maladaptive in a strict biological sense for a male to invest in offspring sired by another male. Accordingly, many mammalian males may show mate-guarding behavior to protect their reproductive prospects and investment.

The variation in reproductive success is generally greater among males than among females, although the degree of this depends on the species. It may be less challenging for females than for males to find willing mates. The potential production of offspring by any female is limited by her lifespan and time and energy taken to gestate, nurse young, and return to fertility after each reproductive cycle. The costs of reproduction may make females generally more cautious in mating than are males. Males are not as constrained, and in theory would be able to inseminate one female after another, given available and receptive females. The major constraint for males is the presence of competing males. This sets the stage for intense intermale competition (see chapter 9).

Species-Specific Adaptations and Bonding

Despite this universal foundation for sex differences in motivation, structured by simple facts of mammalian biology, it would be a mistake to form strong generalizations across species, and especially erroneous to stereotype humans. Social structures and reproductive strategies vary considerably among species (see, for example, Clutton-Brock, 1991; Wilson, 1975). There are several qualities of interaction between the sexes, and parental care also varies enormously in quality. Many species breed only during specific seasons, and the sexes may only associate then, while other species breed throughout the year. Definitions of major forms of male-female affiliation are given in Table 7-1.

In many species there is little or no bonding between the sexes. Rats and house mice, for example, are quite promiscuous. In numerous laboratory

TABLE 7-1. *Major Forms of Male-Female Affiliation*

Promiscuity	Indiscriminate mating
Monogamy	One male bonded to one female
Serial monogamy	Limited duration (e.g., one season) monogamous bond, later replaced
Polygamy	Multiple attachments by both males and females
Polygyny	Some males each have bonds to more than one female
Polyandry	Some females have bonds to more than one male

studies, males and females of these species have been observed to mate rather indiscriminately with any available member of the opposite sex. Rats may even engage in group mating (McClintock, 1984). House mice show virtually no courtship; male mice actively pursue any receptive female, sniffing the hindquarters, then spontaneously commencing attempts to mate within 10 to 30 minutes of the first encounter (deCatanzaro & Gorzalka, 1979).

In other mammals, polygamous or monogamous relationships have various durations and forms. Monogamy is much more common among birds than mammals, and where it is seen, it is closely associated with cooperative biparental care (Clutton-Brock, 1991; Lack, 1968; Orians, 1969). Among mammals, certain carnivores like foxes and coyotes are reputed to be monogamous, as are many humans. Many mammals are polygynous.

Polygyny can be associated with intense competition and dominance hierarchies among adult males, because some males have great reproductive success while others are excluded. In pinnipeds, large aquatic mammals like seals and sea lions, polygyny is at an extreme. A single large elephant seal male, for example, may corral dozens of females into a harem (LeBoeuf, 1974). The majority of males never reproduce, while a small subset experiences enormous success. In male red deer, a few adult males within a herd do all of the mating, while most other males simply watch passively but attentively (A. Brelurut, personal communication, see Brelurut et al., 1990).

Baboons also illustrate the relationship of male dominance and reproductive success (see Hall & DeVore, 1965). A typical group has a few adult males, two or three times as many adult females, and juveniles of both sexes in roughly equal numbers. The unequal adult sex ratio suggests that some adult males are entirely excluded from social groups. Dominant males have primary access to females while they are in *estrus*, the physiological and behavioral state related to ovulation and sexual receptivity, and show mate-guarding. Both males and females initiate copulation. Females most frequently approach the dominant male, who sometimes ignores lower-status females. Males below the dominant male mate less frequently, usually when the female is not in estrus.

Since male-female sex ratios tend to be equal, polygyny means that some males are excluded from relationships with females. In species like gorillas, most individuals live in small groups. The sex ratio within the groups is equal for juveniles, but more adult females are found than adult males, and there is a clear dominance hierarchy among males. Lone adult males may thus be encountered (Schaller, 1965). These males may be found on the periphery of social groups, or they may live as isolates that are entirely excluded from the group.

In other species living in small groups with both adult males and females, there are separate dominance hierarchies for each sex that affect reproductive opportunities. In timber wolves, for example, only the dominant male and the dominant female may reproduce in many seasons, while breeding by subordinate males and females is suppressed (Fentress et al., 1987). Similarly, in marmosets, there are dominance hierarchies among both females and males, and reproduction is suppressed by both behavioral and physiological means in subordinate females (Abbott, 1984).

According to Ewer (1968), mammalian courtship patterns are not fixed; instead they vary dependent on the relative states of sexual readiness when potential partners meet. The courtship may be especially prolonged if a male finds a female before she is sexually receptive. Courtship may also be a one-sided affair, with the male making all of the advances while being evaded by the female. Less commonly, a sexually receptive female encounters a male before he is sexually motivated, although Ewer suggests that this is not exceptional. In such cases, the female may make displays which increase the male's sexual excitement. In all mammals, there is a very central role of odor stimuli, or pheromones, in mammalian courtship and mating behavior (Vandenbergh, 1988).

Chimpanzees, often called our closest relatives, live in dynamic and fluid groups, cooperating with less dominance-oriented behavior than in many other primates. Their mating involves little male-female bonding, unlike many (if not most) human beings. Goodall (1965) described how mating among chimpanzees may be initiated by either sex. If females initiate, they crouch in front of the male and look back, a gesture that males sometimes ignore. If males initiate, they swing vigorously among tree branches, with hair and body-posture erect, in view of the female. In some cases females scream when so approached by males. Goodall remarked that chimpanzees tend to be promiscuous, as some females were observed mating with more than one male in rapid succession, an observation confirmed by other observers (e.g., Reynolds & Reynolds, 1965).

Bonobos are a rare species, once called pygmy chimpanzees. They are sexually active throughout their lives, starting as juveniles, and they can mate several times per day, much more often than they need to conceive (Blount, 1990; Wrangham, 1993). They adopt a variety of sexual positions, including the face-to-face posture that most humans prefer. They engage in both heterosexual and homosexual sex, and show oral and masturbatory sex. As with chimpanzees, there is paternity confusion. It is believed that sexuality has assumed roles beyond reproduction, including social communication and female-female bonding.

The degree and form of male involvement with young also varies substantially among species (see Clutton-Brock, 1991). In many species, the male is gone after mating, and the burden of parenting rests entirely with the mother. In relatively promiscuous species like mice and rats, paternal care is rare. In the laboratory, if male and female mice are confined together, male behavior depends on paternity confidence. If a male mouse has mated with a female and is continuously housed with her, he will peacefully tolerate the litter when it is born and even assist the dam. On the other hand, if a male is placed with a female and her pups when he is not the sire, it is very likely that he will kill the whole litter (Labov, 1980).

Some mammals, especially social herbivores, have *precocial* young, virtually born on their feet, ready to follow the herd and rely on their own resources. There is relatively little maternal care, and virtually no paternal care. Apart from mother's milk, herbivore young tend to graze for food rather than being provisioned by their parents. In *altricial* mammals, on the other hand, young are quite helpless at birth, requiring intensive adult investment simply to survive. We see active parental instruction of young in many carnivores and primates, where the skills of survival are fairly complex. It is in such mammalian species that males may also play a role. Human infants are certainly altricial, because they have no capacity to survive on their own, even after years have passed.

In mammals that live in small cohesive social groups, usually only a few males are affiliated with a group of females, "confidence" of paternity is therefore high, and some male investment in care of young is observed. Adult males may especially play some role in defense of young. For example, in baboon troops, large males will rush to the defense of the group as a whole, placing themselves between the troop and predators such as lions (Hall & DeVore, 1965). Males may also affiliate with young that are no longer nursing, while females are occupied with nursing infants.

Human Strategies

Human beings defy stereotyping. There is diversity within and among cultures in male-female relationships and parental care. In modern cultures, one can easily find all of the patterns described in Table 7-1, although not with equal frequency. There are strong, faithful monogamous unions, some with outside interactions, polygynous males, some polyandrous females, and individuals who are serially monogamous. There are also male homosexuals (from monogamous to promiscuous), lesbians, and persons with various bisexual interests. There are individuals who are asexual, misogynous, androgynous, or hermaphroditic. Some males have little to do with their children, while many others are devoted to them. Devoted mothers are very common, but some mothers abandon or abuse their children.

Our challenge is to account for this diversity fairly. Clearly, cultural patterns and learning have a major bearing. Monogamy has been actively encouraged by the dominant Western and many Eastern traditions, while Islamic and West African cultures have permitted polygyny. However, much of individual motivational variation cannot be explained by culture alone.

Mating is a high-stakes game, and there are many emotions surrounding it, both simple and complex. The potential benefits of a successful relationship are enormous. A new, healthy child, raised in prosperous and stable circumstances, is the ultimate in biological success (see chapters 2 and 11). Arguably, there are many other social and emotional benefits to the couple with a successful relationship. On the other hand, the costs of mating can be devastating. Sexually-transmitted diseases can kill or destroy fertility. A failed relationship can have major costs to both men and women, especially when an individual has invested heavily in it.

Male-female relations are exceedingly complex and idiosyncratic. Courtship can be prolonged, with some pairs maintaining years of platonic friendship before becoming intimate. On the other hand, some pairs impulsively fall into sexual relations shortly after meeting. Eibl-Eibesfeldt (1989) suggested that humans are unique among species in their capacity to fall in love, and that this phenomenon and human courtship in general are inadequately studied from a scientific perspective. We return to this issue in chapter 11.

Human cultures have often been polygynous, meaning that males may bond with more than one female. In one highly cited survey, Murdock (1967) indicated that over 80 percent of human cultures were polygynous. However, this is rather categorical; it does not take into account the relative population size of the cultures and the diversity of individual behavior within them. Eibl-Eibesfeldt (1989) noted that even within those cultures classified as polygynous by Murdock, only a small subset of more affluent men had more than one wife, while monogamous marriages were 2.5 times more common than polygynous ones.

Symons (1979) suggested that humans are by nature secretive about their relationships, while being inquisitive about those of other couples. He argued that the strategies adopted by human males and females differ, in correspondence with general mammalian patterns discussed above. He characterized females as seeking secure relationships, as not being especially interested in casual sex. Males, according to Symons, seek to maximize the number of relationships so as to optimize reproductive success, and hence they are interested in sexual variety.

Buss (1989) provided empirical evidence that supports a view of sexually dimorphic mating psychology. In many cultures, males and females differ in the criteria by which they choose their mates. Females may focus more than do males on attributes that signify possession of resources and fidelity in provision of these resources. Males may focus more than do females on physical appearance, especially on signs that are correlated with fertility, like youthfulness and good health. Males are also very deeply concerned about sexual fidelity, seeking to avoid the risk of investing in children that they have not fathered. Feingold (1992) reviewed numerous studies of human mate selection, reaching conclusions very similar to those of Buss, that males and females choose mates by different criteria. These findings are consistent with the theory that mate selection is influenced by differential investment of males and females in offspring, as discussed above (see also Trivers, 1972). Females are thought to focus more on mates who possess resources that facilitate reproduction and show a willingness to transfer these resources; males are thought to focus more on characteristics of fertility and sexual fidelity.

Humans have been characterized as the only mammalian species in which the female's ovulation is completely concealed from others, including her partner and herself (Short, 1994). Since copulation can occur at any time, the majority of copulations happen when the female is not capable of conceiving. Mating may also occur at any time of the year, unlike many other species, although there are weak seasonal trends in fertility in many cultures (Lam & Miron, 1994; Surbey et al., 1986). It has often been suggested that the constant capacity to mate and hidden ovulation are adaptations that facilitate the formation of pair-bonds.

Humans have brought juvenile development to its most protracted and complex state in nature. The skills of modern adulthood are very complex, so children require an enormous amount of instruction. Despite general sex-differences in reproductive strategies, and gender differences in mate choice, many males in all cultures do invest heavily in their children. In modern times, children of single-parent families are often at a disadvantage (Hetherington, 1989; Wallerstein, 1991). The path to success in adulthood, or economic welfare and reproductive success, begins in childhood and requires competent parenting and schooling. In modern cultures, we have artificially delayed adulthood and created adolescence; individuals are encouraged to postpone reproduction and independence for several years after puberty. This is despite the fact that puberty is occurring at a younger age physiologically, and the result has been "intense social, cultural and religious pressure to bear to suppress this nascent pubertal sexuality" (Short, 1994, p. 418).

Once again, we observe a lag between biological evolution and modern cultural development (see Inset 2-1). This has many other dimensions, including the development of birth control technologies, which further separate sexual activity from its biological "purpose." Previously, mating would almost inevitably lead to pregnancy, with or without a conscious choice to have children. Today, childbearing has become voluntary, controlled in part by cortical processes or decisions rather than simple innate neuroendocrine processes.

NEUROENDOCRINE BASIS OF SEXUAL BEHAVIOR

Sexual behavior is prominent in the motivation of adult animals (see Figure 7-1). Unlike many other forms of motivation that we have discussed, sexual behavior is not homeostatic. Its fulfillment does not restore some balance to the organism as does thermoregulatory behavior, drinking, feeding, or even pain avoidance. Nevertheless, "it is goal-directed (or purposive), intense and persistent, and periodic, and under certain circumstances it can have high priority in the 'motivational time-sharing' of the animal" (Gorzalka & Mogenson, 1977, p. 151).

Human sexual response has been described in most detail by Masters and Johnson (1966). Sexual response itself involves four phases, a complex interplay of parasympathetic and sympathetic nervous system activity. During initial excitation, blood flow and muscle tension increase around the sexual organs. Excitation reaches an upper limit and is sustained at a plateau during mating behavior. Orgasm occurs with a series of rhythmic contractions in the pelvic muscles and there is a subjective experience of pleasure, which in the male is associated with ejaculation. This is followed by resolution, a period of quiescence. Human sexual behavior is often not reproductive in nature. Almost all males and many (if not most) females masturbate. Many people engage in oral sex as well as coitus. Although most adults are primarily heterosexual, there are many variations in individual sexual interests.

Males

Male sexual behavior varies in quality among mammals. There are three general components: mounting, intromitting, and ejaculation. Mounting involves self-positioning on the female such that copulation is possible. Intromitting involves insertion of the erect penis into the female's vagina and the commencement of pelvic thrusting. Ejaculation is a reflex that culminates sexual response, usually with the emission of sperm. The male's ability to intromit can require the female's cooperation, especially in species where the female must be in estrus to mate. The duration of mating varies among mammals and individuals within species. In some species, males show multiple mounts and intromissions before ejaculation, dismounting in between, while in others there may be only one long intromission.

Erection and ejaculation are actually simple spinal reflexes. Spinal transection in the dog, which severs the brain from the spinal cord, leaves these reflexes intact (Hart, 1967), and human male paraplegics are generally capable of these responses (Money, 1961). Erections are also seen in juveniles, even in infants.

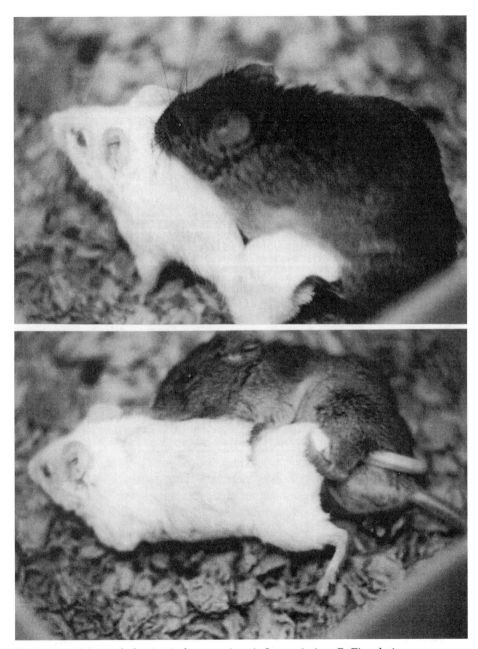

Figure 7-1 Mating behavior in house mice. A: Intromission. B: Ejaculation.

In the male, the gonads are the testes (see Figure 7-2). After puberty, the testes secrete various steroids, predominantly androgens, the best known of which is testosterone. They also can secrete significant amounts of estrogens, which are normally thought of as female hormones, but which in fact are chemically similar to androgens. It is well known that androgens sustain masculine physiology and behavior. The production of androgens is under control of the pituitary and hypothalamus (see chapter 4). The pituitary produces the peptide hormone LH, under control of GnRH (gonadotropin releasing hormone) from the hypothalamus. LH stimulates the production of testosterone from the testes. Testosterone acts on various sites in the body, including the brain, where it selectively binds in various regions of the limbic system. The actions of testosterone at the pituitary and hypothalamus act to regulate subsequent production of LH, through a feedback mechanism that prevents overproduction of testosterone.

There is some seasonal variation in testosterone levels in many mammals, especially in seasonal breeders (Lincoln, 1981). There may even be some

Figure 7-2   The human testis, the source of masculine hormones.

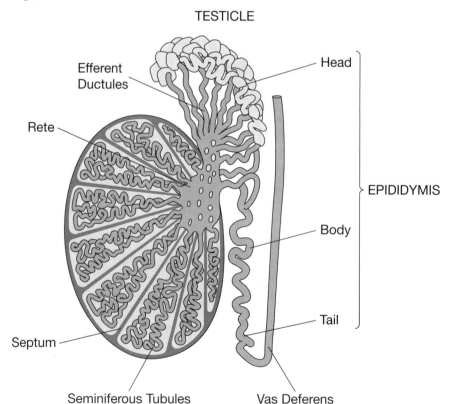

small seasonal trends in human male testosterone levels and sperm counts, depending on latitude and climate (Levine, 1994). Otherwise, the male pattern of hormone release is not cyclical, at least not in the way that it is in females' estrous or menstrual cycle (see below). However, there is a daily cycle in most men. Generally, testosterone levels are highest in the morning and decline over the course of the day, although this may depend upon the individual and the time of year (Reinberg et al., 1975). Such short-term variations probably do not relate directly to sexual appetite, because, contrary to popular misconception, testosterone does not directly control sexual response. Rather, general, longer-term testosterone levels are required for full masculinity, and momentary sexual response is under control of other neural factors and situational variables.

Castration of male mammals generally diminishes male sexual motivation, although the quality and time-course of this can depend on the species, age, and behavioral experience of the individual. In rodents following castration, the ejaculatory response is typically lost first, then later intromissions are lost and subsequently the male will cease even attempting to mount (Whalen et al., 1961). In carnivores such as domestic dogs and cats, some males, especially those with substantial sexual experience, may retain sexual response long after castration, months and even years later (Beach, 1970). Sexual behavior may remain even longer following castration in primates. In castrated rhesus monkeys, 100 percent mounted, 60 percent intromitted, and 30 percent ejaculated three years after the surgery (Phoenix, 1974). Human studies exist; these involve male sexual offenders who have been castrated in jurisdictions where courts have the power to impose such a sentence. Generally, castration has been reported to prevent repetition of rape and child molesting offenses, although not in all cases, and there are methodological concerns about some of these studies (see Heim & Hursch, 1979; Stürup, 1968). Of course, the question of whether castration should be used to treat chronic sexual offenders raises ethical debates outside of the scope of science.

Thus, while castration generally eliminates male sexual response, it may only do so imperfectly. This may be partly due to the adrenal glands, which can also produce significant amounts of androgens, so a source of sex steroids remains after castration. In any event, giving replacement doses of testosterone or other androgens can restore normal male sexual behavior in males that are castrated as adults (deCatanzaro, 1987a; Whalen et al., 1961). Such restorative effects of androgen treatment may require several days or even weeks of daily treatment with the hormone.

Male mammals typically improve in sexual functioning with repeated experience. Male rats show increased efficacy with repeated sexual trials; the proportion of males mounting increases and there is a shorter latency to mounting with repeated trials (Rabedeau & Whalen, 1959). Chimpanzees with no previous sexual experience may not immediately be able to copulate successfully (see Goodall, 1965). Although there is less systematic evidence for humans, there is reason to suspect the same thing on the basis of clinical reports, since transitory concerns of "honeymoon impotence" and premature ejaculation are often reported in the formative stages of human relationships (Masters & Johnson, 1970).

Pheromones, or specific chemicals released by one individual and perceived by another, play a critical role in male sexual arousal and indeed mammalian reproductive behavior in general (see Vandenbergh, 1988). Males in many mammalian species typically sniff the female genital area as a prelude to commencing mating behavior. Females may also sniff the male genital region. Evidence suggests that in the rat, males and females emit substances that act as sexual attractants to the opposite sex (Bronson & Caroom, 1971). Male pheromones are implicated in the stimulation of ovulation (Whitten, 1956) and the acceleration of puberty (Vandenbergh, 1967) in females.

Evidence suggests that male sexual response is under the control of regions of the hypothalamus, particularly the preoptic area (POA). Electrical stimulation of the POA in male rats can facilitate male copulatory behavior (Malsbury, 1971). Electrical changes have been recorded in the neurons of the medial POA of male rhesus monkeys during mating behavior (Oomura et al., 1983). In fact, evidence indicates that the POA is implicated in the control of male sexual behavior in a wide variety of mammals and other vertebrates (Kelley & Pfaff, 1978). In many species, lesioning of the POA can eliminate male sexual response, and testosterone tends to accumulate in this region of the hypothalamus. Below, we will discuss evidence that this region is critical for the masculinity of the brain.

The amygdala and adjacent regions of the cortex may also play a role in male sexual response. In a classic study, Klüver and Bucy (1937) found that rhesus monkeys with extensive damage in the temporal lobes of the brain, including the amygdala and hippocampus, were hypersexual. In cats, the effects of damage to the amygdala depend upon the individual and the site of the lesion, and it may be the adjacent (pyriform) cortex that influences male sexual behavior (Green et al., 1957). Damage to the pyriform cortex can alter the object toward which sexual activity is directed; lesioned tomcat males were observed to mount each other, inanimate objects, and other species. For obvious ethical reasons, because we cannot experimentally manipulate human brains, we do not have a lot of human data. However, there is at least one human case report of hypersexuality in a man who had bilateral temporal lobe lesions (Terzian & Ore, 1955).

Sexual reflexes in males involve a complex interplay of sympathetic and parasympathetic autonomic responses, with brain chemistry also involved. Animal studies suggest that a little bit of stress may actually facilitate male sexual arousal, while a lot of stress tends to inhibit it. Mildly painful stimulation can actually arouse sexual activity in male mammals (Caggiula & Eibergen, 1969). The pituitary stress hormone ACTH, when given artificially directly into the brain, can stimulate erection and ejaculation in mammals (Bertolini et al., 1975). Stimulant drugs also help male sexual arousal in low doses, but have the opposite effect in high doses. The catecholamine neurotransmitter dopamine is believed to play a major role in male sexual arousal. Low doses of drugs that stimulate dopamine activity in the brain, like amphetamine or apomorphine, can facilitate male sexual arousal in mammals (deCatanzaro & Griffiths, 1996; Gessa & Tagliamonte, 1975; Hull et al., 1986; Soulairac & Soulairac, 1975). However, these same drugs may also hasten ejaculation, while higher doses of these drugs tend to reduce male sexual arousal or prevent it altogether.

Females

Female mammals show cyclicity in the secretion of hormones from the ovaries. In many cases there are behavioral changes that accompany this cycle, although the degree and form of this behavioral cycling depends upon the species. For most mammals, we call this cycle the *estrous cycle*. In many primate species, including humans of course, there is uterine bleeding, or menses, at the end of the cycle if fertilization has not occurred, and we call the cycle the *menstrual cycle*.

The female mammalian system involves steroids from the ovaries (see Figure 7-3), acting in concert with peptide hormones from the pituitary gland. In adulthood, the ovaries release estrogens and progesterone in a cycle, the estrous or menstrual cycle. This cycle of ovarian activity occurs in conjunction with activities of the anterior pituitary. LH and FSH are gonadotropins from the pituitary; their release is influenced by GnRH in the local blood supply from the hypothalamus (see chapter 4). There is also a mutual control of these ovarian steroids and pituitary peptides. Generally in mammals, with some variance among species, estrogen and FSH rise in the preovulatory phase of the cycle. Then there is a dramatic surge in levels of the peptide LH at midcycle, which triggers ovulation and progesterone release. Progesterone levels fall toward the end of the cycle unless there has been fertilization. If the female is not pregnant, the cycle ends and recommences, and there is menstruation in women and some other primates. If the female is pregnant, hormonal cycling stops and progesterone remains at sustained high levels.

The relationship of pituitary-gonadal hormones to reproductive motivation is dependent upon the species. It is quite direct in simpler mammals like mice and rats, where estrogen and progesterone have a direct influence on sexual activity, which is constrained to only a portion of the estrous cycle. It is much less direct in humans, where sexual activity can occur throughout the menstrual cycle.

In many mammals, the female is only receptive sexually at a point in the cycle around ovulation. This point is accompanied by vaginal and uterine changes. In the rat, whose sexual behavior has been studied more than that

OVARY

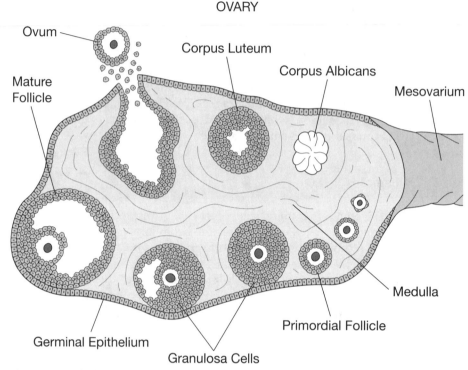

Ovum
Mature Follicle
Corpus Luteum
Corpus Albicans
Mesovarium
Medulla
Primordial Follicle
Granulosa Cells
Germinal Epithelium

Figure 7-3   The human ovary, the source of feminine hormones.

of any other species, there is a close relationship between sexual receptivity and phase of the estrous cycle. In fact, sexual behavior is quite strictly controlled by ovarian hormones. About every five days, a female rat will naturally come into estrus. During this time, she is receptive to the advances of males, and shows a distinct lordosis posture in response to his mounting. Lordosis involves an arching of the back that allows the male to intromit and ejaculate (see Pfaff, 1980). At other phases of the cycle, the female will reject the mounts of the male, failing to show this posture and making evasive movements. However, when she is in estrus, she may actively solicit male attention, showing "proceptive behavior," such as darting, hopping, and ear-wiggling, that tends to elicit male mounting.

If a female rat has her ovaries removed, she will not show sexual receptivity. However, it is a straightforward matter of hormone replacement to bring out sexual behavior. The recipe involves an injection of estrogen a few days before exposure to a male, and an injection of progesterone about six hours before such exposure. Under these circumstances, the female usually shows full sexual receptivity. This recipe essentially mimics the natural cycling of steroid hormones in the female.

It is well known that many other adult female mammals show behavioral changes that are periodic. When they come into "heat," they may actively seek male attention and solicit sexual behavior. Many of you will have observed such behavior in the female domestic cat, for example. The motivational change in feline heat can be quite dramatic. Normally tranquil female cats may howl incessantly and seek to wander outdoors when they otherwise would rest indoors. Many female mammals advertise their sexual receptivity.

In primates, the ovaries may not be as important as the adrenal glands in controlling female sexual response. Removal of the ovaries or menopause may not even influence sexual interests in women. On the other hand, the adrenal glands may be important for primate female sexual response. Everitt and colleagues (1972) have concluded that androgens from the adrenal gland regulate sexual receptivity in female rhesus monkeys much more than do hormones from the ovaries. Women who have had their adrenal glands surgically removed have been reported to show substantial reductions in sexual interest (Waxenberg et al., 1959). This is actually the opposite of the effect seen in rodents; removing the adrenal glands of female rats and mice increases their sexual receptivity (deCatanzaro, 1987b).

In most primates, including humans, the relationship between cycling ovarian hormones and sexual behavior is much weaker than in many mammals. As is well known, women are capable of sexual response at any phase of the menstrual cycle, although individual women may have preferences about when they wish to mate. This ability to mate throughout the cycle is also seen, for example, in rhesus monkeys (Rowell, 1963).

Successful mating behavior, meaning that which leads to fertilization and pregnancy, does not just require insertion of sperm into the female's vagina. A significant amount of female stimulation has been shown to be necessary for sperm to be transported to the mature ova, which are in the fallopian tubes. This may be why mammalian mating behavior is often much longer than might seem necessary, taking hours in many mammals. In mice and rats, longer matings are more fertile; short matings are less likely to produce pregnancy than are those that involve several intromissions (Adler & Toner, 1986; deCatanzaro, 1991a). The cervix in mammals is a significant impediment to fertilization, and may be mechanically and/or hormonally opened by prolonged mating behavior. Moreover, a number of hormonal changes occur in female mammals during sexual activity, including release of LH, prolactin, and oxytocin (Komisaruk & Steinman, 1986). As in several other mammals, oxytocin rises during coitus in humans (Fox & Knaggs, 1969). Oxytocin is known to produce uterine contractions, which could facilitate sperm transport. Accordingly, a female drive to achieve orgasm may in fact have strong adaptive significance.

The hypothalamus, as well as peripheral and brainstem mechanisms, have been established to play a major role in female sexual response. The most thorough analysis has been conducted by Pfaff (1980), who has extensively studied the role of physiological structures in the lordosis reflex of female rats. He established that the ventromedial hypothalamus (or VMH, which you may recall from chapter 5 for its role in feeding behavior) is particularly important for female sexual response. There are substantial numbers of estrogen receptors there, and implantation of very small doses of estrogen directly into the VMH can stimulate sexual receptivity. The preoptic area (POA) of the hypothalamus also exerts some control over release of the hormone LH, and it may play an inhibitory role in sexual receptivity.

The septum also plays an inhibitory role in female sexual behavior (Nance et al., 1975). Large lesions of the lateral septum increase sexual receptivity, while stimulation of this region may inhibit sexual receptivity, at least in laboratory rats. This region may have its influences on sexual behavior through interconnections with olfactory mechanisms, since male odor is among the cues stimulating female sexual response.

Brain monoamines are involved in female sexual response, at least in mammals studied in the laboratory. The transmitter substances, dopamine and serotonin (see chapter 4), may have inhibitory influences on female sexual receptivity, as indicated by studies of pharmacological stimulation of dopaminergic and serotonergic synapses in female rodents (Carter & Davis, 1977; Everitt et al., 1975; O'Connor & Feder, 1983).

As mentioned, many mammals are seasonal in their breeding patterns. Some evidence implicates melatonin, which is an indoleamine like serotonin. Melatonin is released from the pineal gland during darkness. Its levels are thus especially high in temperate and northern zones during the late fall and winter because the photoperiod is short. Evidence suggests that melatonin may suppress functioning of the reproductive tract and sexual behavior in some mammals (deCatanzaro & Stein, 1984; Glass & Lynch, 1981).

How about odor? We mentioned above that male pheromones are implicated in the stimulation of ovulation (Whitten, 1956) and the acceleration of puberty (Vandenbergh, 1967) in females of some species. Does this mean anything for humans? Data collected by McClintock (1971; 1983) suggest that it does indeed. When women are housed together in groups, such as in college dormitories, there is a tendency for their menstrual cycles to synchronize. Furthermore, women's menstrual cycles are also influenced by social contacts with men, with cycles being shorter in women who have more frequent contacts with men. A similar effect has subsequently been found by others (Veith et al., 1983), who reported that women who spent at least two nights with men during a 40-day period exhibited a significantly higher rate of ovulation than did those spending zero or one night with men. There is reason, therefore, to believe that reproductive pheromones operate in human beings, as they do in other mammals. Although the issue is not resolved, there has been some discussion of the possibility that androstenol, an androgen derivative, might serve as a human male pheromone (Benton & Wastell, 1986; Gustavson et al., 1987).

Sexual Differentiation of the Brain

It is well established that the brain is sexually bipotential, but that there is alteration of critical structures prenatally. Most of the major events causing prenatal sexual differentiation into male or female forms are now established (see review by Kelly, 1991). Early in fetal development, the primordial gonad differentiates according to chromosomal sex, and this in turn influences factors in the brain, such that the individual is male or female in form and behavior. Prenatally, there is a surge in testosterone levels in males, which causes masculine differentiation of the hypothalamus that endures for life.

The sex chromosomes of males are XY, while those of females are XX. The short arm of the Y chromosome contains a gene that is known as the testes determining factor (TDF). The TDF sets in motion a series of events that lead to masculine development, acting in conjunction with a number of other genes. Early in fetal development, it causes the gonads, which were previously undifferentiated with potential to become male or female, to become testes rather than ovaries. This induces the external genitals to develop in male form rather than female form. Well after the genitals are formed, in late pregnancy in humans, the femininity or masculinity of the brain will be determined. The brain will either remain in a default feminine form, or it will be masculinized by testosterone and other androgens. Normally (but not always), such androgens are from the fetal testes, so gender is consistent with genital form.

The area of the brain that is most critical is the preoptic area (POA) of the hypothalamus, which we described above for its critical role in male sexual activity and a possible secondary role in female sexual activity. Within the POA is a region called the sexually dimorphic nucleus (SDN), which has been found to be much larger in males than in females in a number of mammals including humans (e.g., Gorski et al., 1978; Swaab & Fliers, 1985). The normal surge in testosterone, occurring as a male fetus develops, causes the SDN-POA to be larger and to respond in a masculine fashion for life. In the absence of a perinatal surge of testosterone, a female cyclical gonadotrophic pattern occurs for life.

Thus, prenatal hormones impose a permanent sex-specific blueprint on the developing nervous system. It is not only the normal surge of testosterone in the male fetus that is of interest. Sexual differentiation of the SDN-POA can be affected by hormones from the mother as well as the fetus. The mother's steroids are small molecules that are able to pass through the placenta (see Weisz & Ward, 1980). The adrenal glands of females can potentially produce substantial amounts of androgens (see discussion of sexual orientation below and chapter 8). In laboratory animals, the sexually dimorphic behavior of both female and male offspring can be affected by androgens from the mother, and from other littermates whose blood passes to the fetus in the uterus (Clark et al., 1993; vom Saal & Bronson, 1980). Accordingly, it is possible for the masculinity or femininity of the brain and adult behavior to be somewhat discrepant with the form of the genitals.

During the critical periods perinatally for steroid influences, other nonsteroidal compounds can potentially masculinize the brain (see Kelly, 1991). Substances under investigation include the synthetic steroid DES that was given to women during the 1950's, the infamous (and now banned) pesticide DDT and other environmental pollutants, and drugs such as barbiturates. This naturally leads to social concerns about the potential for drugs, environmental toxins, and food contaminants to alter natural sexually dimorphic physiology and behavior. The scope of such potential problems in not clearly known at this point.

SEXUAL ORIENTATION

As is well known, not all persons seek mature members of the opposite sex as partners. Male homosexual behavior, in particular, is not rare. Several surveys show that a substantial minority of individuals show homosexual interests and behavior. Homosexuality is not just a modern phenomenon that we could explain simply through cultural evolution. It has been recorded in a number of historical circumstances, such as in classical civilizations, and in anthropological studies of many technologically less-developed cultures (Ford & Beach, 1951; Money & Ehrhardt, 1972). Indeed, in some cultures, male homosexual practices have been actively encouraged, especially during early adulthood before heterosexual marriages take place. Moreover, homosexual behavior is recorded in many other mammalian species. Ford and Beach (1951) reviewed a wealth of evidence documenting this, indicating that males occasionally behave as do females, and that females occasionally behave as do males. They suggested that this is especially common in nonhuman primates. Homosexuality is found in both males and females, although studies suggest that it is probably more common among males. For that reason, there have been many studies of homosexual (or gay) males and relatively few concerning homosexual (or lesbian) females.

The major motivational question that is often posed about homosexuality harkens back to the evolutionary issues raised in chapter 2. Given that reproduction has evolved as a perpetuation of genes over generations, why is it that reproductive drives can so commonly be directed toward the same sex, where they cannot serve the "purpose" toward which they have evolved? Clearly, natural selection directly favors reproductive behavior. Conventional logic suggests that sexual activity has evolved because those who reproduce pass on motivational and emotional tendencies toward this behavior, whereas those who do not reproduce may pass on nothing.

By that logic, reproductive drives should be highly selected for expression exclusively toward objects that serve reproductive goals. Yet homosexuality may be too frequent to dismiss as merely an aberration. Moreover, some homosexual individuals not only show an interest in their own sex, but actually show an aversion toward the opposite sex (Freund et al., 1973). So, no matter how one feels about the issue on a personal basis, there is a major scientific puzzle to solve.

Psychogenic Factors

For a long time, homosexuality was explained by psychosocial factors by most experts in the area. Early explanations from psychoanalytic perspectives suggested that interactions with mother and father during early development were responsible for atypical gender orientation. The psychoanalysts (see Bieber et al., 1962) pointed to distant relations with the father, in conjunction with overly close relations with the mother, in the genesis of male homosexuality. Very few researchers adopt this explanation any more, and the data once taken as support for this theory have been widely criticized. Even though some fathers of homosexual males have been observed to have distant relations with their homosexual sons, this could be a reaction to their sons' condition just as much as a cause of the condition. More modern explanations have been quite different.

One case history has been frequently cited to address the role of upbringing in sexual identity. Money and Ehrhardt (1972) reported cases of twin boys, one of whom experienced a surgical accident as an infant that ablated his penis. After some debate, the parents and physicians decided to raise this child as a girl, and undertook surgery to reform the external genitalia. This case received widespread publicity highlighting the malleability of sexual identity. It was said that the child reared as a boy was masculine and viewed himself as a boy, while the "girl" clearly was feminine and viewed herself as a girl. However, a more recent report (Diamond & Sigmundson, 1997) has presented a follow-up that completely undermines the original conclusion. In fact, the "girl" reported numerous sexual identity problems as a child, including a tendency to stand while urinating and extreme difficulties being accepted as a girl by peers. Upon learning as an adolescent that "she" was in fact chromosomally male, he expressed relief, had surgery to restore masculinity, and continued life as a man, interested in women and ultimately marrying. This case history is now taken as evidence of the importance of prenatal events in sexual identity. When asked as an adult why as a child he had not accepted the identity of a girl: "His answer was simple. Doing so did not feel right. He wanted to please his parents and placate the physicians so he often went along with their decisions, but the conflict between his feelings and theirs was mentally devastating and would have led to suicide if he had been forced to continue." (Diamond & Sigmundson (1997, p. 301).

Many researchers have pointed to mechanisms of learning, especially during adolescence, to explain sexual orientation. In the 1960's and 1970's, as conditioning theory assumed a dominant place in psychology, unusual sexual orientation was often explained in terms of histories of sexual gratification in conjunction with atypical stimuli. Many researchers pointed to a role of masturbatory conditioning in the development of unconventional sexual orientation (e.g., Evans, 1968; Marquis, 1970; McGuire et al., 1965). The basic idea is that specific stimuli are repeatedly associated with sexual fantasy in adolescence during masturbation. The process was seen as one of classical or Pavlovian conditioning. If sexual gratification, especially the pleasure of ejaculation, is repeatedly associated with unconventional stimuli, these stimuli may come to elicit sexual arousal. Such stimuli include members of the same sex in the case of homosexuality, children in the case of pedophilia, or other unusual objects like leather handbags in the case of fetishes. So it was argued that individuals who repeatedly fantasized about, for example, women in black lace, underage children, or members of the same sex during masturbation, would become fixated upon such stimuli as a source of sexual gratification. They would then seek out such sexual objects in the real world.

It was argued that homosexuality could be similarly reinforced during adolescence through repeated sexual gratification in direct sexual encounters with others of the same sex. Essentially, homosexual orientation was seen as developing in adolescence as individuals experimented with sexual play with members of the same sex and found it gratifying. This gratification, through conditioning processes, was seen as progressively orienting sexual desire toward the same sex, so that homosexuality became habitual. At the same time, experiences of rejection from members of the opposite sex could reinforce this process. Negative experiences in social interactions with the opposite sex, such as rejections in invitations to date, were seen as producing anxiety about heterosexual behavior, progressively reinforcing the orientation of sexual activity toward the same sex.

A large literature has developed around the social learning theory of sexual orientation (see reviews by Barlow & Abel, 1981; Redd et al., 1979). This idea that sexual orientation was classically conditioned became the basis for therapies designed to reorient individuals' sexual behavior. Male homosexuals seeking to become heterosexual were treated with therapies associating aversive stimuli with pictures of nude males and more pleasant stimuli with pictures of nude females, and given various treatments designed to improve social skills with members of the opposite sex. Socially problematic sexual deviation, such as pedophilia, was similarly treated, however in a number of instances without success (e.g., Marshall, 1974).

Neuroendocrine Factors

In laboratory rodents, we know how to make males behave as females and females behave as males. This is consistent with the sensitive period for masculinization of the brain discussed above. Regardless of chromosomal or even morphological gender, masculine or feminine behavior in laboratory mammals can be brought to full expression in adulthood with the right combination of adult steroids, as well as steroid levels during the critical period prenatally (perinatally in some mammals like laboratory rats, where the critical period extends from late prenatal development into the first few days after birth). The recipes for this are summarized in Table 7-2.

Remember that the form of the gonads, whether male or female, is determined early in fetal development, as discussed above. The form of the brain, whether masculine or feminine in terms of hypothalamus and pituitary functioning, is determined late in fetal development (and in some mammals also shortly after birth). This critical period for masculinization of the SDN-POA (see above) is discrete, and it has a permanent effect upon sex-characteristic behavior (see Gorzalka & Mogenson, 1977; Kelly, 1991; Quadagno et al., 1977; Whalen et al., 1971). If a male rat is castrated shortly after birth, or treated with drugs that block the masculinization of the hypothalamus, it is permanently affected. It will be less masculine, but it will not be feminine unless it is also given female hormones. If it is given female hormones, estrogen and progesterone, in a timing that mimics the natural estrous cycle, it will show full female sexual receptivity, including the female lordosis response as described above. On the other hand, if a female rat is given a single large dose of testosterone during the critical period perinatally, her brain will be more responsive to testosterone for life. Indeed, if she is also given repeated doses of testosterone during adulthood, she will show masculine behavior, including mounting of females and male-pattern aggression (see also chapter 9).

So, animals can be made to behave like members of the opposite sex, simply by masculinizing the brain or letting it remain feminine during the

TABLE 7-2. *Summary of Hormone Dependency of Adult Masculine and Feminine Behavior in Laboratory Rodents,* showing conditions producing the clearest results. The full expression of masculine behavior in adulthood requires a perinatal testosterone surge and circulating testosterone in adulthood. The full expression of feminine behavior requires the absence of perinatal testosterone as well as estrogen and progesterone cycling in adulthood. Either sex can be made to show either pattern.

	Perinatal	Adult	Adult Behavior
Male:	Intact	Intact (Testosterone)	Masculine
	Castrated		Asexual
	Castrated	Estrogen and Progesterone	Feminine
Female:	Intact	Intact (Estrogen and Progesterone)	Feminine
	Intact	Ovariectomized	Asexual
	Testosterone	Testosterone	Masculine

critical perinatal period for development of the SDN-POA, then also treating them with hormones of the opposite sex during adulthood. We can make a male behave as a female, and a female behave as a male. This has led to much speculation about whether human homosexual behavior might be explained by abnormal prenatal hormones (in us, the sensitive period for alteration of the SDN-POA is believed to be prenatal). This idea is especially interesting because we know that maternal steroids pass to the fetus. In the experimental animal literature, there are reports that maternal stress late in pregnancy can decrease the masculinity and increase the femininity of male rat pups, by disrupting the surge in testosterone normally seen perinatally in males (Ward, 1972).

Money and Ehrhardt (1972) reported studies of developing girls whose mothers had abnormal hormonal conditions during pregnancy. Some of these girls had experienced congenital adrenal hyperplasia (CAH), where the adrenal glands secrete abnormal amounts of androgens. The mothers of other girls had been given synthetic steroids, progestins, to prevent premature labor, and it was later discovered that these drugs could have the effects of androgens. So in both situations, the developing brains of girls had been exposed to unusual amounts of androgens during the critical period of sexual differentiation of the hypothalamus. Money and Ehrhardt reported that the girls were not lesbian in their sexual interests as adolescents, but that they were "tomboys" in their social interests, preferring male playmates and rougher patterns of play that are usually more characteristic of boys. Subsequently, other studies have confirmed that CAH has influences on psychosocial development (e.g., Helleday et al., 1993; Kuhnle et al., 1993), although the reasons for this may be complicated by physical problems of CAH that can include a need for genital surgery and medication for metabolic problems. At least one study (Hines & Kaufman, 1994) has confirmed that girls affected by CAH have somewhat more masculine interests during childhood, reflected particularly in preference for male playmates.

Meyer-Bahlburg and others (1995) examined the effects of prenatal exposure to the synthetic estrogen diethylstilbesterol (DES) upon sexual orientation of women. DES was once widely used for treatment of various at-risk pregnancies until it was banned in 1971 for harmful side effects. Adult women whose mothers were given DES while pregnant were compared to controls without such prenatal exposure. Sexual orientation was assessed by interview. Consistently across samples, more women who were exposed to prenatal-DES were rated as bisexual or homosexual than were controls.

For some time, there has been a concerted effort to find hormonal differences between heterosexual and homosexual men. Very few differences have been found. In particular, there has been no reliable difference in adult levels of testosterone or other sexually dimorphic steroids (see review by Byne & Parsons, 1993). However, Dörner and others (1975) reported that the response of pituitary LH to injections of estrogens differed between heterosexual and homosexual men, with homosexual men showing a pattern that is similar to that found previously for women.

In recent years, there have been reports of differences in brain physiology between male homosexuals and heterosexuals. LeVay (1991) reported a difference in hypothalamic structure, specifically in one of four cell groups of the anterior hypothalamus, which was found in postmortem tissue to be larger in heterosexual than homosexual males. In another study, Allen and Gorski (1992) reported that the size of the anterior commissure in the human brain, part of the band of fibers that connects the two cerebral hemispheres, which is known to differ between men and women, also differs between heterosexual and homosexual men. They suggest that this may relate to differences in cognitive function.

Such differences in perceptual-cognitive skills have been reported by McCormick and Witelson (1991). These researchers examined measures of spatial skills, which typically favor men (on average in the whole population), and measures of verbal fluency, which typically favor women. The pattern of cognitive skills of homosexual men was different from that of heterosexual men, with homosexuals having lower spatial ability relative to fluency. The cognitive pattern of homosexual men did not significantly differ from that of women. The authors viewed these findings as consistent with a neurobiological substrate of homosexuality.

Such recent findings are intriguing, but we still do not know the causes of homosexual behavior. There is a great deal of current research designed to probe further the role of prenatal masculinization or feminization of the brain in sexually dimorphic behavior, and surely the answer will be clearer as this research unfolds in the coming years.

Genetics and Evolution

Recent work has suggested that male homosexuality may have some genetic basis. Bailey and Pillard (1991) conducted a study of concordance for homosexuality among twins and adoptive brothers. They did so by identifying male homosexuals with identical twins, nonidentical twins, or adoptive brothers. Of the relatives whose sexual orientation could be determined, 52 percent of identical twins, 22 percent of nonidentical twins, and 11 percent of adoptive brothers were homosexual.

Some intriguing new evidence suggests that genetic contributions to male homosexual orientation may be passed from mother to son, not father to son. Hamer et al. (1993) examined the families of 114 homosexual men, finding increased rates of same-sex orientation in the uncles and male cousins in the maternal line of these subjects, but not in their fathers or paternal relatives. They examined DNA sequences in the X sex chromosome in 40 families in which there were two gay brothers. They uncovered a region on the X chromosome that appears to contain a gene or genes for male homosexuality.

A genetic explanation for homosexuality, and the frequency of homosexuality in humans regardless of the degree of genetic input, raise some rather fascinating questions from an evolutionary standpoint (see Savin-Williams, 1987; Weinrich, 1987; Wilson, 1978). The issue, put very simply, is why natural selection would tolerate nonreproductive sexuality, when actual reproduction requires heterosexual behavior and is the essence of gene propagation. Explaining some homosexual behavior is not the problem; if individuals are bisexual, or also engage in reproductive sexuality due to cultural practices encouraging universal marriage, they will produce enough children to pass on their genes to successive generations. However, exclusively homosexual behavior, where the person turns down true reproductive opportunity with the opposite sex, does present an evolutionary problem. One idea is that male homosexuality could be a byproduct of polygyny. Given that, historically (especially in primate and indeed mammalian evolution), some males have monopolized females, other males have always been excluded from sexual opportunity. If males excluded from reproductive opportunity engage in nonreproductive sexual behavior, such behavior would have had no adverse effect upon reproductive opportunities and hence might be tolerated by natural selection. It has also been suggested that kin selection (see chapter 2) may have played a role, as homosexual individuals may have historically helped nurture their kin (nieces and nephews), thus indirectly propagating their genes.

Biological theories of homosexuality are currently receiving a great deal of attention. Much of this attention has derived from dissatisfaction with the evidence for earlier psychosocial theories. Nevertheless, some researchers are not fully convinced that the answer lies in the direction of biology. Byne and Parsons (1993) argued that the evidence for biological bases of homosexuality is not yet definitive, just as there is no compelling evidence to support any single psychosocial theory. Bem (1996) suggested a developmental theory of sexual orientation, criticizing but also attempting to accommodate biological approaches. He argued that biological variables, such as genes, prenatal hormones, and brain neurochemistry do not directly code for sexual orientation per se. Instead, they influence childhood temperaments affecting preferences for sex-typical or atypical activities and peers. Bem theorized that this leads children to feel different from opposite or same-sex peers, to be aroused differentially by them, perceiving one sex as exotic, which may transform to erotic activity with adult experience.

In any event, we must conclude that we simply do not have all of the answers at this point, and that we must await the results of ongoing and future research. Tentatively, it might be reasonable to assume that the development of non-reproductive sexual orientation could be due to a number of factors, complex interactions of biological and experiential factors, operating in idiosyncratic fashions depending upon the individual concerned.

MENSTRUATION, PREGNANCY, AND NURSING

Of course, reproduction encompasses many other dimensions beyond sexual activity, particularly the nurturance of young. At this point, we will discuss the fundamental neurohormonal features of menstruation, pregnancy, and nursing. We will discuss the many other very important dimensions of affection and childrearing in later chapters.

The Menstrual Cycle and Emotional Changes

It is widely thought that there are variations in women's emotions over the course of the menstrual cycle. In particular, it is suggested that the phase just prior to menstruation is associated with mood changes, what is widely called the premenstrual syndrome (or PMS). Is this scientific or is it cultural myth?

Physiologically, there are certainly many changes in the premenstrual phase of the cycle. The levels of progesterone are dropping radically, and the uterus is preparing to bleed, to slough off the layer of cells that have been prepared for the possibility of pregnancy. We know that progesterone binds in the brain, including the preoptic area, central hypothalamus, and other regions of the limbic system, and cortex (e.g., Sarrieau et al., 1986; Shughrue et al., 1991). There is evidence that other steroids can alter brain chemistry that may be associated with our moods (see chapters 4 and 8). Accordingly, a hormonal mechanism of PMS-related emotional changes is quite plausible, but this is still unproven (see review by Floody, 1983).

For women, mating behavior and the frequency of orgasm are not evenly distributed over the menstrual cycle, but this is not consistently related to reproductive hormones as in other species (Udry & Morris, 1968). Many other measures show variation over the menstrual cycle as well. Pain sensitivity may vary, with women being more sensitive in the luteal phase, or the latter portion of the cycle after ovulation but before menstruation (Hapidou & deCatanzaro, 1988). Reactions to stress similarly vary; premenstrual women have been found to show greater irritability and anger in response to provocation during the premenstrual period (Van Goozen et al., 1996). The premenstrual phase may have the effect of making some women more susceptible to responding emotionally to negative life events. A study of 82 college women over a 40-day period found relatively positive moods at the middle (ovulatory) phase of the menstrual cycle and relatively negative moods in the week preceding menstruation and during the first few days of bleeding (Rossi & Rossi, 1980). Women taking birth control pills, who therefore do not experience the natural fluctuations in levels of estrogen and progesterone, did not report these mood changes.

One large epidemiological study (Ramcharan et al., 1992) examined a systematic sample of several thousand women in Calgary, Alberta. Although milder influences may have occurred for a larger number of women, severe negative mood changes affected only a small subset of women, about 1 percent, during the premenstrual phase of the cycle. The women most at risk were those between 26 and 35 years of age who had experienced major stressful life changes over the entire past year.

There are also many studies of the frequency of aggressive acts perpetrated by women in relationship to the menstrual cycle (see review by Floody, 1983). Essentially, many of these studies indicate that aggressive behavior is most common in the premenstrual phase. Naturally, this is a very controversial line of research, and there have been many methodological concerns raised about these older studies. It would certainly be unfair to stereotype women on this basis, or to try to predict any individual's behavior on the basis of such statistical generalizations.

Pregnancy

Pregnancy is a unique phase of life for women, and one which may be accompanied by mood and motivational changes. Physiologically, pregnancy commences with a series of hormonal changes that occur subsequent to fertilization of the ovum (or ova). See Figure 7-4 for a visual representation of the female reproductive tract.

It is now clear that the earliest phases of pregnancy are fragile in mammalian species, including humans (see deCatanzaro & MacNiven, 1992). Data from many species indicate that diverse forms of physiological or psychological stress can disrupt this vulnerable process, terminating pregnancy in its earliest phases. In laboratory rodents and farm animals, cessation of early pregnancy has been induced by stimuli like excess heat or cold, physical restraint, predator exposure, social changes, and human handling. Merely exposing a pregnant mouse to a novel male, meaning a male that differs from the one that made her pregnant, can cause the pregnancy to end (Bruce, 1959; deCatanzaro et al., 1996).

Fertilization occurs in the fallopian tubes. In the subsequent days, fertilized ova must migrate down the tubes to the uterus, where they normally set up roots. This process of rooting in the uterus is called implantation. Implantation is the beginning of a major physiological investment by the mother in the pregnancy. It is clear that implantation is sensitive to emotional stress, because such stress upsets the normal balance of estrogen and progesterone that is essential for the ova to survive.

In humans, we know that the vulnerable period of pregnancy extends beyond implantation. Miscarriages occur in a substantial number of women during the first trimester of pregnancy (Llewellyn-Jones, 1974). There are

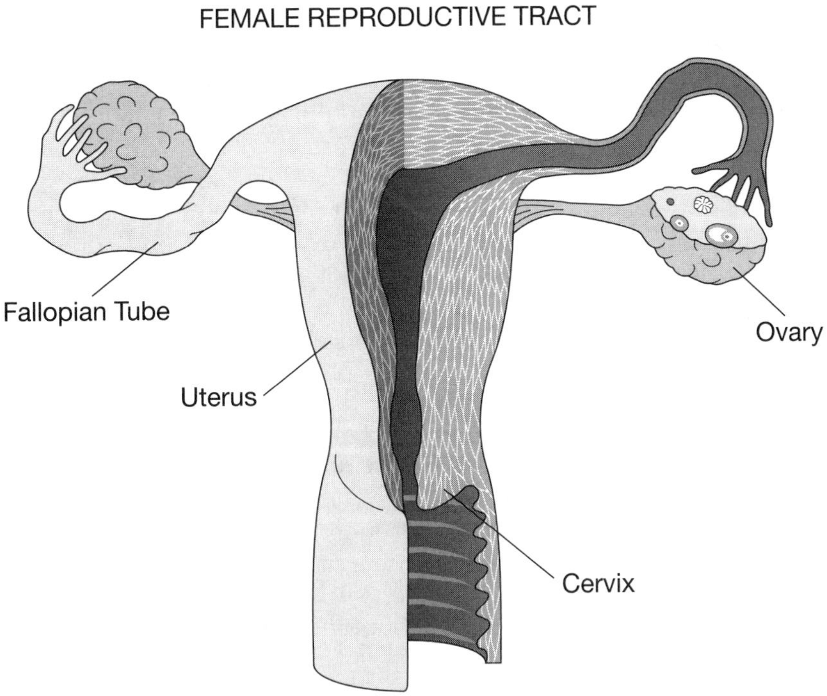

FEMALE REPRODUCTIVE TRACT

Fallopian Tube

Ovary

Uterus

Cervix

Figure 7-4   The human female reproductive tract, showing the uterus, with the two fallopian tubes branching from above, each leading to one of the two ovaries.

probably many reasons for this, such as chromosomal and other viability problems in the fetus and general maternal health, that have nothing to do with psychology or emotions. However, there is a longstanding suspicion that maternal emotions could be relevant. Obviously one cannot do the sorts of experiments that would prove the issue. Although there are many methodological concerns, some correlational studies of women suggest that anxiety and various stressors are related to some problems of pregnancy, including spontaneous abortion, birth defects, and other obstetric complications (Istvan, 1986; Levin & DeFrank, 1988).

Obviously, the emotional reaction to pregnancy is very much dependent upon the social and psychological context. For many women and their partners and families, pregnancy is a source of great joy. This is quite natural given the logic that we explored in chapter 2, because reproduction is a primary drive, and producing a new child gratifies this drive. Many couples strongly desire children, and many achieve this goal only after many months or even years of effort. On the other hand, sometimes pregnancy is not wanted. The circumstances may be wrong, as for example when the mother is young and unmarried, or poor and overburdened by other children. It takes substantial resources to raise a child, and the whole enterprise is most easily accomplished in affluence and ease. As is well known, many mothers are severely distressed by unwanted pregnancy, and they may seek to terminate it through abortion. Accordingly, there is no uniform emotional reaction to pregnancy.

Pregnancy is accompanied by radical changes in the woman's hormones, as progesterone is sustained at high levels and the menstrual cycle is shut down. The pituitary's release of oxytocin and prolactin may also be altered. Moreover, there are physical changes such as morning sickness in early pregnancy, and of course the growing metabolic needs of the developing fetus. Such hormonal and metabolic changes may themselves have a bearing upon moods. Certainly appetite will be affected (see chapter 5), simply through the nutritional demands of rapid growth. Pregnancy may also cause fatigue as metabolic resources are channeled to growth.

There are also other obvious psychological changes that may bear upon moods. These include many things. There is the social announcement of pregnancy (or its conspicuous impact upon the woman's physique), and the subsequent attitudes of spouse, children, family, friends, and coworkers. There is the need to alter habitual activities, such as skiing or bicycling or some types of work. There may be anxiety about the pain of birth or the health and welfare of the new child. Accordingly, for many reasons, pregnancy is associated with many emotions, and these emotions may fluctuate.

Parturition

Birth is a dramatic and traumatic event, both physiologically and psychologically. Despite the stress and pain that inevitably go along with childbirth, it is ultimately usually a euphoric event. If all goes smoothly, the birth of a healthy child is a source of tremendous joy to the family. This is not surprising from an evolutionary standpoint (see chapters 2 and 10), because a new child represents biological "success," the potential for transmission of the parents' and family's genes into future generations. If the child is wanted, and the mother and child are both in good health, and there are positive prospects for raising the child, there may be no greater source of joy or euphoria than childbirth.

Unfortunately for some, childbirth may not be so rewarding. A minority of women suffer severe complications that endanger their own wellbeing. In the absence of modern medicine, and occasionally despite it, substantial numbers of women have died in the process of giving birth (Llewellyn-Jones, 1974). There are many other complications that can occur, including severe loss of blood, discomfort and pain of breech birth, or unexpectedly premature or postmature birth. In modern circumstances, the need to resort to Cesarean section may be a disappointment for women who anticipated natural childbirth.

Then, there are the many unfortunate imperfections that may be evident in the newborn child. The child may be stillborn, and the parents may be thrust immediately into severe grief where they expected joy. The child may be born prematurely, far from the due-date. Prematurity is not necessarily a bad sign for the child's prospects, but it is a risk factor. This and many other neonatal illnesses in the child may leave the parents very anxious and emotionally volatile, because the ultimate outcome is unknown, and as they are forced to visit the hospital to see their new child, disrupting their routines and clouding the joy that would come with uncomplicated birth. Children may be born with severe chromosomal malformations, like Down's syndrome or other conditions that affect intelligence and health. There may be very severe congenital malformations, such as anencephaly or megalocephaly as seen in Figure 5-1. There may be more subtle congenital malformations like cleft palate, conspicuous birthmarks, or ambiguous genitals. Sadly, this is only a small subset of the long list of problems that can occur in newborn children.

Not only do parents have to deal with their own anxiety, disappointment, and/or grief when these malformations and health risks occur, they also have to deal with disruptions to their work, financial strains if they must pay the medical bills, and various social matters that may arise. Normally, friends and acquaintances ask two questions when a child is born: "Is it a boy or a girl?" and "How much does she/he weigh?" If all is well with mother and child, the announcement is made with pride and joy. If the parents have a newborn that is an hermaphrodite, with ambiguous genitalia, or one born after six-months' gestation, clinging to life at one kilogram (2.2 pounds), answering these questions may be difficult.

Immediately subsequent to birth, most women show few emotional problems, and are very often quite relieved and joyful. However, post-partum depression is seen in something like 10 to 15 percent of cases (O'Hara, 1987). We have just discussed some of the problems that could understandably produce negative moods after childbirth. In some cases, however, depression is seen without such obvious causes. There may, of course, be private causes that are not obvious to the researcher or clinician observing the case. For example, marital tensions, financial problems caused by the new responsibility, disruptions in work, disruptions in leisure, or sleeplessness from a crying baby, make birth an enormous change in routine.

There are major hormonal transitions that occur at birth, which may also influence moods. Progesterone levels, which have been exceptionally high through pregnancy, are suddenly much lower. Oxytocin dynamics, and sensitivity of oxytocin receptors, are also involved in birth itself. Shortly after birth, prolactin rises in pulses to prepare for nursing, in conjunction with oxytocin dynamics. These changes alone may alter brain chemistry that is relevant to moods. Moreover, the trauma of birth can cause adrenal hormonal changes, and there is the exhaustion from loss of blood, loss of sleep, and sheer excitement. In chapters 8 and 10, we examine issues of stress, affect, and neuro-hormonal changes in more detail.

Nursing

Naturally, mammalian mothers nurse their infants directly through their breasts. Humans in modern times have had the option of doing so artificially, through infant formulas and baby bottles, although there is a strong movement back to the natural method in light of many recent studies showing that breast-fed babies have advantages over bottle-fed babies (see Inset 5-1). Under natural and ancestral conditions, as reflected in anthropological studies of women's nursing patterns in technologically less-developed cultures, women tend(ed) to nurse their children for as long as three or four years, often using this as a natural method of birth-control or birth-spacing (Eibl-Eibesfeldt, 1989). Many women do not show normal menstrual cycling while breast-feeding, because this disrupts the normal pulsatile release of GnRH from the hypothalamus and hence LH release from the anterior pituitary gland (McNeilly et al., 1994).

There is a large literature on the evolution of parental behavior in mammals (see Clutton-Brock, 1991). There has also been much research concerning the expression of maternal behavior in laboratory mammals (e.g., Bridges, 1984; Fleming et al., 1989; Orpen & Fleming, 1987; Siegel, 1986). Essentially, rat studies show that maternal behavior in females is regulated by a complex interaction of maternal hormones and experience with pups. In the rat, primiparous females (those giving birth for the first time), show the full range of maternal behavior as soon as the young are born. The mother builds a nest and retrieves her young to the nest, and adopts a nursing posture in the absence of any learning experience. Maternal hormones influence attraction to pup-related odors in female rats (Fleming et al., 1989). Of course, we know much less about the physiological and experiential determinants of maternal responsiveness in people, simply because we are limited to observational methods. We return to these issues in chapter 11.

Care of young is not a necessary sequel of birth in many mammals, including people. Infanticide has been observed in many species (see Blaffer-Hrdy, 1979) and across human cultures (Eibl-Eibesfeldt, 1989). We return to this issue in chapter 9.

Chapter 8

AROUSAL AND STRESS

Our bodies and psychology adapt in nonspecific ways to deal with the demands that we face in coping. When we face increased demands, they become revved up. When demands diminish, we wind down and become more sedate. Our circumstances can require both short- and long-term changes in activity levels. In this chapter, we examine how body and brain chemistry changes in response to stress and relaxation, and how this can radically alter both motivation and mood.

Demands of coping produce psychological and neuroendocrine adaptations that go hand-in-hand. We have mechanisms for adjusting to both immediate and long-term pressures of coping. These can alter mood and motivation, transforming an individual's emotions and hierarchy of drives. These mechanisms evolved long ago, as proven by resemblance to mechanisms of other animals. In plain English, we refer to these adaptations as arousal and stress. Modern science indicates that arousal and stress can have many qualities.

Stress and the G.A.S.

Cannon (1915) and Selye (1936) deserve special credit for describing general mechanisms underlying stress. Selye outlined a three-stage process which he called the general adaptation syndrome (GAS). The GAS involves reactions to diverse events, from psychological demands to physical illnesses, which set off a stereotyped set of hormonal reactions that reorient the body's resources. The first stage is Cannon's (1915) *emergency* or *alarm reaction*. This occurs with immediate needs, especially danger, and consists of arousal of the sympathetic nervous system and the release of catecholamines from the adrenal medulla (see chapters 4 and 6). Release from acute stress, or rest, is accompanied by parasympathetic reflexes that reverse stress reactions. The second stage of the GAS is a response to chronic stress, demands to cope that persist for days, weeks, and months. Selye called this the *stage of resistance*. During chronic stress, it is the adrenal cortex rather than the adrenal medulla that is of greatest importance. Selye's third phase of stress is the *stage of exhaustion*. Intense stress cannot persist indefinitely without a serious cost. Ultimately, if chronic stress is too intense for the individual's coping apparatus, there will be bodily failure, illness, and death. Selye's general description remains valid, but today we know much more about the quality of both immediate and protracted reactions to stress.

Defining *stress* is not always straightforward. Most people have some sense of what we mean by stress, but subjective feelings are not adequate for scientific purposes. Selye (1956, 1973) defined stress as the psychophysiological consequence of any event challenging the organism's capacity to cope, citing the stereotyped endocrinological response to diverse stimuli. While most such stimuli are unpleasant, Selye recognized that affectively positive stimuli that exhilarate us can also be stressful. Winning the lottery could thus be stressful, because it causes major changes in a person's life. Stressors have also been defined as any stimuli that disrupt an organism's homeostatic state, requiring adjustment or adaptation (Hinkle, 1977). That definition is, of course, extremely broad and nonspecific, encompassing virtually any significant change in life. Operationally, following Selye's logic, we could define stress in terms of measurable physiological responses, and stressors as stimuli that provoke such responses.

Simple generalizations are elusive. One person's stress can be another's leisure activity. While many people are traumatized by the prospect of speaking to a large crowd, others revel in the spotlight. While many people fear heights, others mountain climb or parachute jump for pleasure. While many students hate mathematics, others choose it as their profession. Nevertheless, some things are stressful to most sane people. Certainly, very few people seek physical illness, death of loved ones, humiliation, poverty, or lack of basic comfort. Even so, a few people show self-injury, commit suicide, kill family members, ridicule themselves, take vows of poverty, or voluntarily live in the streets.

Many people thrive on hard work, and are bored and unhappy when there is nothing to do or little excitement. One feature that is critical for the impact of demanding stimuli is whether one can effectively cope. This may make the difference between successful adaptation in the stage of resistance, and psychological and physiological breakdown in the stage of exhaustion.

SHORT-TERM ADAPTATIONS

Arousal

In plain English, the word *arousal* is meaningful to most of us, and it has a lot to do with the general state of motivation. Although the concept has often been used in psychological science, it is quite vague and abstract. It refers to a variety of processes that control activation, wakefulness, motor behavior, and alertness. It overlaps with the idea of acute stress. Physiologically, arousal includes autonomic activation, hormonal events, mechanisms in the brainstem, and events in the cerebral cortex.

Many theorists have argued that efficiency of human performance bears a relationship to arousal or general activation, but that this is not a simple linear function. Instead, it is suggested that performance relates to arousal through an inverse U-shaped function (Berlyne, 1967; Duffy, 1962; Hebb, 1955; Lindsley, 1957; see also Figure 8-1). Accordingly, too little arousal leads to poor performance, a moderate level of arousal optimizes performance, while overarousal interferes with adaptive behavior. Although this idea has been criticized as being too general and insufficiently concrete (Neiss, 1988), a wealth of observations in general psychology fit this notion approximately.

Consider yourself as a student faced with learning new material. Without enough arousal (even anxiety) about your performance, you might not study and pay attention, and you might fail your course. Some arousal will probably make you do the work that is necessary in order to be prepared for exams. However, sometimes some students become excessively anxious or aroused, to the point that they cannot concentrate, and fidget instead of focus, or have mental blocks. (I hope that you learn enough about emotions through this text to self-monitor and channel your energies positively, avoiding such excess anxiety.)

As Neiss (1988, p. 359) pointed out, "Optimal performance probably results from a state in which tension is low and intensity is high. The difficulty has always been that these two are positively correlated. However, this correlation seems to be quite variable across persons. Indeed, a hallmark of outstanding musicians, dancers, and athletes is their ability to maintain high intensity and remain 'loose'. Many others are unable to do this, instead experiencing a debilitating degree of anxiety in connection with important motor performances—or avoiding them altogether."

The concept of arousal and the meaningfulness of the inverted U-shaped function have been criticized. Not all researchers of motivation use the term *arousal*. Neiss (1988) argued that the concept of arousal as currently used refers to the common variance shared by the physiological components of a number of emotional states, including anger, excitement, sexuality, fear, shame, and sadness. He argued that arousal cannot be created in any pure form for research purposes, nor can causality be attributed to it. Instead, he

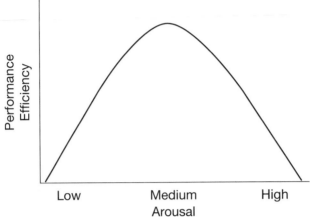

Figure 8-1 The classic hypothetical inverted U-shaped function relating efficiency of performance to level of arousal.

suggested that specific states of emotion and activation have their own properties. Neiss argued that the inverted U-shaped function of arousal and performance is descriptive, rather than explanatory, and that it may be true but trivial. On the other hand, Anderson (1990) debated some of Neiss's assumptions. She agreed that the inverted U-shaped function might be simply descriptive, but argued that too many dimensions of psychological performance fit this function for us to abandon its use in describing such phenomena.

Peripheral Physiology in Arousal and Acute Stress

We discuss the emergency reaction at several points in the book, especially chapters 4 and 6. The reader might wish to refer back to Figures 4-6 and 4-7. The sympathetic portion of the autonomic nervous system tends to fire rapidly during any sudden crisis that demands immediate attention. Reflexes of the sympathetic nervous system affect every organ in the body. They promote catabolic processes, those expending energy from stored reserves. They cause increased blood flow to skeletal muscles and reduction of blood flow to the digestive organs, enabling rapid physical movement. The adrenal medulla secretes norepinephrine and epinephrine into the bloodstream during the emergency reaction, which boosts sympathetic reflexes. Some sympathetic reflexes are subjectively familiar to all of us, and we have already discussed these reflexes in other chapters. The classic signs of sympathetic autonomic arousal include increased heart rate, increased respiration rate, perspiration, pupil dilation, and piloerection, or goose bumps. These responses rapidly mobilize the body to cope with an immediate need or danger.

Modern evidence, much of it based on animal studies, has uncovered mechanisms and chemical systems in the brain that also undergo changes during arousal and acute stress. The brainstem has a number of systems involved in general activation. The reticular activating system (see chapter 4) is a complex web of neurons in the brainstem that projects to higher brain structures. It receives input from various sensory information. For example, some pain fibers (see chapter 6) arrive at the reticular activating system, presumably helping to account for the arousing nature of painful stimuli. Projections from the reticular formation reach upward into forebrain structures, leading to general arousal in the forebrain. It is also probably true that forebrain mechanisms can send information in the other direction, initiating general alertness or arousal in descending pathways.

There are dynamics in monoamine neurotransmitters in the brain that also accompany arousal and the response to diverse acute stressors. Recall that the monoamine systems, especially norepinephrine and serotonin, are heavily concentrated in the brainstem with projections to the forebrain (see chapter 4). The catecholamines in particular act in conjunction with the sympathetic nervous system, and they are directly involved in general activation (Anisman, 1975; Modigh, 1973; Welch & Welch, 1971). Generally, there is an elevation in the release and synthesis of dopamine and norepinephrine during acute stressful stimulation. At some point, if the stress continues unabated for some time, there may be a depletion of such catecholamines, associated with behavioral exhaustion, such that the availability of these catecholamines in the synapses may descend below normal levels.

Stimulant drugs like amphetamines, cocaine, and methylphenidate (Ritalin) artificially stimulate activation and arousal mechanisms in people and other animals. It is well known that these drugs act to stimulate catecholaminergic activity in the brain (Cooper et al., 1991). This, along with many other lines of research, indicates that central catecholamine transmitter systems are involved in arousal, attention, and mental concentration. Typically, such drugs induce sleeplessness, alertness, activation, even agitation. Their effects upon behavior tend to be non-monotonic, following an inverted U-shaped function like that in Figure 8-1. For example, amphetamine's effects upon motor activity in rats present such a function of dose (Snyder et al., 1972). Similarly, amphetamine at moderate doses can stimulate male sexual arousal in mice, but at high doses it completely destroys such arousal (deCatanzaro & Griffiths, 1996).

In addition to changes in the sympathetic and catecholaminergic systems, hypothalamic and pituitary peptides are released during acute stress. ACTH has long been known to be released during acute stress. Its adreno-cortical influences are well known, causing steroids like cortisol to be released in the minutes following stress. However, usually such steroids are thought to be slow-acting in their impact upon physiology and behavior, and steroids are most commonly associated with longer-term stress (see below). However, ACTH itself may have some shorter-term influences, and this hormone also finds its way to cerebrospinal fluid, from where it could have shorter-term impacts on mood and actions (see Dunn & Gispen, 1977). Curiously, ACTH also has the capacity to elicit stretching, grooming, and yawning behavior in a number of mammals via its action through the ventricular system, and in some species yawning is seen in mildly stressful social situations (see Baenninger, 1987; Provine, 1986).

CRF from the hypothalamus stimulates ACTH release via local blood supply, and CRF may also be released locally in the hypothalamus and elsewhere and have other influences of its own (Kupfermann, 1991a; Lenz et al., 1987). Also released during acute arousal or stress, are the endorphins and enkephalins. As was previously discussed (see chapters 4 and 6), these substances have the capacity to dull pain perception and alter mood. Concordant with this is the fact that acute stress can induce natural states of analgesia (Mousa et al., 1981; Urca et al., 1985). Other pituitary hormones like oxytocin have also been observed to rise during acute stressful experience in mammals (Lang et al., 1983); the specific function of this is not clear.

Thus, a combination of sympathetic nervous system arousal and all of its reflexes, release of catecholamine hormones from the adrenal medulla, activation of central catecholamine neurotransmitters, and hypothalamic and pituitary hormones provides a strong activational system in the body. It increases mental alertness, sensory awareness, and muscle readiness, so that we can take fast action and cope with immediate needs. This whole set of systems is dynamic in all of us, more active when we are more active, and less active when we rest.

As many of us who drink coffee know very well subjectively, caffeine also has general stimulating effects upon central nervous system functioning. Scientific literature also supports this assertion, although the effects depend upon personality and time of day (e.g., Revelle et al., 1980). Caffeine and related chemicals are also found in cacao, tea, and some soft drinks, and it may well have addictive properties. As is well known, many individuals use it deliberately to improve their arousal in the morning. The physiological mechanism of action of caffeine does not depend upon the catecholamines, but instead involves vascular changes in the nervous system and an increase in blood pressure.

Do Autonomic Mechanisms Vary in Quality Among Emotions?

Consistent with the idea of general arousal, Cannon (1915) emphasized the common autonomic features of various emotions. Some theorists (e.g., Mandler, 1975; Schachter & Singer, 1962) similarly suggested that autonomic arousal was common to many emotions, and that cognitive and perceptual factors are required to differentiate among the emotions. Schachter and Singer (1962) injected the adrenal hormone, epinephrine (adrenaline), into human subjects. (Epinephrine stimulates sympathetic activation.) They reported that this produced only an undifferentiated emotional state, whose expression depended on the perceptual and social context. Subjects interpreted and labeled their emotion depending on circumstances. One way in which this was manipulated was by having a model display a specific emotion, such as euphoria or anger. Subjects tended to interpret their own emotional state as did the model.

On the other hand, some classic evidence suggests that adrenal epinephrine and norepinephrine might have distinct functions, and that different emotions might produce distinct patterns of autonomic arousal. Funkenstein (1955) studied effects of the drug mecholyl, which stimulates parasympathetic reflexes. He compared its influences in psychiatric patients who had different prevailing emotional problems. When mecholyl was given to "fearful" psychotic subjects, it induced a blood pressure drop like that induced in normal subjects given mecholyl plus epinephrine. When mecholyl was given to "angry" psychotic subjects, the drop in blood pressure was like that found in normals given mecholyl plus norepinephrine. He concluded that epinephrine was more associated with fear, and norepinephrine was more associated with anger. He also cited earlier work indicating that predatory species like lions have high levels of norepinephrine, while less aggressive species like rabbits have high levels of epinephrine.

More recent work by Frankenhaeuser (1975) casts some doubt on Funkenstein's conclusions. Frankenhaeuser measured urinary excretion of metabolites of epinephrine and norepinephrine under a variety of emotional circumstances, finding that norepinephrine release required a higher level of arousal, but that both substances were released under a variety of emotional conditions. She also found no difference in the emotional states elicited in people by artificial infusion of norepinephrine and epinephrine. Clearly, the potentially different roles of the two major adrenal catecholamines has not received enough modern attention.

There may be other differences in autonomic arousal associated with different emotions. In another classic experiment, Ax (1953) covered human subjects in electrodes and wires, ostensibly measuring hypertension. He then surreptitiously gave them some very mild shocks. When each subject reported the sensation, the experimenter came into the room, expressed surprise, pressed a key which caused sparks to jump near the subject, then exclaimed with alarm that there was a high-voltage short-circuit in the system. Naturally, this induced fear! In other cases, he had a technician enter the room and insult the subjects, presumably inducing a state of anger. While such procedures might not survive today's research ethics boards, the results are informative. The profiles of seven physiological measures, including heart and respiration rates, face and hand temperature, skin conductance, and integrated muscle potential during the "fear" and "anger" stimuli were quite distinct.

More recently, using less controversial procedures, Ekman et al. (1983) also found distinct autonomic responses associated with six emotions, anger, fear, sadness, happiness, surprise, and disgust. Emotional states were elicited either by having subjects recall emotional experiences, or by having subjects display the facial expression characteristic of the emotion. Ekman and colleagues found increased heart rate in anger, fear, and sadness, but not in other emotions. They found a distinct elevation of finger temperature in anger but not in other emotions. There were also larger decreases in electrical skin resistance in sadness than in other emotions.

So, there are some distinct autonomic features of specific emotions. We know much less about distinct brain mechanisms associated with emotions, because they are less accessible. However, at several points in this book, we will discuss some evidence of emotion-specific limbic and cortical systems, as well as neurochemical systems, based on animal studies and modern human brain-imaging and pharmacological techniques.

Rebound Mechanisms, Rest, and Sleep

Subsequent to a period of relatively intense arousal, or following the acute stress or emergency reaction, there is typically a parasympathetic rebound which operates to restore homeostasis by temporarily shifting the body into a more vegetative mode. This reverses sympathetic reflexes, often more slowly than they were elicited, and allows recovery from stress. Reflexes throughout the body favor digestion, storage of energy, growth, immunity, repair of damage, and excretion of wastes from cells, organs, and the whole body. Essentially, reflexes of the parasympathetic nervous system cause a flow of resources to the internal organs and away from the brain and muscles.

The parasympathetic system innervates most major organs of the body (see chapter 4), stimulating reflexes that reverse the functions set off by the sympathetic portion. It tends to fire less rapidly than the sympathetic system. While the sympathetic system fires rapidly, in various degrees but as a coordinated whole entity, parasympathetic system reflexes may occur bit by bit and more independently of one another. Recovery from acute excitement and restorative functions may not have to occur as rapidly and suddenly as the defensive responses of the sympathetic system. Acetylcholine is the transmitter substance most associated with the parasympathetic nervous system. It is also a transmitter substance in the brain (see chapter 4), and it is known from many animal studies that this transmitter is involved particularly in the rebound after various short-term stressors (Anisman, 1975).

As everyone knows, there is a daily cycle of activity that normally relates to the light cycle. As diurnal organisms, whose strongest sense is vision, humans are adapted to be active during the light and sleep during the dark. Almost all of us sleep at night and rise in the morning, but of course there are some individual differences in the activity cycle, especially with the advent of artificial light and occupational demands for irregular activity levels. Sleep is undoubtedly a relatively parasympathetic phase of our activity cycle.

There are hormonal cycles that go along with these circadian activity cycles. Darkness sets off pineal-gland secretion of melatonin (Cassone et al., 1993; Reiter, 1983; Trentini et al., 1979). Although we still lack definitive proof, there is longstanding suspicion that this hormone has something to do with sleep onset. There are also distinct circadian cycles in certain steroid hormones. Cortisol (see below) shows a daily cycle, typically being highest in the hours just before we rise in the morning and lowest in the evening (Kandel, 1991c). Men's testosterone levels show a similar cycle (Reinberg et al., 1975).

As we all know subjectively, the desire to rest and sleep can certainly motivate behavior, or a relative lack of behavior (such as sleep) when there is an immediate opportunity to consummate this drive. Most people seek rest daily. When we have been alert and active for about half to two-thirds of the 24-hour day, we generally want to rest, and we are strongly driven to seek relaxing activities and a comfortable bed. The more that we are sleep-deprived, the more overwhelming this drive becomes. On the other hand, few of us want to rest all of the time, as a study by Heron (1957) discussed below clearly indicates.

Boredom

Discussions of boredom as a motivator of behavior are complicated by a lack of agreement among psychologists about exactly what the concept means. Smith (1981) provided a review of early research on boredom and attempts to explain it in physiological terms. The earliest researchers viewed boredom as synonymous with monotony, and caused by "inadequate reflex circulatory adjustments to the boring task" (McDowell & Wells, 1927). Psychologists were mainly concerned with the practical implications of industrial or job-related boredom. Barmack (1937) defined boredom as a tendency to revert to sleep or a sleeplike state (his subjects were university students) caused by inadequate motivation, and his research found amphetamines to relieve boredom. Other psychologists, mainly during the 1960's, defined boredom in terms of increased or decreased arousal, feelings of unpleasantness and constraint, all producing conflicting motivational states. Very little empirical research was done to support any of these hypotheses.

One exception was Heron's (1957) study of sensory deprivation. Heron paid university students to undergo sensory deprivation for as long as they could tolerate it. The subjects had to lie on a bed, with breaks only to eat and eliminate. Sounds were masked by a constant din, vision was restricted by a mask, and touch sensation was diminished by cotton gloves. As time passed, subjects reported that they could not think clearly, that their minds wandered uncontrollably or simply went blank, and that they had very strong hallucinations. When tested after 12, 24, and 48 hours of sensory deprivation, subjects' mental performance on standard tasks such as simple arithmetic became impaired. Emotionally, the subjects were irritable, and usually they demanded to leave the experiment after a few days despite financial incentives to continue.

More recent research has been undertaken to examine some of the physiological changes accompanying boredom induced by vigilance tasks (Bailey et al., 1976). Such tasks involve, for example, constant monitoring of a video screen for rare and unusual events. With increased time in such monitoring tasks, subjects have reported increased irritation and decreased attention. This is accompanied by decreases in heart rate and blood pressure. Braby and colleagues (1993) had subjects monitor videos of airplane instrument panels, and also found subjective reports of work underload to be correlated with a decrease in heart rate. Of course, such studies and the whole issue of boredom-induced attention deficits are of great importance for many practical applications, such as pilots and aircraft controllers who maintain long hours of monotony, occasionally punctuated by moments of severe crisis (see Beaty, 1991).

A Boredom Proneness Scale was developed by Farmer and Sundberg (1986) and has been used by social researchers to identify and study individuals and groups prone to boredom. For example, Watt and Vodanovich (1992) found a significant correlation between boredom proneness and impulsivity. Vodanovich and Kass (1990) used the same scale to examine age and gender differences in boredom proneness. They found that males have a higher need for external stimulation than females, and that older individuals are less prone to be bored. Sundberg and colleagues (1991) administered the Boredom Proneness scale to college students in Australia, Hong Kong, Lebanon, and the United States. Students in Lebanon were the most boredom-prone, followed by those in Hong Kong. Across all cultures, males were more boredom-prone than females. Such general differences surely do not apply to all individuals subsumed by these categories, and the validity of the measure with respect to real-life behavior is not clear.

Surprise

The emotion of surprise has been viewed as a primary, culturally universal emotion by many researchers (e.g., Ekman et al., 1987; Izard, 1991; Panksepp, 1982; Plutchik, 1994). Essentially, surprise arises from a violation of expectancy. Expectancy can be defined as some sort of cognitive-perceptual set about the nature of ongoing events in the individual's environment. An individual expects certain relationships among events on the basis of experience and general knowledge. For example, we all expect darkness to descend in the evening, and light to arise in the morning, but when primitive people first encountered total solar eclipses, they were undoubtedly surprised by darkness at midday. At a common sense level, most of us have a clear understanding of expectation and surprise.

Surprise in reaction to sudden unexpected information is associated with stereotyped facial expressions. It surely is also related to "arousal" mechanisms as we have been discussing. Typically, there is a lifting of the eyebrows, with the eyes agape, as if to prepare for perception of new visual information. The ears may also perk somewhat, although this reflex is probably more visible in your dog or cat than it is in humans. Again, such a reflex may allow the individual to be alert to incoming auditory information. The mouth typically opens during surprise, which could be construed as allowing increased respiration associated with the acute stress response.

Sudden surprising events can produce very simple reflexes, called startling, in both humans and other animals. Startling can be clearly seen in human infants, described as the Moro reflex, wherein an infant throws his or her arms outward and arches the back in response to a sudden noise or physical shock (Hofer, 1981). Many examples have been described for other species; for example, individual baboons suddenly encountering a snake have been observed to leap instantly away with all four limbs clear of the ground (Hall & DeVore, 1965).

Sensation Seeking

Although most individuals generally avoid stress, some directly seek it. Thrill-seeking behavior sometimes carries considerable risk, and surely there are enormous individual differences in such behavior. Although there has been little empirical research done on boredom and its physiological basis, there has been much research on sensation seeking.

Berlyne (1967) posited that human affect, like performance, follows the inverse U-shaped function of arousal and stimulation as pictured in Figure 8-1. He suggested that low levels of arousal or boredom produce negative affect, that a moderate level of arousal coincides with pleasure, but that high levels of arousal and stimulation produce tension and stress. Accordingly, he suggested that people are motivated to escape boredom by seeking environmental stimulation, even if this involves some risk-taking.

A Sensation Seeking Scale was developed by Zuckerman et al. (1964). This includes boredom susceptibility as one factor in sensation seeking, but also includes thrill and adventure seeking, experience seeking, and disinhibition. Zuckerman pointed to very substantial individual differences in this personality trait, implying that there is a genetic basis for thrill-seeking. More recently, Zuckerman (1984) has looked at human sensation seeking using animal models and a comparative biological approach. He noted, for example, the differences in open-field activity in different strains of mice (see chapter 3), and interpreted this in terms of brain neurochemistry and sensation seeking. In humans, preliminary studies have related norepinephrine and related enzymes, particularly monoamine oxidase (MAO) to sensation seeking (see chapter 10 for a discussion of monoamines and mood). Zuckerman suggested a model relating mood, activity, and sociability to activity of central catecholamine neurotransmitters, neuroregulators, and other factors which balance and stabilize arousal systems through feedback loops. Under this model, novelty (in the absence of threat) is rewarding through activation of noradrenergic neurons.

Most people would be quite reluctant to jump out of an airplane, even with a parachute, but others apparently do this just for fun, or perhaps sometimes also to impress other people. The physiological and psychological concomitants of sport parachute jumping have been systematically studied (Fenz & Epstein, 1967; Fenz & Jones, 1972). As might be expected, novice jumpers show much greater signs of autonomic arousal than do experienced jumpers, in terms of heart rate, respiration rate, and skin conductance. In novices, these classic sympathetic nervous system responses are present from the beginning of the day of the jump, rising progressively as the novices arrive at the airport, board the plane, and rise in altitude, reaching a peak at the final altitude just before the jump. In experienced jumpers, these measures indicate less sympathetic arousal, and tend to peak earlier, usually just after takeoff. Among novice jumpers, those who perform better tend to show a pattern of sympathetic nervous system arousal that is closer to that of the experienced jumpers, that is somewhat calmer at the point of jumping. Subjective measures of fear concerning an impending jump also differed between novice and experienced jumpers; the novices were most fearful just prior to jumping, while those with experience were more fearful during the previous night and while reaching the airport but much less so during the flight and jump itself.

Maladaptive Overarousal

There are several manifestations of excessive arousal that yield the downturn in performance seen in Figure 8-1. Many of these problems are described in the clinical literature on anxiety (see Paul & Berstein, 1973; Redd et al., 1979). There may be failures of normally adaptive responses with intense anxiety. Extreme anxiety can, for some individuals, adversely affect diverse functions, including performance on academic examinations, performance in competitive sports like figure skating, musical performance, public speaking, or even sexual response. This is what has informally been called "a case of the jitters." More precisely, there may be excessive sympathetic nervous system and catecholaminergic arousal. This may cause trembling that interferes with motor sequences in an athletic event, or with voice control in public speaking or singing. Anxiety may interfere with the concentration and focus needed for effective performance. It might also cause perspiration, flushing, and/or facial expressions of negative affect that interfere with confident and appealing public demeanor. There may be sleeplessness or appetite disturbances prior to the event, which for some people could impede optimal performance (although, surely, minor sleep and appetite disturbances are common experiences, and many of us who do perform in public find that they have little impact). The sympathetic overarousal may be so severe, and accompanied by irrational or inordinate fear, that it is called a panic attack (see chapter 6).

Performance anxiety can also lead to maladaptive avoidance behavior, where the individual cancels ("chickens out," colloquially), often just prior to the event. This may be seen, for example, in the student who is due to give an oral presentation or the artistic performer who cancels the event at the last minute in order to avoid the anxiety of performance. Of course, this may not make a good impression on the prospective audience. As discussed in chapter 6, excessive avoidance is associated with failure to learn about the matter that is feared, and prevents the realization that it is actually much safer than it is assumed to be.

This is our second examination of anxiety. We first viewed anxiety in chapter 6 as an extension of fear into more complex cognitive functions. We look at this concept a third time in chapter 13 when we discuss decision-making and risk-taking. Anxiety, as a vague and abstract concept, has been used in many different contexts in psychology, and its abandonment has been urged (Sarbin, 1968). However, various researchers have sought operational definitions of this concept in terms of physiological, behavioral, and cognitive components (e.g., Gray, 1982; Redd et al., 1979)

Although knowing this obscure fact may not help those who are anxious, in the worst cases of extreme anxiety or overarousal, it is possible to die of spontaneous cardiac arrest (see reviews by Hughes & Lynch, 1978; Richter, 1957). There are many human anecdotes of individuals who have experienced spontaneous heart attacks during extreme emotional circumstances. Fortunately, this is rare, and the arousal must be exceptionally intense, and the phenomenon probably only occurs in highly susceptible individuals. Sudden-death syndrome has been systematically examined in laboratory animals. For example, rats suddenly placed in inescapable swimming tasks may die spontaneously, without drowning and despite excellent swimming skills (Binik et al., 1977).

LONG-TERM ADAPTATIONS

Selye (1936, 1956) showed a stereotyped endocrine response to diverse *chronic* changes, including physiological changes such as surgery or anaesthesia, environmental events like extreme cold, and psychological situations such as social conflict. Such stimuli were labelled as *stressors*, and the result in the organism as *stress*. While generalized neuroendocrine reactions to chronic stressors are well established, we now know that there are also qualitative variations in chronic stress reactions that depend upon the individual and the nature of the stressor.

The Pituitary-Adrenocortical System

Long-term stress causes steroid changes which affect our energy and neurochemistry, often helping us cope. They temporarily inhibit digestion, reproduction, immunity, and growth to favor muscular activity and alertness.

Psychological events that arouse emotions impinge on the limbic system and hypothalamus. Stressful events cause CRF release in small quantities from the hypothalamus, as the first stage in the pituitary-adrenocortical response. CRF is transmitted via the local blood supply to the pituitary, setting off release of ACTH. ACTH, as discussed above, may have some influences of its own, but its best known action is to stimulate hormone production and release by the adrenal cortex. The adrenal cortex releases corticosteroids like cortisol and corticosterone. These corticosteroids go throughout the body, and are picked up again at the hypothalamus and pituitary, where they provide feedback that can dampen further release of ACTH, such that the system does not become overactive. Corticosteroids also exert actions on the adrenal medulla, increasing its capacity to produce epinephrine.

Corticosteroids cause numerous changes in body chemistry. They alter the metabolism of carbohydrates, proteins, and fats. They diminish inflammatory or immune responses, reducing the body's response to infection and damage. They suppress reproductive processes in both males and females, even to the point of reducing sperm production and disrupting the menstrual or estrous cycle. They may even suppress growth. These losses of normally adaptive processes are the prices paid for channeling resources to deal with the stress. For while these processes are inhibited, resources in the body flow to the brain and muscles as needed, liberating energy for dealing with the crisis. Essentially, the body channels its resources to cope effectively with the original stress. Usually this is highly adaptive, because the suspension of long-term projects of growth, reproduction, and immunity is temporary, and a small price to pay for the benefit of increased energy and alertness that helps the individual cope with the immediate problem.

   The adrenal cortices actually release numerous steroids, and the balance of these steroids may have critical influences upon brain chemistry and our moods. Figure 8-2 summarizes some of the major biosynthetic processes in the adrenal cortex. In addition to the production of aldosterone (discussed in chapter 5 with respect to its roles in thirst and sodium metabolism), and production of corticosteroids, the adrenal cortex has the capacity to produce a host of sex steroids, including progesterone, testosterone, androstenedione, DHEA,17β-estradiol, and others.

   Cortisol in humans is the hormone most closely associated with chronic stress. Cortisol levels are elevated in diverse psychosocial and other demanding situations, particularly conditions that are unfamiliar to the individual, frightening situations, and conditions associated with uncertainty or anticipation of unpleasant events (Fredrikson et al., 1985; Kirschbaum & Hellhammer, 1989). For example, cortisol levels are elevated in air force crews (Leedy & Wilson, 1985) or in persons experiencing phobic anxiety (e.g., Nesse et al., 1985). In children, cortisol levels can be indicative of general levels of stress, and have been found to be elevated, for example, in children living with stepfathers rather than natural fathers (Flinn & England, 1991). It is a fair bet that they are elevated in many students during examination periods.

   Steroids go to various peripheral targets in the body, but they also go to the brain. As small molecules, they are not impeded by blood-brain barrier mechanisms (see chapter 4). Instead, they circulate freely in the brain, but their receptors are concentrated in specific regions. There are specialized cells with specific intracellular receptors for steroids. Such receptors are concentrated in regions of the brain that are associated most with motivation and emotion, the hypothalamus and the limbic system. Cortisol and corticosterone have receptors in the hypothalamus and pituitary, and also in other limbic sites like the hippocampus, amygdala, and septum (deKloet et al., 1990; Sarrieau et al., 1986; Seckl et al., 1991). Sex steroids (estrogens, testosterone) have receptors in parts of the hypothalamus, such as the ventromedial region and preoptic area, and also reach other limbic sites such as the septum and amygdala (Pfaff, 1980; Simerly et al., 1990). Remember that steroids are generally fat-soluble molecules, and thus are metabolized and excreted slowly. In keeping with this, many of the effects of steroid hormones are long-term (days, weeks, and months), with chronic influences over the general organization of motivation and behavior.

   Steroids can have modulating effects on brain chemistry that in turn influence emotion and motivation. Corticosteroids can naturally inhibit MAO (Parvez & Parvez, 1973; Rastogi & Singhal, 1978). Recall that MAO is an enzyme that breaks down the monoamine neurotransmitters in the brain (serotonin, norepinephrine, and dopamine). Thus, steroids like cortisol could elevate activity of monoamine neurotransmitters by inhibiting MAO. As is made explicit in chapter 10, MAO inhibition could have influences that elevate our affective state, that is, make us somewhat happier, by increasing

BIOSYNTHETIC PATHWAYS FOR ADRENAL STEROIDS

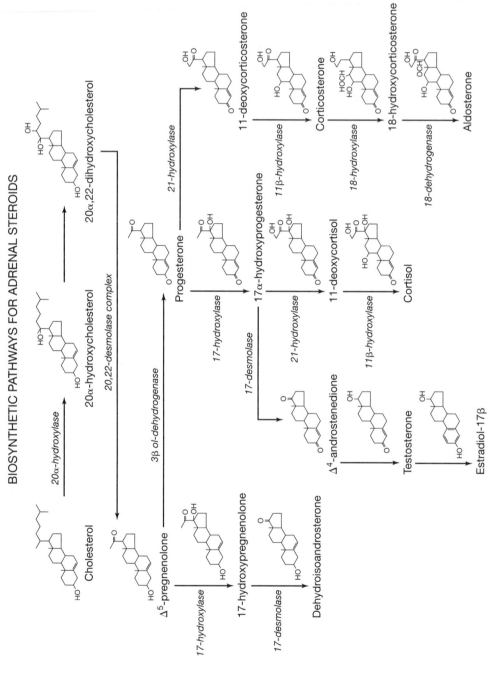

Figure 8-2 A subset of the major biosynthetic pathways for steroids in the adrenal cortex. The adrenal cortex can produce a variety of sex steroids as well as glucocorticoids like cortisol and mineralcorticoids like aldosterone.

availability of these monoamine transmitters at their receptors. However, the effects of cortisol levels on moods are probably nonmonotonic, meaning that increased levels at some point are associated with the opposite effect (another example of an inverted U-shaped function). In fact, chronically elevated cortisol levels are actually associated with psychological depression, as we discuss in detail in chapter 10.

There are neurochemical dynamics associated with various degrees of chronic stress that fit this picture (Anisman, 1975; Welch & Welch, 1969; 1971). Under moderate levels of chronic stress, or ongoing demands from the environment with which the organism can cope, there are elevations in the synthesis and turnover of brain catecholamines, norepinephrine and dopamine, and possibly also of serotonin. However, in animals that have been exhausted and are failing to cope with the demands placed on them, we see depletions of these same monoamines in the brain. That is, levels and activity of these monoamines are reduced to subnormal levels, perhaps because mechanisms for their production and release are simply exhausted. This profile is seen, for example, in laboratory mice that have been repeatedly defeated in aggressive encounters or exposed to electric shock.

Also consistent with this profile are direct actions of the hormone ACTH on the brain. As discussed above, ACTH via cerebrospinal fluid has influences that amplify actions of the catecholamines (Dunn & Gispen, 1977).

The adrenal androgen DHEA is currently receiving a lot of attention for its possible effects upon health and mood (Kalimi et al., 1994). DHEA is one of many adrenal androgens and estrogens. Such steroids are only partly under the influence of ACTH, being also influenced by other factors that are not known. DHEA has effects that suppress actions of stress hormones like cortisol, and it may thus undo or modulate influences of hormones associated with stress. Various effects on mood and metabolism are under study, but it may be too early to form strong conclusions about its actions.

Figure 8-3 gives a summary of the systems involved in both short- and long-term stress mechanisms. There are many interactions among the sympathetic portion of the autonomic nervous system, the hypothalamus and pituitary, the adrenal gland, and central brain mechanisms, especially those involving catecholamines. These systems act in concert in both short-term and long-term activational processes, in turn affecting motivation and emotion.

Limits to Reproduction

It may be no coincidence that steroids mediate both reproduction (through the gonads) and stress (through the adrenal cortex). Many dimensions of reproductive activity are impaired by stress. One classic demonstration is that of Calhoun (1949). Calhoun gave rats unlimited food resources in a small room, then observed what happened to their population over time.

BASIC STRESS SYSTEMS

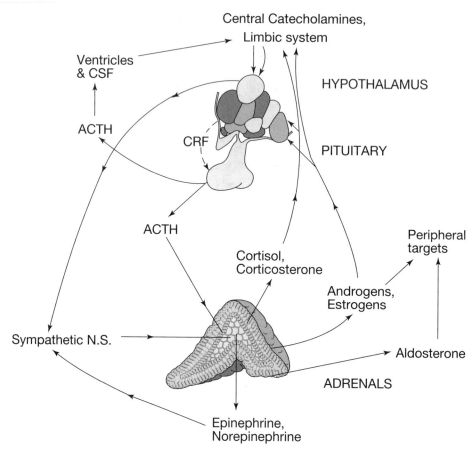

Figure 8-3   A summary of systems involved in stress. The main short-term mechanisms involve activation of the sympathetic nervous system, which rapidly stimulates many reflexes, with secretion of catecholamines from the adrenal glands and activation of brain catecholamines. The first part of the long-term response also occurs in immediate stress: Release of CRF by the hypothalamus into local circulation stimulates release of ACTH by the pituitary gland into general circulation and cerebrospinal fluid. The response of the adrenal cortices involves steroids, like cortisol and adrenal sex steroids, which enter general circulation, passing throughout the body and to the limbic system of the brain, causing long-term adaptations.

Initially, their population grew rapidly, until the room was quite full of rats. After that, even though food was abundant, the population stabilized, because various dimensions of reproduction began to fail.

Reproduction is vulnerable to stress in both sexes, but probably much more so in females than males. Female fertility is inhibited by stress. For example, some women show temporary menstrual disturbances during academic examinations, with menstruation being early, late, or missed altogether (Dalton, 1968). The majority of female Nazi concentration camp inmates, who endured exceptionally severe conditions, failed to menstruate throughout their incarceration, but resumed normal functioning sometime after their freedom was regained (Matussek, 1975). As discussed in chapter 7, pregnancy is also vulnerable to stress. The most vulnerable period is during the days immediately following fertilization, when the ova either set up roots in the uterus or perish (deCatanzaro & MacNiven, 1992). In diverse mammals, early pregnancy is very vulnerable to psychological stress, such as excess heat or cold, physical restraint, environmental or social changes, nutritional shortage, or exposure to predators. These effects are clear in laboratory rodents and domestic herbivores like sheep and cattle, and there are probably also comparable effects in women. Of course, it may be optimal not to continue pregnancy in the face of severe stress, because the young may not thrive. The human miscarriage rate is high during the first trimester of pregnancy. There are probably many causes of this phenomenon, but one of these causes may be maternal stress (cf. Istvan, 1986; Levin & DeFrank, 1988; Llewellyn-Jones, 1974).

Health Effects of Emotions and Chronic Stress

Achievement often requires hard work and stress, and surely many people do well in life because they are willing to drive their bodies into modes of high performance, hormonally and neurochemically akin to Selye's "stage of resistance." With appropriate phases of rest and relaxation, there is probably no harm in hard work and moderate states of chronic stress. Moreover, the productivity of hard work and the enjoyment of the many benefits that it brings could often outweigh some costs to other qualities of life. Nevertheless, certain forms of chronic stress, especially unrelenting, uncontrollable, and frustrating forms, can bring severe costs to health and welfare.

There is little question that many health problems are correlated with chronic stress. There is a wealth of evidence that cardiovascular disease is related to an accumulation of stressful life events and psychological difficulties (Byrne, 1987; Glass, 1977). Indeed, proneness to coronary failure has been linked to Type A behavior, which is a constellation of attributes including urgency and impatience, competitiveness and ambitiousness, need for achievement, poor frustration tolerance, hostility and aggression, and high occupational involvement (Friedman & Rosenman, 1974). Experimental studies with animals also show that stomach ulceration is precipitated by chronic uncontrollable stress; indeed, rats that can predict or control repeated shock delivery develop fewer ulcers than do rats that receive the same amount of shock without prediction or control (Weiss, 1971). Experimental tumor growth in mice has been shown to be enhanced by chronic stress (Sklar & Anisman, 1980). Moreover, poorer prognosis of diseases such as human breast cancer is correlated with social stress, lack of social support, fatigue, and psychological depression (Levy et al., 1987). Diverse forms of psychopathology also are at least partly caused by stressful life experience. There is evidence for contributions of stressful experience to a wide range of childhood and adult problems, ranging from psychotic behavior to psychophysiological problems to affective disorders (see Davison & Neale, 1996; Wicks-Nelson & Israel, 1997). As we discuss in chapter 10, states of psychological depression are often precipitated by chronic coping problems and correlated with high cortisol levels.

It may be fair to say that many life stressors diminish physical health and longevity, and that negative emotions can diminish immunity and resistance to disease (Miller, 1988; Solomon, 1987; Solomon & Amkraut, 1983). One important dimension of this is social support from family members and valued friends (Berkman, 1984; Cobb, 1976; Dimsdale et al., 1979; Kaplan et al., 1977). Social support can be defined in terms of an individual's sense that he or she is cared for, loved, esteemed, and a member of a network of mutual obligations (Cobb, 1976). Although the progression of some forms of disease is probably independent of social support networks, a substantial amount of evidence suggests that individuals with frequent social contacts with concerned friends and relatives often have a better prognosis than do those with fewer contacts, in the face of comparable disease and injury. Thus, there may be truth in the statement *Friends make good medicine.*

An example of such data comes from a nine-year study of social networks and mortality in Alameda County, California (Berkman & Syme, 1979). A random sample of 6,928 adults was surveyed in 1965, and social and community ties were assessed. The findings were that those people who lacked social ties were more likely to die in the follow-up period than were those having such ties. This association was statistically independent of physical health at the start of the study, socioeconomic status, and health-related practices such as smoking, drinking, and physical activity. Another study (Blazer,1982) similarly found that within a sample of elderly persons in North Carolina, individuals with greater social support tended to live longer than those with less social support, which was statistically independent of demographic and socioeconomic variables. Of course, such correlations, even with appropriate statistical control for potentially confounding factors, do not absolutely prove causal relations between social support and longevity.

Other data that provide stronger support for a causal relationship come from a prospective epidemiological study, part of the Tecumseh Community Health Study (House et al., 1982). In this study, social relationships and activities were initially reported during interviews and medical examinations in 1967–1969, with mortality over the succeeding 9 to 12 years examined in a cohort of 2,754 adult men and women (aged 35–69 at the start of the study). The assessment of social relations included considerations of social isolation, marriage, and contacts with friends, kin, and community. After statistical adjustments for age and mortality risk factors, the data showed that men reporting higher social involvement were significantly less likely to die during the follow-up period. The trend was present regardless of age, occupation, and health. A similar trend relating social involvement and mortality was evident for women, but was insignificant when age and other risk factors were controlled.

Grief can also increase the probability of mortality. In folklore, there are many anecdotes of cases where individuals die shortly after they have lost their beloved spouses. In fact, there is supportive scientific evidence. Parkes and colleagues (1969) studied 4,486 widowers 55 years of age or older for nine years following the death of their wives in 1957. Of these, 213 died during the first six months of bereavement, which was 40 percent above the expected rate for married men of the same age. The greatest cause of this increase during the first six months was coronary thrombosis and other heart disease. Also, Helsing et al. (1981; 1982) conducted a prospective epidemiological study of 4,032 persons over 18 years of age who became widowed between 1963 and 1974 in Washington County, Maryland, and an equal number of married persons matched for race, sex, age, and geographical location. Mortality rates based on years at risk were about the same for widowed as for married women, but were significantly higher for widowed males than for married males, even after adjustment for demographic, socioeconomic, and behavioral variables. Mortality among widowed males who remarried was significantly lower than among those who did not. Living alone was especially correlated with mortality. Deaths from infectious diseases, accidents, and suicides were significantly higher than expected among widowed males, and deaths from cirrhosis of the liver were significantly higher than expected among widowed females. Although behavioral variables are surely involved in suicide (see chapter 10) and accidents, and may play a role in cirrhosis of the liver via alcohol consumption, it may be harder to account for mortality from heart and infectious diseases without invoking emotionally induced changes in neuroendocrine variables.

Another rather fascinating finding is that the timing of death may be briefly delayed by positive socioemotional factors, being postponed until after significant events have occurred. Phillips and King (1988) studied the number of deaths in various subpopulations in California before and after the Jewish holiday of Passover during 1966 to 1984. In a Jewish sample, there were significantly fewer deaths than expected in the week before Passover, and significantly more than expected in the week after. This "dip-peak" pattern was found exclusively in people with Jewish background but was not found in various control groups, including Blacks, Asians, and Jewish infants. Phillips and Smith (1990) similarly examined mortality in various subpopulations in California before and after the traditional Chinese holiday, the Harvest Moon Festival. Mortality among persons of Chinese ancestry and traditions was found to dip by 35.1 percent in the week before the festival and to peak by a similar amount (34.6 percent) in the week following the festival. Among causes of death, cardiovascular diseases showed the greatest dip-peak pattern, followed by diseases of the heart, followed by malignant neoplasms. These trends were not seen for control samples of other ethnic backgrounds. The authors suggest, essentially, that death takes a holiday, being postponed until after symbolically meaningful events!

At the other end of the lifespan, in neonatal development, some evidence suggests that vulnerable infants may be more likely to thrive when they receive regular visitation from their family members (Brown et al., 1991; Fanaroff et al. 1972; Zeskind & Iacino, 1984). Hospitalization of low birth weight infants has often led to an unnatural separation of mother and infant. Although the evidence does not show a definitive relationship between visitations and survivorship, and causative mechanisms are very difficult to determine, there are indications that greater numbers of visitations by mother are associated with better developmental outcome.

Aging, Senescence, and Limits to Self-Preservation

It is clear that stress interacts with aging and death. This leads to deeper discussion about why, from an evolutionary perspective, we age and die. It is an obvious fact of nature that in late adulthood, our bodies slowly degenerate or senesce, no matter how hard we try to deny or fight it. This may cause new stresses as we try to cope while our coping apparatus is deteriorating.

One idea is that aging is just wear and tear on the body. Accordingly, just like an old car, we fall apart in many ways with age. This idea was formally discussed as a cause of senescence by Comfort (1964). Although it is not a comforting thought, degeneration and death are inevitable for all of us.

Another idea came from Fisher (1950), Medawar (1957), Williams (1957), and Hamilton (1966). These evolutionary biologists suggested that degradation of optimal health is inevitable in the postreproductive state, because all that genes need do to get passed on over generations is to achieve copies of themselves, by having the individual survive and reproduce. What genes do after reproductive age is less affected, if at all, by natural selection, and so their expression may degrade from optimal expression to randomness in postreproductive years.

More formally, consider a concept, "reproductive value," developed by Fisher (1950). In simple terms, this is the probability of reproducing beyond a certain age. Reproductive value can be computed by integrating actuarial statistics, that is the proportion of any age cohort (e.g., all persons born in 1968) surviving and reproducing beyond any specific age (see Figure 8-4). For example, consider the average number of offspring that all infants who

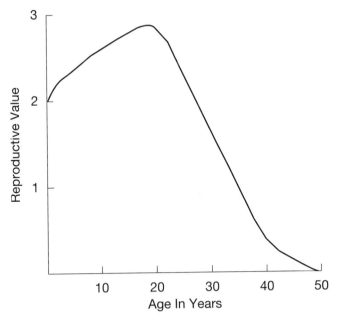

Figure 8-4 A typical curve of reproductive value (see deCatanzaro, 1991b; Fisher, 1950; Hamilton, 1966), which represents prospective reproduction at specific ages, as an integral of the proportion of each age cohort surviving to reproductive years and reproducing in future. Reproductive value increases during the juvenile period, as a function of mortality, peaks at the commencement of adulthood, then declines rapidly thereafter.

are six months old today will produce in their lifetimes. Because some will die before reaching adulthood, this is less than the average number of future offspring of all people who are 24 years old, because they have already survived childhood and are on the threshold of peak reproductive years. Consider 40-year-olds, many of whom have already reproduced, but that is considered irrelevant in this statistic. Future number of *new* offspring, on average, is much less for 40-year-olds than for 24-year-olds (especially for women). By age 50, reproductive value is zero for women because of menopause (although modern technologies can alter this fact), and also getting low for men.

Reproductive value is an important consideration for many dimensions of social motivation, as we shall see in later chapters. At this point, let us relate it to self-preservation and aging. The point made by Medawar (1957), Williams (1957), and Hamilton (1966) is that any gene is more often expressed at younger ages than at older ages, simply because mortality of an age cohort (e.g., all persons born today) cumulates with increasing age. The effects of genes' expression in youth thus carries more weight than their expression at later ages. With increasing age, especially post-reproduction, genes may not affect their own propagation over generations. Accordingly, genes with healthy effects in youth, but degenerative or random effects later on, can be passed on over generations. With randomness comes less optimal self-preservation, senescence, and ultimately death.

Motivation and emotion, as well as physiology, may change in postreproductive years. Some changes may result from health changes. Other changes arise as children age, and careers progress. Senescence theory also suggests biological reasons, as we will revisit in future chapters. Age may bring less attention to reproduction, more attention to the welfare of family instead of oneself, and greater acceptance of death as inevitable.

The story of limits to self-preservation must be elaborated in the light of modern inclusive fitness theory (deCatanzaro, 1991b). In highly social species like ours, where nurturance of children involves heavy investment over many years, individuals' survival is often essential beyond the mere act of reproduction, well into the post-reproductive years, insofar as kin are dependent. Natural selection thus bears on survival in postreproductive years when it affects dependent kin. In theory, therefore, self-preservative genetic expression is expected in individuals with prospects of benefit to close kin. However, consider the conjunction of low reproductive value and lack of contact with kin, or worse, a sense of being unwanted by kin. In evolutionary theory, this is where limits to self-preservation motivation can arise (see deCatanzaro, 1981a; 1991b; 1995).

Although many people try to live forever, defying their inevitable ultimate destiny, it cannot happen. Our lives are very short in an evolutionary time scale, and there may be more important goals in life that surpass those of immediate selfish survival. We revisit this issue in chapter 10, in order to understand why some people sometimes give up the struggle to live, or even seek to die.

POST-TRAUMATIC STRESS SYNDROME

Severe stress can have longlasting impacts upon an individual's emotional state. Sometimes, these effects endure long after the stress itself has abated, although like many of the impacts of severe stress, the long-term effects vary greatly among individuals.

Post-traumatic stress disorder (PTSD) was first recognized and studied in soldiers who were affected mainly in trench warfare during World War I. Interest waned after the war, but with the outbreak of World War II there was a renewed interest in finding out what had become of the World War I veterans. This resulted in some extensive studies by Kardiner (1941) documenting the symptoms of soldiers who had been incapacitated by their war experiences. He described two phases of post-traumatic stress: the acute phase, immediately following the traumatic event, and the stabilized phase, developing two weeks to six months later and lasting many years in some cases. Acute symptoms included shock, terror, delirium, paralysis, sensory disturbances, and even coma. The stabilized phase could have many different manifestations. Kardiner describes symptoms such as delusions and paranoia, which he categorized as schizophrenia. He grouped symptoms such as irritability, depression, tempers, phobias, and sensitivity to noise together as "transference." He described many case studies of veterans suffering from autonomic disturbances such as sweating, headaches, and enuresis. Others had sensorimotor disorders such as deafness, speech disorders, and constricted vision. His documentation of symptoms and case studies was thorough, although his psychoanalytic interpretations might now be viewed with skepticism.

More recent studies of war-related PTSD have been conducted on American veterans of the Vietnam war. Many of the same symptoms described by Kardiner are identified in these veterans (Weathers et al., 1995). A significant finding was that a majority of veterans suffering from PTSD were also diagnosed with other disorders, including alcoholism, drug dependence, antisocial personality, and depression (Sierles et al., 1983).

In situations of war, many people besides soldiers experience trauma. More recent studies have also focused on concentration camp survivors, torture survivors, and refugees. A thorough study of the adjustment, health problems, and psychiatric problems of survivors of Nazi concentrations camps was conducted between 1958 and 1962 by Matussek (1975). Matussek's methods differ from those of other studies because he tracked down survivors to interview rather than only using those who had sought medical certificates. Nevertheless, he concluded that the number of "psychologically healthy" survivors was very small. Subjects suffered from a broad spectrum of physical and psychological complaints persisting many years after liberation, and there was no single specific syndrome that could be statistically identified. Large numbers of survivors suffer somatic illnesses, primarily falling under "internal disorders" and "gynecological disorders." The most common psychological disturbances included a chronic general state of exhaustion, and feelings of mistrust, paranoia, and social isolation. Many survivors reported feelings of resignation and despair, apathy, and aggressive-irritable moodiness. A relationship was found between the severity of psychological disturbance of inmates and their ability to reintegrate successfully into society. All former inmates reported problems in their social lives.

One of the most common and specific complaints of almost all individuals suffering from PTSD is that of sleep disturbances. A study of torture survivors from Iran, Iraq, Palestine, and Afghanistan used polysomnography to study sleep patterns (Astrom et al., 1989). All subjects had abnormal sleep patterns compared with normal age- and sex-matched controls. They had shorter total sleep time and woke frequently from REM (dream) sleep. These findings probably account for frequent nightmares and chronic exhaustion reported by most survivors of traumatic stress. Similarly, a study of concentration camp, combat, and sea disaster survivors found longer than normal latencies to fall asleep and to commencement of REM sleep, and larger than normal amounts of "awake" and "movement" time within sleep periods in such survivors (Hefez et al., 1987).

Recently, studies have begun to look at PTSD in populations not involved in war. A predominant factor contributing to PTSD in the general population of the United States has been found to be violent crime (Breslau et al., 1991). Resnick and colleagues (1993) estimated that the lifetime PTSD prevalence for a representative national sample of 4,008 women was 12.3 percent. Moreover, they estimated that 30 percent of sexual assault victims and 40 percent of violent assault victims met diagnostic criteria. Other studies show that victims of violent crime also show high rates of substance abuse, depression, and sexual dysfunction in the case of rape victims (see review by Hanson et al., 1995). Many studies attempting to link violent crime victimization and emotional health have been criticized, however, because of poor sampling techniques, numerous confounding variables, and failure to establish whether mental health problems preceded or resulted from the crime episode (Hanson et al., 1995).

By some estimates, almost 2 million households in the U.S. each year are affected by natural or technological disasters, such as fire, flood, hurricane, structural collapses, or transportation accidents (Green & Solomon, 1995). Although initial reactions among most victims range from surprise and confusion to helplessness and anger, these reactions usually resolve within a few months, with a smaller number sustaining longer-term psychological effects. Pre-disaster data rarely exist for the affected population, so studies of impacts rely on finding matched control populations. In one such study, Shore and colleagues (1986) compared 500 community survivors of the Mount St. Helens volcanic eruption with a control population, and found higher rates of depression, anxiety, and PTSD in the disaster survivors. In the survivor population who had experienced death of a family member or extreme property damage, rates of PTSD were 21 percent for women and 11 percent for men. In an example of a technological disaster, Green and colleagues (1990) studied survivors of a dam collapse that had killed 125 people. They also found much higher rates of depression, anxiety, and PTSD in the exposed population than in a control population.

Many victims of other, more common types of accidents, also show signs of psychological impact, including PTSD (Scotti et al., 1995). The most common causes of non-fatal accidental injury, as recorded in hospital admissions, are falls and motor vehicle accidents. Victims show a continuum of responses from none to severe, with PTSD only one possible outcome. Other diagnoses include panic attacks, obsessive-compulsive disorder, phobias, and substance abuse. In studies of motor vehicle accident survivors, Goldberg and Gara (1990) found 43.6 percent to exhibit depression and 14.5 percent full PTSD. Other studies reviewed by Scotti and colleagues (1995) found PTSD rates in the range of 46 to 65 percent.

Stress and arousal are thus complex processes with both short- and long-term dimensions. We elaborate on many of the themes of this chapter as we move into discussions of aggression (chapter 9) and affective behavior (chapter 10).

Chapter 9

ANGER, HATE, AND AGGRESSION

People, like members of other species, have always had to partition limited resources among individuals and groups. Demands upon resources are typically greater than the supplies, because of a constant tendency toward overreproduction (see chapter 2), which naturally leads to conflict among individuals. Several motivational and emotional phenomena relate to social status and the allocation of resources, in both self-assertion and self-defense. In plain English, we have several terms for emotions and drives related to these matters, in threat and appeasement or aggression and defense.

Forms of Threat and Aggression

A very important distinction between threat and aggression is clear from studies of animal behavior. Conflict and division of resources often occur without any outright fighting, through gestures of threat and appeasement. Outright fighting is potentially very costly, to winners as well as losers. There are no hospitals in nature, no antibiotics or nurses, and even a small scratch can become infected and lead to death. Entering into an actual fight is thus very risky, even when victory is likely. Accordingly, most conflict within species is settled by gestures, displays of body posture and vocalization that determine which animal is dominant and has access to resources, and which is subordinate and walks away.

Aggressors, and those attempting to defend territory against intrusion, typically try gestures of threat first, and only will launch an outright attack if gestures fail. Rattlesnakes rattle their tails, giving a warning and chance to escape before biting. Most domestic dogs bark loudly and persistently, and growl and bear their teeth, and will only bite or attack if extremely provoked (or may never do so if you call their bluff). In many species (see, for example, Ewer, 1968) animals on the attack show self-maximizing postures that make their bodies appear larger, including piloerection (hair standing on end), which gives an illusion of even greater size. They show a "threat-stare," emit roars or other loud vocalizations, and make aborted chase movements toward the opponent.

On the other hand, animals backing down may simply flee and yield territory to the aggressor. Or, if they share a common territory with the aggressor because they are members of the same social group, they may show gestures of appeasement. These often include self-minimizing gestures such as crouching movements. These are readily apparent in the domestic dog, and are often shown to their human masters (see Figure 2-1). In primates, we often see female sexual gestures, such as presentation of the hindquarters, used as appeasement gestures by both males and females. Somehow these have acquired over evolution a secondary function, being used to placate dominant males, perhaps because sexual arousal is normally incompatible with aggression.

True aggression does occur, of course. *Aggression*, as used in plain English, has many meanings. In scientific use, it also refers to many distinct phenomena. Moyer (1968) discussed seven different forms of aggression, depending on the object under attack and the situation provoking attack:

1. Predatory aggression, which is almost always between species and is used to gather food
2. Intermale aggression, which is related to dominance and partitioning food, other resources, and mates
3. Territorial aggression, which is also usually among males, and similar to #2, and may involve scent-marking and other manners of defining the boundaries of physical territory
4. Defensive or fear-induced aggression, such as might be shown as a last resort by prey in the face of a predator
5. Maternal aggression, displayed by a lactating animal in defense of its young
6. Irritable aggression, which is elicited by frustration or pain
7. Instrumental aggression, which is more dispassionate, and is learned or developed by conditioning procedures and influenced by rewards

The different forms of aggression are clearly motivated by distinct factors, and although there may be some overlap, the scientific causes need to be considered separately.

We focus here mostly on threat and aggression within the species. Humans are historically predators, and have also been subjected to predation. The motivation of hunting for food is obvious, related to issues in chapter 5. We need not say much more about it here, except to note the curious fact that hunting, as a sport, appeals to some individuals, usually male, even when they are quite well fed. Also, we will note below that predatory aggression in mammals has distinct neurological features from those involved in dominance-related or intermale aggression. Defensive motivation was discussed in chapter 6. We are obviously motivated to shelter ourselves against animal predators, ranging from microorganism-induced diseases, to biting insects, to the very few large predatory mammals that still confront some people, to competitive human organizations. Within the species, fear interacts directly with aggressive motivation, in determining decisions to stand and fight or run away, and thus in dominance and subordination.

Once again, we look at other mammalian species as well as ourselves, because it is quite clear that the roots of human anger and aggression run deep in evolution, although as usual, modern human evolution has produced some interesting modulations. Gestures of threat and appeasement, corresponding to aggressiveness and fearfulness, have been described by ethologists for many species. In Figures 9-1 and 9-2 are given some classic pictures of postures shown by domestic cats and elephants.

Dominance and Subordination

The concept of *dominance* has a long history in the study of animal behavior (see review by Bernstein, 1981). It is used to describe a variety of competitive interactions, including threat and aggression related to territoriality, especially among animals that cohabit the same territory within a social group and therefore must partition resources and females among themselves. It has been observed in numerous species that some individuals get more than do others, move more freely and show less fear or avoidance of other members of the group, and that this status is established and maintained by aggression and defeat and/or threat and appeasement gestures. It is often observed that dominance hierarchies, particularly among males, are associated with differential access to females, and hence that dominance relates to reproductive success. There is an enormous literature on examples from animal behavior; we discuss just a few mammalian cases and then turn our attention to human beings.

Dominance-oriented behavior is especially pronounced in mammalian males, although it can also be described, usually in milder forms, among females. As we discussed in chapter 7, in most mammals there is far more variation in reproductive success among males than there is among females. This derives from a degree of polygyny among males, where some enjoy a great deal of reproductive success while others are excluded altogether from reproduction. This fact of nature sets the stage for extreme competition among

Figure 9-1   Expressions of threat and fear in domestic cats.

From Leyhausen (1956). *Zeitschrift für Tierpsychologie*, Beiheft 2, pp. 136–137, copyright © 1956, Blackwell Wissenschafts-Verlag, reprinted with permission.

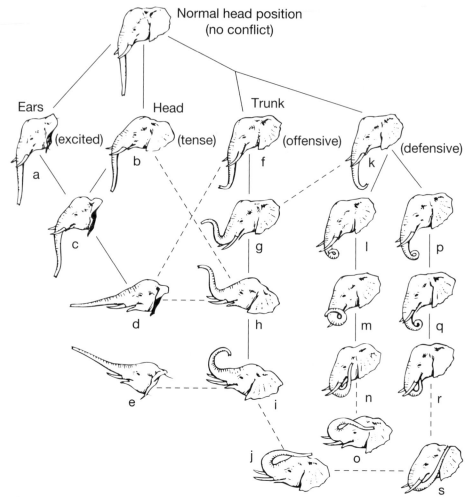

Figure 9-2   Expressions of threat and fear in elephants.

From Kuhme (1963), *Zeitschrift für Tierpsychologie* 20, 66–79, copyright © 1963, Blackwell Wissenschafts-Verlag, reprinted with permission.

males for reproductive success, and is widely viewed as the evolutionary basis for intermale aggression. Some males reproduce, other do not, and to be among those that do, one often must defeat competitors. So, over generations, the males who are aggressive and dominant tend to pass on their genes, while those that are less aggressive or less successful in competition with other males may fail to pass on their genes. Thus, there are strong evolutionary pressures, at least among nonhuman animals, favoring aggressive tendencies among males.

One of the strongest examples is found in elephant seals, where inter-male aggression dramatically determines reproductive success (LeBoeuf, 1974). Some large males get all of the reproductive success, corralling harems of females and expending considerable effort to exclude other males and sustain their dominance, while other males get nothing. This sets up strong evolutionary pressures among males, favoring the replication of whatever characteristics produce reproductive success, and selecting out any unsuccessful characteristics.

Baboons have been described as showing dominance hierarchies among males that determine reproductive success, but according to Hall and DeVore (1965, p. 55), the definition is not straightforward: "Dominance is a complex conception assessed by observations of the frequency and the quality of several types of behavior in various kinds of situations, with reference both to the other animals within the group and to external events." Hall and DeVore presented data showing that animals that rank first within a group have the most sexual opportunities with females that are in full estrus, receive submissive female sexual gestures ("presenting") most often from females, juveniles, and males within the group, and are involved in the greatest number of aggressive episodes. The facial expression of threatening animals involves staring, sometimes accompanied by a quick jerking of the head down and then up. Grinding of the teeth and yawns that widely display the teeth are also often seen during aggressive encounters. There may also be displays of vigorous shaking of tree branches and vocalizations described as grunting and loud roaring. On the other hand, subordinated or "fearful" animals may show a "fear grimace," characterized by retraction of the lips so that the teeth are exposed but not separated, while the ears may be flattened against the head. This fear grimace is rarely seen in adult males. Subordinated animals may often run away screeching, while the dominant animal gives chase.

Among humans, social dominance is often difficult to define, and in modern civilized life it may be quite divorced from aggressiveness. It was probably much easier to define social dominance within simple hunting-gathering groups than it is in complex modern society. Within small groups today, such as street gangs, a pecking order may not be hard to define, and aggression may still play a role. Within a small company, who is boss is clear, but aggression (in the sense of violence) is usually quite irrelevant. Dominance may be situation-specific; the department chair may not be captain of the department baseball team. Within larger organizations and society in general, socioeconomic factors and chains of command may be said to provide some sort of hierarchy. However, in terms of rising in the hierarchy, violent aggression and even many forms of threat are usually counterproductive, because they are illegal and socially sanctioned (when identified).

For people, expression of anger acts as a threat, but outright aggression is usually not the enforcer of the threat. Except for less civilized quarters of the species, such as in street gangs or among prison inmates, anger most often is not a prelude to violent behavior. In interpersonal relations, there are often other ways of carrying out threats, if need be. For example, we can stop giving business to a rude salesperson, or we can terminate a friendship when abused by the other party. Within most families, temporary anger is often expressed, and although some parents employ corporal punishment, others correct their children's misbehavior through more sophisticated means, withdrawing privileges if threats are not sufficient. In civilized society, it is permissible to express irritation, annoyance, and even restrained anger in conjunction with verbal statements of our grievances. Those in authority within institutions often have other mechanisms to carry out their threats, like firing, demotion, withdrawal of privileges, or embarrassment.

Human Anger and Expression

In people, direct expressions of anger clearly act as threat gestures, intended to modify other people's behavior. Modern civilized adults can often achieve a lot merely with words, but more primitive expressions of anger can be visible in our faces and body language.

The physical manifestation of anger appears to be innate and constant across cultures, and descriptions have not changed much over the years. Darwin (1872, p. 256) describes that in anger "the action of the heart is a little increased, the colour heightened, the eyes become bright . . . the wings of the nostrils are somewhat raised to allow of a free indraught of air . . . the mouth is commonly compressed, and there is almost always a frown on the brow." He (p. 257) describes the posture of an angry person as "ready for attacking . . . his head erect, with his chest well-expanded, with his feet planted firmly on the ground." He goes on to describe the hand and arm positions and movements, but claims that these are the only aspects of the posture that are variable in different cultures: "With Europeans, the fists are commonly clenched."

In more modern descriptive research, Izard (1991) points out that anger triggers identical muscle movements in infants and adults. The skin of the forehead is pulled tight by muscles that lower the brows, and the brows are drawn sharply downward and inward creating a bulge above the nasal roof. The lowered brow makes the eyes appear narrow. He suggests that with maturity we learn to modify the face of anger, particularly the mouth expression, which changes from an open square or rectangular shape in young children to tightly closed with clenched jaws in adults.

Argyle and Cook (1976) describe how gaze is used in dominance displays by many species, and also in aggressive encounters. This is also characteristic of angry humans, who may show a "hate stare." They suggest that this gaze is a deliberate breaking of the usual taboo against staring at strangers in public places.

The human voice may also change in nature during anger, with the quality depending on whether it is "hot anger" or "cold anger" (see review by Kappas et al., 1991). In irritation or cold anger, there may be an increase in mean pitch and high-frequency energy as well as a tendency toward downward-directed contours, that is reducing the pitch toward the end of sentences. In rage or hot anger, the pattern may be consistent with that of cold anger, but with greater variation in pitch, indicative of sympathetic nervous system arousal.

Appeasement, the other side of the coin in humans, may be expressed in many fashions, from verbal statements of deference to compliant behavior to body language. Appeasement may have characteristics of fearfulness, which we discussed in chapter 6. Smiling has been suggested to serve as an appeasement gesture, among other meanings (Freedman, 1979; see chapter 10).

Sex Differences and Neuroendocrine Substrata

Men, on average, are historically far more aggressive than are women. It is well known that in almost all cultures, men much more than women go to war, commit homicide, or engage in barroom brawls. Nevertheless, one must not stereotype either sex on this basis; there are many gentlemanly men and some women who engage in physical violence.

In children, this is reflected in an average difference between boys and girls in the level of what is known as rough-and-tumble play, which is found in diverse cultures (DiPietro, 1981; Hines & Kaufman, 1994; Mazur, 1983). This is generally characterized as rough, active, outdoor play. It includes playful physical assault involving hitting and shoving the other child without harmful intent, physical assault on objects such as balls, and playful wrestling involving overall body contact. It is usually among boys, although like other sexually dimorphic behavior, there are exceptions. This sort of rough intermale play is also described in juvenile males of other primate species.

The general male-female difference in aggressiveness is found in most mammals, and perinatal testosterone and gross adult levels of this hormone are proven to be relevant for many species. In fact, it is very well known that tomcats are far more aggressive and "uncivilized" than neutered male cats. Neutered males can make excellent house pets, but tomcats wander for long periods in search of females, scent-mark with foul-smelling emissions, and are prone to fight other males. Similarly, most knowledgeable people would rather deal with a steer than a bull, or a gelding instead of a stallion.

In mice and rats, the relationship of androgens and aggression is well understood (see Inset 9-1; also chapter 3). In these species, especially mice, aggressive behavior is sexually dimorphic, being displayed by males toward other males. Indeed, it follows closely the androgen dependency described in chapter 7 for male sexual behavior, being dependent on a conjunction of perinatal androgenization of the brain during a critical period and circulating androgens in adulthood (see Brain & Benton, 1983; Quadagno et al., 1977). Castration can eliminate intermale aggression, and testosterone injections can restore it. Females can be made to show intermale aggression simply by giving an injection of testosterone during the critical perinatal period, followed by repeated injections of testosterone in adulthood.

Despite much effort to uncover possible relationships between testosterone and human aggressiveness, it is not at all clear that human aggressiveness is androgen dependent (Albert et al., 1993; Archer, 1991). Individuals who are high and low on measures of aggressiveness do not consistently differ in levels of testosterone. Several studies have looked at prisoners incarcerated for violent offenses, comparing their testosterone levels to nonviolent prisoners or members of the general public; these studies have not yielded conclusive findings. Aggressiveness in boys does not consistently change at puberty, when there is a major increase in levels of testosterone. Human studies of castration of male sexual offenders indicate a reduction in male sexual behavior and recidivism, but the impact of such surgery upon subsequent aggressive behavior is unclear (see Heim & Hursch, 1979; Stürup, 1968). In their thorough review, Albert et al. (1993) suggest that, unlike the situation in nonprimate mammals where testosterone does play a clear role in aggressiveness, a relationship of human and even other primate aggressiveness to testosterone activity does not clearly exist.

Nevertheless, more individual men commit aggressive acts than do individual women, and not all researchers believe that testosterone is irrelevant. One report (Van Goozen et al., 1995) indicated that cross-sex steroids influence aggressiveness. Transsexual individuals voluntarily taking steroids characteristic of the opposite sex were examined before and after treatment. Androgen administration to females increased self-reports of aggressiveness in paper-and-pencil survey measures, while ovarian hormones given to genetic males decreased anger- and aggression-proneness. Of course, the meaning of such measures for real-life experiences is not established, nor is it clear whether expectations of the subjects might have influenced their responses.

Endocrine Changes in Response to Social Status

In a simple species such as mice, dominance in intermale encounters has enormous impact upon subsequent behavioral initiative, and it transforms physiology. Behaviorally, male mice that have previously won aggressive encounters with other males tend to be much more assertive with other mice, more likely to initiate new attacks against other males in comparison to subordinated mice (see Brain & Benton, 1983). They are also more likely to initiate mating behavior than are subordinates when given free access to receptive

Inset 9-1   Intermale competition in house mice

The most highly studied form of aggressive behavior is that shown by common European house mice (*Mus musculus*), a domesticated species for which we have developed numerous genetic strains in the laboratory. We described in chapter 3 how this behavior occurs in male mice in a stereotyped form in the absence of any learning, and that we know that it has a genetic basis.

Male mice are extremely competitive for reproductive success, and there is every reason to believe that aggressive behavior evolved because more aggressive mice enjoyed greater reproductive success than did nonaggressive mice. Several studies indicate that this behavior is greatly enhanced by the presence of sexually receptive females. If male mice are allowed brief sexual encounters with female mice, they are far more aggressive than those that have not had contact with females, when placed with other males in a neutral arena (deCatanzaro, 1981b). Having been with females makes males more aggressive. In fact, we have found that the very best recipe for murderous aggression in mice is to house two males together, beside a female mouse that neither male can access because of a wire-grid separation. Under these circumstances, one male is usually found dead within two days of making this social arrangement.

It is well known that such intermale aggression in mice is dependent on androgens, because castrated males and females tend not to fight (Brain & Benton, 1983). Male mice that are dominant in intermale encounters become substantially different in physiological makeup from males that are repeatedly defeated or subordinate. In subordinated mice, the adrenal glands may be more active, the testes may be less active, the male sex accessory glands are smaller, and the turnover of brain catecholamines may be higher than in males that are housed alone or are dominant in aggressive encounters. Dominant and subordinate males also differ in their behavior. Dominant males are more assertive, more likely to initiate aggressive behavior, and more likely to mate with females (deCatanzaro & Gorzalka, 1979).

When male mice mate, they deposit a large sperm plug in the female after the sperm. This coagulates and hardens, making it difficult for other males to inseminate the female. Thus, males have evolved a mechanism to prevent competition from other males even after they have completed mating and left the scene. This may not be the end of intermale competition, because even females that are already pregnant can be targeted by other males for pregnancy blocks. In what is known as the "Bruce effect" (Bruce, 1959; deCatanzaro et al., 1996), males other than the sire of the pregnancy may direct pheromones at females that are already pregnant, and this will in many cases terminate the pregnancy by blocking intrauterine implantation of fertilized ova. By ending the pregnancy, the novel male sends the female back into estrus, so that she can quickly become pregnant again with his progeny.

If all of these mechanisms have failed to prevent other males from siring a female's young, a novel male is likely to kill the newborn pups if he encounters a parturient female whose young were sired by another male (Gandelman, 1983; Labov, 1980). This behavior is dependent on androgens, being eliminated by castration and restored by testosterone administration. This again makes it likely that the female will return quickly to estrus, so that the new male, the one that killed the pups, has a chance of siring a new litter. Of course, the female does not allow such infanticide without putting up a fight; the one circumstance in which females most reliably fight is in defense of their pups (Svare & Mann, 1983).

So males in this species are in rather brutal competition for females' reproductive benefits, actively trying to beat the other males at several phases of the reproductive process.

---

females (deCatanzaro & Ngan, 1983). Similar effects have been reported in deer mice, where dominant males completed more copulations than did less aggressive males competing with them for access to a female (Dewsbury, 1981). Repeated exposure to aggression and defeat tends to lead to substantial drops in plasma and pituitary levels of luteinizing hormone (LH) in mice (Eleftheriou & Church, 1967), which could subsequently lead to reduced gonadal activity. Adrenal activity tends to be greater in mice that are subordinate, consistent with the idea that they are more stressed (Benton et al., 1978; Leshner, 1983). Even brain chemistry is affected. Brain catecholamines are active during aggressive encounters, and subsequent to defeat, may be very depleted (Welch & Welch, 1969; 1971).

Studies of rhesus monkeys show some interesting patterns in the relationship of testosterone levels and social dominance (Bernstein et al., 1983). Testosterone levels are very dynamic in this species, showing patterns in relation to the breeding season. They also show a marked diurnal rhythm, with a peak in the night prior to dawn, a decline over the day, and a rise again in the evening. The presence of females, especially those in estrus, has a significant influence on the testosterone levels of males. Simply presenting males to females in estrus causes their testosterone levels to rise, independent of whether they begin to show sexual behavior.

The most remarkable feature of testosterone levels in rhesus monkeys is their responsiveness to changes in social status. Social defeat can be as strong an influence as sexual stimulation on testosterone levels, but acting in the opposite direction. In several systematic studies conducted in collaborations of Rose, Bernstein, and Gordon (see review by Bernstein et al., 1983), testosterone has been measured in monkeys within stable heterosexual groups and related to dominance, and then the dominance structure has been experimentally disrupted by moving animals among colonies. Dramatic testosterone declines were observed when males were taken from familiar groups and introduced into all-male groups, where they were promptly defeated in aggressive encounters. The new monkey in an established group typically enters the dominance hierarchy with the lowest rank. When males were similarly introduced into an established heterosexual group, they were also defeated, and any positive influence of female exposure was more than offset by the defeat. Thus, social experience regulates androgen levels. Alterations in hormones may in turn have some role in the initiation of social behavior, as the subordinated male may be more timid in approaching other males and females as a consequence of defeat.

Some fascinating data suggest that human androgen levels are also responsive, at least in the short term, to social conditions and successes and failures. Serum testosterone levels were found to increase after victory in tennis matches, especially if individuals were pleased with their performance (Booth et al., 1989). Cortisol levels were not related to winning and losing, but did tend to be lower in more competent and experienced players. In another study (Elias, 1981), competitive fighting (wrestling) among men has been reported to have similar effects upon testosterone levels. Male seniors in medical school showed relative rises in testosterone during the few days after they received their M.D. degrees (Mazur & Lamb, 1980). On the other hand, new male army recruits and officer trainees show substantial declines in testosterone levels compared with control populations, presumably due to stress, male grouping, and degraded status in training (Kreuz et al., 1972). Thus stress may lower androgen levels in men, while positive mood and success may raise androgen levels.

Neurological Substrata of Aggression

Hess (1954) first studied the effect of electrical brain stimulation on behavior. He was able to elicit coordinated movement sequences that were the same as natural behavior patterns, simply by stimulating specific regions of the cat brain. One of the most reliable patterns elicited was a "rage" sequence, involving hissing and teeth-baring.

Delgado (1969) conducted experiments in which stimulation of the lower brain centers of macaques and chimpanzees left free in their social groups resulted in what he called "false rage." This was purely a motor response which, although it looked like anger, was not acted upon by other members of a social group.

Flynn and colleagues (1970) distinguished two forms of aggressive stereotyped action patterns in cats. The first form, affective attack, is more dramatic. This involves the "Halloween cat" posture depicted in the classic picture in Figure 2-1, with an arched back, piloerection, dilated pupils, and bared teeth. It is often accompanied by screams and is a prelude to attacks with the claws. This is a ragelike response often seen in fights among tomcats. The second form, quiet-biting attack, is very different, and seems to be more predatory, lacking emotional display. This may involve searching, stalking, and quiet pouncing, as many people have observed in their domestic cats when they predate on mice or birds. Electrical stimulation of the brain could induce one or the other of these forms of attack, depending on the location of the electrodes. Panksepp (1971) has similarly elicited two forms of attack in the rat. Affective attack is more often produced by medial hypothalamic stimulation, whereas quiet biting attack is more often produced by stimulation of the lateral hypothalamus.

Obviously, we cannot conduct this sort of experiment with humans, but there are many "natural experiments" that occur when people suffer misfortunes such as brain tumors or acquired brain injuries, or when they have psychosurgery to treat tumors or conditions like severe epilepsy. Albert and colleagues (1993) have reviewed these data and compared them to laboratory animal studies. Human cases with tumors in the medial hypothalamus have been associated with extreme aggressiveness, including rage in the presence of stimuli that most people would view as merely annoying. Lesions of the septum in rats are well known to produce defensive rage reactions; there are human case studies of septal tumors that similarly produced heightened defensiveness, with outbursts of temper and violence. The amygdalas and adjacent temporal lobes also apparently play a role in modulating aggressiveness. Several case reports link temporal-amygdaloid seizures with outbursts of violence, and there are comparable data from other mammalian species. The amygdalas seem to play a major role in mammals in the balance of fearfulness and aggressiveness (see chapter 6).

Frustration and Irritation

Frustration is a word that we apply to a mood arising when we fail to achieve some gratification where it is expected. Frustration is subjectively familiar to all of us, and is almost always viewed as unpleasant. Frustration comes from a discrepancy between expectation and reality, where some effort has not produced the reward that was anticipated. Scientifically, frustration can be defined as an activation of behavior that occurs when an individual fails to be rewarded for a response (see Amsel, 1992). Typically, there is reason to anticipate reward, for example due to a history of receiving reward for the same response in the same circumstances. Even in nonhuman species, failure to deliver response-contingent reinforcement in a context where the response previously produced reinforcement produces a measurable activation of behavior.

A classic theory contends that frustration leads to aggression (Dollard et al., 1939). The idea is that individuals who fail to receive gratification may act out impulsively in some aggressive manner. A related suggestion is that experiences with aversive stimuli may facilitate aggression (Berkowitz, 1974).

The probability of an aggressive response is said to be enhanced when individuals experience an aversive stimulus. This is what Moyer (1968) called irritable aggression.

Certainly, there are data from animal studies that show that aggressive responses may be facilitated by aversive stimuli (see review by Conner et al., 1983). Numerous experiments show that when male rats are paired together and then given several inescapable footshocks, they will spontaneously begin to fight. This effect has also been found in several other mammalian species. Thus, experiencing a painful stimulus can clearly increase the probability of aggression.

A Role of Learning in Aggressiveness

Despite evidence for biological factors in aggressiveness, there is ample evidence that aggressiveness is influenced by social learning. In a classic series of studies, Bandura and colleagues (see Bandura, 1977) have shown that observational learning influences children's aggressive responses in controlled laboratory settings. Nursery schoolchildren were placed in standardized situations where they observed other children playing with inflatable dolls. The model children either behaved in a peaceful fashion with the dolls, or punched them in an aggressive fashion. The observers were subsequently placed in the room with the dolls themselves. Those that had seen nonaggressive behavior tended to be peaceful in their own patterns of play with the dolls, but those who had observed the aggressive models tended to be aggressive themselves. The same effect has been obtained when children simply observed filmed models. So, young children tend to mimic aggressive play when they see others behaving that way.

It is often suggested that parents who use corporal punishment set an example that their children will imitate. Certainly, several studies show that there is a correlation, whatever the cause, between aggressiveness in developing children and family patterns of aggressive behavior. Bullying and antisocial aggression are more commonly displayed by children, usually boys, who have observed high rates of aggressive behavior in their homes (Patterson et al., 1989), and who have had relatives in previous generations who acted in aggressive fashions (Huesmann et al., 1984). These and many other recent studies have led to social and political concern about the amount of violence that children observe on television.

Homicide

Acts of outright murder are the epitome of the motivation to do harm to others. As is well known, and in many jurisdictions a source of legal distinction, homicide can occur as an impulsive act of passion, or it may be a more calmly calculated and premeditated act. The circumstances of homicide are varied and multifarious, and the subject of numerous fictional novel plots as well as real-life dramas.

In Figure 9-3 are given statistics from 1991 homicide victims in the United States, broken down by age and sex. You may also wish to refer to chapter 13, where these rates are given in the context of additional data from Canada and Mexico, in comparison to rates of death by accident, suicide, and infectious disease, from World Health Organization statistics. Several issues are clear from these data. In all three countries, despite substantial national differences in overall rates of homicide, male victims predominate. This is true at almost all ages, except in infancy, where the sex ratio is closer to being equal. Infancy is one age of comparatively high risk, but this does not match the very high rate of risk for young adult males, especially in the United States and Mexico. In Mexico, males of all adult ages are at comparatively high risk of death by homicide, and so curiously are aged females.

In terms of motivational theory, killing others who obstruct one's access to resources or mates is not hard to understand, even though it is certainly illegal and most of us find it utterly repugnant, unethical, and unacceptable. If an individual stands to gain in some manner from committing homicide, and anticipates that he or she can evade detection and justice, and the victim is not of kin, the act can be seen as fitting within self-serving psychology. As

Figure 9-3   1991 homicide victims in the United States, broken down by age and sex.
Source: World Health Statistics Annual–1994, W.H.O. (1995).

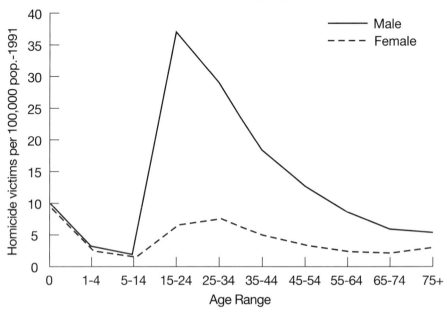

with other decisions about potential actions, we can presume a tradeoff of potential costs and benefits to the individual's fitness (see chapters 2 and 13). Killing in self-defense is not only rational but generally excused legally. Killing for self-gain takes many other forms which are not so easily forgiven by society, such as murder of a stranger to gain his property, or killing a person with knowledge that could incriminate you, or killing a rival for a lover.

Many instances of homicide are domestic, which naturally raises the question: Why kill those sharing your genes, whom you are supposed to love? Daly and Wilson (1988) have addressed this issue in some depth. Among other samples, they analyzed the relationship of homicide to kinship in a sample from Detroit in 1972. Of 508 "closed cases" where the relationship of victim and offender was known, 243 (47.8 percent) were unrelated acquaintances, 138 (27.2 percent) were strangers, and 127 (25.0 percent) were "relatives." However, closer inspection indicated that of the 127 victims related to their killers, only 32 were consanguinal relatives (genetically related). Of the remaining 95, 80 were spouses (36 women killed by husbands and 44 men killed by wives), while 10 were in-laws and 5 were step-relations. So, in fact, only a minority of homicides (6.3 percent of the total homicides) were actually genetically related. The 32 victims of kin included 8 who were children of their killers, 11 who were the killer's parents, 9 brothers, 1 sister, 1 cousin, and 2 nephews.

A classic analysis of homicide in Africa was provided by Bohannan (1960). Bohannan and his collaborators reported on several tribes from various regions of Africa where careful records were kept by colonial administrators in the early- to mid-twentieth century. The vast majority of homicides were perpetrated by males, and the victims were also usually male, although of course there were exceptions. For example, in his report of the Tiv of central Nigeria, Bohannan (pp. 35–36) reported that "women are involved in homicide even less than they are in European countries, the number of killings done by more than one person is very small, and the number of 'unsolved murders' is very small indeed." At least to the colonial administrators, for what it is worth, the motives for murder were usually conspicuous. In all of the tribes analyzed, the motives were diverse. Some victims were thieves (or believed to be), some victims were wives with whom there were quarrels (very few husbands were killed by wives), some victims were rivals or long-established enemies, some victims were brothers. As Africans were rarely allowed access to guns in those times, most murders were committed by stabbing or beating.

Bohannan (1960, pp. 242–246) also conducted interesting analyses of homicides of kin. Of course, kin are usually more proximate to an individual than are strangers, and some rate of homicide among kin may simply reflect the fact that these are the persons with whom an individual interacts. Many victims who were defined as kin in anthropological terminology were in fact affines, related by marriage rather than by genetics of common descent. Of a total of 197 cases of homicide of "kin" from six tribes, 60.4 percent were actually directed toward affinal kin. When true genetic kin were killed, about half (48.7 percent) of them were of the ascending (older) generation, and fewer were of the same generation (35.9 percent) or descending generation (15.4 percent). When those related only by marriage (affines) were killed, 82.4 percent were of the same generation, most of which were wives of the perpetrator, while fewer were of the ascending (13.4 percent) or descending (4.2 percent) generations.

Modern technology has surely made murder easier to commit in some ways, at least at an emotional level. Struggling with another individual to stab or beat him involves directly viewing the agony of the victim and some risk that he might retaliate in self-defense. At some point in the process, the perpetrator could be inclined to desist in revulsion with the feedback from the act. However, poisons or guns simplify the act; one need merely to pull a trigger or lace food with chemicals. The perpetrator can thus be more frail than the victim, and he may not need to view the consequences of the act. This could facilitate more impulsive homicides, again illustrating the principle of evolutionary lag discussed in Inset 2-1, that our modern technological and cultural change has occurred so rapidly that our emotions and impulses may sometimes be maladaptive and out of historical context.

Human Infanticide and Child Abuse

Daly and Wilson (1988) have analyzed infanticide within human families. In a review of the ethnographic data, they enumerated 112 stated circumstances of infanticide from a cross-cultural sample of 35 societies. Of these, 20 cases related to doubts about the paternity, including 15 involving adulterous conception, 3 a nontribal sire, and 2 where a new husband demanded the death of a child sired by a previous husband. In 21 other cases, an infant was deformed or very ill. Another 56 cases were classified as involving doubtful circumstances for childrearing, such as twin births, too many siblings, lack of male support, the mother being unwed, the death of the mother, or economic hardship. The remaining 15 cases involved various other circumstances, such as the infant being female, conception in incest, and ritual deaths.

Daly and Wilson (1988) also analyzed contemporary Canadian data concerning infanticide and child abuse. The risk of infanticide by the mother's or father's hand is far greater when the child is very young. This trend is especially pronounced for mothers, who perpetrate substantially more acts of neonatal infanticide than do fathers. For fathers, the decline in frequency by age of the child is more gradual. Daly and Wilson suggest that paternity uncertainty may be one of the factors that contributes to male-perpetrated infanticide; that in fact, many cases may involve "fathers" killing children whom they know or suspect were actually sired by another man. Their analyses of reported instances of child abuse bolster this assertion. Data from the United States and Canada clearly indicate that per capita rates of child abuse are far greater for children living with one parent and one step-parent than for children living with two natural parents.

According to Frodi (1985), child abuse may relate to infant quality, being associated with factors like low birth weight that can diminish infant attractiveness to parents. In particular, aggression toward the child may be elicited by especially aversive forms of persistent crying. For some parents and infants, the normal empathy-evoking qualities of infant crying that promote caregiving may give way to impulsive aggression elicited by aversive features of the crying.

Child-abuse and infanticide clearly have culture-specific dimensions. In Japan, corporal punishment of children is rare, and the occurrence of child abuse and neglect is quite infrequent compared to the United States (Wagatsuma, 1981). This is consistent with very low rates of violence and homicide in Japan, and may partly be due to the close-knit nature of extended family in that country. Somewhat more common are cases of child abandonment and infanticide in Japan, which in most instances are perpetrated by the biological mother. In contrast, in New Guinea, there are many common practices of child treatment that would surely be viewed as unacceptable within technologically developed cultures, including: "infanticide, initiation rites, child mutilations, sale of infants for both marriage and sacrifice, and forced homosexuality, to name only the more dramatic examples" (Langness, 1981, p.14). One not uncommon practice in New Guinea was the cutting off of small girls' finger joints during mourning ceremonies.

Eibl-Eibesfeldt (1989), from a broad cross-cultural perspective, confirms that maternal infanticide is seen in many cultures, generally shortly after birth and before the mother has had time to form attachment to the infant. Infanticidal behavior has very deep evolutionary roots, being seen in many other species under a definable set of circumstances that resemble those characteristic of human cases (Blaffer-Hrdy, 1979). Maternal infanticide is seen in many mammalian species, and is most likely to occur shortly after birth, especially when the newborns are not well-formed or when the mother is stressed or lacks resources necessary to effectively rear young. Male-perpetrated infanticide is most likely to be associated with nonpaternity. The phenomenon is probably most thoroughly described for laboratory mice, where dams occasionally kill part or all of their own litters, while males are prone to kill litters which they did not sire (Gandelman, 1983; Labov, 1980; see Inset 9-1). There are ethological descriptions for many other mammals (Blaffer-Hrdy, 1979). For example, one classic instance of infanticide is seen in male lions who defeat other males, taking over a pride of females and killing cubs sired by the displaced males, which sends the females into sexual receptivity once they are no longer lactating (Schaller, 1972).

Accordingly, many experts believe that there is an ancient evolutionary logic behind infanticide, one which may sometimes surface in modern human behavior despite proscription by legal and ethical codes. Although under the vast majority of circumstances, females will nurture and vigorously protect their young, there can be some tendency to terminate the process in circumstances where resources are not favorable for nurturance. Males, on the other hand, are seen as likely to endanger young that are not their own, especially insofar as this increases their own prospects of propagating their genes.

Warfare, Human Evolution, and a Soldier's Motivation

One of the most unique features of our species is the fact that we have so often competed on a group level through violence and warfare. Among animals, we have achieved a place at the top of the food chain without major competitors (except for the disease microorganisms that parasitize us). Our greatest dangers have come from members of our own species. Throughout history, we have organized aggression and defense at a group level within the species. There is some evidence that our motivational and emotional character has been altered by these facts.

Evidence suggests that warfare may have long characterized our species. Although it is difficult to be absolutely definitive about the extent of warfare in human evolution, there is substantial evidence suggesting that warfare has long been in our nature (Durham, 1976; Roper, 1969; Vayda, 1974). There are skeletal remains from hundreds of thousands of years ago suggesting that human ancestors died of injury by stone hunting tools, and ancient cave paintings depicting scenes of warfare. Technologically less-developed Amerindian and African cultures observed in the 17th through 20th centuries were known to practice frequent intergroup warfare.

Although many of us abhor warfare, especially in its manifestations in current history, it may be factual to state that warfare has been an integral part of human evolution. Bigelow (1969; 1972) has described intergroup conflict as one of the main driving forces of human evolution. He suggested that, paradoxically, intergroup conflict has favored the development of within-group cooperation. This is because cohesive groups could be more successful in intergroup conflict than fractious groups.

Consider that human ancestors probably lived for millions of years in hunting-gathering groups (see Inset 2-1), small groups of something like 50 to 150 individuals, most of whom were strongly linked by kinship ties. Progressively, as agricultural and other technologies have advanced during the past 10,000 years (see also Flannery, 1972), we have come to live in larger and larger groupings and higher density. Bigelow (1969, 1972) argued that this has brought on an increasingly greater need for within-group cooperation and altruism. He suggested that as groups of varying size and states of technological and cultural advancement encountered one another, those that were larger, more technologically advanced, and more cohesive tended to supplant those that were smaller, less technologically advanced, and less cohesive. This occurred partly due to technology, as better weapons would defeat less-advanced weapons, and group size, as larger groups had more power than smaller groups. Social cohesion also played a critical role, according to Bigelow, because the more cohesive group would always be able to coordinate a better effort than would a more fractious group of comparable size. Accordingly, Bigelow suggested that within-group cooperation evolved in conjunction with between-group conflict, because more cohesive and technologically advanced groups tended to supplant less cohesive and less advanced groups.

There is no doubt that there has been dramatic dynamism of human demographics during the recent historical period, including eras of colonization right through twentieth-century world war. Within groups, there is a strong tendency for antisocial motivation to be sanctioned by the group. Legal and moral systems may have arisen in conjunction with civilization (Bigelow, 1969; Flannery, 1972), discouraging and punishing individuals who act in less cooperative fashions, while rewarding those who behave in more prosocial fashions (see also chapter 14).

On a related issue, how is it that people (almost always men) have been motivated to put their own lives on the line and go into battle? Durham (1976) has addressed this issue. There may be at least two reasons, the first being a more defensive and the second being, well, more offensive.

First, from a defensive perspective, a risk of death may readily be understood within the context of inclusive fitness maximization (see chapter 2), if one's life is potentially traded to save those of kin. Death in defense of kin may be very well justified by the fact that kin contain copies of one's own genes, probably in most instances more copies than exist in oneself. An individual who sacrifices his or her life to save three children is certainly behaving in an adaptive fashion from the perspective of inclusive fitness, because approximately 1.5 times as many genes exist in those children as in oneself. To die for the benefit of one's extended family, who may have an even greater relative representation of one's genes compared to oneself makes sense from modern evolutionary theory (see chapters 2 and 10).

The second reason, historically, for going into battle, also makes sense from what is certainly a more "selfish" perspective. That is the possibility that in victory, there may be spoils of battle that lead to a major increase in inclusive fitness. In defeating another group, males in historical/evolutionary perspective may have gained property and access to women, thus gaining in inclusive fitness as a consequence of risking death. Chagnon (1968) described warfare among preliterate, technologically primitive native peoples of the Amazon, the Yanomamö. Typically, parties of men from one village undertook raids upon a rival village. The object of the raids was to kill one or more of the members of the enemy, and to escape if possible before suffering any losses. Naturally, this could lead to retaliatory raids, direct conflicts between rival parties, and a cycle of recurrent warfare among villages. Often, women were abducted after men were killed, and sometimes raids were undertaken explicitly to capture women, who would subsequently be raped by many men then given to one of them as a wife. According to Chagnon, the Yanomamö regarded fights over women as the primary cause of their wars.

Chapter 10

HAPPINESS, SADNESS, AND COPING STRATEGIES

There are many qualities of joy and sadness. We call this whole dimension of attitude and behavior *affect*. We have many plain-English terms for pleasant moods associated with satisfaction, such as happiness, joy, bliss, euphoria, elation, gladness, cheerfulness, contentment, being in an elevated or uplifted mood, having high spirits. Others connote unpleasant moods associated with discontentment, such as sadness, dysphoria, unhappiness, grief, melancholy, the blues, depression, being down or downhearted or dispirited. These terms carry various shades of meaning about degree and quality of mood, but of course none has scientific precision. Our affective states occur in various short- and long-term forms, generally in response to important life events, and they affect our strategies of coping and our social interactions.

Common sense and a wealth of evidence tell us that affective states are responsive to significant events in our lives, particularly our social adaptation. In common terms, "up" and "down" analogies follow success and failure. Successes in adaptation tend to elevate our affective state, while failures tend to lower it. The events that evoke these elevations and depressions are often of clear biological and social significance. This explains the nature of affective state from a functional, evolutionary perspective.

Consider some of the most reliable stimuli that evoke strong affective changes. The birth of a healthy, wanted child is often a source of enormous joy to family, and this of course represents a significant improvement in biological fitness (see chapter 2). The death of a cherished, young, healthy member of the family typically evokes severe grief, and this is a clear loss in biological fitness. Events associated with improved welfare and increased comfort level generally elevate our moods, while those associated with significant losses to welfare and comfort may lower our moods. In courtship and mating, young adults may react with joy to the establishment of a successful new relationship, and with depression to a rejection or breakup of a cherished relationship. The news that one has gained a desired job, a social position, or money can be uplifting, but the news of a layoff, loss of status, or financial loss can be depressing. People generally react with mood elevations to praise and positive social attention, but with mood depressions to criticism, denigration, and social rejection.

This chapter presents evidence that affective states are usually reactions to significant events, involving changes in activation, direction of motivation, and social demeanor. The evidence suggests that affective dimensions are predispositions, derived from natural selection more than culture, to react to ongoing life events.

AFFECTIVE DISPLAYS

Facial expression

Affective state can be "written all over your face." As we all know subjectively, facial expressions like smiling and frowning communicate our disposition to others. Some of the earliest scientific descriptions came from Duchenne (1862) and Darwin (1872), and there has been much research since the early 1970's.

Smiling, according to Darwin (1872, p. 213), involves "the raising of the upper lip, the cheeks are drawn upwards. Wrinkles are thus formed under the eyes . . . as a gentle smile is increased into a strong one . . . the wrinkles in the lower eyelids and those beneath the eyes are much strengthened or increased." He also describes how the skin on the bridge of the nose becomes wrinkled, and the eyes become bright and sparkling. There are, of course, many variants of smiling and lip movements. Many of these were described, without ascription of function, by Seaford (1978). As well as classic smiles with upturned contours of the mouth, there are movements such as pursing of the lips and tongue to lip movements. Seaford attempted to develop a taxonomy of smile forms, identifying several consistencies across individuals.

As was touched on in chapter 2, evidence suggests that smiling in pleasure is innate and culturally universal. Freedman (1979) and Izard (1991) reviewed literature supporting these ideas. Both indicated that smiling appears reflexively within hours or at most a few days after birth. By about five weeks, a smiling response is elicited in response to a number of stimuli, with the human face being the most reliable. By four or five months, the infant begins to discriminate among faces and smiles only to some of them, usually familiar ones. As discussed in chapter 3, smiling can be seen very early in development in blind as well as sighted infants, particularly in response to attention from caregivers (Fraiberg, 1974; Freedman, 1964). Freedman (1979) found more smiling on the part of females than males, beginning in infancy, and discussed ethnic differences in the frequency of the smile. Freedman suggested that the smile has many meanings, as a gesture of appeasement, an assurance that "I mean you no harm," and an expression of interpersonal unity.

Ekman and Friesen (1982) distinguished "felt, false, and miserable" smiles. The *felt* or *genuine smile* involves relatively involuntary actions of the zygomaticus major muscles pulling up the lip corners. This happens in conjunction with the orbicularis oculi muscles which surround the eye, whose contraction creates wrinkles that radiate from the outer corners of the eye. The cheeks are raised and the eye fissures narrowed. This smile of true delight is often now called the Duchenne smile. In the *false smile* there is no raised cheek or eye wrinkles, and in the *miserable smile* facial features associated with negative affect are readily apparent. They suggested that genuine smiles differ from other smiles, which may be more deliberate, polite, and masking of actual feeling. Only genuine smiles involve the orbicularis oculi, and the smile forms may also differ in the time taken for the response to appear and dissipate.

Fox and Davidson (1988) reported that 10-month-old infants show genuine (Duchenne) smiles in response to mother's approach, whereas strangers more often elicited other sorts of smiles. In EEG measures of activity in the cerebral hemispheres, only genuine smiles were associated with left-frontal cortical activation, a pattern which their data suggest is characteristic of positive affect.

Eibl-Eibesfeldt (1989) described a rapid gesture of the eyebrows often seen in smiling, that is associated with positive regard and greeting. This is the brief upward eyebrow flash. He contended that this is found in numerous cultures, as displayed in Figure 10-1.

Frowning, on the other hand, is associated with displeasure. Two main aspects of frowning are raising of the eyebrow inner ends and drawing down of the corners of the mouth. Darwin (1872, p. 188) indicates that muscle actions "draw the eyebrows together, their inner ends become puckered into a fold or lump." Furrows form on the forehead. Meanwhile, in the lower face, muscle contraction "draws downwards and outwards the corners of the mouth, including the outer part of the upper lip, and even in a slight degree the wings of the nostrils. When the mouth is closed and this muscle acts, the commissure or line of juncture of the two lips forms a curved line with the con-

Figure 10-1 Eibl-Eibesfeldt suggested that a sign of positive greeting in diverse cultures is the "upward eyebrow flash."

From Eibl-Eibesfeldt, Irenäus. *Human Ethology* (New York: Aldine de Gruyter). Copyright © 1989, Irenäus Eibl-Eibesfeldt. Reprinted with permission.

cavity downwards, and the lips themselves are somewhat protruded, especially the lower one" (Darwin, 1872, pp. 201–202).

Knapp (1980) similarly suggested that sadness is expressed on the face with the inner corners of the eyebrows drawn up, the skin below the eyebrows triangulated with the inner corners up, and the upper eyelid inner corner is raised, while the corners of the lips are down or the lip is trembling. Izard (1991) claimed that the expression of sadness or frowning is often more fleeting than is the feeling, which may linger, and that older children and adults will attempt to inhibit these facial expressions.

Voice

The voice during speech is also a clue to a person's affective state (see reviews by Kappas et al., 1991; Scherer, 1986). Vocal language is sung to some extent, not just delivered in a monotone, and it has many qualities of pitch, intensity, and timbre. Among affective states, normal contentment or "peaceful enjoyment" may not involve clear voice patterns, but states of elation and sadness do. During active joy or elation, there tend to be increases in voice pitch, much variability of pitch, and loudness of the voice. These characteristics may reflect general sympathetic nervous system arousal. During sadness and dejection the voice also shows some strong and consistent trends. This includes decreased frequency (pitch), a decreased range in frequency such that the voice is more monotone, and diminished intensity or loudness. Sadness may also involve downward directed contours, a tendency to lower the pitch toward the end of each sentence.

Of course, music and accompanying lyrics convey rich emotional messages that elaborate upon these simpler dimensions of affective communication in speech. This may say something profound about the meaning of music as a motivational system, that it provides a strong, dynamic, and evolving mode of affective communication. Popular and traditional music cultures are replete with emotional messages that are well known subjectively to many people, but less understood scientifically.

Laughter

Laughter is a primitive form of communication which is found in and understood by all human cultures (see review by Askenasy, 1987). Although some authors suggest that laughter is exclusively human, Goodall (1968) describes how a form of laughing (a series of staccato panting grunts) frequently accompanies bouts of wrestling and tickling in chimpanzees. In humans, laughter appears within the first four months of life (Weisfeld, 1993), with some researchers placing the onset as early as five to eight weeks after birth (Izard, 1977). It decreases somewhat with maturity. The facial expressions associated with laughter are stereotyped across cultures.

The physiology of laughter involves a combination of complex facial muscle changes, often evolving out of a smile, and abrupt expiration due to contraction of the intercostal muscles (Sveback, 1975). The resultant breathing causes the vocal chords to add short and broken sounds. In a hearty laugh, the head may get tossed back. The brain mechanisms are not entirely known, but we do have some ideas. Askenasy (1987) suggests the existence of a laughter pacemaker in the reticular system, with this central location explaining the simultaneous facial expressions, vocal sounds, and heart rhythmic changes during laughter. There is some supportive evidence from laughing behavior in patients with brainstem tumors. Weisfeld (1993) suggests laughter mediation occurs in the hypothalamus and limbic structures, again citing evidence from case studies of laughing in individual patients with damage in these areas. Both Askenasy and Weisfeld emphasize that the importance of jokes in producing laughter implies input from higher neocortical areas.

Laughter appears to cause changes in levels of many hormones. In one study (Berk et al., 1989), experimental subjects viewed a humorous video, while control subjects simply spent time in a similar room. Blood was collected every 10 minutes for hormone analysis. Mirthful laughter in response to the video reduced serum levels of cortisol, epinephrine, and growth hormone relative to controls, possibly reversing the classical stress hormone response. Immune factors may also respond positively to laughter. One study (Dillon et al. 1985) found that salivary immunoglobin A (IgA) concentration increased significantly after subjects viewed a humorous video, but did not change when they viewed a serious documentary. Another study (Labott et al., 1990) also found increased levels of IgA in subjects who viewed a humorous video, while subjects who cried in response to a sad video had lower levels of IgA than controls. Studies of infant chimps (Berntson et al., 1989) showed that they respond to chimpanzee laughter with vocalizations and a cardioaccceleratory response similar to sympathetic activation, and that these responses decline with age.

The early age of laughter emergence and specieswide distribution suggest that laughter is innate. This has led to speculation as to the possible adaptive function (see review by Weisfeld, 1993). Darwin (1872) suggested that laughter in infants rewards caretaking by adults, thus promoting survival. Freud (1905) thought that laughter served to release energy from inhibited tension. Laughter is an almost exclusively social activity (Bergson, 1911), and is found in a social context 95 percent of the time. It probably is used to influence others, to amuse, to compliment, to show appreciation, and to appease. However, Lorenz (1963) noted that laughter can either enhance or divert aggression. People can either "laugh at" or "laugh with" others. Laughter itself has been found to reduce anxiety and anger, thus diffusing aggression, and perhaps serving a social function of communicating group safety (Weisfeld, 1993). In contrast, Eibl-Eibesfeldt (1989) suggested that some forms of laughter and ridicule increase aggression and are commonly found in primitive warfare. He also suggested a role for laughter in courtship, where women tend to laugh more, perhaps as a signal of submission. Another possible adaptive function of laughter is the enhancement of the immune system and healing processes as supported by studies mentioned above (Dillon et al. 1985; Labott et al., 1990). Thus, no single evolutionary function for laughter has been identified. There are costs to the organism associated with laughter, because laughing consumes energy, is noisy, and can attract unwanted attention (Weisfeld, 1993).

Several different types of humor were identified by Weisfeld (1993), which may have different roles in survival and development. These ranged from the simplest forms of tickling found in both chimpanzees and humans, which reliably produce laughing in infants and may provide practice in defending vulnerable bodily areas. More advanced situations involve social play such as chasing and wrestling, which provide practice of obvious benefit to fitness. He suggested that joking provides practice for social competition and avoiding embarrassment since jokes are often about social situations. Word play serves a function in language development. Humor may also play a role in social control by illustrating and correcting deviant behavior, and in promoting group solidarity through shared jokes about shared values.

Crying

Crying is innate behavior which begins at birth in human infants, as we discussed previously (chapters 2 and 3). There has been a considerable amount of research on infant crying because of its usefulness as a diagnostic tool for abnormalities in newborns. Crying has been described as the highest state of arousal on a continuum from sleep to wakefulness (Lester, 1985). It is a complex behavior involving interactions of the central nervous system, respiratory system, peripheral nervous system, and a variety of muscles. The importance of the CNS is demonstrated by the fact that infants with CNS disorders have characteristic high-pitched cries (Zeskind, 1985).

Crying within the first half hour of life has a distinctive sound, described as one or two gasping inspirations, often voiceless or flat (Newman, 1985). Its function is probably to assist in ductal closure and the reorganizing of the cardiovascular system following birth. After about half an hour the quality of the cry changes to a typical infant cry of long stressful wails, sustained at 50 to 70 utterances per minute, and lasting for several minutes. The pattern and sound are distinctive enough that most mothers can identify their own babies by cry after 48 hours of exposure (Formby, 1967).

Crying is found in infant mammals of diverse species besides humans, including cats, bats, elephant seals, and reindeer (Buchwald & Shipley, 1985). It is used mainly as a distress signal when isolated, hungry, or cold. Mammals probably evolved this mechanism because of the prolonged period of intense attachment necessary between mother and infant for suckling and survival. Buchwald and Shipley (1985) compared the pain cries and hunger cries of human infants and kittens, and found similar variability and range of sounds. The maternal responses invoked by the cries were also similar between the two species. Primate infants also have a cry response, with the cries of apes being most similar to those of humans (Newman, 1985). Particularly strong in apes is the isolation call, which occurs when an infant loses visual contact with its mother, and consists of a long, loud cry of continuous tonality which aids the mother in retrieval of the infant.

The adaptive value of infant crying is obvious. It elicits maternal attention, feeding, and warmth, increasing the chances of survival of the crying infant. The physiological responses of mothers to infant crying were measured by Donovan and Leavitt (1985). They found a significant decrease in heart rate in mothers shown a videotape of a crying infant, and interpreted this as the cardiac component of the orienting response. They also found in follow-up studies that this physiological response was a good predictor of maternal behavioral responses, although these were also influenced by cognitive and experiential variables.

Crying surely diminishes with age, but nevertheless occurs in many distressed children and adults of all ages. The phenomenon in adulthood is less well studied, but it is commonly mentioned in the context of grief and depression, as we discuss below. Like other affective expressions, its adaptive function in adulthood probably has to do with its role in communication and altering the response of others. Although it may often evoke sympathy, this may not be a reliable outcome, as older children sometimes apply derisive terms such as *crybaby*, and adults too may view it as immature and manipulative.

Body Postures and Behavioral Activation

According to Darwin (1872, p. 207), "Joy, when intense, leads to various purposeless movements—to dancing about, clapping the hands, stamping, etc., and to loud laughter." On the other hand, Darwin (1872, pp. 186) described persons in a state of low spirits, dejection, and despair as: "remaining motionless and passive, or may occasionally rock themselves to and fro. The circulation becomes languid; the face pale; the muscles flaccid; the eyelids droop; the head hangs on the contracted chest; the lips, cheeks, and lower jaw all sink downwards from their own weight." Many modern sources (e.g., Davison & Neale, 1996) give very similar descriptions of hy-

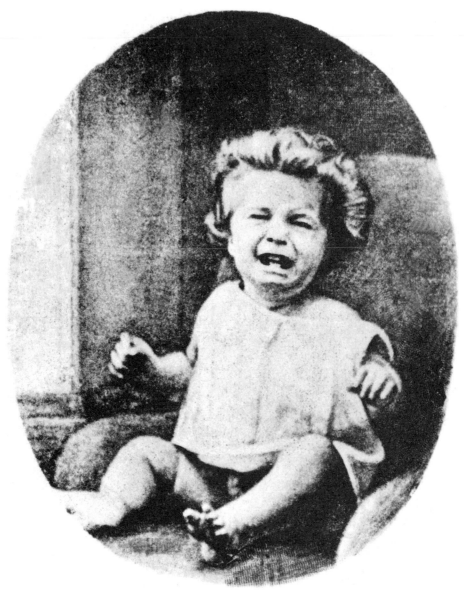

Figure 10-2   A crying infant.
From Darwin (1872).

perexcitement and excess physical activity in mania, and slowed movement and inactivity in depression.

Stooped or downcast postures, with head hanging and hunched body are often described as characteristic of depression, while upright postures with head held high may be associated with confidence and positive affect. These gestures are reminiscent of themes in chapter 9, where we discuss how many species show characteristic changes in body posture in relationship to threat and appeasement, and dominance and subordination. Upright, self-maximizing postures, seen in numerous species, are described in conjunction with social dominance. On the other hand, many of the same species show self-minimizing postures in association with appeasement and social subordination.

There are many gestures that communicate affective state as well as other dimensions of mood and situation (see, for example, Rimé & Schiaratura, 1991). We discuss some other forms in later chapters. One interesting example is the shoulder shrug. Darwin (1872, p. 277) noticed that helplessness and impotence could be expressed as follows: "When a man wishes to show that he cannot do something, or prevent something being done, he often raises with a quick movement both shoulders. At the same time, if the whole gesture is completed, he bends his elbows closely inwards, raises his open hands, turning them outwards, with the fingers separated."

AFFECTIVE STATES

Affective states, at least within normal ranges, are natural responses to gains and losses that develop during the course of life. These reactions vary with the individual's personality and genetic makeup. Some people's affect is "flat" or less variable, while others are more volatile and dynamic. Some soldier on cheerfully in the face of stressors, while others react to the same stressors with severe depression. Very few people escape some ups and downs in mood, states of transitory joy and sadness. Few people escape unexpected stress, most of us at some point experience death of loved ones, and we all take gains and losses in ongoing adaptation.

Regardless of personality, some people have good fortune, while others follow a downward course or have a bumpy ride in life. Appearance, aptitude, health, family, education, socioeconomic status, and plain luck all bear upon success and failure in well-known, obvious ways. Sometimes, however, success and failure may be relative to an individual's personal expectations rather than any absolute standards. An "A" student may be upset by receiving a B, while other students are happy just to pass.

Strategies of Confidence and Success

Most research has focused on states of negative affect or depression, because of the attention of psychiatrists and clinical psychologists. Thus, there is very little literature on states of confidence, success, happiness, and contentment.

Success is energizing and can encourage effort, especially repetition of successful strategies. This surely relates to themes of reward and inhibition to be discussed in chapter 12. "Jumping for joy" may be wasted energy (unless you need the exercise), and spontaneous mania without cause is often viewed as a disorder. Nevertheless, being energized by true success over the longer term can surely spur an individual on to even greater success. Initiative, courage to endeavor, self-confidence, persistence, and relentless pursuit of objectives are the essence of great achievement. It is well known that these characteristics can lead to great social and financial success, as proven in innumerable biographies of leaders and innovators. On the other hand, I pose another simple question: Where would poetry, art, literature, and music be if various artistic people had never suffered from depression?

Below we discuss how some people get locked in a vicious cycle of depression, because failure leads to inhibition, which leads to lack of effort, which perpetuates failure because problems do not get solved. On the other hand, it is possible to conceive of a virtuous cycle, where success leads to initiative, which encourages effort, which perpetuates success because problems are solved and creative energy is unleashed. Nevertheless, no one escapes setbacks and disappointments in life, and it can be unwise to persist with an unrealistic objective. Faced with failure of some effort, it can be adaptive to inhibit, step back, regroup, strategize, and set a new course.

Bereavement

People usually react with grief to the death of a valued loved one. This may be one of the most difficult emotional experiences that a person faces in life. Effects of grief may be prolonged, lasting weeks, months, and even years. Nevertheless, grief is viewed as a normal and healthy reaction to a genuine loss. It resembles "depression" due to other causes.

The degree of grief generally relates to the closeness of the relationship, usually being most severe for a genetic relative or spouse (see Parkes, 1972; Van Dyke & Kaufman, 1983). It may also relate to the reproductive value of the deceased (Crawford et al., 1989; see chapter 8). The sudden death of a young, vital relative can be a devastating experience, as is clear to any parent who has lost a child. On the other hand, when an aged grandmother dies after a full life, mourning may be absent or much less severe, and may indeed be replaced by a sense of relief if coping had become difficult or uncomfortable for the individual.

Adaptation to the sudden loss of a young, close relative is often extremely hard. The initial reaction of acute grief after a loss is characterized by somatic distress and tearfulness in waves lasting from 20 to 60 minutes (Lindemann, 1944). This may include feelings of shortness of breath, stom-

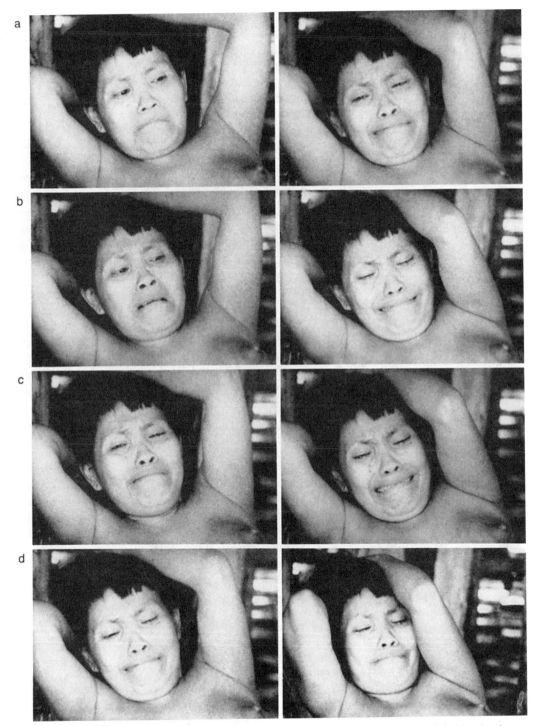

Figure 10-3 A face of a woman in grief. This woman has just received news of the death of a loved one.

ach emptiness, lack of muscular strength, and excruciating mental pain. There may be a sense of unreality and emotional distance from other people, and a paradoxical sense of the presence of the lost one. There may be preoccupation with guilt feelings about some aspect of interactions with the deceased, behavioral disorganization, and bouts of agitation, anger, irritation, and anxiety.

The more chronic reaction of mourning is depression. Normal routines are disturbed, and the individual may lose initiative. There may be a phase in which the individual is apathetic, with a loss of goal-direction, especially if many of the individual's activities prior to the loss were organized in conjunction with the lost loved-one (Parkes, 1972). These reactions can last for months and even years, and there may be sudden bouts of crying upon recollections of the loss. As discussed in chapter 8, there can be an increased vulnerability to illness and even death during the period of bereavement. Bereavement can also cause permanent changes in the motivation and attitude of the individual suffering the loss, especially where an individual's motivation was oriented around activities with the deceased person.

Signs of grief and depression in response to loss of a loved one are known to occur in infancy, provided a child has reached an age of clear attachment to a mother figure. Spitz (1946) described a syndrome of "anaclitic depression" in infants aged 6 to 10 months who were separated from their mothers. These infants cried persistently, then with time showed signs of severe anxiety and psychomotor inactivation, including social withdrawal, failure to react to the environment, insomnia, anorexia, weight loss, and retardation in growth and development. Bowlby (1969, 1973) subsequently described a similar syndrome in infants separated from their mothers. The initial reaction to separation is one of *protest*, characterized by crying that cannot be consoled by other caretakers and restless attempts to find mother. This is followed by a phase of *despair*, with the apparent realization that mother is not immediately returning, with signs of depression, anxiety, psychophysiological disturbances of sleep and appetite, loss of interest in the environment, and social withdrawal. Bowlby described the third phase as *detachment*, which affected children variably, some being self-absorbed and resistant to new attachments and others investing in new relationships. Of course, the presence of other supportive family members modulates the outcome.

Anaclitic depression in response to loss of mother has also been observed in infant monkeys (Harlow, 1974; Kaufman & Rosenblum, 1969). Monkeys have been found to show a classic grief reaction like that seen in children. There is initially agitation, violent crying vocalization, and random locomotion. After a day or so, this initial protest phase gives way to a prolonged period of "despair," which is characterized by decreased activity levels, and a characteristic hunched or huddling posture with self-clasping.

There is social withdrawal lasting at least one month, with a dramatic inhibition of play behavior. A few infant monkeys have been observed to die in these circumstances, although most ultimately recover if they are in a social network.

It has often been suggested that early parental loss can have a profound impact upon the emotional development of some affected people. In particular, there are reports that depression in childhood and adolescence is correlated with early parental loss or separation, especially the death of the child's mother (Caplan & Douglas, 1969; Seligman et al., 1974).

Depression, Psychological Pain, Inhibition, and Regrouping

Withdrawal and pensive behavior could help healing to psychosocial assaults, analogous to the value of pain in healing physical damage. This can be adaptive if it leads to inhibition of failed responses and subsequent launching of new coping strategies.

Many people report brief or prolonged "anguish" or "psychological pain" provoked by unpleasant memories or current situations. These concepts may overlap somewhat with concepts of "grief" and "depression." Psychological pain is very subjective and difficult to define operationally (in terms of concrete, measurable events). Thornhill and Thornhill (1989) cited examples from women who have experienced mental pain after being victims of rape, noting that many individuals report that psychological pain can be at least as intense as is actual physical pain. They speculate that, in an evolutionary context, psychological pain is analogous in function to physical pain: It serves to draw the individual's attention to significant social events provoking the pain and promotes correction of these events and evaluation of future courses of action.

Clinical psychologists and psychiatrists who study depression often label it as illness, in need of treatment and medication. This medical model derives from the express purposes of these professions to heal. In contrast, strictly scientific approaches seek merely to understand rather than to intervene. Intense sadness and temporary depression provoked by real losses, unsatisfying situations, and personal tragedies may be much too natural and common to call illness. It is surely a matter of severity, and the presence or absence of an objective stressor that sets off the depression, and whether temporary reduction of activity, withdrawal from social situations, and pensiveness serve toward adaptive restructuring of behavior.

Certainly, in its most severe instances, "depression" can assume the qualities of illness, insofar as there is a breakdown in natural behavior that impedes normal functioning. Many individuals have been described as being locked in a self-perpetuating cycle of inactivity, lack of initiative and problem-solving behavior, social isolation, failure to work and groom themselves, and psycho-physiological disturbances of sleep and appetite (Davison & Neale, 1996).

Many cases of "depression" are elicited by stress (Anisman & Zacharko, 1982), and as we discuss below, the physiology of depression often resembles that associated with chronic stress. On the other hand, clinicians have often pointed to a small minority of "endogenous" cases of depression where there are no obvious eliciting stressors, which may simply be due to neurochemical imbalance (Kandel, 1991c).

Suarez and Gallup (1985) suggested that depressive mood often derives from reproductive difficulties, and that this makes evolutionary sense given the critical role of reproduction in the pursuit of biological fitness. They suggest that this accounts for several dimensions of depression. Depression is more common among women, while women biologically and traditionally play a greater role in reproduction through pregnancy, nursing, and nurturance. It could account for acute dysphoria associated with menstruation, and more prolonged dysphoria at the time of menopause. Suarez and Gallup note that both women and men often experience intense depression following miscarriages, stillbirth, and neonatal death, or following the birth of a defective child. Their idea also explains bereavement as discussed above. Furthermore, rejections from desired members of the opposite sex can provoke dysphoria and depression, as can the undesired break-up of an established heterosexual relationship.

Paradoxically, there may be moments of post-partum "blues" for some women who have just given birth, and more prolonged post-partum depression for a small minority of women (O'Hara, 1987). Although definitive reasons for momentary dysphoria in the midst of what can be a very joyful event are not established, many researchers point to the hormonal upheavals associated with birth. The rarer forms of more severe post-partum depression may relate to earlier psychological problems, relationship to spouse, and other stressors. The relationship of maternal depression to infant health and robustness has apparently not been investigated.

Other stressors that can elicit depression are well known, and indeed commonsense. These include termination of employment, consistent academic failure relative to either objective standards or personal standards, social denigration and shame, more complex interpersonal difficulties including conflict with family, poverty, poor health, and a host of other personal difficulties. These sorts of factors consistently emerge in the literature on severe depression preceding suicide (deCatanzaro, 1981a; Maris, 1981), as we discuss below.

Difficulties in social interactions and interpersonal skills are correlated with depression, and could be both causes and consequences. The quality of social bonds, past and present, is seen as crucial to susceptibility to depression. This is illustrated by a study (Billings et al., 1983) which compared 409 men and women entering psychiatric treatment for depression with a demographically matched group of 409 nondepressed men and women. Depressed persons reported significantly more stressful events than controls, and experienced more severe life strains associated with their own and their family members' physical illness, more difficulties in family relationships, and more stress in their home and work situations. These differences were consistent for both men and women.

Social Learning and Cognition in Depression

A number of theorists have pointed to cognitive distortions and learning processes in the origins of depression. A common theme is that histories of learning and false attributions cause individuals to fail to cope with normal stresses and problems.

One very influential idea came from Beck (1967). He argued that depressed individuals commit logical errors that distort events in their lives. They tend to see catastrophes in minor setbacks. They become self-deprecating and self-blaming in the face of events that normal people would view as merely irritating and inconvenient. Beck viewed depressed persons as the victims of their own illogical self-judgments. He said that they form arbitrary inferences rather than logical deductions. They magnify small problems, while minimizing their own achievements and potential. They form selective abstractions, focusing on only a subset of data rather than the whole picture, and make sweeping generalizations ("Nobody likes me, this situation is hopeless, and I can't do anything right").

Another highly cited idea, proposed by Seligman (1975), is that depression is caused by "learned helplessness." Seligman originally conducted experiments with dogs, where essentially he taught them not to avoid aversive stimuli. First, the animals were repeatedly given inescapable shocks. With numerous shocks, as time passed, the dogs stopped trying to jump out of the chamber or otherwise escape, and simply froze as shocks were delivered. Later, they were put in a new chamber where they received shock in one side, but simply had to walk to the other side to escape the shock. However, they failed to move when shock was delivered. Because of the history of inescapable shocks, the animals would not make a simple response that would let them flee the shock. Seligman said that these dogs had learned that they were helpless, and therefore later failed to cope when they could.

This led to speculation that humans who are depressed also behave as if they believe themselves to be helpless. They fail to make coping responses even when these responses are possible, essentially because they have learned that their own behavior has no impact on their welfare. Helplessness, inhibition of behavior, and lack of effort were said to result from repeated experiences that personal welfare is beyond control. Of course, lack of initiative can be quite maladaptive, because problems tend to accumulate for anyone who does not solve them. Seligman and colleagues later presented a somewhat reformulated and more cognitive model (Abramson et al., 1978), suggesting that cognitive distortion about fate in life causes some people to fail to make coping responses, and consequently to become depressed. These researchers hypothesized that a particular attributional style, a tendency to make "internal, stable, and global causal attributions" about negative events, causes some people to fail to try to control their lives and solve their problems. Accordingly, helpless and depressed people think that their problems are due to uncontrollable factors, so the problems remain unsolved and the stresses deepen.

One other influential psychosocial theory, based on learning processes, was formulated by Lewinsohn (1974). According to this idea, individuals who are depressed generally have inadequate social skills. They thus receive insufficient rewards or reinforcement from other people. This low level of reinforcement elicits depressive responses, such as fatigue and loss of initiative. In a vicious cycle, both activities and rewards decrease. Some of the symptoms of depression, such as social withdrawal, expressions of negative affect, failure to groom oneself, and failure to work, tend to harm relations with others, making them react negatively. This perpetuates the low level of social reinforcement, which causes the depression to deepen. The person fails to show the initiative and responses that would help them to cope and escape this downward cycle.

These ideas seem to converge to some degree, and may help to explain why some people have difficulty escaping from the natural sadness and demotivation that can accompany disappointing and stressful experiences. There has been much research to address these theories.

There is support for the idea that problem-solving behavior relates inversely with depression. For example, Gotlib and Asarnow (1979) examined interpersonal and other problem-solving skills in nondepressed, mildly depressed, and clinically depressed university students. They found that depression was negatively correlated with interpersonal problem-solving ability. Differences were found only for interpersonal and not other forms of problem-solving skills. The nondepressed students performed best on the interpersonal skill measure, while the clinically depressed group performed worst. Billings et al. (1983) found that depressed people were less likely to use problem-solving and more likely to resort to emotional coping responses than were matched nondepressed controls. They also found that depressed people had fewer and less supportive relationships with friends, family members, and coworkers.

It is much less clear that cognition and attribution alone can explain depression. Although a number of studies (e.g., Cutrona, 1983) have shown a correlation between attributional style and depression, they have not always confirmed that life stressors are misinterpreted. Hammen and Cochran (1981) compared moderately depressed college students, nondepressed students who had encountered high levels of personal stress, and nondepressed controls. They examined causal attributions in response to naturally occurring life stressors, in dimensions of perceived control and locus of causation. Contrary to cognitive attribution models of depression, the groups did not differ in their ascription of causes to the stresses experienced. Layne (1983) suggested that although depressed people are consistently pessimistic, they are not always cognitively distorted. Layne reviewed many relevant studies, suggesting that most studies actually show that depressed people show *less* cognitive distortion than do normals, while commenting that reality is often painful.

Physiology of Depression

To gain insight into relationships between psychosocial and physiological factors in depression, consider the dramatic neurohormonal changes in response to psychosocial conditions described in chapters 8 and 9. Stress physiology is very dynamic, responding to psychological factors during ongoing development. Consider the pituitary-adrenal system and its interactions with brain monoamines discussed in chapter 8. Consider how mice that are socially dominant become distinct from subordinates in behavioral initiative, brain monoamines, and hormones, and the similar data from monkeys and humans in chapter 9.

As we have discussed, there are clear signs of coping difficulties and stress in the personal lives of most depressed people. Indeed, many depressed people show classic hormonal signs of the chronic stress syndrome. In particular, cortisol levels have been observed in many severely depressed people to be substantially higher than those of nondepressed normal people. Kandel (1991c) estimated that 40–60 percent of depressed patients show excessive secretion of cortisol. Normal people show a circadian (daily) rhythm in cortisol, with high levels in the early morning as the day begins, and gradually declining levels over the course of the day. This circadian rhythm is often upset in severely depressed people, with high levels found throughout the 24-hour period.

Other evidence for disturbance in adrenal functioning in severely depressed people comes from the dexamethasone suppression test (Carroll, 1982). Dexamethasone is a drug, a potent synthetic steroid that can block pituitary ACTH production, by acting on the natural feedback mechanisms that keep cortisol and ACTH in homeostasis (see chapter 8). When dexamethasone is given, most normal people subsequently will show a drop in natural cortisol levels. However, in many but not all depressed subjects, there is an abnormal result in cortisol levels following dexamethasone administration. This suggests a disturbance in the hypothalamic-pituitary-adrenal system. In some cases the adrenal glands have become so hyperactive that they have lost some of the normal control exerted by the pituitary gland.

Several lines of evidence suggest that psychological depression is associated with reduced activity of the serotonergic neurotransmitter system, and possibly a secondary role is played by reduced activity of norepinephrine (see reviews by Kandel, 1991c; Owens & Nemeroff, 1994).

Measures of serotonergic activity in depressed individuals have implicated reduced activity of this neurotransmitter in depression (Owens & Nemeroff, 1994). There are reports of reduced concentrations of metabolites of serotonin in cerebrospinal fluid of depressed people, reduced concentrations of serotonin and its metabolites in postmortem brain tissues of depressed people, and inverse correlations of depression with measures of plasma tryptophan, the amino acid that is the metabolic precursor of serotonin (see chapter 4).

Perhaps the strongest evidence for a role of monoamines in human affect comes from the known mechanisms of action of drugs that some people willingly self-administer (see Cooper et al., 1991). Many of these drugs are illegal. Some artificial euphoria-inducing and hallucinogenic drugs, like LSD, psilocybin, DMT, and bufotenine, are known to stimulate serotonin receptors, because of their chemical shape and conformity to serotonin's natural postsynaptic receptors. The notorious and powerful substance LSD conforms to the serotonin receptor but is otherwise chemically quite dissimilar from serotonin, which may make it difficult to metabolize and account for its hallucinogenic and indeed dangerous effects. Some other euphoria-inducing drugs, including amphetamines, cocaine, and mescaline, act on norepinephrine and other catecholamine receptors. This suggests that it is possible to stimulate affective changes artificially, strictly through chemical means.

Pharmaceutical treatment of depression, employed by physicians, relies on modulation of monoamine neurotransmission. Some of the oldest antidepressant drugs are MAO inhibitors (see chapters 4 and 8). MAO is an enzyme which degrades monoamine neurotransmitters, that is, dopamine, norepinephrine, and serotonin. MAO thus breaks down the substances directly involved in nervous system arousal, activation, and positive affect. So MAO inhibitors, if taken for some time, can artificially keep people happier by unblocking monoamine activity, keeping monoamine levels high.

Other commonly used drugs for treatment of depression are monoamine reuptake inhibitors, which prevent recycling of monoamines into their presynaptic cells. More recently, some drugs have been specific serotonin reuptake inhibitors, which act to prevent natural removal of serotonin from its synapses in the brain. Serotonin is active when it is released into the synapse. Once there, it has its action by interacting with postsynaptic receptors. Reuptake is a process whereby serotonin is taken back into the presynaptic cells, a sort of recycling that takes serotonin out of circulation. So, such drugs keep serotonin where it is active, by preventing its recycling, and artificially make people happier. Of course, no drug alone solves people's problems, and drug treatment is not a natural cure for depression.

Foods that contain tryptophan (precursor to serotonin) and tyrosine (precursor to the catecholamines dopamine and norepinephrine) are naturally preferred by many people, and probably have an impact on mood. This remains an open question. The role of diet in human mood is obviously important but insufficiently studied. The physiological integration of specific foods into ongoing brain chemistry involves many dimensions, including general metabolism, blood-brain chemistry dynamics, and enzymes involved in amino acid transport and transmitter synthesis. It has long been suggested that favored foods like chocolate, wines, alcohol and sugars, spices, etc. have actions increasing monoamine activities.

Other evidence pointing to a monoaminergic substrate of affect comes from numerous clinical reports on uses of the drug reserpine (see review by Goodwin & Bunney, 1971). Reserpine was one of the very first tranquilizers, derived from a natural plant used for centuries in India. This drug was employed during the 20th century by physicians to treat diverse disorders, including high blood pressure, mental excitement, and psychosis. Reserpine is established to deplete monoamines in the brain, including serotonin, norepinephrine, and dopamine. Thus it reduces activity of the monoamines whose actions are associated with more positive moods. As higher doses were tried, numerous independent reports surfaced indicating that a substantial minority of patients were rendered depressed by this drug, when there were no objective reasons to be downhearted. The onset of this effect typically occurred after a few weeks of treatment, and was not universal. However, in some of those affected, there were complaints of sadness, discouragement, crying spells, dejected and apathetic mood, loss of interest in usual activities, and even suicidal thoughts.

A rarer form of depression, manic-depression or bipolar depression, involves an unregulated cycle of high and low moods, and may have a distinct physiological basis. Episodes of depression are similar to those of the more common unipolar depression as just described, while phases of euphoria or mania are characterized by an elevated, overactive, sometimes reckless, and irritable mood lasting over a week. There is usually no psychosocial factor that precipitates the mood swings. Treatments with lithium salts are generally very effective in leveling out mood swings in such persons, especially by preventing the manic phase. The source of the problem is thus thought to be a neurochemical imbalance, and affected individuals often take lithium on a continuing basis. Lithium is thought to modulate neuronal firing and restore neurochemical balance (Kandel, 1991c), possibly by facilitating norepinephrine reuptake by cells that release it (Cooper et al., 1991).

SAD

Another form of mood upset is the phenomenon known as seasonal affective disorder (SAD). In northern temperate and Arctic climates, some people suffer negative affect during late fall and winter. There could be many

SEROTONERGIC SYNAPSE

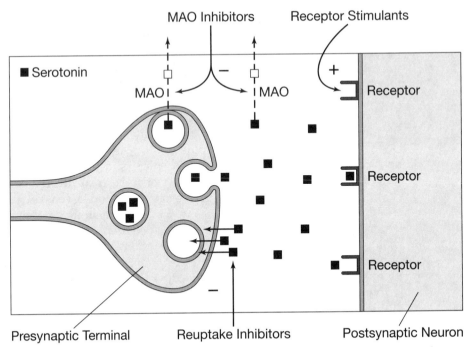

Figure 10-4 A model of serotonin's action at its synapses, showing a presynaptic nerve ending and postsynaptic receptor, and the natural actions of MAO and reuptake. The mechanisms of drug action are shown for MAO inhibitors, receptor stimulants, and reuptake inhibitors.

factors responsible for this, including annual work cycles, the thwarting of outdoor activities during the cold and dark months, and the isolation that can be associated with extreme northern living. But these are also the darkest months of the years in such latitudes, with the fewest hours of sunshine.

In everyday culture, brightness and sunshine are often associated with happiness. A "sunny disposition" comes when there is "sunshine in our lives," so we are "bright and cheerful." This is much better than being "gloomy," in a "dark mood," because a "dark cloud is hanging over us." Few weather reports in popular media are presented with dispassionate objectivity. Instead, it is often assumed that moderate warmth and sunshine are uplifting to our moods, while coldness, wetness, and darkness are dispiriting (farmers may have other opinions, as may those in very arid and hot climates). Poetry and musical lyrics are full of similar allusions.

Of course, the pineal, the ancient gland in the middle of the brain, is also very responsive to dark and light, because it is triggered by darkness to secrete melatonin (Cassone et al., 1993). The pineal is a secretor of indoleamines (see chapter 4), especially melatonin. Melatonin is derived from serotonin and ultimately from dietary tryptophan. All of this suggests another possible way in which indoleamines (serotonin and melatonin) modulate human affect.

Light therapy has often been reported to help those affected by SAD. We cannot yet complete the story, pinpointing any precise role of pineal indoleamines in mood and a relationship to SAD. An upset in normal melatonin rhythm has not been clearly implicated in SAD (e.g., Checkley et al., 1993), but some evidence suggests that dynamics of serotonin may be involved (Coiro et al., 1993).

LIFE-THREATENING BEHAVIOR

Suicide

Some humans reach a point in development at which voluntary mechanisms to seek death somehow overcome instincts of self-preservation. As we discuss in detail in chapters 5 and 6, the body is full of mechanisms that serve to preserve life. Most of us would surely fight with all of our energy to save our lives, but some people actively seek death. This turn in motivation is associated with chronic stress and unsolvable problems, reproductive difficulty, poor health, severe depression, guilt and shame, and difficulties with family.

In Figure 10-5 are given data for rates of suicide by age and sex in a typical year in the United States. If you refer ahead to chapter 13, you will see these rates given in the context of rates from Canada and Mexico, and in comparison to rates of death by accidents, homicides, and infectious diseases, from all three countries, taken from World Health Organization statistics. Almost no suicides are reported among young children. In all three countries, consistent with broad international data, suicide is much more common in males than in females, which is true without exception at all ages. In the United States and Mexico, older men are at greater risk than are younger men, with the highest rates being found among the elderly. In recent years this trend has not held in Canada, where rates are fairly constant during adulthood. Among women, the rates by age have been much more constant across adulthood, with a small peak in numbers in the age range 45–54 in the United States and Canada.

Suicide is not just a modern phenomenon, and we cannot therefore just ascribe it to stresses of modern life or maladaptive behavior in the presence of modern technologies. It has accounted for a substantial number of deaths in all carefully surveyed cultures. It was documented in numerous technologically less-developed cultures at the point of first contact with European colonialists (Steinmetz, 1894), and it has been observed throughout recorded human history (Rosen, 1971). The rates recorded in technologically less-advanced or "primitive" cultures (e.g., Bohannan, 1960; Elwin, 1943; Firth, 1961; Leighton

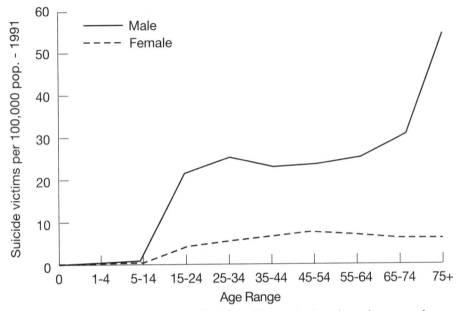

Figure 10-5   1991 suicide victims in the United States, broken down by age and sex.
Source: *World Health Statistics Annual—1994,* World Health Organization (1995).

& Hughes, 1955) generally approach those observed in modern, technologically advanced cultures. Within countries where records have been kept for many years, overall rates appear to have been remarkably stable for over a century, despite massive changes in technology (see review by deCatanzaro, 1981a). What has happened is not a change in frequency but rather in methods; in countries like the United States and Britain, it was once the case that most suicides were committed by self-hanging, but now most suicides occur with firearms and poisons.

Suicides are often associated with unsuccessful heterosexual relationships, chronic infirmity, social isolation, social disgrace, and failures of major endeavors (deCatanzaro, 1981a; Maris, 1981). It has been established since the classic work of Durkheim (1897) that suicide bears relationships to social-ecological variables like aging, marital status, number of children, contact with family, and integration into social networks. In general, across numerous cultures and history, persons who are younger, with stable family relations and marriages, and with more positive social contacts are least likely to commit suicide. Social isolation is thus an important predictor of suicides. This is illustrated by Seiden's (1966) comment that, not infrequently, suicides by college students were not discovered for weeks after the death, in that no one was sufficiently involved with the person to notice that he or she was missing.

Beck and colleagues (1975) suggested that cognitively, people who are suicidal have a sense of "hopelessness," with a negative view of present and future prospects. This is in contrast to merely depressed but nonsuicidal persons, who typically view the present as bad, but often retain some hope of future improvement. Suicide is usually preceded by severe depression, but many if not most depressed persons are not suicidal.

Much evidence points to reproductive and family variables, or rather the lack of success in these areas, as correlated with suicide. My students and I (deCatanzaro, 1984; 1995) have studied this through large-sample surveys of the general public of Ontario, and samples of high-suicide-risk groups, including elderly, psychiatric, criminal psychiatric, and homosexual populations. Subjects have been given questions probing reproductive behavior, quality of family contacts, and suicidal ideation. Within each sample, variance in contemplation of suicide correlated reliably with questions about reproductive status and family-social variables. Poor relations to the opposite sex, social isolation, and poorer contact with family significantly predicted suicidal ideation. Across all samples, the most reliable predictor was perceived burdensomeness toward family.

There are some cultural variations in suicide, but studies from diverse cultures show circumstances comparable to those in modern Western cultures. For example, Bohannan (1960) reported on suicides in four African tribes from colonial records in the early- to mid-twentieth century. About two-thirds of suicides were committed by males. Unlike most Western data, many of the suicides occurred in domestic situations, usually married people. Apparent causes were diverse, often involving recent quarrels with spouse or lover, sexual impotence, chronic disease, shame, or insanity. As with almost all technologically less-advanced cultures, the most common method of suicide was self-hanging. Meer (1976) conducted an extensive analysis of suicide in Durban, South Africa during 1940 to 1970, when separate statistics were kept for the four so-called races separated under apartheid. Comprehensive analyses of the data indicated that regardless of ethnic background, suicide frequency was much higher among single, widowed, and divorced individuals than among those who were married. Meer suggested that, just as in most other cultures, stable marriage and family restrain suicide.

It is not just severe chronic stress that sets off a failure of self-preservative motivation. People have endured extremely terrifying, depriving, and humiliating circumstances, such as in Nazi concentration camps, and retained a strong will to live (Matussek, 1975). Suicidal ideation and behavior does occur in a small subset of people in such circumstances, but the vast majority try to survive. Self-preservation may be eroded more by the specific forms of chronic stress constituted by social isolation, and low reproductive value in conjunction with burdensomeness toward kin.

Some evidence suggests that genetic dynamics underlie the propensity to react to certain life stressors with suicide (see reviews by Lester, 1986; Roy,

1992). Roy and coworkers examined 176 twin pairs in which one twin had committed suicide. In nine pairs, both twins had committed suicide. Seven of these nine pairs were among the 62 monozygotic (MZ) twins. Thus, concordance rates were 11.3 percent for MZ and 1.8 percent for DZ (dizygotic) twins. In another study in Denmark by Schulsinger et al. (1979), 5,483 cases of adoption registered in Copenhagen between 1924 and 1947 were studied. Of these cases, 57 eventually died of suicide. These cases were matched on demographic factors with 57 control cases from the adoptees. Of the 269 identifiable biological relatives of the adoptee suicides, 12 (4.5 percent) committed suicide, whereas only 2 (0.7 percent) of 269 biological relatives of controls committed suicide. None of the adoptive relatives of either group committed suicide. These data indicate some genetic contribution to suicide, suggesting that it does run in families. However, no one would contend that genetics directly cause suicide, and there is some evidence that imitative learning can influence individual cases of suicide (Phillips, 1974). Rather, it is more plausible that relevant personality factors are heritable, and that these surface in reaction to extreme psychosocial circumstances.

There is mounting evidence of neurochemical factors subserving affective variation and indeed suicide, showing a pattern that is strongly consistent with the evidence discussed above implicating brain monoamines, especially serotonin, in affective variation. Generally, such studies (Arango et al., 1995; Motto, 1986; Stanley et al., 1986) show that serotonin levels are substantially depleted in the brains of suicide victims, in comparison to control brains of persons of similar age and sex who have died from other sudden violent causes.

To summarize so far, suicide reflects a profound change in motivation that arises under very limited circumstances. It is especially related to loss of purpose in life, as reflected in poor ties to kin and the opposite sex, and a psychological sense of failure and hopelessness.

Parasuicide

In addition to true acts of suicide, where the individual dies as the result of a discrete act, there are many more cases of survived "suicide attempts," or parasuicides. Unlike suicides, which typically are recorded by coroners and reported by each nation to the World Health Organization, parasuicides are generally observed by individual hospitals and psychiatrists, and there are no centrally compiled statistics. There are more and different biases than those affecting suicide data. Some less serious cases may go unreported, there may be some confusion with accidents, an unrepresentative sample of persons may present themselves to psychiatrists, and some cases may be covered up to avoid embarrassment.

There surely are cases of true attempts to commit suicide that are inadvertently survived, but many experts believe that the motivation behind most parasuicides is something quite different from that behind true suicide. Sublethal "suicidal" gestures may not involve any intention to die, but instead may be motivated by rewards expected after survival. In particular, Stengel (1973) and Kreitman (1977) have forcefully argued that many so-called suicide attempts are deliberately survived, and that those committing such acts anticipate that they will be rewarded for this behavior by increased attention from other people.

One fact that strongly suggests a distinction from suicide is a striking difference in the demographic profiles of suicide and parasuicide. Several studies (e.g., Kreitman, 1977; Parkin & Stengel, 1965; Pederson et al., 1973) show that the sex ratio for parasuicide is quite the opposite of that for suicide; far more females commit parasuicidal acts than do males. These same studies show that the peak rates for parasuicide are in young adulthood, with relatively low rates among the elderly, in contrast to suicide frequency which increases or remains stable with age.

Like suicide, parasuicide is associated with psychological depression and stressful circumstances. Kreitman (1977) analyzed parasuicides in Edinburgh, Scotland. He examined a large sample of cases of sublethal drug overdoses at a poison control center, excluding those who had taken drugs accidentally. He suggested that parasuicide is related to such factors as divorce, overcrowding, low socioeconomic status, unemployment, and juvenile delinquency. Since parasuicide is most commonly reported by psychiatrists, there are naturally many studies that correlate it with various psychiatric diagnoses.

Another way in which to assess the relationship of parasuicide to suicide is to examine how many individuals making nonlethal attempts later indeed do commit true suicide. Kreitman (1977) reported follow-up data for one year after parasuicide, finding that only 1 percent committed suicide. Dahlgren (1977) followed up 229 cases of parasuicide occurring between 1933 and 1942 in Malmo, Sweden, tracing more than 95 percent of cases for 35 years. During the first 12 years, 9.7 percent of males and 3.7 percent of females committed suicide. After 35 years, only 10.9 percent of the total male and female cases had committed suicide. Tefft et al. (1977) conducted a thorough follow-up of parasuicides in Monroe County, New York. Mortality patterns were examined for 11 years, with a comparison of suicide attempters, a psychiatric population without suicide attempts, and a general population without psychiatric problems. From early adulthood to age 54, the suicide attempter population showed the highest mortality due to all causes, while the psychiatric population showed the second highest rate. After age 54, the suicide attempter group showed the lowest mortality. Suicide accounted for about 29 percent of deaths among the suicide-attempter group, but the majority of suicides in Monroe County during the study period were committed by persons with no previous records of suicide attempts.

Accordingly, many researchers believe that in the majority of cases, parasuicidal acts do not actually predict later suicide. This could be due to many factors, of course, because people's circumstances may improve. Without doubt, there are cases of ambivalent motive, confusion, and inadvertent actions. But researchers contend that many parasuicides represent an epiphenomenon of suicide, a mimicry of the act with very distinct motivation. Many parasuicides may be cries for help, gestures resembling suicide which do not truly have suicidal intent, but instead are designed for social impact.

Self-Injurious Behavior

People occasionally do various things that are less than optimal for survival. A long list could be developed, and would include abuse of dangerous drugs, risk-taking with cars or guns or chemicals (see chapter 13), and self-mutilation.

One peculiar form of behavior that is well-described in the literature is persistent self-injurious behavior (see reviews by deCatanzaro, 1981a; Winchel & Stanley, 1991). This behavior takes many forms, including head-banging, head-hitting, self-scratching, and self-biting behavior. Such unusual behavior is most commonly observed in institutionalized mentally retarded and psychotic populations. It has been seen at all levels of functioning, but it is most common at the very lowest levels of intelligence, where it is associated with various genetic, congenital, and developmental malformations that severely affect the nervous system. Comparable forms of behavior have been observed in primates raised in extremely abnormal environments, especially prolonged social isolation.

Often self-injurious behavior is stereotyped and repetitive. Individuals have been observed to strike their heads with their fists, or to bang their heads against hard objects such as the floor or walls, in some cases hundreds of times per hour. This behavior may come in waves, often being elicited during stress, crying, and tantrum spells. In modern circumstances, such people are often kept in physical restraints and heavily sedated in institutions to prevent serious injury.

There are some specific disorders, such as the Lesch-Nyhan syndrome, in which the individual may bite repeatedly at his or her own lips and scratch themselves, apparently unable to inhibit such obviously self-damaging behavior. However, head-banging, head-hitting, and self-scratching are seen in association with diverse causes of mental disability and institutionalization. There is no single genetic, congenital, or developmental cause.

Early explanations of such unusual behavior invoked learning mechanisms, citing reinforcement of the behavior by caretakers, who would attend to every instance of the behavior. Behavior like head-banging naturally provokes strong emotional responses in observers, who are often inclined to intervene and pay attention to the self-injurious person. This mechanism may help to explain some cases, but more recent attention has turned to biological factors. These factors include problems with pain perception or avoidance and lack of voluntary motor control due to severe neurological malformation. We still do not have complete answers about the causes of this behavior.

Evolutionary Limits to Self-Preservation

A broad evolutionary perspective may help to explain why self-preservation has limits. Although self-preserving mechanisms pervade motivation, and natural selection obviously supports this, there may be restricted circumstances under which this breaks down. We began to see why at the end of chapter 8.

Our lives are very short in an evolutionary time scale, and there may be more important goals that surpass immediate selfish survival. Consider the following question: Since you cannot avoid death, what can you do to protect your truly long-term interests, those beyond your death? In chapter 2, we discuss a scientific answer to this. Any organism's afterlife is found in its offspring, and in the offspring of close kin, which carry the individual's genes into future generations. Natural selection favors survival of an individual only insofar as this survival brings genes into future generations. Maximizing inclusive fitness, the representation of one's genes in future generations, may not always require survival, and sometimes survival might even get in the way (deCatanzaro, 1991b).

Thus, there sometimes may be better ways to promote inclusive fitness than to survive. Consider a mother defending young against a threat. Three young contain more of the mother's genes than she does herself. Trading her life for their defense is thus an adaptive act from the perspective of inclusive fitness. If age makes her reproductive value much lower than that of her young, her self-sacrifice may be worth saving just one or two young. The same logic may explain a soldier's willingness to sacrifice himself in defense of kin and community. The benefit to inclusive fitness involved in dying sometimes outweighs the loss.

In theory, the same is true if one has poor reproductive prospects, or low reproductive value, at the same time as being burdensome toward kin, perhaps by consuming resources that might otherwise be available for young kin of high reproductive value. In these conditions, a person's survival impedes his or her inclusive fitness, because it lowers the chances of his or her genes getting passed on to future generations. There is no reason natural selection would favor motivation to survive in such circumstances. Over numerous instances and generations, natural selection might even favor a turn in motivation toward death in these circumstances. Indeed, a mathematical function exists, integrating ideas of reproductive value, senescence theory, and inclusive fitness, that explains how natural selection might have affected variations in survival motivation recurring in our ancestors over numerous generations (deCatanzaro, 1991b; see also chapter 8).

Freud (1924) gave us the notion of a "death instinct" in human psychology on the basis of his clinical observations. While he was unable to explain how such an instinct might evolve, today the idea is plausible from an evolutionary standpoint. Such an instinct could have evolved, but only if it were expressed where death brings a net benefit to inclusive fitness.

An evolutionary perspective could not possibly account for all aspects of modern suicides. Stable ancestral conditions rather than novel modern conditions are relevant to genetic expression. Truly maladaptive suicides may result from social transitions, psychopathology, and novel dangers like guns, drugs, and cars. We cannot always expect fully adaptive behavior in the presence of evolutionarily novel conditions. Natural selection has not had time to prepare people to behave with full adaptiveness in the presence of guns, drugs, cars, and toxic chemicals (see Inset 2-1). These things may allow some people to take their own lives quite impulsively, where it is not at all in the interest of their inclusive fitness.

Nevertheless, evolutionary concepts do roughly fit with the known social ecology of suicide, which as described above is most often found in socially isolated males, in people with poor reproductive relationships, and under conditions of alienation from family and community. It may be that there is some kind of emotional switch that alters our motivation away from survival, but only under limited circumstances.

Chapter 11

LOVE AND ATTACHMENT

Like many of the other plain terms used for emotions, *love* has many meanings, and thus for scientific purposes we must more precisely define our subject matter.

Most psychologists define a number of distinct types of love and attachment. Harlow (1971) differentiated three basic forms of affection. Maternal-infant bonding is the most fundamental form, essential for survival. Peer bonding occurs among siblings and like-age playmates. Heterosexual bonding is the reproductive bond between unrelated members of opposite gender.

In fact, we can differentiate more finely among forms of attachment, identifying many types. The bond between mother and infant is an interwoven mesh, but it can be viewed from two perspectives, infant's and mother's. Paternal attachment and nurturance of young is variable, but many children enjoy strong biparental care and supportive relations with father. Extended family structures exist in all cultures, albeit with much variation, and there are often close ties, for example, between grandparent and child. Sibling interactions are both supportive and competitive. Sibling ties can provide the basis of peer interactions in childhood, and can often continue as lifelong ties. There are many forms of friendship and alliance among peers. One universal form is the tendency of juveniles to affiliate with others of like age, sex, and stage of development, without genetic relationship. Sexual attraction and bonding have many forms (see chapter 7). Pre-courtship and courtship phases, or "romantic love," can involve intense emotions. This is differentiable from stable heterosexual companionship that occurs over many years, which can be supported by family and mutual interests. There are of course many forms of adult friendships, alliances, and associations.

PARENT-CHILD RELATIONS

Infant's Bond to Mother

Maternal-infant bonding is the deepest and most essential feature of human social behavior. It is the basis of mammalian nature, ancient in evolution and necessary for survival. Although in modern times we could probably nurture children with artificial milk-formula dispensing machines, and remove their waste and regulate their environments in factories, no one would dare suggest wisdom in that idea. The strongest bond in human nature has critical value far beyond the mere satisfaction of physical needs.

There are coordinated behavior patterns of mother and infant that are universal across human cultures. Mother love involves warm and gentle cuddling, provision of nourishment, removal of discomfort, and emotional exchange with the infant. This includes nursing, other physical contact, and emotional communication through mutual eye-gazing, facial expression, and voice intonation. During the first few months of life, an infant's attachment to mother is promoted by built-in behavior that elicits proximity and caregiving (Bowlby, 1969). This includes the infant's intense crying and facial displays signalling discomfort, and conversely displays of soothing or successful comforting. As we discussed in chapter 3, newborn young of most mammals vocalize in response to the mother's withdrawal, stimulate her return through such crying, and generally cease crying upon being comforted.

Normally, the human infant is held in the mother's arms and breast-fed, which is accompanied by eye contact and smiling exchanged between mother and infant. The mother regulates the infant's physiology and comfort, controlling factors such as nourishment, temperature, vestibular sensation through rocking and handling, and tactile stimulation through holding and touching (Hofer, 1981). She also regulates emotional and arousal states, by providing comfort in response to the infant's signs of distress.

The human infant's ability to identify one mother figure is not clearly established for some time. It is well known that it is easiest to place a child for adoption in early infancy, before specific attachment to mother has occurred, and that an infant will show similar response to nurses and other substitute caregivers who successfully provide nourishment and comfort. The infant's attachment to a single mother-figure is not instantaneous or automatic. There is no "imprinting" process or rapid infant fixation on a specific mother during a critical period. Instead, the human infant's attachment to a single figure is progressively reinforced by comfort, closeness, and need-satisfaction.

By about 3 to 5 months of age, the baby typically shows more discriminate attachment behavior. At this age, a baby can tell one face from another, and will smile to familiar faces and not others. He or she is more easily soothed by familiar persons, usually mother and family. By about 6 or 7 months, most babies have a clear attachment to a single figure, usually the mother, who alone has the power truly to sooth. The child typically has some locomotor behavior emerging at this point (crawling), and will base around the mother in exploration. There is clear emergence of fear of separation from mother, and many children also show fear of strangers. These fears are manifested in facial expression, vocalization (crying), and activation of motor behavior oriented toward the mother or caretaker. Fear of maternal separation and fear of strangers are often said to peak at about 8 months of age, although there are substantial individual differences, and experts debate this age profile (Ainsworth et al., 1978; Bowlby, 1969; Buechler & Izard, 1983). As discussed in chapter 10, Bowlby (1973) described how infants separated from their mothers initially protest, crying without being consoled by other caretakers, showing restless attempts to find mother.

After 12 months, babies show increased interest and calmer attention to other persons, including father, siblings, other family members, and babysitters. One longstanding perspective toward such attachment has explained it in terms of conditioning (see chapters 3 and 12). Progressively, as other people are associated with need gratification and security, they become a source of gratification in themselves, as conditioned reinforcers. In theory, anyone who is repeatedly associated with positive reinforcement becomes reinforcing.

Maternal Attachment to Infant

Parental attachment to a new infant is also progressive. Many children are wanted long before they are born. From the mother's point of view, there is again no simple imprinting on a new child. In a few mammals like sheep, a permanent bond to young may occur through olfactory imprinting at birth. With humans, there appears to be no such all-important period. Instead, it is now generally accepted that maternal-infant bonding occurs over a substantial period of time (Crouch & Manderson, 1995). Nevertheless, some evidence suggests that contact with the baby during the hours and few days immediately after birth may be especially important for the mother to develop normal maternal affection (Klaus & Kennell, 1976).

Lactation and the intimate behavior of nursing surely play an ongoing major role in attachment. Biologically, the natural hormonal consequence of birth sets the stage for lactation, with dynamics in pituitary hormones, including oxytocin and prolactin, and a subsequent intimate physical interaction between mother and nursing child. This hormonal state continues

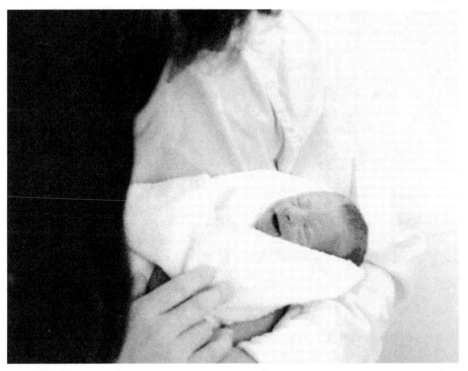

Figure 11-1   This child was born prematurely, at about seven months' gestation. This picture is taken three days after birth, with the parents holding her surrounded by extended family on their first visit. All observers interpreted the spontaneous facial expression as a smile.

Courtesy R. Bather.

through lactation, often suppressing menstruation. There is a unique interplay of maternal and infant need states, because the mother can need to lactate and be relieved by the infant, and lactation is actually stimulated by the infant's crying. This can continue for months and even years after birth, and may be used by the mother as a natural method of birth-spacing (see Eibl-Eibesfeldt, 1989). Of course, we interfere with this process if artificial infant formulas are substituted for mother's milk.

The suggestion has been made that the posterior pituitary hormone, oxytocin, could play a role in maternal-infant bonding, as well as filial bonding and heterosexual attachment processes as discussed below (see Carter et al., 1992). Oxytocin is well known for physiological roles in conjunction with pregnancy, birth, and lactation. Its pulsatile actions are related to uterine contractions and milk release, and thus related to primary mother-infant interactions. Work in the prairie vole, which is relatively monogamous, is consistent with the idea that oxytocin release is associated with a number of

Figure 11-2   An infant reacting to his mother's playful attention.

attachment processes, especially those associated with reproduction and kin (Carter et al., 1995).

Mutual gaze plays an important role in bonding (see Figure 3-3). Argyle and Cook (1976) discuss the central role of gaze in attachment behavior. People gaze more at those they like, beginning with mother-infant interactions. The amount of gaze is an important signal of affection. Human infants fixate and smile to human eyes by the end of four weeks. Shifts in gaze and interruptions in mutual gaze play an important part in games between mother and infant.

Fleming et al. (1990) conducted a longitudinal study of new human mothers from late pregnancy to 16 months postpartum, using interviews and questionnaires to assess mood patterns. Although most mothers' mood scores remained fairly consistent from one time point to the next, there was a general improvement in mood at 3 and 16 months postpartum relative to mood during pregnancy and 1 month postpartum. Positive feelings about the infant, especially, increased linearly with time from birth, probably reflecting im-

Figure 11-3 For the child (about six months of age) on the right, temporary separation from mother caused distress, and the introduction of a peer was not yet a meaningful distraction.

proved health and feelings of competence. Fleming and Corter (1988) studied hormones, moods, and attitudes of first-time mothers during pregnancy, and found no significant relations between several major hormones and mothers' attachment to the fetus. Mothers who had positive maternal attitudes prenatally showed more affectionate behavior postpartum. Attempts to relate postpartum moods to changes in specific hormones at birth were largely unsuccessful, but this is probably constrained by difficulties in methodology. Animal studies, where hormonal levels and maternal contact can be manipulated, show that maternal behavior is regulated by a complex interaction of maternal hormones and experience with young. The onset of maternal behavior at birth is facilitated by hormonal changes at the end of pregnancy, but the behavior is sustained with experience, even in the absence of hormones (e.g., Bridges, 1984; Fleming et al., 1989; Orpen & Fleming, 1987; Siegel, 1986).

Paternal Attachment to Children

Evidence suggests that fathers' attachment to their children can be as powerful as mothers' attachment, at least by the age of 7 months and beyond

(Lamb, 1977). Of course, this is variable, dependent on the individual family and the individual father's style of interaction with the child. Some men neglect their children. Many other men are highly motivated to be fathers, being elated by pregnancy, attending the child's birth, assisting the mother through the process, actively protecting children, and working toward the benefit of their children through development. In terms of motivation to promote inclusive fitness (see chapter 2), it is equally in a father's interest as in a mother's to support their own offspring. There are numerous examples of extensive paternal investment in offspring in the animal kingdom, supported by the benefits to offspring quality brought about by biparental care (Clutton-Brock, 1991).

Insight into family composition and paternal care is gained from studies like that which Flinn (1992) conducted in a Caribbean village. Fathers in Grande Anse, Trinidad, "make important contributions to the welfare of their children, although they usually do not spend much of their time . . . involved in direct care of infants and preadolescents" (p.78). There is wide variation in household composition, including nuclear (biparental), single parent (usually mother), and extended grandparental households. Male parental behavior is highly variable, "with some fathers providing extensive resources and care for their children, while others provide little or none" (p.57). Males distinguish between step and genetic children, and "usually interact more frequently and less agonistically with their genetic children than with their stepchildren" (p.79). Co-residence facilitates the interaction of father and child. Fathers treat their infant sons and daughters equivalently, but may exert influence over their teenage daughters' relationships and interact more frequently with their adult sons. Remarriage and parent's absence from the home can interfere with child-parent relations.

Modeling of roles from parent to child may have powerful influences, according to classic psychodynamic theory and common sense, in ways that go beyond the scope of this book into other areas of psychology. Even though there can be same-sex identification and sex-characteristic modeling in parent-child relations, there may be important dynamics across sexes. Boys from father-absent situations more often display behavior difficulties and social adjustment problems as adolescents (Hetherington, 1989). Girls' relations to fathers may be especially important for their self-esteem (Bee, 1981), and may shape their expectations concerning their own adulthood relations with men.

Attachment Quality and Emotional Development

Early bonding to family can have substantial impacts upon subsequent emotions and personality. Numerous findings suggest that emotional adjustment in life is profoundly influenced by the quality of bonding to mother and family.

Harlow's (see Harlow, 1965; 1971; 1974; Harlow & Harlow, 1969) famous studies with rhesus monkeys showed the profound importance of maternal care. Infant monkeys were separated from their mothers for various periods of time, generally with devastating effects. Despite proper nutrition and a clean environment, the monkeys showed very disturbed behavior. They showed stereotyped nonfunctional patterns, such as rocking back and forth in a corner, clasping their own bodies, or biting their fingers and skin. They often screeched and cried. As adults, infants raised without mothers were socially maladept, incapable of normal sexual or maternal behavior. When the maternally deprived infants were offered a surrogate cloth mother, they became attached to this figure. Contact with this soft surface provided some improvement in behavior. These data indicate that attachment to mother has innate components, and is not just totally conditioned by need satisfaction.

In public orphanages and in institutions for the mentally retarded, like those found decades ago in developed countries and still seen in some poorer countries, people have at times raised children in virtual factories, with sterile environments and low staff:child ratios. The effects psychologically upon children are generally devastating, retarding their development and sending many children into psychomotor depression (Spitz, 1946) and even self-injury (van Velzen, 1975; see chapter 10).

There are individual differences in attachment and dependency among infants. Ainsworth and colleagues (1978) have studied year-old babies, confronting the child with a "strange situation" in the laboratory, alone or in the presence of mother and/or a stranger. Most children of this age have a tendency to return to mother and cling in a novel setting. Securely attached babies seek and maintain contact with mother in this situation, especially when reunited after brief separation. They clearly prefer mother over the stranger, and greet mother with a smile or cry after separation. On the other hand, insecurely attached babies may react in other ways. They may avoid or ignore mother at reunion, treat the stranger more like the mother, and not cling or resist if picked up. Other less securely attached babies may be ambivalent about mother, both seeking and resisting contact, but can be very distressed when alone. These individual differences have been found to persist for at least a few years when babies are retested. Further research has shown that socioemotional competence is clearly dependent on the quality of mother-infant attachment. Securely and insecurely attached infants differ in physiological measures of stress, such as cardiac activity and adrenocortical response (see Hertsgaard et al., 1995; Spangler & Grossmann, 1993).

Harlow (1971) suggested that the quality of the mother-infant bond may establish an infant's basic sense of trust. Harlow and Mears (1983) discussed broad emotional sequences and consequences, interactions during development between early attachment and fearfulness and aggression. They suggested that there were several alternative pathways in emotional development, with the maternal-infant bond having a critical and abiding impact upon subsequent emotional development.

As we discussed in chapter 9, parental care of newborns is not a perfectly reliable process. One of the most common forms of homicide is maternal infanticide. As we discussed, infanticidal behavior has deep evolutionary roots, being seen in many mammals where it is most likely to occur shortly after birth, especially when newborns are not well-formed or when the mother lacks resources necessary to rear young (Blaffer-Hrdy, 1979). Some humans show impulsive aggression toward the child, often elicited proximately by aversive features of crying (Frodi, 1985).

For most fathers, paternity confidence is critical for investment in children. We discuss the evolutionary roots of this in chapter 7, and how male-perpetrated violence and infanticide can be associated with nonpaternity in chapter 9. Infanticide has also been perpetrated by the father in various circumstances more closely resembling those affecting the mother, such as infant quality and timing, number of other children, and resource availability.

Individual parents differ in the level of "warmth" that they display toward their children. This may be under the partial control of genetic factors that influence the behavior of both parent and child (Kendler, 1996). The level of parental protectiveness and authoritariness also varies substantially among individuals, and may have more to do with family background, including attitudes and culture, than genetics per se. Parent-child relations are dynamic and interactive, controlled by the child as well as the parent. Within families, there are different patterns of interaction with different children.

Some parents are abusive to their children or may simply neglect them (see chapter 9). Some parents treat some of their children more favorably, while neglecting others (Daly & Wilson, 1980). Child abuse and inferior treatment may relate to infant quality, factors diminishing infant attractiveness to parents, or by unwanted sex or timing of birth, or other stressors. Poor treatment by parents certainly sets the stage for disadvantaged development (Wicks-Nelson & Israel, 1997). Children of single-parent families are often at a disadvantage (Hetherington, 1989; Wallerstein, 1991). Successful parenting requires substantial investment and careful guidance over many years. The path to success in adulthood, which is linked to economic welfare and reproductive success, begins in childhood and requires competent parenting and schooling.

Familial Bonds and Conflict

Although relatives share much of their genetic fate, their interests can conflict. A parent's interest is not always the same as that of his or her child. This is a well-known fact of nature, displayed at several points in maturation, especially weaning (Clutton-Brock, 1991; Ewer, 1968). There are tensions whenever it is in one party's interest to sustain a relationship, while the other party has reason to exit. A potentially weanling baby has reason to continue the metabolically cheap source of nourishment, but for the mother this can diminish future fertility or distract from her freedom.

Adolescence is a period of transition to adulthood (see Weisfeld & Berger, 1983), with many changes in motivation and attachment. There is emergence of sexual dimorphism and bimaturism, intergenerational friction, same-sex aggregation but intense interest in the opposite sex, and greater aggressiveness of males. There is conformity at the same time as individuation and emergence of role specialization. In modern circumstances, we have delayed adulthood, or at least the culture has encouraged its members to postpone reproduction and independence from parents until an age well past puberty. This is despite the fact that puberty is occurring at a younger age physiologically, and the result has been intense socio-cultural pressure to delay adulthood. Parent-child interests can certainly diverge and conflict at this time, especially in modern circumstances where there are pressures to delay independence, leaving a lag between physical maturity and the age at which independence is feasible.

SIBLING AND PEER RELATIONS

Sibling Relations

Dunn (1988, p.119) suggested that "the relationship between young siblings is distinctive in its emotional power and intimacy, its qualities of competitiveness, ambivalence, and of emotional understanding that can be used to provoke or to support." There is a high frequency of interaction and imitation. Siblings have direct impact upon one another, and indirect impact through interactions with the parents. They are also often among a child's most immediate and constant playmates.

Sibling interactions can have many positive qualities of mutual support. Older siblings can assist parents in raising children in many ways. They provide models to imitate. They can assist in teaching skills to younger siblings, passing on information about language, motor skills, and social behavior that they have already mastered. They provide company and stimulation when other peers are absent. They can guard each other in more challenging situations. They can support each other in disputes with other children (or even with parents!).

On the other hand, rivalry among brothers and sisters is found in most if not all families with more than one child. It can be defined in terms of competition between siblings for love, affection, attention, or other gain from parents (Leung & Robson, 1991). It may be more common between opposite-sex siblings, more intense in smaller families, most common in young children (ages 2–4), and often displayed most by the eldest child, although family patterns are quite variable.

Aggression among youthful siblings is also well known, and indeed is one of the most common forms of human aggression (Felson, 1983). It may emerge first when an older sibling is displaced from mother's attention by a younger sibling. Property, division of labor, and objectionable behavior are common causes of immediate disputes. Parental intervention may paradoxically increase overt displays of sibling rivalry (Felson, 1983). With a more laissez-faire approach by parents, an older sibling may dominate a younger sibling, who submits. Intervention can embolden a younger sibling to challenge an older one, and hence to make more of a display to parents. Of course, children, just like kittens, puppies, and juvenile monkeys, engage avidly in play-fighting, which is not to be mistaken for true aggression. Such playfulness is surely mutually adaptive in gaining rudimentary physical coordination and social skills, in line with other forms of play as we discuss in chapter 12.

Jealousy generally occurs where individuals are dependent upon a relationship, feel insecure within the relationship, and when there is some threat to the relationship (see Clanton & Smith, 1987; Parrott & Smith, 1993). There is a form of jealousy that is seen very early in development. Young children may show this concerning rivals for their mothers' attention. Masciuch and Kienapple (1993) reported on the emergence of jealousy in children four months to seven years of age. They videotaped children while their mothers paid exclusive attention to another child or praised another child's work. They showed that the emotional state of jealousy can be inferred from consistent and reliable behavioral expressions in these circumstances. This included direct expressions of negative affect, especially in the younger children. There were also changes in gaze, verbalization, and action induced in this mother-peer triangle, many of which were interpreted by independent observers as attempts to solicit the mother's attention.

A distinction is commonly drawn between jealousy and envy (Parrott & Smith, 1993). Jealousy is associated more with fear of loss, distrust, anxiety, and anger, and is necessarily found in interpersonal relations. Envy is more associated with recognition of someone else's superiority in some domain. The emotional outcome of envy is variable and hard to stereotype, but may include feelings of inferiority, longing, resentment, ill-will, and guilt and denial concerning the emotion.

Friendship and Affiliation

Interactions with nonrelated peers are qualitatively different from those among siblings, who share kinship. Common interest links individuals who lack genetic commonality, especially peers at comparable phases of development. Peer-attachment is seen in developing children, emerging progressively, especially after 3 to 5 years of age. Comparable peer attachment is well known in other species (and best studied in rhesus monkeys; Harlow, 1971).

In evolutionary perspective, peers have long interacted because of mutual interests. Trivers (1971) discussed evolution by *reciprocal altruism* as explaining origins of alliances and altruism projected onto non-kin, as we will explore in more detail in chapter 14. Developmental experience also plays a major role. The general tendency to seek friendship may be explained by evolution, but specific alliances and friendships are probably formed in part by simple mechanisms of reinforcement learning. If the company of another remains rewarding, it is sustained. If not, it may be supplanted by more rewarding actions. With age and experience, trust is one of the most important features of friendship and alliance. Peer attachments are often less reliable and enduring than family bonds.

We will discuss the important roles of play and imitation during development in chapter 12. Peers are a continual source of information, stimulation, challenge, and feedback about social, perceptual, language, cognitive, and physical skills. They face the same challenges of development at the same time, and can exchange information and imitate one another. Kids often challenge one another, criticize each other bluntly and directly, demonstrate and model physical skills, and provide socialization of emotions. For example, they yell 'crybaby' at infantile emotional expression that seems inappropriate, but immediately help or run for help in any real crisis. They exert social control over one another, and practice skills of compromise and dominance-subordination.

Body language communicates friendship and attachment. Eye-contact is especially important (Argyle & Cook 1976). Eyes and eye-spots act as social signals in many species. In almost all animals, gaze produces arousal and indicates that an interaction or response is expected. It can display intentions which range from threatening to friendly to sexual. It can also be used to establish dominance. In people, visual contact serves to regulate the flow of communication, with eye contact often signalling that interaction is welcome. When used by a speaker to a listener, it can indicate that the speaker requires feedback or that it is the listener's turn to speak. Gaze has important meaning in interpersonal exchanges in all human cultures. In some cultures, such as Japan and Northern Europe, gaze avoidance is taught. Gaze serves as a signal for interpersonal attitudes and emotions. People look more at those they like, and generally people who look more (and with longer looks) create a more favorable impression, although there are many exceptions to both these generalizations. There are individual differences. Extroverts gaze more frequently, especially while talking, and females gaze more than do males in many situations, but again especially while talking (Argyle & Cook, 1976).

Miscellaneous

The strong tendency for humans to affiliate and bond also projects onto other species. There have been many objective economic benefits of domestic animals (see chapter 3), but many people, especially in affluent countries, keep pets simply for companionship and affection. As is well known, such an apparent need for affection is seen in many children and adults alike. It is difficult to classify this as peer or parental bonding, but it has elements resembling both. Dogs and cats show behavior that begs attention, including whimpering or meowing in babylike fashions, and that communicates soothing and comfort, like tail-wagging or purring. In the case of dogs, we have taken a species that shows strong natural familial bonding (the wolf), and bred them such that many project familylike bonding onto specific humans (cats are naturally more solitary, but have also been bred for contact). We have associated with these species for at least tens of thousands of years. For many people, there can be a dependency (or surrogate dependency) between human and pet, with emotional communication that relies on each species' specific repertoire of gestures and vocalizations.

PAIR BONDING

Evolutionary Roots

We began to describe mating processes in chapter 7. Recall how human mating, like that of other species, is risky and competitive. It is structured at its most basic level by mechanisms of mammalian sexual attraction. But there is something much more than that when bonds form. Eibl-Eibesfeldt (1989) suggests that humans are unique among species in their capacity to "fall in love."

Nevertheless, pair-bonding is seen in the majority of bird species, while among mammals, monogamous bonding is restricted to a minority of species (Clutton-Brock, 1991). Heterosexual bonding generally occurs in conjunction with biparental care. Biparental care is especially advantageous for the young of species that require more protection, nurturance, and instruction to cope as adults. Social attachment, including heterosexual pair-bonding, is seen in a few small mammals, such as prairie voles, as well as several carnivore species, including foxes and wolves, and of course many humans. Human man-woman relations are exceedingly complex and idiosyncratic. They have basic dimensions in common with those of other species, but also many unique qualities in deriving from complex human cognitive, socio-emotional, personality, and economic interplay.

As we discuss in chapter 7, human courtship can be very prolonged, with some pairs maintaining years of friendship before becoming intimate, while others bond quickly. Perhaps Eibl-Eibesfeldt was referring to the prolonged and often unrequited infatuation and longing (the big crush) that can occur before a relationship is even founded, or that can be sustained long after a relationship is severed. This phenomenon is inadequately studied from a scientific perspective, but there is of course a great volume of literature, poetry, and music devoted to the subject.

Recall the sexually dimorphic psychology of mate attraction that we discussed. General strategies adopted by human males and females differ, in correspondence with mammalian patterns, with females typically seeking secure and supportive relationships, while some males show interest in plural relationships and focus on sex, as might have once optimized reproductive success (Symons, 1979). Empirical evidence (Buss, 1989; Feingold, 1992) supports this view. In many cultures, males and females differ in the criteria by which they choose their mates. Females may focus more than do males on attributes that signify possession of resources and fidelity in provision of these resources. Males may focus more than do females on physical appearance, especially on signs correlated with fertility, youthfulness, and good health. Males are also deeply concerned about sexual fidelity, seeking to avoid the risk of investing in children that they have not fathered.

Of course, social norms and cultural rules also structure the ways in which people bond. Almost all cultures have marriage rituals, and many have courtship rituals. Human adults often bond, in idiosyncratic manners and sometimes polygamously, as influenced by biology and cultural norms, in the interests of common children and companionship.

Romantic Versus Companionate Love

The physical manifestation of love was described by Darwin (1872, p. 224–225) as being "one of the strongest of which the mind is capable." However, it is less stereotyped and universal than other emotions, and often expressed by "a gentle smile and some brightening of the eyes. A strong desire to touch the beloved person is commonly felt."

In courtship or formative phases of relationships, emotions can be intense and volatile. Most people distinguish such passion from companionate love, a more stable, less intense, and longstanding attachment based on mutual dependency.

Romantic or passionate love is known by many names, such as *having a crush*, *lovesickness*, *infatuation*, or *obsessive love*. According to common lore, of course, such feelings do not always last long. Sometimes one bit of new information, or one rejection, can make all those imperfections, conveniently repressed by the idealization of the crush, become prominent! On the other hand, sometimes a crush can become an obsession.

According to Hatfield & Sprecher (1986; see also Carlson & Hatfield, 1991; Hatfield & Rapson, 1987), passionate love can be defined by cognitive,

Figure 11-4 A woman's sequence of eye and facial movement during flirtation.

From Eibl-Eibesfeldt, Irenäus. *Human Ethology* (New York: Aldine de Gruyter). Copyright © 1989, Irenäus Eibl-Eibesfeldt. Reprinted with permission.

emotional, and behavioral components associated with longing for union. Cognitive components involve preoccupation with the person loved, idealization of the other, and desire to be known by the other. Emotional components involve attraction (especially sexual), positive feelings when things go well, negative feelings when things go badly, a longing for reciprocity, a desire for complete and permanent union, and physiological arousal. Behavioral components include attempts to determine the other's feelings, studying of the other, assisting the other, and attempting to establish or maintain physical closeness.

Sexual attraction leads to both gaze and pupil dilation due to autonomic arousal. Gaze is also important in communicating the nature of interpersonal relationships. It is used extensively in courtship and love. Studies have shown that engaged couples use mutual gaze more than casual acquaintances, and that longer glances are perceived by others as indicative of a longer relationship (Argyle & Cook, 1976).

In contrast, companionate or conjugal love is less intense and more stable. It is based more on common interests, long-established friendship, and interdependency. The common interests in established pair-bonds often include children and family. According to Carlson and Hatfield (1991), successful intimate relationships have cognitive, emotional, and behavioral dimensions. The cognitive dimensions include self-disclosure with one another, especially revelation of the most intimate facets of self, including idiosyncrasies, strengths and weaknesses, hopes and fears. The emotional characteristics involve deep caring for the partner, which brings with it a power to hurt one another and evoke jealousy, especially given extensive knowledge about the partner's weaknesses. Profound trust also characterizes successful relationships, but there is often risk of betrayal, which can have irreparable consequences. The behavioral characteristics include comfort with physical proximity, including sexuality.

The suggestion has been made that oxytocin could play a role in heterosexual bonding as well as other social attachment processes (see Carter et al., 1992). Oxytocin is released during sexual behavior in mammals, including humans, and may be associated with orgasmic responses in both sexes (Fox & Knaggs, 1969; Komisaruk & Steinman, 1986). According to Carter (1992, p.131), "oxytocin and/or the neural events surrounding the release of oxytocin may have behavioral effects during sexual arousal, orgasm, sexual satiety and other aspects of sociosexual interactions." During sexual activity, oxytocin release occurs in conjunction with autonomic nervous system activity and spinal reflexes. Sexual satisfaction has often been thought to have a bonding effect.

Work in the prairie vole suggests that oxytocin is associated with attachment processes associated with reproduction and kinship (Carter et al., 1995). It also points to possible adrenal involvement in partner preference (DeVries et al., 1996), an effect that is sexually dimorphic, as concurrent stress or corticosterone injections facilitate males' preference for females, while stress or such injections inhibit formation of females' preference for specific males. In chapter 7, we discuss how male mammals can be sexually stimulated by brief stress and catecholamine activation. Interestingly, there is some evidence for heightened human sexual attraction under conditions of high anxiety (Dutton & Aron, 1974).

We cannot easily study the brains of romantically obsessed persons, and it may be very hard to find any comprehensive animal model of human romance. We do know a lot about sexual attraction, as discussed in chapter 7. Olfactory cues relate to sexual attraction and individual recognition in most mammals. With respect to human bonding, we know little about neural processes. Although the evidence is not formal, there may be some hint about the neurochemical substrata of affection from subjective reports of experimental (and usually illegal) use of pharmacological agents that interact with brain monoamines, particularly some euphoria-inducing substances (see Liebowitz, 1983).

We discuss evidence that illustrates the potential depth of companionate attachment in chapters 8 and 10, found in the literatures on bereavement and widowhood. In chapter 8 we discuss several studies showing that death rates increase due to all causes during the immediate months and years after bereavement (Helsing et al., 1981; 1982; Parkes et al., 1969).

Attachment interacts with many other emotions, both positive and negative. An individual's self-esteem certainly is related to regard from significant others. This includes mother, family, and peers, and in adulthood is especially sensitive to attitudes of esteemed members of the opposite sex. In chapter 10, we discuss a profound relationship of negative self-esteem to psychological depression and life-threatening behavior.

Sexual Jealousy

Like its parallel in children, adult jealousy occurs among individuals who depend upon a relationship but feel insecure about it (see Clanton & Smith, 1987; Parrott & Smith, 1993). In adults, jealousy can unleash a torrent of emotions, many of which are viewed as negative both in subjective and social terms, including love-hate ambivalence, anger, fear, anxiety, sorrow, shame, humiliation, confusion, depression, or a desire for vengeance. Jealousy is probably most severe when the rival is viewed as high in prestige, resources, and attractiveness (McIntosh & Tate, 1992).

Jealousy may be somewhat sexually dimorphic. Both sexes have concern about disease risks and risk of partner alienation through sexual and emotional infidelity. However, as discussed in chapter 7, there are evolutionary reasons for sexual dimorphism in mating psychology. Males typically guard against infidelity, protecting themselves from investment in offspring that might not be their own (Daly et al., 1982). By nature, male bonding is related to paternity confidence. For females, who by nature carry the greater weight in reproduction and nurturance, the possibility of alienation of affection can cause concern for loss of support and resources. Both sexes are concerned about sexual infidelity and potential emotional infidelity, but males, more than females, are found to be more distressed by the thought of sexual infidelity as opposed to deep emotional or love infidelity (Buss et al., 1992). There has been some debate about contributions of evolution and social learning to this sexually dimorphic psychology (see Hupka & Bank, 1996; Weiderman & Allgeier, 1992).

It is well known that jealousy can, in some individuals, set off rage responses, as is well documented in case histories of homicides prominently displayed in the news media. In chapter 9, data are presented that show a link between homicide rate and reproductive situation, in humans and other species. Love triangles can present volatile situations.

Intersexual relations, like other critical relations starting with those to mother, influence an individual's self-esteem. As we discussed in chapter 10, broken heterosexual relationships are often associated with psychological depression and even life-threatening behavior. So are general difficulties with the opposite sex and a sense of rejection from family (deCatanzaro, 1995). Affect is clearly related to reproductive condition, in terms of sexual relations, bonding, and family ties. Family provides support.

We explore social impacts on motivation and emotion in more detail in chapter 14, as well as the large individual differences in social relations, personality, and social motivation.

Chapter 12

MOTIVATION TO LEARN

Human infants are altricial, born helpless and entirely dependent on parents for care. People are at an extreme in nature in this regard. It takes at least 15 years to mature and learn the skills necessary for independence. In modern circumstances we have extended this even further, such that it may take as many as 25 years of formation before individuals are ready for fully independent adult functioning. Indeed, with ever-advancing technologies and competitiveness in the job market, many adults today must continually learn to keep abreast of change.

Successful human development has always required the acquisition of numerous skills. It can be shown that we are driven to learn, through curiosity and play. We have mechanisms that favor learning, reward and inhibition processes in the brain, and a strong tendency to imitate other people and learn socially.

Exploration and Curiosity

Any mammal set free in unknown territory tends to explore and actively gather information about the new environment. This has obvious benefits, because it is much easier to cope effectively with an environment that is understood. It also has obvious dangers, simply because potential perils are unidentified. If you were suddenly plopped in the middle of an island and forced to cope, you would soon need to know where to find water, food, and shelter, and you would also want to know whether there were poisonous snakes, cliffs, or landmines.

A rat or mouse, when placed in an open field, tends to move about the new territory, sniffing and cautiously approaching any features. As we discuss in chapter 3, formal data from these laboratory species show that genetics strongly influence individual differences in exploration and emotional reflexes (Broadhurst, 1975, 1976; DeFries et al., 1978). Some animals placed in an open field are more venturous while others are more timid, tending to freeze and to defecate. Defecation has often been viewed as a sign of emotionality or fearfulness because it is correlated with less exploration and is known to be reflexively associated with emotional arousal.

Your cat or dog probably explores similarly (minus the defecation, one hopes) if you set it free in a new house or yard. Most domestic pets confronted with new territory move about it, more or less cautiously depending on the individual and circumstances, and gather information from the senses. Cats sniff and visually inspect strange objects, and may bat them with their paws, often drawing back then approaching tentatively again.

Humans also use simple locomotor behavior, visual and olfactory inspection, and manipulation, but we also explore in much more complex fashions. Naturally, the simpler animal forms of exploration are most readily seen in crawling infants and toddlers, while many more complex forms develop with age and experience. Such sophisticated adult activities as reading the newspaper or inquisitive conversation (even gossip) can be construed as curiosity-driven exploration. There can be no doubt that a drive to learn about the environment is highly adaptive, because information gathering means preparation for effective coping.

Play

Play is readily seen in developing children as a strong emergent drive. Of course, adults also do things that we call play. Play has information-gathering and skill-development value, as a natural mode of learning.

Play behavior is found in the young of most mammalian species, including almost all primates, carnivores, and ungulates (Ewer, 1968). There seems to be some controversy over whether rodents play, or how to define the concept in birds, and doubt about relevance of the concept to amphibians, reptiles, or fish (Smith, 1982). This may be in part due to lack of data on many of these species, but it also surely is due to less neurological sophistication and simpler modes of adaptation.

Most of us have definite ideas about what is meant by the word *play*, but as usual scientific precision requires more careful definition of terms. The word in the ethological and psychological literature is often used in vague and conflicting ways, and definitions vary or are lacking altogether. Smith (1982), in a review of play, defined it as behavior that has no clear, immediate benefit, and is characterized by some variability or inefficiency. Bernstein (1982) defined it as any activity lacking a consummatory response or a clear goal. Both these definitions include a huge range of behaviors, perhaps many more than most of us would include when we think of play.

Assuming play is innate, it is interesting to speculate about its function. Certainly, the costs of play can be great, including energy expenditure, exposure to predators, and potentially serious injuries. The benefits may be more long term. Fagen (1977) argues that it is for this reason that play should be found mainly in K-selected species (see chapter 2), where the long lifespan maximizes benefits, while the protection of young minimizes costs.

Most researchers agree that the main benefits of play are physical training for future endurance and strength (Fagen, 1976) and training for social competition. Exercise play and social play include muscles otherwise used mainly in physically vigorous adult activities. Among other functions of play may be the socialization of emotional responses (Buck, 1983). In social primates, play provides experience with affective behavior, providing social feedback. Elements of adult social behavior can appear during play, including sexual posturing, aggressive and threat gestures, and submissive behavior (Harlow, 1971).

Symons (1978) made extensive observations of rhesus monkeys in the field, and found practicing fighting skills to be particularly common and intense in young males. During play chases he noted locomotor patterns typical of intraspecific aggression and probably of predator avoidance. He noted a "play face" that consistently preceded all playful interactions, which probably signals nonaggressive intentions. In addition, carnivores, such as the domestic cat, play practice stalking, pouncing, biting, and shaking skills (West, 1974). Among primates, manipulative play and tool use practice are prominent.

In contrast to other mammals, Symons (1978) contends that adult human fights are not rehearsed in the play fights of children, since in all human societies serious adult violence is characterized by the use of weapons, and learned cooperative combat. Play fights in children involve more primitive tactics such as trying to get on top of one's opponent, with kicking, hitting, and grappling, but little biting (Aldis, 1975), and are more common in boys than girls. Symons also notes that humans actively teach each other many games, and that only humans appear to play in teams. Certainly, the physical training aspects of play appear to hold even in modern human culture. Manipulative play is strongly developed in human infants, with both exploratory and playful aspects, providing practice for tool making and use (Smith, 1982). The extensive use of fantasy in play, in which physical actions and objects are given nonliteral qualities, is probably unique to humans, and its function is not clear. Smith (1982) suggests that it provides safe goals for the play behavior, and problem-solving practice. It also may play a role in language development and social behavior.

Other researchers argue that play also has short-term benefits, in that it increases sensory input and arousal when they are below optimal levels (Mason, 1965). Thus play would serve a role in relieving boredom, and could perhaps be included as a sensation-seeking behavior. This suggestion has come under criticism, since it may be difficult to define an optimal level of arousal (although see chapter 8), and understimulated children often actually play less than do others (Smith, 1982).

Habituation, Sensitization, and Classical Conditioning of Emotions

As we interact with environmental features, our emotional response often changes, one way or another. Through very well-known, simple mechanisms of learning, our emotional response to stimuli modulates. One basic

Figure 12-1 A child learning architecture on a beach in Spain.

Figure 12-2 A toddler playing with her father.

process is *habituation*. There are many laboratory experiments showing that, although a stimulus might provoke a response when it is first encountered, the response tends to diminish as we become accustomed to it. So, for example, although the sensations of riding in an airplane may at first evoke strong emotions, frequent flyers are more blasé. Although you might find a particular new song or taste of ice cream arousing, you may later find it boring. On the other hand, sometimes the opposite effect occurs, especially when the stimulus is traumatic. *Sensitization* occurs when repeated exposure to a stimulus elicits a greater response to it. This is found for some people with allergies. It also occurs with some traumatic stimuli, as for example the shell-shocked soldier who jumps with each loud noise.

These processes are closely related to classical conditioning (Terrace, 1973; see also chapter 3). Each recurrence of a stimulus with an unconditioned response can potentially alter the stimulus' power to evoke responses in future. Arbitrary stimuli that are paired in time with natural unconditioned stimuli that elicit responses can themselves come to have power over behavior. There are many formal laboratory demonstrations of this, starting with

Pavlov's (1927) eliciting salivation in dogs by presenting the ringing of a bell, a sound previously paired with food. Less formally, you may find that hearing particular old songs recalls moods that once were associated with those songs.

Clinicians who work with people who have emotional difficulties, such as irrational phobias, generally assume a role of sensitization and classical conditioning in the origins of these difficulties, and also exploit the same principles to countercondition emotional responses (Redd et al. 1979; Wolpe, 1958). This line of research provides some of the richest formal evidence of emotional conditioning. *Systematic desensitization* is a successful procedure that exploits natural relaxation reflexes to countercondition anxiety or fear reactions to particular stimuli. So, if a person fears *x*, he/she can be desensitized to *x* by thinking about and interacting with *x* after being brought into a state of deep relaxation by the therapist. Thus, *x* comes to be associated with relaxation rather than fear, where *x* is anything from snakes to escalators to dogs to sexual intimacy.

We also learn to habituate ourselves to potential stressors by interacting with them and acquiring skills, hence making ourselves better able to cope with challenges in later life. Such *stress-innoculation* is seen informally as a broad educational principle in diverse realms, such as preschool programs, school examinations, swimming lessons, or military training, and it has also been studied as a treatment procedure in clinical psychology (Craighead et al., 1981; Redd et al. 1979). Play and formal education surely involve elements of desensitization and stress-innoculation, in the context of skill development, such that individuals become prepared to deal effectively with adult challenges.

Reinforcement and Punishment

A basic principle of psychology is that organisms tend to repeat responses that are rewarded and inhibit responses that are punished. As we discussed in chapter 3, this general mode of learning is known as instrumental or operant conditioning. The idea is that the consequences of behavior shape future behavior. Numerous experiments have shown that animals, including people, can learn through processes of reward and punishment (see Craighead et al., 1981; Nevin & Reynolds, 1973).

In general, responses which are followed by a reward are reinforced, or increase in frequency. It is often possible to sustain an established response with *intermittent reinforcement*, that is, where reward occurs only some of the times that a response is displayed. For example, a teenager may persistently ask to borrow his parents' car, even though they infrequently yield to this demand. If a response is consistently not reinforced for some time, it will ultimately decrease in frequency and cease occurring, or *extinguish*. At first, nonreward of a previously rewarded response can lead to a "frustration" effect (Amsel, 1992), which involves an activation of the response, but ultimately, if the reward never occurs, the response usually ceases.

Responses can also be increased in frequency if they cause an aversive stimulus to stop, a process called *negative reinforcement*. Formal examples from animal experiments are abundant in the scientific literature, for example where termination of an electric shock rewards a locomotor response and increases its frequency. I suppose that a good common-sense human example is seen in the behavior of swatting flies or mosquitoes; we habitually repeat this behavior because it terminates an unpleasant sensation.

Responses become conditioned in the context of specific cues, or prompts, which provide *stimulus control*. Many formal experiments show that instrumental responses tend to occur in the specific stimulus context in which they are rewarded, but less or not at all in contexts in which they are not rewarded. Informal examples of prompts are also commonplace. A cat may learn that noises made by a can opener mean that food is imminent, and may start to meow and rub against its owner's leg whenever it hears a can opener. People learn, almost automatically, to apply a car's brakes when they see a red light or the brake lights of the car in front of them. Seeing a clock indicating that it is 12 noon provokes many people to rise from their chairs and go for lunch, even in the absence of internal hunger cues. Thus, in a sense, conditioning can cause external cues to stimulate motivational states and behavior.

Punishment is the converse process of inhibiting responses which are followed by aversive events. It may involve either the application of an aversive event contingent on a response, or the removal of a positive event contingent on a response. Many animal experiments show that punishment works to inhibit responses upon which it is made contingent (Fantino, 1973). Of course, punishment is also commonly used by parents and teachers to control unruly children, and indeed by the courts to control unruly adults. The formal human literature also shows the effectiveness of punishment procedures, but raises issues about side effects.

Craighead and colleagues (1981) listed a number of conditions that enhance the effectiveness of punishment. These include immediate application of punishment after the undesired response, punishment of each and every occurrence of the response, and introduction of the contingent punishing stimulus at maximal intensity rather than with gradual increases in severity. Punishment is also more effective if there is concurrent removal of the positive motivation for the response, provision of another more positive means of gaining the rewards that the punished response was seeking, reinforcement of responses that are incompatible with the punished response, and a verbal description of the punishment contingency. Suppose, for example, that a parent wishes to discourage a young child from stealing toys from other children. Accordingly, it would be optimal to catch each instance of stealing and immediately withdraw major privileges (for example, by placing the child in his or her room away from friends). It would also help to find a legitimate way for the child to gain access to similar toys, to reward the child for sharing and gift-giving, and to explain exactly why it is wrong to steal and what will happen if he or she does so in the future.

The traditional concerns that have been raised about punishment have to do with its side effects. These include emotional impacts of punishment, avoidance of the punishing agent, and imitation of the use of punishment. A boy whose father uses harsh physical punishment may respond with intense crying and other emotion, may learn to avoid his father, and may grow up and use the same severe strategy with his children.

It is clear that many of the stimuli that constitute reinforcers and punishers are things that we have discussed in detail in previous chapters. The best reinforcers are generally events that satisfy drive states. Food, water, comfort, sexual gratification, and even praise and attention are motivators and reinforcers when given contingent on responses, and punishers when withdrawn contingent on responses. Similarly, we can understand aversive events, those whose withdrawal reinforces behavior or whose application punishes behavior, as those eliciting pain, discomfort, and fear. All of these stimuli, positive and negative, are the very sorts of things used by animal trainers and humans wishing to modify others' behavior.

Neural Substrata of Reinforcement and Inhibition

Modern evidence shows neural substrata underlying the tendencies to repeat successful responses and suppress unsuccessful responses. Such data suggest that the brain contains mechanisms that subserve reinforcement and punishment.

One of the most remarkable findings is that animals' responses can be rewarded merely by delivering mild electrical stimulation to the brain. Olds and Milner (1954) inadvertently found this effect while inquiring whether electrical brain stimulation might increase arousal. They found that, when the electrodes were placed in the septal area and other regions of the limbic system, rats returned to the place in which the mild shocks were given. They then gave the rats levers that they could press, with each press producing electrical brain stimulation. The rats pressed the levers at very high rates, hundreds and even thousands of times per hour.

Olds and Milner noted that this effect was very similar to positive reinforcement. Their studies and those of several other researchers have indicated that there are some distinctive properties of such behavior. For example, some rats that press the lever for electrical brain stimulation at a high rate one day were found to ignore it entirely the next day. But if they were given a few response-independent stimulations, they immediately began to press again. Sometimes animals pressed obsessively, to the exclusion of other adaptive behavior like eating and drinking. However, motivational manipulations, like food or water deprivation, can under some circumstances alter the frequency of responding for electrical brain stimulation.

Research has shown that stimulation of several areas of the brain can produce reinforcement, but the most effective site for the electrodes is the medial forebrain bundle (MFB) (Olds & Fobes, 1981). The MFB is an important collection of axons that interconnect areas in the central base of the brain, travelling from the midbrain through the lateral hypothalamus to the base of the forebrain. The MFB provides communication between midbrain and forebrain structures, and it also has ascending catecholaminergic and serotonergic axons rising from the brainstem and projecting to various forebrain areas.

Often electrical brain stimulation also elicits species-characteristic behavior. In particular, natural stereotyped action patterns are seen. Electrical stimulation can elicit consummatory responses, including eating, drinking, and copulation, and it can also produce fighting, gnawing, or exploratory behavior. The particular behavior patterns that are manifested depend partly on the location of the electrode tips, but also are strongly affected by the nature of the animal's immediate environment (see Caggiula, 1970; Valenstein, 1973). Even with electrodes constantly in the same position, a stimulated rat will do different things depending on the objects in its environment.

In contrast, electrical stimulation of other parts of the brain can be highly aversive. If an animal has been trained to press a lever, and it is then arranged that this response produces electrical stimulation of certain brain areas, the animal will avoid pressing the lever again. Thus, an inhibitory effect, like that of punishment, can also be produced by electrical brain stimulation. In general, brain stimulation that produces inhibition also elicits stereotyped species-characteristic responses. We discussed some of this evidence in chapters 6 and 9. For example, Clemente and Chase (1973) described how stimulation of the dorsal hypothalamus will produce flight behavior, accompanied by rapid breathing, pupil dilation, and urination and defecation. Others (e.g., Panksepp, 1971) described how aggressive responses could be elicited with electrodes in various regions such as the medial hypothalamus.

Subsequent research on rewarding brain stimulation has focused on identification of the optimal electrical parameters, neural pathways, and neurochemical substrata (see reviews by Bielajew & Harris, 1991; Carlson, 1994). There has been much attention to catecholamines, especially dopamine, based on several facts. Many of the brain areas that are associated with rewarding electrical brain stimulation are associated with catecholaminergic neurotransmission. Drugs that block dopaminergic action generally tend to block reinforcement processes, and these effects can be produced even when very small quantities of these drugs are introduced locally in the brain. Moreover, drugs like amphetamine and cocaine are catecholaminergic stimulants, and they can also be used to reinforce behavior. Use of such stimulants can also set up artificial motivation, perhaps by affecting brain reinforcement mechanisms.

In any event, it is clear that the brain contains mechanisms of reinforcement and inhibition. It is possible to tap into these systems artificially in animal brains, and thus to influence fundamental processes that underlie motivation.

Conditioned Reinforcement and Acquired Goals

Some stimuli are innately rewarding, but others become rewarding through experience. Many of the goals that organisms seek have acquired their capacity to influence behavior through some history of association with drive satisfaction. Stimuli can acquire power to reinforce or punish, even though they once were neutral.

A classic conception distinguishes between *primary* and *conditioned* reinforcers. Many stimuli that motivate organisms, like food and water for hungry and thirsty animals, have their power over behavior for biological reasons, which we amply discuss in other chapters. Stimuli with a natural capacity to affect behavior, like food, water, sexual gratification, pain relief, and temperature moderation have been called *primary reinforcers*. On the other hand, it is possible to make stimuli that were once neutral come to influence behavior. This phenomenon has been called *conditioned reinforcement*.

Conditioned reinforcement has clearly been demonstrated with laboratory animals (see reviews by Dinsmoor, 1983; Hendry, 1969; Nevin & Reynolds, 1973). A rat will normally not work to hear a tone or see a light flash. However, if the tone or light is repeatedly paired with the presentation of food, it may later be used on its own to motivate behavior.

Of course, we humans also develop acquired goals through histories of learning and experience. Surely, cognitive learning and social learning, as well as simple conditioning, play major roles in this process. As individuals age, develop, and differentiate, they acquire distinctive goals and preferences.

No modern book on motivation of behavior could fairly neglect one other very grand motivator of human behavior: Money! Money can be called a generalized conditioned reinforcer, because we make it convertible for almost all goods and services. As we all know, many people avidly seek money. We work for it, are rewarded by receiving it, and can be distressed and punished by its loss. Economists' perspectives on motivation see money as the broad influence on individual and collective behavior. Their very valid perspectives on human motivation go beyond the scope of this book, where we are concerned with more biological dimensions. Such economic perspectives on motivation are entirely consistent with biological perspectives, but elaborate upon collective dimensions of motivation in advanced modern societies.

Educators also have their currency. If you are reading this text as a student, you might reflect upon the fact that you have been under the control of marks or grades, which superficially are just numbers or letters on paper, but which signify status and are potentially convertible for career advancement. Clinical psychologists and many other would-be behavior modifiers and authorities have provided many demonstrations of control of classroom and other institutional behavior through mini-economies using various tokens and symbols (see Craighead et al., 1981). Institutional behavior in schools, prisons, hospitals, group-homes, and the military has been controlled, to a degree, by stars, points, status symbols, rank, and so forth. Such token economies work because the symbols are convertible to goods, services, privileges, or status.

Intrinsic Versus Extrinsic Control

Very often, more than one contingency of reward and/or punishment bears upon the same behavior. These contingencies may work together or they may pull in opposite directions. We elaborate on this theme in chapter 13, where we discuss conflicts among motivations. Here, let us consider one important distinction, that between *intrinsic* control, by factors immediately and naturally bearing upon behavior, and *extrinsic* control, by factors that are superimposed, often by social matters.

Many activities have rewards or aversive features as natural, direct, and intrinsic consequences. This is certainly true of any response that leads to immediate drive satisfaction. For example, eating sweet food has its own reward, as do many other consummatory behaviors. It is conditional on current state, as we discuss throughout this book. When tired, resting and sleeping are rewarding, but when alert and bored, seeking entertainment and stimulation are more likely.

This is opposed to externally imposed consequences, usually of a social nature. A parent, teacher, or employer might impose rewards that encourage a particular form of behavior. These are extrinsic factors structured not by the immediate consequences of the behavior, but by outside encouragement. Intrinsic and extrinsic factors may work in concert, or in opposition. The intrinsic rewards may only be discovered after extrinsic factors get the behavior off the ground, as when parents encourage eating broccoli with the extrinsic reward of dessert, and the child later decides that he likes broccoli.

Going into the shade on a hot day is intrinsically reinforcing, but suppose that you are required by your job as a harvester to stay in the sun in the fields. Behavior thus has two conflicting demands upon it, one very intrinsic and related to comfort, and the other controlled somewhat more extrinsically by the need to earn money. A child may play piano because he or she loves to hear the music produced. On the other hand, parents and teachers may actively encourage piano playing, and thus a child may play not for enjoyment, but rather to please others. University students may attend a lecture because the material is intrinsically interesting, or because they need to learn it for the more extrinsic reason of passing examinations. Not all controlling factors neatly fit into labels of intrinsic or extrinsic, but the distinction is often useful.

Educators often argue that maximization of intrinsic motivation is important for classroom learning (Stipek, 1993). Many tasks of learning potentially offer intrinsic rewards, but an extrinsic motivator is necessary to get the task under way. For example, many people who have not used computers are reluctant to start, and may require extrinsic motivation by a teacher or employer to start. However, subsequently, with some mastery of their use, computers may gain more intrinsic appeal.

A more probable behavior can be used to motivate a less probable behavior. This is often called Premack's principle, which occurs whenever the opportunity to perform the more intrinsically rewarding response follows from performing the less intrinsically rewarding response. Formal research shows that animals can be motivated by making a more probable response contingent on a less probable response (see Premack, 1959). The literature concerning human behavior modification also shows that Premack's principle can be very effective (Craighead et al., 1981). This principle is commonly used by teachers and parents and even employers. A simple example is the parent who makes a child's access to the TV contingent on doing homework, when the child wants to watch TV but not do homework. This principle also rather naturally occurs in many situations, where hard, unpleasant work leads to comfort, consummation, and pleasure.

Contagion, Imitation, Vicarious Learning, and Culture

We often do things simply because others around us are doing them. This is certainly true of some simple, stereotyped forms of behavior, like yawning (Baenninger, 1987; Provine, 1986) and laughing (Askenasy, 1987). Imitation is seen early in human development, in selective mimicry of adult facial expressions (Field et al., 1982; see Figure 3-3). Learning through observation is seen in many primates, which have the capacity to learn without the actual performance of responses (Menzel, 1973).

In many experiments, Bandura (1977) and others have demonstrated that people can transcend the simple methods of learning (direct reinforcement and punishment) that constrain learning in more simple species. Our behavior can change merely because we observe other people's behavior. Observation of a performed response can increase the frequency of the same sort of response in observers. Seeing the response being rewarded is an even more potent model, while seeing the response being punished can inhibit the same response in observers. Through *vicarious learning*, behavior can be motivated and its frequency can change without any direct experience with rewards and punishers.

We readily see imitation in various fads that diffuse through culture, especially with modern media. This is seen in style of dress, hairstyles, slang expressions, and recreational patterns like the hula-hoop or the Macarena. Humans can imitate very complicated responses, those that had initially to be learned by someone in more difficult ways, perhaps by trial and error. Historically, the whole industrial revolution is a tale of manufacturers imitating and elaborating technology and modes of production.

Imitation can be a powerful motivator. It is certainly one of the most important ways in which we learn new responses (Bandura, 1977). We copy what we see others do, and we also copy on the basis of verbal or written descriptions of what other people have done. We especially emulate prestigious and successful persons. Imitation is a rapid shortcut in the acquisition of new responses, in comparison to tedious trial and error. Each individual does not have to "reinvent the wheel" each time he or she learns a new skill. Instead, the information is passed on from other people, by example, description, demonstration and modeling, or active instruction. This is the basis of culture, and clearly one of the reasons for human success as a species.

Nevertheless, the human tendency to imitate can lead people astray. The clearest example of this is found in historical cases of mass suicide. In Jonestown, Guyana in 1978, several hundred men, women, and children simultaneously committed suicide, mostly by poison. Although some of the cult leaders may have arrived at the psychological conditions favoring suicide (see chapter 10), and some cult members may have been coerced or murdered, there is little doubt that many people were simply swept up in the mass psychology of the situation. In fact, there have been many cases of mass suicide in recorded history (deCatanzaro, 1981a). There are also cases of clustered suicides. For example, there is statistical evidence of increased frequency of suicide following cases publicized in the news media (Phillips, 1974).

Incentives Versus Reinforcement in Intelligent Animals

We humans take this ability to learn by representation much further, because of our advanced language and cognitive skills. We can be motivated to perform complicated responses just on the basis of ideas.

Just the notion that some behavior will lead to reward can make the behavior happen. Remember that in nonhuman studies of conditioning, new response acquisition and behavioral change require a history of direct experience with reinforcers and punishers. Humans can clearly circumvent this experience through verbal and other social transmission, and indeed cognitive representation.

This point has been made by many theorists (e.g., Bandura, 1977; Cofer, 1972; Bolles, 1967). They suggested that intelligent organisms can learn new responses in anticipation of rewards that they have never actually experienced. In cognitively simpler animals, an individual must experience a contingent consequence before behavior frequency changes. *Incentives* operate especially with more intelligent and sophisticated humans, generally older children and adults. It is possible to perform new responses because they learn, through language, culture, and observation of others, that certain forms of behavior can potentially lead to rewards. Accordingly, behavior can be motivated and its frequency can change without any direct experience with rewards and punishers. What is needed is some cognitive representation of potential reward or punishment.

People may buy lottery tickets because they hear or read that a ticket could be worth a lot of money. In most cases, they have never been reinforced for this behavior by actually winning anything. Instead, the concept of potentially winning is enough to motivate the behavior. This is a good example of incentives in action, but it is generally not an example of incentives acting adaptively, because most people lose money in the long run by buying lottery tickets. Clearly, the behavior is sustained in many people, so the incentive is more powerful than the actual punishment.

Thus, humans change behavior without direct experience with contingencies of reinforcement and punishment, through incentives and disincentives. These concepts imply some cognitive representation of potential rewards and punishers, not previously experienced. We learn through language, culture, and observation that certain forms of behavior can lead to various consequences. Insight and intelligence can allow us to perform new responses in anticipation of such potential consequences.

Again, a university student might get insight into the situation by considering subjectively his or her own motivation. There are many potential rewards of going to university. Some of these are more intrinsic and immediate, such as social aspects, opportunities to emulate others, intrinsic interest in the curriculum, and family encouragement. Nevertheless, the decision to invest years and substantial amounts of money in advanced training is also probably influenced strongly by long-term concerns for employability and social advancement. It is common knowledge that education improves career prospects. This knowledge is spread through language, culture, and examples of others. An incentive operates insofar as a student works in response to a mental picture of a better life following advanced education. The real reward is not experienced until the culmination of years of investment in training. The reward is anticipated, but not yet received, yet it sustains years of behavior. This is incentive, not reinforcement, guiding behavior.

The entrepreneur who invests her life savings in a new business venture, hoping to market a better mouse trap to the universe, takes a major gamble based merely on an idea of potential rewards. Any foundling business can take substantial cost in time and money before any reward is reaped. One would be very hard pressed to explain such behavior through simple operant conditioning. Instead, it is clear that intelligent people can work hard because of a cognitive image of potential success, showing anticipation and insight never seen in other animals. This is rational if there is a reasonable probability that the mousetrap will sell, although there is some risk of loss of investment. The fact that people can engage in such incentive-driven behavior, without immediate rewards, is a testimony to the sophistication of our cerebral cortices.

Education, Cognitive Development, and Achievement

Family, peers, formal schooling, and public media all actively influence any individual, particularly in early development. They channel the expression of natural drives and emotions. Most of us are heavily socialized, each by his or her own individual social milieu. As we explore further in chapters 13 and 14, our "animal instincts," the subject matter of earlier chapters of this book, are extrinsically modulated by acculturation. This begins with parenting, is progressively influenced by peers during child development, and in modern times is also mediated by formal education and mass media.

In modern times, the practice of active conceptual instruction has obvious value, elevating us above simpler emotions and improving skills of adaptation. The drive to learn may have strong adaptive value, and be cognitively driven, implicating the cerebral cortices. This provides override of subcortical neuroendocrine mechanisms that subserve our more primitive drives and emotions.

Social encouragement can be one of the strongest motivators of human behavior. This may certainly not be true for all individuals, as there are psychopathic or sociopathic personalities. But for most individuals, praise or criticism, acceptance or contempt, love or fear of others, encouragement or discouragement all act as powerful influences, when their source is from valued family members, peers, or organizations. We return to this issue in detail in chapter 14.

Many strategies are employed to encourage developing children and adults to strive for growth and achievement. This is a modern educational issue, and there are many practical perspectives on motivation that go beyond the scope of the present book (see Pintrich & Schunk, 1996; Stipek, 1993).

Chapter 13

CONFLICTS AMONG MOTIVES

An individual rarely has just one goal on her or his agenda. Moreover, conflicting impulses often drive us in opposite directions, so decisions must be made.

Approach-Avoidance

Many problems in life present two or more conflicting motives. Classic work of Miller (1959) suggested that conflict arises from competing tendencies to approach and avoid. The closer that one is to a goal, the greater is its pull. However, if it also has aversive features, there is also repulsion. According to Miller, the pull of approach increases gradually as the goal is nearer. Repelling factors present much steeper gradients with proximity of the object.

Miller actually defined three major kinds of conflict. In an *approach-approach* conflict, there are two possible rewards, one of which must be relinquished in order to accept the other. Animals in experiments can be placed in this situation by having two goal boxes at either end of a runway, placing the animal between them. Typically, animals oscillate back and forth a few times before making a decision (as you might in a dessert bar). In an *approach-avoidance* conflict, the same goal has both positive and negative consequences, as for example when it delivers both food and electric shock. Typically, animals approach such a goal box and then halt, again hesitating, oscillating back-and-forth before acting (as you might in front of a cold lake on a hot day). In an *avoidance-avoidance* conflict, there are two aversive options, and a choice must be made. This is of course an "unhappy" situation, and animals may seek a third option, such as jumping out of the box, failing which, they oscillate back-and-forth for a long time before making a decision.

In all of these simple conflict situations, animals tend to hesitate, approach, then retract, repeatedly, before resolving the conflict with a decision. Humans also often hesitate when in conflict. This may not be a bad thing, because it is important to gather information about options before lurching into a decision. On the other hand, indecisiveness can mean that problems do not get solved. The tradeoff depends upon the nature of the options and the urgency of the decision.

In humans, some evidence suggests that there is cerebral asymmetry in processes that might relate to approach and avoidance. In particular, the left and right frontal hemispheres may show differential responses in the two cerebral hemispheres, as indicated by measures such as lateral gaze shifts and EEG readings, depending on the affective content of stimuli (Davidson, 1983).

Multiple Approach-Avoidance, Worry, and Anxiety

Mundane human problems involve decisions about alternatives with both positive and negative potential outcomes. Worry and anxiety may relate to the incomplete information that often enters into these decisions.

Suppose, after graduating, that you find yourself with two job offers. One option is near your family, pays more, and looks more secure. The other is preferred by your spouse, is in a more pleasant climate, and you like your prospective colleagues better. Your spouse and family are trying to convince you of opposite choices.

Conflicting impulses, emotions, and drives are commonplace. Adaptation is rarely static. Most individuals are constantly challenged to solve problems. Throughout development, there is a need to learn and make choices; usually without complete information about the consequences of decisions. This is especially true in adult life, because children usually have adults who make important decisions for them. This chapter will give us a third perspective toward "anxiety," which we also discuss in chapters 6 and 8.

Cortical Inhibition and Enhancement of Emotions

Logic may support behavior that is contrary to emotional inclinations. For example, if individuals acted upon every sexual and aggressive impulse, they might face severe social disapproval. Knowledge of propriety and the law often inhibits lower emotional impulse.

Modern diet provides other examples. Should you buy that donut or walk on by? Knowledge of nutrition is stored at a high cognitive (cerebral cortical) level, but impulses for sweets and fats come from much more primitive, ancient, neuroendocrine levels (see chapter 5). An individual who is concerned about weight and health can direct eating behavior from a high-order cortical level, with intelligence and self-control. However, this will conflict with impulses, such as salivation and activation of digestive juices at the mere odor of baking cookies or fried chicken. Cortical control over impulses can bring internal conflict. Self-discipline often comes with maturity, although not all children lack self-discipline and not all adults have it!

Other examples are covered in our discussion of fear and courage in chapter 6. Soldiers must often override fear, directing behavior instead by training, social control, and wits, for example when they jump out of airplanes (see also chapter 8) or walk onto battlefields. At the amusement park, many people go through perceptually frightening physical experiences, reassured by knowledge that the rides are usually safe.

Our cognitive control helps us to transcend lower emotional impulses. As we discuss in chapter 12, intelligent humans change behavior through incentives and disincentives, cognitive representations of potential rewards and punishers that have not previously been experienced. We learn through language, culture, and observation. Insight lets us perform new responses in anticipation of potential consequences. Self-consciousness helps to substitute cortical control for primitive lower-brain control. As children mature, they often learn to substitute polite verbal requests for crying fits, as means of controlling their parents.

Higher perceptual and cognitive processes direct our emotions. We respond differently to the presence of a venomous snake depending on whether it is under the bed or behind glass at the zoo, or to a bus ride depending on whether or not someone tells us that the driver is drunk, or to an absent child depending on whether we know where he or she is. The influence of arousal upon human emotions depends upon an interaction with cognitive and situational variables. People may interpret and label emotion depending upon knowledge and perception (see Schachter & Singer, 1962).

Moreover, knowledge and reason set off emotions. We may feel angry and upset when we learn that there has been an environmental disaster, even when we do not directly see, feel, or smell it in our own neighborhood. Mere words can alter emotions, as when an individual learns that his favored political candidate has won, or when he reads that his bank account is overdrawn, or that she received an A on an exam. When we are complimented on an important performance, or denigrated and ridiculed by our peers, we often respond emotionally in ways that exhilarate or depress us (see chapter 10).

Knowledge and impulse often summate to "mixed feelings" and ambivalence. Many situations contain both intrinsic and extrinsic controls (see chapter 12) that pull in more than one direction. Most of the time, human beings can make decisions, try not to look back, and act with wisdom as integrated whole organisms, balancing multiple primitive impulses and intelligent insights! Surely, this is one of the attributes that makes some individuals more successful in life than are others.

Delay of Gratification

Very often, individuals must postpone gratification in order to persist in working toward long-term goals. It has probably always been true, but it is especially so in modern competitive circumstances, that it is advantageous to ignore control by immediate intrinsic rewards and focus instead on long-term objectives. This may require higher cognitive control, and suppression of immediate pleasure. Hence, we have the common expression, *Short-term pain for long-term gain.*

It is fair to say that developing children and adolescents with impulse-control deficits are generally disadvantaged relative to their peers, more likely to have academic and social difficulties, and more prone to delinquency (Wicks-Nelson & Israel, 1997). No doubt, this can be even worse for excessively impulsive adults, who might overspend their budgets or take care of health less than optimally. That, of course, does not mean that "all work and no play" is a successful strategy, or that some hedonism in off-hours is a bad thing.

Commonsense examples are abundant. Going to work or classes may involve short-term discomfort for long-term benefit. Staying in bed may be more immediately and intrinsically gratifying than getting up and going to work, or perhaps it is sunny and pleasant outside and you would rather play than read this book, or maybe you would rather read this book than study for your calculus test. Medical and graduate students often choose short-term financial loss for long-term career and financial success. Diet and exercise regimes provide other clear examples of self-discipline paying off in the long run. It may be intrinsically and immediately rewarding to eat potato chips, chocolate, and greasy food. But this is traded against conscious awareness that bad diet will make you fat and unhealthy. Primitive emotions say one thing, higher cortical control says another.

Mischel and colleagues (1989) reviewed data concerning the development of delay of gratification in children. They characterize infants as impulse-driven, unable to delay gratification and demanding immediate satisfaction. They suggested that future-oriented self-control develops with maturation, while coexisting with some impetuousness. They found enduring individual differences in such self-control as early as four years of age, and that those preschoolers who delayed gratification "developed into more cognitively and socially competent adolescents, achieving higher scholastic performance and coping better with frustration and stress" (p. 933).

Defense Mechanisms and Irrational Resolutions

Cognition and emotion can summate in some odd fashions to produce irrational results. Freud (1977) made several observations. Although his methods were perhaps not the best of modern science, some of his ideas have been validated through many other case histories recorded by subsequent observers. These logical-emotional twists are certainly not seen equally in all people.

Repression is cognitive avoidance of unpleasant memories, such as forgetting traumatic events. In post-traumatic stress, survivors of extremely horrific experiences bury memories and discuss them very reluctantly (see in chapter 8, concentration camp survivors, Matussek, 1975). Vivid recall of traumatic events sets off conditioned responses and is psychologically painful. Repressive defensiveness has also been described as "a coping style in which verbal reports about affect are commonly dissociated form other indices indicative of affective state" (Davidson, 1983, p.122). Many other psychological defense mechanisms have been described. *Denial* has many forms, like repression, designed to ignore unpleasant realities, for example by immersing oneself in work to escape family or social problems. A *reaction formation* is the expression of the opposite emotion to that initially felt, such as changing from love to hate following rejection (see discussion of sexual jealousy in chapter 11). *Projection* is the attribution of your thoughts to another person. This is seen in the person who has a romantic crush on another, but claims to friends that the admired person is the one with the crush. *Displacement* is the direction of an emotion at a safer target, such as kicking the dog instead of your boss. *Regression* is reverting to a less mature developmental stage to avoid adult responsibilities, such as using baby-talk in an argument to avoid an angry response or win a point. *Compensation* is the tendency to react to a shortcoming by excelling in a similar area, such as the disabled person who becomes an athlete. *Atonement* is the attempt to make up for a shortcoming by striving in another area, such as the emotionally neglectful parent who lavishes a child with gifts.

Cognitive Dissonance

Cognitive dissonance occurs when there is a discrepancy between our actions and our beliefs, but we feel they ought to be consistent. If we cannot or will not modify our actions, then we change our beliefs or values (Festinger & Carlsmith, 1959). An example is a study in which subjects are paid to tell others that a particular task (actually very dull and repetitive) is not boring; in other words, they are paid to lie. Most subjects actually change their own attitude to the task, in order to avoid the cognitive dissonance involved in lying.

Another example of cognitive dissonance would be an environmentally conscious person who wishes to drive to work or use air-conditioning, although aware of the environmental damage these cause. The dissonance can be resolved in several ways. One way would be to stop driving or using an air conditioner, that is, to change behavior. Another option would be to modify your environmental beliefs and convince yourself that ozone depletion and climatic change are under control or unimportant. A third, and perhaps most common, option is to add new cognitive elements. This would include convincing yourself that your one car or one air-conditioner will not have a significant impact, or that scientists will have a solution to the problem before it gets too bad. All these options allow you to reestablish cognitive consistency.

Mook (1987) lists some other interesting strategies that some people use to avoid cognitive dissonance. These include blaming the victim, commonly used in revisionist histories, such as portraying native Americans as the culprits when describing their genocide. Another problem is "woodenheadedness," or refusing to consider facts which conflict with one's preset ideas. Of course, the surest way to guard a theory from data is to make sure that the data are never collected.

Rational Decision-Making

Rational decision-making usually occurs without full information. Even though we cannot completely predict the future, we often are faced with important choices that are mutually exclusive, such as taking one career direction or another. Choice often produces internal conflict, especially when the stakes are high.

Although careful rational deliberation would seem to be wise when there is some difficult choice to be made, we may not always act with such deliberation. When faced with a required choice, people sometimes decide rapidly on the basis of sentiment, without much reflection (Zajonc, 1980). Decision-making on the basis of intuition is essential for coping, and often results in reasonable and appropriate choices. It has been suggested that, although a careful weighing of the "pros and cons" is often beneficial, intuition can sometimes be superior, as introspection can sometimes reduce the quality of preferences and decisions (Wilson & Schooler, 1991).

Many important decisions, however, are based on careful weighing of options. When a difficult decision is demanded, people often seek a compelling rationale for making a choice. People actively seek and construct reasons in order to resolve the conflict and justify their choice, to themselves and others (Tversky & Shafir, 1992). Often, when the decision is especially difficult and conflict is high, people delay making the choice, and they may also seek new alternatives or stay with a default option if one exists (Shafir et al., 1993).

Of course, sometimes choices are not optimal. One perspective on this comes from studies of patients' decisions when confronted with medical decisions that involve some risk (see Redelmeier et al., 1993). People sometimes treat danger and safety categorically, failing to recognize relative risks and the fact that high and low levels of the same thing (e.g., salt, sugar, or alcohol in diet) often have very different consequences. People often discount risk reductions, failing to recognize the value of factors that diminish risk probabilistically, while seeking absolute safety or zero risk. Thus, for example, they may attempt to eliminate salt and sugar from their diet, rather than simply to reduce the intake.

Worry "fulfills a useful purpose in helping to motivate health-related behaviors, yet sometimes it serves only to decrease quality of life without any medical gains" (Redelmeier et al., 1993, p. 75). Sometimes fears produce extreme and irrational behavior, where there is a mismatch between objective degree of danger and subjective intensity of worry. This has been documented, for example, in epidemiological studies relating electromagnetic fields to the incidence of cancer; the risks may have been exaggerated by the news media (Jauchem, 1992). Many people in Britain and Europe stopped eating beef after the scare about "mad cow disease" in the early 1990's, on the basis of a very small number of affected human cases; time will tell whether this was rational or not.

Drive Hierarchies

The needs of individuals vary with their affluence, culture, individual circumstances, and stage in the life cycle. Obviously, first and foremost, people must take care of biological needs, those related to survival. These include functions we discuss in detail in chapters 5 and 6, appetitive behavior of hunger and thirst, defense from harsh elements, and maintenance of physiological homeostasis. Only if one is capable of surviving to reproductive age, and is in good health and has sufficient resources, does attention turn to needs of chapter 7, reproduction. Thus far, we have discussed simply essential biological needs that apply to any species.

If you lived in Bangladesh or Burma or the Congo, your motives in life may go no further, because these basic issues of day-to-day survival present a constant struggle. Those of us who live in affluence, particularly in modern developed nations, find that most of these fundamental problems of life are easily solved and we are left with time on our hands. There then become finer motivations of the sort that we experience only in modern technologically developed cultures. We must remember that merely 100 years ago, even in the most developed western countries, most people were engaged in agriculture and other subsistence activities. So we return again to the issue of evolutionary lag.

Maslow (1968) was one of the first to address the hierarchy of needs that arises as basic problems are solved, and one moves on to finer needs. He suggested that human motivation is guided by a hierarchy or ladder of needs. These begin with the most basic physiological needs, such as hunger and thirst. When these needs are met, we begin to concern ourselves with safety, including physical, financial, and even political or social stability. The next to emerge once these needs are met, is the need for love and social affiliation. The need for esteem emerges after this, which can come from productive and useful work, or success in many endeavors. Finally, and perhaps most controversially, the highest need emerges, which is the drive for self-actualization, through the fulfilling of personal potentials and talents. Of course, the meaning of *self-actualization* is very abstract and vague; modern science requires that we seek greater precision.

Off hand, self-actualization would seem to be an idiosyncratic matter. We seek many specialized roles in modern developed societies, dependent on our individual aptitudes, training, and personality.

Risk-Taking

Almost any activity in life carries some risk. I suppose that you could stay in bed in the morning, simply to escape a world that carries too many risks. But even that would leave you at risk that your body and brain would atrophy, and hygiene would deteriorate, and your house could catch fire. You could have a stroke or heart attack just by rising from bed, or you could trip and hit your head.

To give a broad epidemiological perspective on risk, in Table 13-1 are given some of the major causes of death for people from the U.S., Canada, and Mexico, by age and sex.

Causes of death are not entirely independent, and "accidents" may not be pure happenstance. Tabachnick (1973) suggested that many accidents involve some component of suicidal motivation. Given that there are many more accidents than official suicides, the number of additional suicides could be quite high. This notion of "subintentioned death" has also been promoted by Shneidman (1968) and Mellinger (1978).

We must live with some risk in order to perform tasks that are essential for achieving major goals in life. To provide some in-depth examples, transportation risks and risks of reproduction are discussed in Insets 13-1 and 13-2.

Most of us avoid excessive risks, but clearly some individuals take more risks than do others. As any insurance company can tell you, young unaffiliated males are the greatest risk-takers. This certainly is unfair as a generalization to individuals, but statistically it is true. Some people have more to lose than do others by rash and desperate actions. This applies in a notorious fashion to the psychology of unaffiliated adult males, even across species. As

TABLE 13-1   *Age-Sex-Specific Death Rates per 100,000 Population Due to Various Causes in Canada (1992), the U.S.A. (1991), and Mexico (1992)*

Age:		0	1–4	5–14	15–24	25–34	35–44	45–54	55–64	65–74	75+
All accidents (including their adverse effects)											
Canada	M	10.3	13.6	10.3	46.0	39.8	34.3	34.3	38.9	51.0	197.0
	F	12.4	9.5	5.3	14.0	9.5	10.5	12.2	16.7	29.5	160.1
U.S.A.	M	26.4	20.1	13.6	62.0	54.0	46.2	41.4	45.7	61.4	172.7
	F	20.2	14.8	6.7	21.0	14.9	13.9	14.6	18.2	31.3	115.7
Mexico	M	49.1	28.0	20.0	68.3	87.7	91.8	100.2	116.7	160.7	365.3
	F	38.9	18.1	8.8	11.3	11.9	14.1	18.7	28.2	60.5	212.9
Motor vehicle accidents											
Canada	M	2.4	3.0	5.4	31.4	19.3	13.8	13.0	12.9	15.5	31.4
	F	3.6	3.1	3.2	11.0	6.0	6.3	6.7	7.0	11.1	15.6
U.S.A.	M	4.2	5.2	6.7	44.8	31.2	21.8	19.5	19.2	22.3	43.3
	F	4.0	4.7	3.9	17.8	10.4	8.4	8.5	9.2	13.1	19.4
Mexico	M	2.2	6.9	7.7	28.4	37.0	35.8	38.7	42.8	50.0	94.1
	F	3.7	4.9	3.5	5.0	5.9	7.1	7.9	12.1	18.8	28.5
Homicide											
Canada	M	2.4	0.9	0.6	3.3	4.4	4.1	3.8	1.9	1.5	1.6
	F	2.1	0.8	0.6	1.5	2.0	2.0	1.4	1.4	0.6	0.2
U.S.A.	M	9.8	3.0	1.8	36.8	28.5	18.1	12.7	8.6	6.1	5.6
	F	8.7	2.6	1.0	6.9	7.5	5.0	3.8	2.6	2.4	3.4
Mexico	M	5.0	2.5	2.8	43.8	62.1	58.8	53.0	48.9	38.8	43.4
	F	3.6	1.9	1.1	4.2	4.5	5.1	5.0	5.0	6.2	10.3
Suicide and self-inflicted injury											
Canada	M	—	—	1.3	24.7	28.8	27.3	24.7	26.2	20.5	27.2
	F	—	—	0.4	6.0	6.2	7.9	9.1	6.6	5.9	4.2
U.S.A.	M	—	—	1.1	21.9	25.0	23.0	23.7	25.3	30.7	56.0
	F	—	—	0.3	3.8	5.4	6.5	7.6	6.5	6.0	5.9
Mexico	M	—	—	0.4	5.7	7.1	6.4	6.7	7.6	9.8	18.0
	F	—	—	0.2	1.3	1.2	1.0	0.7	1.0	1.1	1.1
All infectious and parasitic diseases											
Canada	M	6.9	1.8	0.7	0.8	0.8	2.2	2.6	6.7	18.5	56.0
	F	8.8	0.8	0.7	1.1	0.5	1.1	1.5	5.6	10.2	46.8
U.S.A.	M	20.4	1.9	0.5	0.8	3.3	7.3	9.6	18.8	39.5	123.0
	F	17.3	1.5	0.5	0.8	2.0	2.9	5.3	12.4	27.3	105.0
Mexico	M	233.1	29.4	4.9	4.6	10.4	19.3	36.5	68.0	139.8	451.9
	F	200.6	27.7	4.6	5.1	7.8	12.5	22.1	46.0	87.3	325.4

Source: World Health Statistics Annual—1994, W.H.O. (1995).

Inset 13-1   Risks and conflicts: Cars and planes

Situations of conflicting potential benefits and losses occur for all of us in everyday life. Every time that we travel, we take a small risk of serious injury or death, weighed against the much more likely outcome that we will gain something through our journey.

A small vacation and a change of scenery surely help us to maintain good physical and mental health. By journeying, we can place ourselves in new environments that may be more relaxing, stimulating, comfortable, or recreational.

Nevertheless, there is a small risk that you will not make it home at all, or that you will come home diminished in well-being through injury or loss of a loved one. Much as it is unpleasant to contemplate, the pleasures of a vacation can carry a small risk of intense pain and loss. This is also true for commuting to work and for business travel, which bring economic benefits, and there are many professions such as mining, piloting, and transport-truck driving that carry inherent risks.

The risks almost all of us face through automobiles are well known. Automobile accidents killed 17 out of every 100,000 Americans in 1991 and 11.6 out of every 100,000 Canadians in 1992 (World Health Organization, 1995). The vast majority of victims were males aged 15 to 35. Countless others are maimed every year. There were more than 1.3 million motor vehicle accident victims in Canada alone in 1993, of which 45 percent reported injuries requiring medical attention (Millar, 1995).

During 1996, there were several highly publicized major air catastrophes. Worldwide, there have been hundreds of civilian air crashes during the past 25 years, many of which have killed all passengers and crew (Barlay, 1990; Beaty, 1991; Forman, 1990). Nevertheless, the vast majority of commercial flights reach their destinations without incident, and airplanes transport hundreds of thousands of persons safely to their destinations for every one that they kill.

Cars, planes, trains, boats, bicycles, and even being a pedestrian carry some risk. Add to that the risks of robbery, disease, and financial imprudence and there is a "down-side" to tourism. Most people have some sense of these risks, yet they travel unnecessarily, not because it is critical for their livelihood, but rather just for fun. The news media regularly remind us of grisly accidents, and many of us have direct knowledge of accidents that have harmed our acquaintances.

It is clear that we accept some risk to achieve a greater quality of life. Most of us take precautions to reduce the risk, such as fastening the seatbelt, maintaining good tires, and avoiding drunk driving. Nevertheless, some risk remains, and many people hop in the car for frivolous reasons. Although cases of fear of automobiles are known (e.g., Cornelius, 1996), cars are so ingrained in modern life that most of us are well inured to them. Fear of flying is probably much more common, affecting 20 to 27 percent of passengers on commercial flights (Forman, 1990), not to mention those who refrain from flying. This fact is curious, because objectively, flying on commercial aircraft is much safer than driving in automobiles. Neither cars nor planes are natural, having evolved largely during this last century.

The car was preceded by the buggy and train, and takes us several times our maximum bipedal speed. Jet aircraft travel accomplishes something that is utterly amazing in evolutionary context, allowing intercontinental travel in a matter of hours to a mere terrestrial mammal. The unnatural sensations of high speed takeoff, high altitude, and landing may help explain why planes are feared much more than cars. Perhaps the most interesting question is why cars are feared so little, when objectively driving is one of the greatest dangers in modern life.

---

we discuss in chapters 7 and 9, striving for reproductive success has always been competitive for mammalian males. In each generation, a subset of males is typically excluded from reproduction. It has been frequently suggested that desperado male psychology is associated with high-risk behavior, simply because males without territory, resources, and mates have relatively little to lose (see chapters 7–10).

Should you sell the family farm and use the money to buy lottery tickets? If the lottery offers a prize of $1 million with a $10 ticket and 500,000 tickets are sold, who will probably win? Obviously, this is not a rational bet, as you can calculate for yourself.

Rational risks involve weighing costs and benefits of outcomes without the risk taken versus outcomes with the risk taken. There is clearly a tradeoff between cost and its probability, and the potential benefit and its probability. Rationally, whether one undertakes a risk depends upon a balance of the value of potential benefits, weighted by the associated probability, as opposed to the value of the potential costs, also weighted by the associated probability.

Inset 13-2 Risks of childbearing

Conceiving and bearing a healthy child is the most essential activity for genetic or reproductive success. However, there are many risks associated with each phase of the process. Sexual activity, pregnancy, labor and delivery, and child care, are all to some extent "risky" endeavors.

Sexual activity involves the obvious risk of contracting diseases, many of which can lead to infertility or even death. The life-threatening risks of HIV are now well known. There are also diverse diseases like hepatitis, chlamydia, gonorrhea, and many viruses that can be transmitted by intimate contact. Many venereal diseases may pose little risk of death, but there is probably a substantial risk of infertility from infections and scar tissue resulting from sexual activity, although precise statistics are not kept.

Pregnancy, labor, and delivery also have associated risks. Maternal death rates in 1991 were 2.9 and 8.2 per 100,000 live births in Canada and the U.S., respectively (United Nations, 1995). These rates are among the lowest in the world, and can be compared with rates like 51 per 100,000 for Mexico or 152 per 100,000 for Paraguay. The most common causes of maternal death are complications of the puerperium, accounting for 91 deaths in the U.S. and 10 in Canada in 1992 (World Health Organization, 1995), followed by hemorrhage of childbirth (36 and 3 deaths in the U.S. and Canada, respectively) abortion (54 and 1 deaths, respectively), toxemia of pregnancy (65 and 2 deaths, respectively), and other obstetric causes (69 and 3 deaths, respectively). Again, although the risk of death is quite low, many of the complications of pregnancy and childbirth result in subsequent infertility.

Assuming that the mother successfully conceives and herself survives pregnancy and childbirth, there is still a risk that her investment can be lost. The pregnancy rate in Canada in 1992 was 77.4 per 1,000 women aged 15 to 44, but the live birth rate was only 58.7 per 1,000 (Wadhera & Millar, 1996). Although most of the losses were due to deliberate abortions, 4.6 percent of pregnancies ended in miscarriages and stillbirths. These statistics include only hospitalized miscarriages and therefore probably significantly underestimate the loss rate. Worldwide, late fetal deaths (28 weeks or more gestation) have been tabulated by the United Nations (1995). The number of fetal deaths per 1,000 live births ranges from 2.8 in Germany and 3.9 in Canada in 1990, to 4.7 in the U.S. in 1989 and on to 10.7 in Brazil in 1990 and 19.4 in Ecuador in 1989.

A liveborn infant still runs risks of not surviving. Infants under age 1 had a death rate in Canada in 1993 of 6.85 per 1,000 live births for males and 5.57 per 1,000 for females (Wilkins, 1995). Most deaths (72 percent in 1993) were due to perinatal causes, such as prematurity, or to congenital anomalies, such a structural defects of the heart (Wilkins, 1995). Infant death rates in the U.S. in 1991 were 10 per 1,000 live births for males and 7.8 for females. These rates can be compared with rates of 21 and 16.4 for male and female infants in Mexico in 1992, 43.8 and 34.3 in Brazil in 1990, and an estimated 112.2 and 102.8 in Pakistan in 1988 (United Nations, 1995).

Chapter 14

SELF, FAMILY, AND COMMUNITY

In this chapter, we examine some of the highest-order emotions that people have. These emotions are rare in other species, and they certainly do not occur equally among all individual people. These emotions illustrate our highly evolved and complex social nature, and our uniqueness as a species.

ORIGINS OF HIGH-ORDER SOCIAL EMOTIONS

Evolution of Selfishness and Altruism

We must first look at evolution to understand the origins of selfishness, altruism, and social emotions. Natural selection operates through differential reproduction of individuals. However, kinship, reciprocity, and social structure impose evolutionary restraints on pure selfishness. Of course, modern culture also impinges on individual behavior, such that motivation and emotion are socialized during development.

As discussed in chapter 2, selfish behavior involves advancement of one's own prospects of survival and reproduction. This is very often in conflict with the interests of others, both between and within species (see also chapter 9). Selfish behavior can be understood through basic Darwinian processes, as individuals struggle to survive and reproduce in competition with others. Survival-oriented motivation (hunger, thirst, pain, fear) is easily explained by natural selection. So is a drive to reproduce.

Natural selection also has provided a basis for more complex social behavior and even altruism. Recall the modern notion, from general biology, that the ultimate motivator of behavior is *inclusive fitness maximization*. Individuals of any species have been fashioned by natural selection to strive to maximize the representation of their genes in future generations. Kin share interests in replication of common genetic material. This mutual genetic interest sets the stage for the evolutionary process of kin selection, which leads to nepotistic behavior, the preferential treatment of close kin.

Parental behavior is obviously in the reproductive interest of the parents, because children represent the genetic future of the parents. Family-oriented helping behavior can also be seen as serving genetic interests when shown, for example, by grandparents, aunts, and uncles. Nepotism occurs in all human cultures and also in many other social species. Altruistic behavior benefiting relatives is no mystery, because the benefits fall on copies of the same genes that are found in the altruist (Hamilton, 1964). Gene sharing among relatives means that direct reproduction is not the only way to bring one's genes into future generations. Individuals can also replicate their genes by helping their relatives reproduce.

Reproduction and kinship are the foundation of social behavior. As we discuss in chapter 11, maternal-infant bonding is the most reliable bond, an ancient mammalian feature that is necessary for survival. This is enhanced via biparental care and male-female bonding, and by family bonds among kin. Coefficients of relatedness (see chapter 2) of one-half prevail among nuclear family members, between parent and child and among siblings. Coefficients of relatedness of one-quarter (grandparent-child, aunt/uncle-niece/nephew) and one-eighth (first cousins, etc.) prevail in extended family ties that are meaningful in all cultures.

Trivers (1971, p. 35) defined true altruism as "behavior that benefits another organism, not closely related, while being apparently detrimental to the organism performing the behavior, with benefit and detriment being determined in terms of contribution to inclusive fitness." This concept does not usually include sacrifices of parenting and kin-directed favors. Trivers suggested that evolution via *reciprocal altruism* could explain helping in crisis, such as saving a drowning stranger. Reciprocal altruism can also explain alliances among non-kin. It can be mutually beneficial if non-kin show favors to one another, because of the synergy in their alliance. Both parties can achieve increased inclusive fitness. In theory, genetic attributes that produce a risk of self-sacrifice while benefiting non-kin, can develop. That is true provided that there is a reasonable expectation of reciprocity, and if the benefit to the recipient strongly outweighs the risk to the altruist. The stranger who saves a drowning man takes some risk of drowning himself, but potentially causes an enormous benefit to the recipient. Trivers suggested that this principle could operate with kin and non-kin. Indeed, it could summate with kin-ship to produce altruism.

Nevertheless, selfish motivation has strong roots in competition for individual reproductive success. Even a brother or sister has only half of one's genetic makeup, relative to the variable genetic features of the population. Abundant biological evidence shows interindividual competition as ongoing in the evolution of all species. This is moderated by kinship, reciprocity, and social alliance. In humans, cultural factors also play a strong role, as explored below.

Ancestral and Modern Emotional Ecology

Ours is a highly social species, like other primates and many carnivores and herbivores, where group living evolved long ago because of interdependencies among individuals. Humans normally live in a family and community setting.

We must consider evolutionary and historical conditions of expression to understand the adaptiveness of our emotions. Over the majority of human evolution, we existed in small hunting-gathering societies consisting largely of kin, perhaps 50–200 familiar individuals linked by genetics, marriage, and alliance. A tendency to cooperate and help other people in the community, as a personality trait, makes evolutionary sense, simply because most people with whom one had contact were probably kin. At the same time, out-group members were often threatening, as shown by the long history of human warfare (see chapter 9).

Only recently have we embarked on a course of increasing social density in conjunction with technological and cultural change (see Alexander, 1979; Flannery, 1972). During most of our evolution, we lived in low density. Agricultural practices, especially during the past 10,000 years, allowed us to settle in larger villages, and our capacity to use tools facilitated this. Cooperative role specialization has permitted more complex social organization and effective exploitation of resources for community development. Civilization, within the past 5,000 years, has brought high-density living, which puts people in greater contact with one another, often as strangers.

We are in a situation of substantial evolutionary lag (see chapter 2, Inset 2-1), where genetic change is behind cultural change. In large cities, we each interact with many unfamiliar persons, and relations to family may have changed. People are challenged in many ways by rapid social and technological change. These changes have brought many benefits in standards of living to many people; these benefits are well known and too numerous to enumerate. On the other hand, modern circumstances have brought new forms of coping and emotional problems to some people.

Both social isolation and crowding can be stressful. Social isolation can have debilitating effects. When people must live and work alone for long periods in extreme environments, stress and depression are common (Palinkas & Browner, 1995; Rothblum, 1990). Lonely and socially isolated individuals, living in modern communities but with inadequate social contacts, are highly susceptible to psychological depression and suicide (see chapter 10). This is especially so for those rejected by family, peers, and/or the opposite sex. Social isolation during early development, and lack of critical bonds such as that to mother generally have devastating effects on development and adaptation (see chapter 11). Rejections from peers and abusive treatment by family impede children's development (see Wicks-Nelson & Israel, 1997). Social contact is not unequivocally rewarding, and crowding is also certainly stressful. When one is trying to concentrate on a demanding task, social contact can be a distraction. In crowded circumstances, other people can impede personal progress. Aggression may relate to social density, resource shortage, and competition (see chapters 2, 8, 9, and 10). It is possible to be "lonely in the crowd," if surrounded by uncaring and unfamiliar faces.

Civilization, Law, Religion, and Culture

Progressively larger cultures have evolved over the past 10,000 years. Modern social and technological environments can limit the adaptiveness of some of our primitive impulses, and cognitive (cerebral cortical) control may often produce superior adjustment as discussed in chapter 13.

Beginning with parental guidance during development, and enhanced by schooling and various public institutions, individuals are acculturated, encouraged to channel drives and emotions in socially acceptable manners. We actively teach values to developing children, through all of the methods of learning described in chapter 12. Culture thus bears upon more primitive impulses to socialize children, such that they behave within guidelines deemed appropriate by family and society.

Legal and ethical systems involve explicit prescriptions bearing upon motivational and emotional inclinations. Sociocultural influences tend to inhibit motives and emotions that are not in the broader culture's interests, for example by outlawing violence, unbridled sexuality, and self-serving behavior that harms the community. Societies reward those who behave toward group interests and punish those who behave contrary to group interests. It may therefore be no mystery that legal and ethical systems, the conscious teaching and encouragement of cooperativeness, have developed historically in conjunction with civilization. High-density living requires intragroup cohesiveness and suppression of selfish actions that are contrary to the group's interest. Political and social order involve teaching rules to developing children, and enforcing these rules in both adults and children through sanctions.

There is thus a strong cultural component to appropriate social motivation. Social control over behavior is profound, written in our emotions as described at several points in this book. Individuals are extensively socialized and acculturated; extrinsic social control guides intrinsic impulses. Social experience modifies human motivation and emotion. The communities in which we live have explicit and implicit rules about appropriate behavior. Of course, not all cultures teach children the same values. For example, the values taught to the Hitler youth in Nazi Germany differ radically from those that most of us would want to encourage in modern, enlightened cultures.

Thus, there are both biological and cultural factors favoring something other than purely selfish behavior. Cooperativeness with family and proximate community has ancient evolutionary roots. Cultural mechanisms reinforce tendencies toward unselfish behavior, through socialization and explicit cultural codes of conduct enforced by social sanctions.

EXPRESSIONS OF HIGH-ORDER SOCIAL EMOTIONS

Contagion and Vicarious Emotion

We often do things simply because others around us are doing them. This is certainly true of some very simple stereotyped forms of behavior, like yawning (Baenninger, 1987; Provine, 1986) and laughing (Askenasy, 1987; Weisfeld, 1993). As discussed in chapter 12, a strong tendency to imitate pervades human behavior, affecting simple emotions and also many complex responses. Indeed, imitation is one of the foundations of human learning and culture.

Very often, people react emotionally when they observe other people's emotional experiences. This point is made in several chapters, where we discuss facial and bodily expression. Emotions are often much more than just personal subjective experiences. They occur within a social network, and they modulate the behavior of others. The emotions experienced by an observer may be the same or different from those seen in a model. This phenomenon is readily measurable in changes in autonomic activity, like heart rate, or levels of hormones like cortisol, which change dynamically when people watch other people. Indeed, we can see it when people watch films, especially those with emotional content. Autonomic and neuroendocrine measures, as well as subjective reports, indicate that filmed dramatic plots are emotion-inducing (Hubert & de Jong-Meyer, 1991; Wittling & Pflüger, 1990). Of course, this fact should not surprise anyone who watches television or movies.

Empathy

The basis of empathy may be the accurate detection of emotional information being transmitted by another person (Levenson & Ruef, 1992). Empathy differs from sympathy, which is compassion or concern stimulated by the distress of another. Empathy, as used by many people, involves identification with the other person, and awareness of one's own feelings after the identification.

Although we actively train children to understand others, empathy may have a partial biological basis. Human infants show imitation of different emotional facial expressions (Field et al., 1982, see Figure 3-3). A basis for empathic responses may exist in other primates. Infant rhesus monkeys deprived of normal social contact from birth can distinguish among facial expressions of conspecifics shown on slides, although this ability fades by about four months of age without other social input (Sackett, 1966). Experiments show that chimpanzees can understand role-reversals in human-chimpanzee pairs, but that rhesus monkeys cannot (Povinelli et al., 1992a; 1992b). In each pair, only one partner could see which of several trays contained a food reward, and the other could pull handles to get the reward, but could not see the contents. The roles were then reversed. Three of four chimpanzees immediately understood their new social roles, and responded accordingly, however none of the rhesus monkeys did. Also, although it is not definitive scientifically, there are case studies from primate behavior in the literature (see review by O'Connell, 1995), showing numerous examples of empathy across a wide range of circumstances, including rescuing an individual from a dangerous social or physical situation.

Parenting behavior may modulate the development of empathy. One experiment with human infants (Boccia & Campos, 1989) was designed to determine whether a mother's reaction to a stranger influenced the child's reaction, at an age of about eight months, when most infants would normally show fear of strangers. Half the mothers were instructed to approach the stranger with a broad smile and cheery vocalizations, the other half with a frown and a worried greeting. The infant's heart rate, gaze, crying, and smiling were all monitored. The mother's expressive pose was found to significantly affect the infant's expressive behaviors, with infants showing much more smiling and motor activity when mothers posed joy, although heart rate was not significantly different.

Observations of children in nursery or daycare settings suggest that there is parental guidance in empathy development. In one study (Kestenbaum et al., 1989), children who exhibited more empathic responses to distressed peers tended to have more "secure attachment" relationships with their mothers. In another study, mothers' reactions to conflict and distress situations were compared to the reactions of their children, with complex and inconclusive results

(Miller et al., 1989). When mothers responded with low-level arousal and prosocial suggestions, their children showed sad facial reactions to distress in peers. When mothers responded with high-level arousal, it tended to be more negatively related to distressed facial reactions. Negative control practices by mothers (spanking, pulling) hindered empathic responding. Generally, most observational studies report that girls show empathic responses more than do boys, and that this gender difference increases with age, which may be influenced by societal expectations, and learned inhibition of responses by boys.

Studies of adults show that observing another person in distress can produce signs of autonomic nervous system arousal. In one study (Eisenberg et al., 1989), married subjects watched videotaped sessions of naturalistic marital interactions. They continuously rated the affect of themselves and a target in the video. Several physiological measures were also compared between the subject and target. The greater the physiological linkage between subject and target, the greater the accuracy of the subject's rating of the target's negative affect. Skin conductance and pulse were the measures most highly correlated with accuracy of affect rating. For ratings of positive affect, women were more accurate than men.

Brothers (1989) summarized medical syndromes which include defects in interpersonal emotional communication. Patients with temporoparietal cortical lesions show an inability to understand emotion in voice quality. Patients with right-hemisphere lesions in areas connected with limbic structures reported that they felt emotions but could not convey them. Infantile autism is a syndrome partly defined by a defect in empathy, but its physiological substrate is not fully known (see also Wicks-Nelson & Israel, 1997). The amygdala may play a role in social emotional communication, including empathy (see chapters 6 and 9). For example, free-range monkeys with bilateral lesions of the amygdala could perform most survival-oriented tasks but did not respond appropriately to approaches from other animals, and eventually isolated themselves (Kling, 1972).

Approval and Contempt

We influence and control one another through facial expressions and gestures, sometimes accompanied by explicit verbal information, providing feedback to other people about their behavior. We discuss the particulars of this topic from other perspectives in chapters 9 to 12.

Approval or praise, as almost anyone knows, can be shown by smiling, cheering, clapping of hands, other vocalizations, and laudatory verbal expressions. This can have a powerful reinforcing effect on the person being praised, evoking pride, pleasure, euphoria, and tangible social benefits.

Disapproval is also shown in well-known fashions. Darwin (1872, p. 267) suggested that humans display contempt as follows: "The nose may be slightly turned up, which apparently follows from the turning up of the upper lip; or the movement may be abbreviated into the mere wrinkling of the nose." Darwin (1872, p. 270) said that disgust is stronger, and consists mainly of "movements around the mouth . . . generally accompanied by a frown."

Embarrassment

Embarrassment is a complex social emotion, quite common but nevertheless poorly understood compared to other emotions. It is often associated with other self-conscious emotions such as anxiety, shame, and guilt. By most definitions, embarrassment involves interpersonal exposure; it is only possible to be embarrassed in the presence of others (Edelman, 1981). Body language displays this emotion. People who are embarrassed tend to cast their eyes downward and reduce eye contact with other people. They may put their hands in front of their faces. They may show increased body motion, speech disturbances, and smiling. Blushing may or may not be present.

While simple emotions such as happiness and sadness appear during the first year of life, more complex emotions like embarrassment do not emerge until the middle of the second year, and then increase with age during early childhood. Lewis and colleagues (1991) found embarrassment (measured as a combination of smiling, gaze aversion, and nervous body movements) in 52 percent of two-year-olds and 82 percent of three-year-olds. It was elicited in a number of situations from observing themselves in a mirror to being asked by the experimenter to dance. At three years of age, there were no differences in frequency of embarrassment between boys and girls. In a study with children aged 5 to 13, Bennett (1989) found increasing reports of embarrassment with age, and that 5- and 8-year-olds reported more embarrassment at the prospect of an active (ridiculing) audience than a passive audience, whereas 11- and 13-year-olds were equally embarrassed by any audience. Bennett attributed this to increasing self-criticism with age.

In one of the few studies of physiological responses during embarrassment, Buck and colleagues (1970) induced embarrassment by threatening subjects with the prospect of sucking an infantile oral object, then measured skin conductance and heart rate. There was some increase in skin conductance, but less than in subjects threatened with electrical shocks. Heart rate in embarrassed subjects decreased.

Fear of embarrassment can have the obvious effect of inhibiting behavior that is potentially embarrassing. This can range from the extreme of avoiding any social interaction, to the more subtle. For example, Edelman and colleagues (1984) set up contrived situations where overloaded females dropped a package, and looked at helping (retrieval) behavior of subjects. When the dropped package was potentially embarrassing (a box of tampons), significantly fewer subjects retrieved the package than when the package was neutral (tea). An individual who exhibits embarrassment has an effect on the behavior of others who are present. For example, subjects who were forced to inform a second person that the person had performed poorly on a task, reported least discomfort when the person reacted with embarrassment (gaze aversion and fidgeting) (Edelman, 1982).

Some research indicates that there may be some crosscultural differences in the occurrence of and reaction to embarrassment. Blushing, gaze aversion, and smiling were most frequently reported by subjects from the United Kingdom, and least frequently by subjects from southern Europe (Edelman et al., 1989). However, these results are based only on self-reports from five European countries. Clearly, much more research is needed.

Blushing has been studied since Darwin (1872), who considered it to be uniquely human, but heritable among humans, and associated with embarrassment. He was reluctant to include a function for blushing, although it has been suggested to serve as a public social warning signal that the rules of the group have been violated. Leary and Meadows (1991) considered blushing to serve to diffuse possible negative reactions through appeasement. There has been little work on the physiological changes which accompany blushing. In one study, cheek and ear coloration (measured photoplethysmographically), cheek temperature, and finger skin conductance were measured in subjects before and after viewing videos of themselves singing (Shearn et al., 1990). All measures were higher during the video than before or after.

Pride, Guilt, and Shame

We have other insufficiently studied emotions that appear in response to social appreciation or condemnation. Emotions such as shame, guilt, and pride, like embarrassment, are considered to be secondary or self-conscious emotions, developing later than more primary emotions such as fear, happiness, or sadness. They depend highly on social interaction, especially with family members. It is probable that these emotions have evolved only in the most highly social species, perhaps only humans (possibly something similar exists in some higher primates and carnivores). Their function may be to help establish and communicate hierarchical status, with gestures of shame and embarrassment communicating appeasement.

Guilt has been argued by many psychoanalysts to be an exclusively self-imposed emotion in response to infractions of internalized standards. However, more recent empirical studies show that in fact it occurs almost exclusively in response to the infliction of harm, loss, or distress to a significant partner. Thus, it serves to strengthen social bonds by enforcing communal norms, by allowing even subordinate members of a family or group some influence, and by distributing or sharing emotional distress (Baumeister, 1994).

One study (Keltner & Buswell, 1996) had subjects categorize events into different emotional categories. In general, embarrassment was associated with transgressions of conventions in public interactions, shame was caused by failure to meet important personal or family standards, and guilt was caused by actions that harm others or violate duties. Observers shown pictures of facial expressions of these emotions were able to accurately identify embarrassment and shame, but guilt less reliably. In another study (Miller & Tangney, 1994), subjects sorted descriptive statements into shame or embarrassment categories. Incidents considered embarrassing were relatively trivial, usually involving surprise, and produced humor, smiles, and jokes. Shame was a more intense emotion, resulting when events revealed one's deep-seated flaws, and produced responses of disgust, anger, and apologies.

Extreme shame is a powerful emotion that can lead to dramatic changes in motivation. Indeed, looking at studies from numerous cultures, extreme shame over some social transgression is one of the most common predictors of suicide (deCatanzaro, 1981a).

These secondary emotions may be seen in young children (see Figures 14-1 and 14-2). One study (Graham et al., 1984) examined development of several emotions in children, including pity, anger, and guilt. Children as young as six perceived anger as resulting from controllable events, and pity from uncontrollable events. Guilt was reported by the youngest children in response to both deliberate and accidental events when the outcome was "wrong", whereas older children only reported guilt when their actions were deliberate, thus implying a development of the concept of responsibility for actions. In another study (Lewis et al., 1992), 3-year-olds were presented with easy and difficult tasks. Independent observers rated success or failure, and the child's reaction. Significantly more shame was shown (as measured by facial expression and posture) when subjects failed easy tasks than when they failed difficult tasks, and more pride was shown when they succeeded on difficult tasks.

Emotions such as pride, shame, guilt, and embarrassment present interesting evolutionary issues that have not been thoroughly investigated. Their self-revealing nature and early emergence in the context of family may suggest a role of kin selection.

"Psychopathy"

We are certainly not all empathetic, or susceptible to finer emotions of social responsibility. Some individuals, often criminals, exhibit persistent and extreme antisocial behavior. This condition is related to genetic, other familial, and environmental factors.

A defining feature of psychopathy is abnormal or deficient emotional responding. Diagnostic criteria include absence of nervousness, lack of empathy

Figure 14-1   A child first walking, being assisted and cheered by parents.

or remorse, egocentricity, and a general poverty in major affective reactions. Another defining characteristic is extreme impulsiveness, or an inability to delay gratification of psychological and biological needs, no matter what the consequences to oneself or others (Hare, 1970). Psychopaths may show impaired emotional responsiveness, as measured by startle-elicited eyeblinks during presentation of slides depicting pleasant, neutral, and unpleasant scenes. Nonpsychopathic students showed greatest startle responses during unpleasant slides and least during pleasant slides, but this effect was absent in psychopathic convicted sexual offenders (Patrick et al., 1993). Studies employing measures of cardiac, electrodermal, and facial muscle responses to imagery of emotional situations show that psychopathic prisoners show less response to emotional images than do more empathetic prisoners (Patrick et al., 1994).

Some evidence suggests that serotonergic dysfunction accounts for many of the symptoms of psychopathy (Lewis, 1991). Psychopaths tend to show little anticipatory fear and do poorly at passive-avoidance learning. Animal studies show that decreases in CNS serotonergic activity impair passive-avoidance

Figure 14-2 A baby first standing, being cheered by parents, and clapping for himself.

learning. Also, some adults with volatile, deviant behavior have been shown to have low levels of specific serotonin metabolites in cerebrospinal fluid (Virkkunen, 1988). Brain-wave activity of some psychopaths has been described as similar to that generally found in children, leading to the hypothesis that cortical immaturity or underarousal relate to psychopathy (Hare, 1970). Some research suggests that many psychopaths are unable to develop conditioned fear responses, and do not learn responses motivated by fear.

PERSONALITY AND CIRCUMSTANCE

It would be a mistake to think that the same rules of motivation and emotion apply equally to all individuals. People differ in their temperaments, emotional qualities, and motives. It is surely the case that evolution has promoted polymorphism in human personality structure, and that enormous variance in experience throughout the life span profoundly enriches that diversity.

There are vast differences among individuals in personality characteristics, many of which are related to motivational and emotional traits. Evidence suggests that these differences have a partial basis in genetics. Different individuals respond idiosyncratically to the same sorts of life-history events. For example, some people react with depression to minor events while others soldier on with a cheerful disposition despite major stressors. High familial concordance is found for diverse affective traits (see Lester, 1986; Nurnberger & Gershon, 1981; Rice et al., 1987; Rosenthal, 1970). Similarly, there is evidence for some degree of familial concordance for traits such as anxiety (Slater & Shields, 1969) and schizophrenia (Gottesman & Shields, 1982; Kety, 1976; 1987), although these conditions are complex and experience is certainly important. Some children are stressed by social contact, socially shy and reserved, while others are much more outgoing (Schmidt et al., 1997). Extraversion versus introversion, a characteristic related to sociability, impulsiveness, and liveliness may have a genetic substrate (Henderson, 1982; Lykken, 1982; Pederson et al., 1988). In fact, evidence suggests that diverse personality factors have a basis in individual genetics (Tellegen et al., 1988).

The development of drives and emotions is a complex interaction of genetics and experience. We discuss in previous chapters (especially 8–13) how experiences alter drives and emotions, including neuroendocrine changes, conditioning, and social learning, that adapt motivation and emotion to the environment. It is fair to conclude that, among many of the major drives and emotions discussed in this book, there are substantial individual differences in the constellation and quality of motivation and emotion.

REFERENCES

Abbott, D.H. (1984). Behavioral and physiological suppression of fertility in subordinate marmoset monkeys. *American Journal of Primatology, 6,* 169–186.

Abramson, L.Y., Seligman, M.E.P., & Teasdale, J.D. (1978). Learned helplessness in humans: Critique and reformulation. *Journal of Abnormal Psychology, 87,* 49–74.

Adebonojo, F.O. (1975). Studies on human adipose cells in culture: Relation of cell size and multiplication to donor age. *Yale Journal of Biology & Medicine, 48,* 9–16.

Adelman, S., Taylor, C.R., & Heglund, N.C. (1975). Sweating on paws and palms: What is its function? *American Journal of Physiology, 229,* 1400–1402.

Adler, N., & Toner, J.P., Jr. (1986). The effects of copulatory behavior on sperm transport and fertility in rats. *Annals of the New York Academy of Sciences, 474,* 21–32.

Adolph, E.F. (1939). Measurement of water drinking in dogs. *American Journal of Physiology, 125,* 75–86.

Adolph, E.F. (1950). Thirst and its inhibition in the stomach. *American Journal of Physiology, 161,* 374–386.

Adolphs, R., Tranel, D., Damasio, H., & Damasio, A. (1994). Impaired recognition of emotion in facial expressions following bilateral damage to the human amygdala. *Nature, 372,* 669–672.

Ainsworth, M.D.S. (1972). Attachment and dependency: A comparison. In J.L. Gewirtz (Ed.), *Attachment and Dependency* (pp. 97–137). Washington, D.C.: Winston.

Ainsworth, M.D.S., Blehar, M., Waters, E., & Wall, S. (1978). *Patterns of Attachment.* Hillsdale, NJ: Lawrence Erlbaum Associates.

Albert, D.J., Walsh, M.L., & Jonik, R.H. (1993). Aggression in humans: What is its biological foundation? *Neuroscience and Biobehavioral Reviews, 17,* 405–425.

Aldis, O. (1975). *Play Fighting.* New York: Academic Press.

Aldrich, C.A., Norval, M.A., Knop, C., & Venegas, F. (1946). The crying of newborn babies. IV. A follow–up study after additional nursing care had been provided. *Journal of Pediatrics, 27,* 89–96.

Alexander, B.K., Beyerstein, B.L., Hadaway, P.F., & Coambs, R.B. (1981). Effects of early and later colony housing on oral ingestion of morphine in rats. *Pharmacology Biochemistry and Behavior, 15,* 571–576.

Alexander, R.D. (1979). *Darwinism and Human Affairs.* Seattle: University of Washington Press.

Allen L.S., & Gorski, R.A. (1992). Sexual orientation and the size of the anterior commissure in the human brain. *Proceedings of the National Academy of Sciences USA, 89,* 7199–7202.

Altmann, S.A. (1968). Primates. In T.A. Seboek (Ed.), *Animal Communication: Techniques of Study and Results of Research* (pp. 466–522). Bloomington: Indiana University Press.

Amsel, A. (1992). *Frustration Theory.* Cambridge, U.K.: Cambridge University Press.

Anand, B.K., & Brobeck, J.R. (1951). Localization of a "feeding center" in the hypothalamus of the rat. *Proceedings of the Society for Experimental Biology and Medicine, 77,* 323–324.

Anand, B.K, Chinna, G.S., & Singh, B. (1962). Effect of glucose on the activity of hypothalamic "feeding centers." *Science, 138,* 597–598.

Anderson, K.J. (1990). Arousal and the inverted-U hypothesis: A critique of Neiss' "Reconceptualizing arousal." *Psychological Bulletin, 107,* 96–100.

Andersson, B. (1955). Observations on the water and electrolyte metabolism in the goat. *Acta Physiologica Scandinavica, 33,* 50–65.

Andersson, B., & Larsson, B. (1961). Influence of local temperature changes in the preoptic area and rostral hypothalamus on the regulation of food and water intake. *Acta Physiologica Scandinavica, 52,* 75–89.

Andrew, R.J. (1963). The origin and evolution of the calls and facial expressions of the primates. *Behaviour, 20,* 1–109.

Andrew, R.J. (1965). The origins of facial expressions. *Scientific American, 213,* 88–94.

Anisman, H. (1975). Time-dependent variations in aversively motivated behaviors: Nonassociative effects of cholinergic and catecholaminergic activity. *Psychological Review, 82,* 359–385.

Anisman, H., & Zacharko, R.M. (1982). Depression: The predisposing influence of stress. *The Behavioral and Brain Sciences, 5,* 89–137.

Appel, M.A., Holroyd, K.A., & Gorkin, L. (1983). Anger and the etiology and progression of physical illness. In L. Temoshok, C. Van Dyke, & L.S. Zegans (Eds.), *Emotions in Health and Illness: Theoretical and Research Foundations* (pp. 73–87). New York: Grune & Stratton.

Arancibia, S., Rage, F., Astier, H., & Tapia-Arancibia, L. (1996). Neuroendocrine and autonomous mechanisms underlying thermoregulation in cold environment. *Neuroendocrinology, 64,* 257–267.

Arango, V., Underwood, M.D., Gubbi, A.V., & Mann, J.J. (1995). Localized alterations in pre- and postsynaptic serotonin binding sites in the ventrolateral prefrontal cortex of suicide victims. *Brain Research, 688,* 121–133.

Archer, J. (1979). Behavioural aspects of fear. In W. Sluckin (Ed.), *Fear in Animals and Man* (pp. 56–85). New York: Van Nostrand Reinhold.

Archer, J. (1991). The influence of testosterone on human aggression. *British Journal of Psychology, 82,* 1–28.

Argyle, M., & Cook, M. (1976). *Gaze and Mutual Gaze*. Cambridge: Cambridge University Press.

Askenasy, J.J.M. (1987). The functions and dysfunctions of laughter. *Journal of General Psychology, 114*, 317–334.

Astrom, C., Lunde, I., Ortmann, J., Boys, G., & Trojaborg, W. (1989). Sleep disturbances in torture survivors. *Acta Neurologica Scandinavica, 79*, 150–154.

Ax, A.F. (1953). The physiological differentiation of fear and anger in humans. *Psychosomatic Medicine, 15*, 433–442.

Baenninger, R. (1987). Some comparative aspects of yawning in *Betta splendens, Homo sapiens, Panthera leo*, and *Papio sphinx*. *Journal of Comparative Psychology, 101*, 349–354.

Bailey, J.M., & Pillard, R.C. (1991). A genetic study of male sexual orientation. *Archives of General Psychiatry, 48*, 1089–1096.

Bailey, J.P., Thakray, R.I., Pearl, J., & Parish, T.S. (1976). Boredom and arousal: Comparison of tasks differing in visual complexity. *Perceptual and Motor Skills, 43*, 141–142.

Bandura, A. (1969). *Principles of Behavior Modification*. New York: Holt, Rinehart and Winston.

Bandura, A. (1977). *Social Learning Theory*. Englewood Cliffs, NJ: Prentice Hall.

Banich, M.T. (1997). *Neuropsychology: The Neural Basis of Mental Function*. Boston: Houghton-Mifflin.

Barash, D.P. (1982). *Sociobiology and Behavior* (2nd ed.). New York: Elsevier.

Barkow, J.H., Cosmides, L., & Tooby, J. (1992). *The Adapted Mind: Evolutionary Psychology and the Generation of Culture*. New York: Oxford.

Barlay, S. (1990). *The Final Call*. London: Sinclair-Stevenson.

Barlow, D.H., & Abel, G.G. (1981). Recent developments in assessment and treatment of paraphilias and gender-identity disorders. In W.E. Craighead, A.E. Kazdin, & M.J. Mahoney (Eds.), *Behavior Modification: Principles, Issues, and Applications* (2nd ed., pp. 337–356). Boston: Houghton Mifflin Company.

Barlow, G.W. (1968). Ethological units of behavior. In D. Ingle (Ed.), *The Central Nervous System and Fish Behavior* (pp. 217–232). Chicago: University of Chicago Press.

Barmack, J.E. (1937). Boredom and other factors in the physiology of mental efforts: An exploratory study. *Archives of Psychology, 218*, 6–81.

Bates, M.S., Edwards, W.T., & Anderson, K.O. (1993). Ethnocultural influences on variation in chronic pain perception. *Pain, 52*, 101–112.

Baumeister, R.F., Stillwell, A.M., & Heatherton, T.F. (1994). Guilt: An interpersonal approach. *Psychological Bulletin, 115*, 243–267.

Beach, F.A. (1955). The descent of instinct. *Psychological Review, 62*, 401–410.

Beach, F.A. (1970). Coital behavior in dogs. VI. Long-term effects of castration upon mating in the male. *Journal of Comparative and Physiological Psychology Monograph, 70*(3.2).

Bear, M.F., Connors, B.W., & Paradiso, M.A. (1996). *Neuroscience: Exploring the Brain*. Baltimore: Williams & Wilkins.

Beaty, D. (1991). *The Naked Pilot: The Human Factor in Aircraft Accidents*. London: Methuen.

Bechara, A., Tranel, D., Damasio, H., Adolphs, R., Rockland, C., & Damasio, A.R. (1995). Double dissociation of conditioning and declarative knowledge relative to the amygdala and hippocampus in humans. *Science, 269*, 1115–1118.

Beck, A.T. (1967). *Depression: Clinical, Experimental and Theoretical Aspects*. New York: Harper & Row.

Beck, A.T., Kovacs, M., & Weissman, A. (1975). Hopelessness and suicidal behavior: An overview. *Journal of the American Medical Association, 234*, 1146–1149.

Bee, H. (1981). *The Developing Child*. (3rd ed.). New York: Harper & Row.

Beecher, H.K. (1956). Relationship of significance of wound to pain experienced. *Journal of American Medical Association, 161*, 1609–1613.

Bem, D.J. (1996). Exotic becomes erotic: A developmental theory of sexual orientation. *Psychological Review, 103*, 320–335.

Bennett, M. (1989). Children's self-attribution of embarrassment. *British Journal of Developmental Psychology, 7*, 207–217.

Benton, D., Goldsmith, J.F., Gamal-El-Din, L., Brain, P.F., & Hucklebridge, F.H. (1978). Adrenal activity in isolated mice and mice of different social status. *Physiology and Behavior, 20*, 459–464.

Benton, D. & Wastell, V. (1986). Effects of androstenol on human sexual arousal. *Biological Psychology, 22*, 141–147.

Bergson, H. (1911). *Laughter: An Essay on the Meaning of the Comic*. New York: Macmillan.

Berk, L.S., Tan, S.A., Fry, W.F., Napier, B.J., Lee, J.W., Hubbard, R.W., Lewis, J.E., & Eby, W.C. (1989). Neuroendocrine and stress hormone changes during mirthful laughter. *American Journal of Medical Sciences, 298*, 390–396.

Berkman, L.F. (1984). Assessing the physical health effects of social networks and social support. *Annual Review of Public Health, 5*, 413–432.

Berkman, L.F., & Syme, L. (1979). Social networks, host resistance, and mortality: A nine-year follow-up study of Alameda County residents. *American Journal of Epidemiology, 109*, 186–204.

Berkowitz, L. (1974). Some determinants of impulsive aggression: Role of mediated associations with reinforcements for aggression. *Psychological Review, 81*, 165–176.

Berkun, M.M., Kessen, M.L., & Miller, N.E. (1952). Hunger-reducing effects of food by stomach fistula versus food by mouth measured by a consummatory response. *Journal of Comparative and Physiological Psychology, 45*, 550–554.

Berlyne, D.E. (1967). Arousal and reinforcement. In D. Levine (Ed.), *Nebraska Symposium on Motivation* (pp. 1–110). Lincoln: University of Nebraska Press.

Bernardis, L.L., & Bellinger, L.L. (1996). The lateral hypothalamic area revisited: Ingestive behavior. *Neuroscience and Biobehavioral Reviews, 20*, 189–287.

Bernstein, I.S. (1981). Dominance: The baby and the bathwater. *The Behavioral and Brain Sciences, 4*, 419–457.

Bernstein, I.S. (1982). Hypotheses about play. *The Behavioral and Brain Sciences, 5*, 158–159.

Bernstein, I.S., Gordon, T.P., & Rose, R.M. (1983). The interaction of hormones, behavior, and social context in nonhuman primates. In B.B. Svare (Ed.), *Hormones and Aggressive Behavior* (pp. 535–561). New York: Plenum Press.

Berntson, G.G., Boysen, S.T., Bauer, H.R., & Torello, M.S. (1989). Conspecific screams and laughter: Cardiac and behavioral reactions of infant chimpanzees. *Developmental Psychobiology, 22*, 771–787.

Berridge, K.C. (1996). Food reward: Brain substrates of wanting and liking. *Neuroscience and Biobehavioral Reviews, 20*, 1–25.

Berry, S.L., Beatty, W.W., & Klesges, R.C. (1985). Sensory and social influences on ice cream consumption by males and females in a laboratory setting. *Appetite, 6*, 41–45.

Bertolini, A., Gessa, G.L., & Ferrari, W. (1975). Penile erection and ejaculation: A central effect of ACTH-like peptides in mammals. In M. Sandler & G.L. Gessa (Eds.), *Sexual Behavior: Pharmacology and Biochemistry* (pp. 247–257). New York: Raven Press.

Bieber, I., Dain, H.J., Dince, P.R., Drellich, M.G., Grand, H.C., Gundlach, R.H., Kremer, M.W., Rifkin, A.H., Wilbur, C.B., & Bieber, T.B. (1962). *Homosexuality: A Psychoanalytic Study*. New York: Random House.

Bielajew, C.H., & Harris, T. (1991). Self-stimulation: A rewarding decade. *Journal of Psychiatric Neuroscience, 16*, 109–114.

Bigelow, R.S. (1969). *The Dawn Warriors*. Boston: Little, Brown.

Bigelow, R.S. (1972). The evolution of cooperation, aggression, and self-control. In J.K. Cole & D.D. Jensen (Eds.), *Nebraska Symposium on Motivation, 20*, 1–57.

Bignami, G. (1965). Selection for high and low rates of conditioning in the rat. *Animal Behaviour, 13*, 221–227.

Billings, A.G., Cronkite, R.C., & Moos, R.H. (1983). Social-environmental factors in unipolar depression: Comparisons of depressed patients and nondepressed controls. *Journal of Abnormal Psychology, 92*, 119–133.

Binik, Y.M., Theriault, G., & Shustack, B. (1977). Sudden death in the laboratory rat: Cardiac function, sensory, and experiential factors in swimming deaths. *Psychosomatic Medicine, 39*, 82–92.

Birch, L.L. (1989). Developmental aspects of eating. In R. Shepherd (Ed.), *Handbook of the Psychophysiology of Human Eating* (pp. 179–203). Chichester U.K.: John Wiley & Sons Ltd.

Blaffer-Hrdy, S. (1979). Infanticide among animals: A review, classification, and examination of the reproductive strategies of females. *Ethology and Sociobiology, 1*, 13–40.

Blass, E.M. & Epstein, A.N. (1971). A lateral preoptic osmosensitive zone for thirst in the rat. *Journal of Comparative and Physiological Psychology, 76*, 378–394.

Blazer, D.G. (1982). Social support and mortality in an elderly community population. *American Journal of Epidemiology, 115*, 684–694.

Bligh, J. (1973). *Temperature Regulation in Mammals and Other Vertebrates*. Amsterdam: North-Holland.

Blount, B.G. (1990). Issues in bonobo (*Pan paniscus*) sexual behavior. *American Anthropologist, 92*, 702–714.

Boccia, M., & Campos, J.J. (1989). Maternal emotional signals, social referencing, and infants' reactions to strangers. In N. Eisenberg (Ed.), *Empathy and Related Emotional Responses* (pp. 25–49). San Francisco, Jossey-Bass.

Bohannan, P. (1963). *Social Anthropology*. New York: Holt, Rinehart and Winston.

Bohannan, P. (Ed.) (1960). *African Homicide and Suicide*. Princeton, NJ: Princeton University Press.

Boissy, A. (1996). Fear and fearfulness in animals. *Quarterly Review of Biology, 70*, 165–191.

Boissy, A., & Bouissou, M.F. (1994). Effects of androgen treatment on behavioral and physiological responses of heifers to fear-eliciting situations. *Hormones and Behavior, 28*, 66–83.

Boissy, A., & Bouissou, M.F. (1995). Assessment of individual differences in behavioural reactions of heifers exposed to various fear-eliciting situations. *Applied Animal Behavior Science, 46*, 17–31.

Bolles, R.C. (1967). *Theory of Motivation*. New York: Harper & Row.

Bolles, R.C. (1970). Species-specific defense reactions and avoidance learning. *Psychological Review, 77*, 32–48.

Booth, A., Shelley, G., Mazur, A., Tharp, G., & Kittok, R. (1989). Testosterone, and winning and losing in human competition. *Hormones and Behavior, 23*, 556–571.

Bowlby, J. (1969). *Attachment and Loss (Vol. 1): Attachment*. New York: Basic Books.

Bowlby, J. (1973). *Attachment and Loss (Vol. 2): Separation*. New York: Basic Books.

Boyd, R., & Richerson, P.J. (1985). *Culture and the Evolutionary Process*. Chicago: University of Chicago Press.

Braby, C.D. , Harris, D., & Muir, H.C. (1993). A psychophysiological approach to the assessment of work underload. *Ergonomics, 36*, 1035–1042.

Bradwejn, J. (1993). Neurobiological investigations into the role of cholecystokinin in panic disorder. *Journal of Psychiatry & Neuroscience, 18*, 178–188.

Brain, P.F., & Benton, D. (1983). Housing, hormones, and aggressive behavior. In B.B. Svare (Ed.), *Hormones and Aggressive Behavior* (pp. 351–372). New York: Plenum Press.

Breland, K., & Breland, M. (1961). The misbehavior of organisms. *American Psychologist, 16*, 681–684.

Brelurut, A., Pingard, A., & Thériez, M. (1990). *Le Cerf et son Élevage*. Paris: INRA.

Breslau, N., Davis, G.C., Andreski, P., & Peterson, E. (1991). Traumatic events and post-traumatic stress disorder in an urban population of young adults. *Archives of General Psychiatry, 48*, 216–222.

Bridges, R.S. (1984). A quantitative analysis of the roles of estradiol and progesterone in the regulation of maternal behavior in the rat. *Endocrinology, 114*, 930–940.

Broadhurst, P.L. (1975). The Maudsley reactive and nonreactive strains of rats: A survey. *Behavior Genetics, 5*, 299–319.

Broadhurst, P.L. (1976). The Maudsley reactive and nonreactive strains of rats: A clarification. *Behavior Genetics, 6*, 363–365.

Brobeck, J.R. (1948). Food intake as a mechanism of temperature regulation. *Yale Journal of Biology and Medicine, 20*, 545.

Bronson, F.H., & Caroom, D. (1971). Preputial gland of the male mouse: Attractant function. *Journal of Reproduction and Fertility, 25*, 279–282.

Brook, C.G.D., Lloyd, J.K., & Wolf, O.H. (1972). Relation between age of onset of obesity and size and number of adipose cells. *British Medical Journal, 2*, 25–27.

Brothers, L. (1989). A biological perspective on empathy. *American Journal of Psychiatry, 146*, 10–19.

Brown, L.P., Gennaro, S., York, R., Swinkles, K., & Brooten, D. (1991). VLBW infants: Association between visiting and telephoning and maternal and infant outcome measures. *Journal of Perinatal and Neonatal Nursing, 4*, 39–46.

Brown, R.E. (1994). *An Introduction to Neuroendocrinology*. New York: Cambridge University Press.

Bruce, H.M. (1959). An exteroceptive block to pregnancy in the mouse. *Nature, 184*, 105.

Buchwald, J.S., & Shipley, C. (1985). A comparative model of infant cry. In B.M. Lester & C.F. Boukydis (Eds.), *Infant Crying: Theoretical and Research Perspectives* (pp. 279–305). New York: Plenum Press.

Buck, R. (1983). Emotional development and emotional education. In R. Plutchik & H. Kellerman (Eds.), *Emotion: Theory, Research, and Experience. Volume 2: Emotions in Early Development* (pp. 259–292). New York: Academic Press.

Buck, R.W., Parke, R.D., & Buck, M. (1970). Skin conductance, heart rate and attention to the environment in two stressful situations. *Psychonomic Science, 18*, 95–96.

Buechler, S., & Izard, C.E. (1983). On the emergence, functions, and regulation of some emotion expressions in infancy. In R. Plutchik & H. Kellerman (Eds.), *Emotion: Theory, Research, and Experience. Volume 2: Emotions in Early Development* (pp. 293–313). New York: Academic Press.

Bult, A., & Lynch, C.B. (1996). Multiple selection responses in house mice bidirectionally selected for thermoregulatory nest-building behavior: Crosses of replicate lines. *Behavior Genetics, 26*, 439–446.

Burghardt, G.M. (1973). Instinct and innate behavior: Toward an ethological psychology. In J.A. Nevin & G.S. Reynolds (Eds.), *The Study of Behavior* (pp. 322–400). Glenview, IL: Scott, Foresman.

Buss, D. (1989). Sex differences in human mate preferences: Evolutionary hypotheses tested in 37 cultures. *Behavioral and Brain Sciences, 12*, 1–49.

Buss, D., Larsen, R.J., Westen, D., & Semmelroth, J. (1992). Sex differences in jealousy: Evolution, physiology, and psychology. *Psychological Science, 3*, 251–255.

Bykov, K.M., & Gantt, W.A.H. (1957). *Cerebral Cortex and Internal Organs.* New York: Chemical Publishing Co.

Byne, W., & Parsons, B. (1993). Human sexual orientation: The biological theories reappraised. *Archives of General Psychiatry, 50*, 228–239.

Byrne, D.G. (1987). Personality, life events and cardiovascular disease. *Journal of Psychosomatic Research, 31*, 661–671.

Caggiula, A.R. (1970). Analysis of the copulation-reward properties of posterior hypothalamic stimulation in male rats. *Journal of Comparative and Physiological Psychology, 70*, 399–412.

Caggiula, A.R., & Eibergen, R. (1969). Copulation of virgin male rats evoked by painful electrical stimulation. *Journal of Comparative and Physiological Psychology, 69*, 414–419.

Calhoun, J.B. (1949). A method for self-control of population growth among mammals. *Science, 109*, 333–335.

Campfield, L.A., Brandon, P., & Smith, F.J. (1985). Online continuous measurement of blood glucose and meal pattern in free-feeding rats: The role of glucose in meal initiation. *Brain Research Bulletin, 14*, 605–616.

Campfield, L.A., Smith, F.J., Rosenbaum, M., & Hirsch, J. (1996). Human eating: Evidence for a physiological basis using a modified paradigm. *Neuroscience and Biobehavioral Reviews, 20*, 133–137.

Camras, L.A., Malatesta, C., & Izard, C.E. (1991). The development of facial expressions in infancy. In R.S. Feldman & B. Rimé (Eds.), *Fundamentals of Nonverbal Behavior.* Cambridge, UK: Cambridge University Press.

Cannon, W.B. (1915). *Bodily Changes in Pain, Hunger, Fear and Rage.* New York: Appleton.

Cannon, W.B., & Washburn, A.L. (1912). An explanation of hunger. *American Journal of Physiology, 29*, 444–454.

Caplan, M., & Douglas, V. (1969). Incidence of parental loss in children with depressed mood. *Journal of Child Psychology and Psychiatry, 10*, 225–232.

Capps, W.H. (1976). *Seeing With a Native Eye: Essays on North American Religion.* New York: Harper & Row.

Carlson, J.G., & Hatfield, E. (1991). *Psychology of Emotion.* Fort Worth, TX: Harcourt Brace Jovanovich.

Carlson, N.R. (1994). *Physiology of Behavior* (5th ed.). Newton, MA: Allyn & Bacon.

Carr, W.J., Martorano, R.D., & Krames, L. (1970). Responses of mice to odors associated with stress. *Journal of Comparative and Physiological Psychology, 89*, 574–584.

Carroll, B.J. (1982). The dexamethasone suppression test for melancholia. *British Journal of Psychiatry, 140*, 292–304.

Carter, C.S. (1992). Oxytocin and sexual behavior. *Neuroscience and Biobehavioral Reviews, 16*, 131–144.

Carter, C.S., & Davis, J.M. (1977). Biogenic amines, reproductive hormones and female sexual behavior: A review. *Biobehavioral Reviews, 1*, 213–224.

Carter, C.S., DeVries, A.C., & Getz, L.L. (1995). Physiological substrates and mammalian monogamy: The prairie vole model. *Neuroscience and Biobehavioral Reviews, 19*, 303–314.

Carter, C.S., Williams, J.R., Witt, D.M., & Insel, T.R. (1992). Oxytocin and social bonding. *Annals of the New York Academy of Sciences, 652*, 204–211.

Cassone, V.M., Warren, W.S., Brooks, D.S., & Lu, J. (1993). Melatonin, the pineal gland, and circadian rhythms. *Journal of Biological Rhythms, 8*, S73–S81.

Chagnon, N.A. (1968). *Yanomamö: The Fierce People*. New York: Holt, Rinehart and Winston.

Charlesworth, W.R., & Kreutzer, M.A. (1973). Facial expression of infants and children. In P. Ekman (Ed.) *Darwin and Facial Expression* (pp. 91–168). New York: Academic Press.

Chaturvedi, S.K. (1987). Prevalence of chronic pain in psychiatric patients. *Pain, 29*, 231–237.

Checkley, S.A., Murphy, D.G.M., Abbas, M., Marks, M., Winton, F., Palazidou, E., Murphy, D.M., Franey, C., & Arendt, J. (1993). Melatonin rhythms in seasonal affective disorder. *British Journal of Psychiatry, 163*, 332–337.

Chevalier-Skolnikoff, S. (1973). Facial expression of emotion in nonhuman primates. In P. Ekman (Ed.), *Darwin and Facial Expression* (pp. 11–89). New York: Academic Press.

Chomsky, N. (1972). *Language and Mind*. New York: Harcourt Brace Jovanovich.

Clanton, G., & Smith, L.G. (1987). *Jealousy*. Lantham, MD: University Press of America.

Clark, M.M., Bishop, A.M., Vom Saal, F.S., & Galef, B.G., Jr. (1993). Responsiveness to testosterone of male gerbils from known uterine positions. *Physiology and Behavior, 53*, 1183–1187.

Cleckley, H. (1955). *The Mask of Sanity* (3rd ed.). St. Louis, MO: Mosby.

Clemente, C.D., & Chase, M.H. (1973). Neurological substrates of aggressive behavior. *Annual Review of Physiology, 35*, 329–356.

Clutton-Brock, T.H. (1991). *The Evolution of Parental Care*. Princeton, NJ: Princeton University Press.

Cobb, S. (1976). Social support as a moderator of life stress. *Psychosomatic Medicine, 38*, 300–314.

Cofer, C.N. (1972). *Motivation and Emotion*. Glenview, IL: Scott, Foresman.

Cohn, C., & Joseph, D. (1962). Influence of body weight and body fat on appetite of "normal" lean and obese rats. *Yale Journal of Biology and Medicine, 34*, 598–607.

Coiro, V., Volpi, R., Marchesi, C., DeFerri, A., Davoli, C., Cafferra, P., Rossi, G., Caffarri, G., Davolio, M., & Choidera, P. (1993). Abnormal serotonergic control of prolactin and cortisol secretion in patients with seasonal affective disorder. *Psychoneuroendocrinology, 18*, 551–556.

Comfort, A. (1964). *Ageing: The Biology of Senescence*. London: Routledge & Kegan Paul.

Conner, R.L., Constantino, A.P., & Scheuch, G.C. (1983). Hormonal influences on shock-induced fighting. In B.B. Svare (Ed.), *Hormones and Aggressive Behavior* (pp. 119–144). New York: Plenum Press.

Cook, M., & Mineka, S. (1989). Observational conditioning of fear to fear-relevant versus fear-irrelevant stimuli in rhesus monkeys. *Journal of Abnormal Psychology, 98*, 448–459.

Cook, W.T., Siegel, P., & Hinkelmann, K. (1972). Genetic analyses of male mating behavior in chickens: 2. Crosses among selected and control lines. *Behavior Genetics, 2*, 289–300.

Cooper, J.R., Bloom, F.E, & Roth, R.H. (1991). *The Biochemical Basis of Neuropharmacology* (6th ed.). New York: Oxford University Press.

Cornelius, R.R. (1996). *The Science of Emotion*. Upple Saddle River, NJ: Prentice Hall.

Corodimas, K.P., LeDoux, J.E., Gold, P.W., & Schulkin, J. (1994). Corticosterone potentiation of conditioned fear in rats. *Annals of the New York Academy of Sciences, 746,* 392–393.

Craighead, W.E., Kazdin, A.E., & Mahoney, M.J. (1981). *Behavior Modification: Principles, Issues, and Applications* (2nd ed.) Boston: Houghton Mifflin.

Crawford, C.B., Salter, B.E., & Jang, K.L. (1989). Human grief: Is its intensity related to the reproductive value of the deceased? *Ethology & Sociobiology, 10,* 297–307.

Crouch, M., & Manderson, L. (1995). The social life of bonding theory. *Social Science and Medicine, 41,* 837–844.

Cutrona, C.E. (1983). Causal attributions and perinatal depression. *Journal of Abnormal Psychology, 92,* 161–172.

Dahlgren, K.G. (1977). Attempted suicide: 35 years afterward. *Suicide and Life-Threatening Behavior, 7,* 75–79.

Dalton, K. (1968). Menstruation and examinations. *Lancet, 2,* 1386–1388.

Daly, M., & Wilson, M. (1980). Discriminative parental solicitude: A biological perspective. *Journal of Marriage and the Family, 42,* 277–288.

Daly, M., & Wilson, M. (1983). *Sex, Evolution, and Behavior* (2nd ed.). Belmont, CA: Wadsworth.

Daly, M., & Wilson, M. (1988). *Homicide*. New York: Aldine de Gruyter.

Daly, M., Wilson, M., & Weghorst, S.J. (1982). Male sexual jealousy. *Ethology and Sociobiology, 3,* 11–27.

Dantzer, R.P., & Mormède, R.M. (1981). Pituitary-adrenal correlates of adjunctive activities in pigs. *Hormones and Behavior, 16,* 78–92.

Darwin, C. (1859). *On the Origin of Species*. London (Facsimile ed.). New York: Atheneum, 1967.

Darwin, C. (1868). *The Variation of Animals and Plants under Domestication*. New York: Orange Judd.

Darwin, C. (1872). *The Expression of Emotions in Man and Animals*. London: Murray.

Davidson, R.J. (1983). Affect, repression, and cerebral asymmetry. In L. Temoshok, C. Van Dyke, & L.S. Zegans (Eds.), *Emotions in Health and Illness: Theoretical and Research Foundations* (pp. 123–135). New York: Grune & Stratton.

Davison, G.C., & Neale, J.M. (1996). *Abnormal Psychology* (5th ed.). New York: Wiley.

Dawkins, R. (1978). *The Selfish Gene*. London: Granada.

deCatanzaro, D. (1981a). *Suicide and Self-Damaging Behavior: A Sociobiological Perspective*. New York: Academic Press.

deCatanzaro, D. (1981b). Facilitation of intermale aggression in mice through exposure to receptive females. *Journal of Comparative and Physiological Psychology, 95,* 638–645.

deCatanzaro, D. (1984). Suicidal ideation and the residual capacity to promote inclusive fitness: A survey. *Suicide and Life-Threatening Behavior, 14,* 75–87.

deCatanzaro, D. (1987a). Differential sexual activity of isolated and grouped male mice despite testosterone administration. *Behavioral and Neural Biology, 48,* 213–221.

deCatanzaro, D. (1987b). Alteration of estrogen-induced lordosis through central administration of corticosterone in adrenalectomized-ovariectomized rats. *Neuroendocrinology, 46,* 468–474.

deCatanzaro, D. (1991a). Duration of mating relates to fertility in mice. *Physiology and Behavior, 50,* 393–395.

deCatanzaro, D. (1991b). Evolutionary limits to self-preservation. *Ethology and Sociobiology, 12,* 13–28.

deCatanzaro, D. (1995). Reproductive status, family interactions, and suicidal ideation: Surveys of the general public and high-risk groups. *Ethology and Sociobiology, 16,* 385–394.

deCatanzaro, D., & Gorzalka, B.B. (1979). Isolation induced facilitation of male sexual behavior in mice. *Journal of Comparative and Physiological Psychology, 93,* 211–222.

deCatanzaro, D., & Gorzalka, B.B. (1980). Effects of dexamethasone, corticosterone, and ACTH on lordosis in ovariectomized and adrenalectomized-ovariectomized rats. *Pharmacology Biochemistry and Behavior, 12,* 201–206.

deCatanzaro, D., & Griffiths, J. (1996). Differential sexual activity of isolated and group-housed male mice: Influence of acute *d*-amphetamine sulfate administration. *Pharmacology Biochemistry and Behavior, 54,* 601–604.

deCatanzaro, D., & MacNiven, E. (1992). Psychogenic pregnancy disruptions in mammals. *Neuroscience and Biobehavioral Reviews, 16,* 43–53.

deCatanzaro, D., & Ngan, E.T. (1983). Dominance in intermale encounters and subsequent sexual success in mice. *Journal of Comparative Psychology, 97,* 269–278.

deCatanzaro, D., & Stein, M. (1984). Suppression of the lordosis reflex in female rats by chronic central melatonin implants. *Hormones and Behavior, 18,* 216–223.

deCatanzaro, D., Zacharias, R., & Muir, C. (1996). Disruption of early pregnancy by direct and indirect exposure to novel males in mice: Comparison of the influences of preputialectomized and intact males. *Journal of Reproduction and Fertility, 106,* 269–274.

DeFries, J.C., Gervais, M.C., & Thomas, E.A. (1978). Response to 30 generations of selection for open-field activity in laboratory mice. *Behavior Genetics, 8,* 3–13.

deKloet, E.R., Reul, J.M.H.M., & Sutanto, W. (1990). Corticosteroids and the brain. *Journal of Steroid Biochemistry and Molecular Biology, 37,* 387–394.

Delgado, J.M.R. (1969). Offensive-defensive behaviour in free monkeys and chimpanzees induced by radio stimulation of the brain. In S. Garattini & E.B. Sigg (Eds.), *Aggressive Behavior* (pp. 109–119). New York: Wiley.

Dembroski, T.M., MacDougall, J.M., Eliot, R.S., & Buell, J.C. (1983). Stress, emotions, behavior, and cardiovascular disease. In L. Temoshok, C. Van Dyke, & L.S. Zegans (Eds.), *Emotions in Health and Illness: Theoretical and Research Foundations* (pp. 61–72). New York: Grune & Stratton.

Denton, D. (1982). *The Hunger for Salt.* New York: Springer-Verlag.

Desor, J.A., Maller, O., & Greene, L.S. (1977). Preference for sweet in humans: Infants, children, and adults. In J.M. Weiffenbach (Ed.), *Taste and Development: The Genesis of Sweet Preference* (pp. 161–172). Bethesda, MD: U.S. Department of Health, Education, and Welfare.

DeVries, A.C., DeVries, M.B., Taymans, S.E., & Carter, C.S. (1996). The effects of stress on social preferences are sexually dimorphic in prairie voles. *Neurobiology, 93,* 11980–11984.

Dewsbury, D.A. (1981). Social dominance, copulatory behavior, and differential reproduction in deer mice (*Peromyscus maniculatus*). *Journal of Comparative and Physiological Psychology, 95,* 890–895.

Diamond, M., & Sigmundson, K. (1997). Sex reassignment at birth. *Archives of Pediatric and Adolescent Medicine, 151,* 298–304.

Dillon, K.M., Minchoff, B., & Baker, K.H. (1985). Positive emotional states and enhancement of the immune system. *International Journal Psychiatry in Medicine*, *15*, 13–17.

Dimsdale, J.E., Eckenrode, J., Haggerty, R.J., Kaplan, B.H., Cohen, F., & Dornbusch, S. (1979). The role of social supports in medical care. *Social Psychiatry*, *14*, 175–180.

Dinsmoor, J.A. (1983). Observing and conditioned reinforcement. *The Behavioral and Brain Sciences*, *6*, 693–728.

DiPietro, J.A. (1981). Rough-and-tumble play: A function of gender. *Developmental Psychology*, *17*, 50–58.

Dobzhansky, T. (1963). Cultural directions of human evolution. *Human Biology*, *35*, 311–316.

Dodd, J., & Role, L.W. (1991). The autonomic nervous system. In E.R. Kandel, J.H. Schwartz, & T.M. Jessell (Eds.), *Principles of Neural Science* (3rd ed., pp. 761–776). Norwalk, CT: Appleton & Lange.

Dollard, J., Doob, L.W., Miller, N.E., Mowrer, O.H., & Sears, R.R. (1939). *Frustration and Aggression*. New Haven, CT: Yale University Press.

Donovan, W.L., & Leavitt, L.A. (1985). Physiology and behavior: Parents' response to the infant cry. In B.M. Lester & C.F. Boukydis (Eds.), *Infant Crying: Theoretical and Research Perspectives* (pp. 241–261). New York: Plenum Press.

Dörner, G., Rohde, W., Stahl, F., Krell, I., Masius, W.-G. (1975). A neuroendocrine predisposition for homosexuality in men. *Archives of Sexual Behavior*, *4*, 1–8.

Douglas, M. (1975). *Implicit Meanings: Essays in Anthropology*. Boston, MA: Routledge.

Duchenne, G.B. (1862). *The Mechanism of Human Facial Expression*. Edited and translated version by R.A Cuthbertson (1990). Cambridge: Cambridge University Press.

Duffy, E. (1962). *Activation and Behavior*. New York: Wiley.

Dunn, A.J., & Gispen, W.H. (1977). How ACTH acts on the brain. *Biobehavioral Reviews*, *1*, 15–23.

Dunn, J. (1988). Sibling influences on childhood development. *Journal of Child Psychology and Psychiatry*, *29*, 119–127.

Durham, W.H. (1976). Resource competition and human aggression, part I: A review of primitive war. *Quarterly Review of Biology*, *51*, 385–415.

Durham, W.H. (1991). *Coevolution: Genes, Culture, and Human Diversity*. Stanford: Stanford University Press.

Durkheim, E. (1897). *Suicide*. (Republished in 1951), Glencoe, IL: Free Press.

Dutton, D., & Aron, A. (1974). Some evidence for heightened sexual attraction under conditions of high anxiety. *Journal of Personality and Social Psychology*, *30*, 510–517.

Ebert, P.D., & Hyde, J.S. (1976). Selection for agonistic behavior in wild female *Mus musculus*. *Behavior Genetics*, *6*, 291–304.

Edelman, R.J. (1981). Embarrassment: The state of research. *Current Psychological Reviews*, *1*, 125–138.

Edelman, R.J. (1982). The effect of embarrassed reactions upon others. *Australian Journal of Psychology*, *34*, 359–367.

Edelman, R.J., Asendorpf, J., Contarello, A., Zammuner, V., Georgas, J., & Villanueva, C. (1989). Self-report of embarrassment in five European cultures. *Journal of Cross-Cultural Psychology*, *20*, 357–371.

Edelman, R.J., Childs, J., Harvey, S., Kellock, I., & Strain-Clark, C. (1984). The effect of embarrassment on helping. *Journal of Social Psychology*, *124*, 253–254.

Egger, M.D., & Flynn, J.P. (1963). Effect of electrical stimulation of the amygdala on hypothalamically elicited attack behavior in cats. *Journal of Neurophysiology*, *26*, 705–720.

Eibl-Eibesfeldt, I. (1961). The interactions of unlearned behaviour patterns and learning in mammals. In J.F. Delafresnaye (Ed.), *Brain Mechanisms and Learning* (pp. 53–73). Oxford: Blackwell.

Eibl-Eibesfeldt, I. (1989). *Human Ethology*. New York: Aldine de Gruyter.

Eiseley, L. (1958). *Darwin's Century*. New York: Doubleday.

Eisenberg, N., Fabes, R.A., Miller, P.A., Fultz, J., Shell, R., Mathy, R.M., & Reno, R.R. (1989). Relation of sympathy and personal distress to prosocial behavior: A multimethod study. *Journal of Personality and Social Psychology, 57,* 55–66.

Ekman, P. (1973). Cross-cultural studies of facial expression. In P. Ekman. (Ed.), *Darwin and Facial Expression* (pp. 169–222). New York: Academic Press.

Ekman, P. (1994). Strong evidence for universals in facial expressions: A reply to Russell's mistaken critique. *Psychological Bulletin, 115,* 268–287.

Ekman, P., & Friesen, W.V. (1971). Constants across cultures in the face and emotion. *Journal of Personality and Social Psychology, 17,* 124–129.

Ekman, P., & Friesen, W.V. (1981). The repertoire of nonverbal behavior: Categories, origins, usage, and coding. In T.A. Sebeok, J. Umiker-Sebeok, & A. Kendon (Eds.), *Nonverbal Communication, Interaction, and Gesture* (pp. 57–105). The Hague: Mouton Publishers.

Ekman, P., & Friesen, W.V. (1982). Felt, false, and miserable smiles. *Journal of Nonverbal Behavior, 6,* 238–252.

Ekman, P., Friesen, W.V., O'Sullivan, M., Chan, A., Diacoyanni-Tarlatzis, I., Heider, K., Krause, R., LeCompte, W.A., Pitcairn, T., Ricci-Bitti, P.E., Scherer, K., Tomita, M., & Tzavaras, A. (1987). Universals and cultural differences in the judgements of facial expressions of emotion. *Journal of Personality and Social Psychology, 53,* 712–717.

Ekman, P., Levenson, R.W., & Friesen, W.V. (1983). Autonomic nervous system activity distinguishes among emotions. *Science, 221,* 1208–1210.

Eleftheriou, B.E., & Church, R.L. (1967). Effects of repeated exposure to aggression and defeat on plasma and pituitary levels of luteinizing hormone in C57BL/6J mice. *General and Comparative Endocrinology, 9,* 263–266.

Elias, M. (1981). Serum cortisol, testosterone, and testosterone-binding globulin response to competitive fighting in human males. *Aggressive Behavior, 7,* 215–224.

Elwin, V. (1943). *Maria Murder and Suicide*. London: Oxford University Press.

Epstein, A.N., Fitzsimons, J.T., & Rolls, B.J. (1970). Drinking induced by injection of angiotensin into the brain of the rat. *Journal of Physiology (London), 210,* 457–474.

Estes, W.K., & Skinner, B.F. (1941). Some quantitative properties of anxiety. *Journal of Experimental Psychology, 29,* 390–400.

Ewer, R.F. (1968). *Ethology of Mammals*. London: Elek Science.

Evans, D.R. (1968). Masturbatory fantasy and sexual deviation. *Behaviour Research and Therapy, 6,* 17–19.

Everitt, B.J., Fuxe, K., Hökfelt, T., & Jonsson, G. (1975). Studies on the role of monoamines in the hormonal regulation of sexual receptivity in the female rat. In M. Sandler & G.L. Gessa (Eds.), *Sexual Behavior: Pharmacology and Biochemistry* (pp. 147–159). New York: Raven Press.

Everitt, B.J., Herbert, J., & Hamer, J.D. (1972). Sexual receptivity of bilaterally adrenalectomized female Rhesus monkeys. *Physiology & Behavior, 8,* 409–415.

Eysenck, H.J. (1960). *Behaviour Therapy and the Neuroses*. New York: Pergamon Press.

Fagen, R.M. (1976). Exercise, play, and physical training in animals. In P.P.G. Bateson & P.H. Klopfer (Eds.), *Perspectives in Ethology* (pp. 189–219). New York: Plenum Press.

Fagen, R.M. (1977). Selection for optimal age-dependent schedules of play behavior. *American Naturalist, 111,* 395–414.

Fanaroff, A.A., Kennell, J.H., & Klaus, M.H. (1972). Follow-up of low birth weight infants—The predictive value of maternal visiting patterns. *Pediatrics, 49,* 287–290.

Fantino, E. (1973). Aversive control. In J.A. Nevin & G.S. Reynolds (Eds.), *The Study of Behavior* (pp. 239–279). Glenview, IL: ScottForesman.

Fantino, E., Sharp, D., & Cole, M. (1966). Factors facilitating lever pressing avoidance. *Journal of Comparative and Physiological Psychology, 62,* 214–217.

Fantz, R.L. (1963). Pattern vision in new-born infants. *Science, 140,* 296—297.

Farmer, R., & Sundberg, N.D. (1986). Boredom proneness—The development and correlates of a new scale. *Journal of Personality Assessment, 50,* 4–17.

Faust, I.M., Johnson, P.R., & Hirsch, J. (1980). Long-term effects of early nutritional experience on the development of obesity in the rat. *Journal of Nutrition, 110,* 2027–2034.

Feine, J.S., Bushnell, M.C., Miron, D., & Duncan, G.H. (1991). Sex differences in the perception of noxious heat stimuli. *Pain, 44,* 255–262.

Feingold, A. (1992). Gender differences in mate selection preferences: A test of the parental investment model. *Psychological Bulletin, 112,* 125–139.

Felson, R.B. (1983). Aggression and violence between siblings. *Social Psychology Quarterly, 46,* 271–285.

Fentress, J.C., Ryon, J., McLeod, P.J., & Havkin, G.Z. (1987). A multidimensional approach to agonistic behavior in wolves. In H. Frank (Ed.), *Man and Wolf: Advances, Issue, and Problems in Captive Wolf Research* (pp. 253–274). Dordrecht, Netherlands: W. Junk Publishers.

Fenz, W.D., & Epstein, S. (1967). Gradients of physiological arousal in parachutists as a function of an approaching jump. *Psychosomatic Medicine, 29,* 33–51.

Fenz, W.D., & Jones, G.B. (1972). Individual differences in physiological arousal and performance in sport parachutists. *Psychosomatic Medicine, 34,* 1–8.

Ferguson, N.F.L., & Keesey, R.E. (1975). Effect of quinine-adulterated diet upon body weight maintenance in male rats with ventromedial hypothalamic lesions. *Journal of Comparative and Physiological Psychology, 80,* 478–488.

Festinger, L., & Carlsmith, J.M. (1959). Cognitive consequences of forced compliance. *Journal of Abnormal and Social Psychology, 58,* 203–210.

Field, T.M., Woodson, R., Greenberg, R., & Cohen, D. (1982). Discrimination and imitation of facial expressions by neonates. *Science, 218,* 179–181.

Fields, H.L. (1987). *Pain.* New York: McGraw-Hill.

Figlewicz, D.P., Schwartz, M.W., Seeley, R.J., Chavez, M., Baskin, D.G., Woods, S.C., & Porte, D. (1996). Endocrine regulation of food intake and body weight. *Journal of Laboratory and Clinical Medicine, 127,* 328–332.

Firth, R. (1961). Suicide and risk-taking in Tikopia society. *Psychiatry, 24,* 1–17.

Fisher, R.A. (1950). *The Genetical Theory of Natural Selection.* New York: Dover.

Fitzsimons, J.T., & Simons, B.J. (1969). The effect on drinking in the rat of intravenous infusion of angiotensin, given alone or in combination with other stimuli of thirst. *Journal of Physiology (London), 203,* 45–57.

Flannery, K.V. (1972). The cultural evolution of civilizations. *Annual Review of Ecology and Systematics, 3,* 399–426.

Fleming, A.S., Cheung, U., Myhal, N., & Kessler, Z. (1989). Effects of maternal hormones on "timidity" and attraction to pup-related odors in female rats. *Physiology and Behavior, 46,* 449–453.

Fleming, A.S., & Corter, C. (1988). Factors influencing maternal responsiveness in humans: Usefulness of an animal model. *Psychoneuroendocrinology, 13,* 189–212.

Fleming, A.S., Ruble, D.N., Flett, G.L., & vanWagner, V. (1990). Adjustment in first-time mothers: Changes in mood and mood content during the early postpartum months. *Developmental Psychology, 26,* 137–143.

Flinn, M.V. (1992). Paternal care in a Caribbean village. In B.S. Hewlett (Ed.), *Father-Child Relations.* New York: Aldine de Gruyter, pp. 57–84.

Flinn, M.V., & England, B. (1991). Childhood stress as measured by radioimmunoassay of cortisol levels in saliva. *American Journal of Physical Anthropology,* (Suppl. 12), 73.

Floody, O.R. (1983). Hormones and aggression in female mammals. In B.B. Svare (Ed.), *Hormones and Aggressive Behavior* (pp. 39–89). New York: Plenum Press.

Flynn, J., Vanegas, H., Foote, W., & Edwards, S. (1970). Neural mechanisms involved in a cat's attack on a rat. In R.F. Whalen, M. Thompson, J. Verzeano, & J. N. Weinberger (Eds.), *Neural Control of Behavior* (pp. 135–173). New York: Academic Press.

Ford, C.S., & Beach, F.A. (1951). *Patterns of Sexual Behavior.* New York: Harper and Row.

Forman, P. (1990). *Flying into Danger: The Hidden Facts about Air Safety.* London: Heinemann.

Formby, D. (1967). Maternal recognition of infant's cry. *Developmental Medicine and Child Neurology, 9,* 293–298.

Fox, C.A., & Knaggs, G.S. (1969). Milk ejection (oxytocin) in peripheral venous blood in man during lactation and in association with coitus. *Journal of Endocrinology, 45,* 145–146.

Fox, N.A., & Davidson, R.J. (1988). Patterns of brain electrical activity during facial signs of emotion in 10-month-old infants. *Developmental Psychology, 24,* 230–236.

Fraiberg, S. (1974). Blind infants and their mothers: An examination of the sign system. In M. Lewis & L.A. Rosenblum (Eds.), *The Effect of the Infant on its Caregiver.* New York: Wiley.

Frankenhaeuser, M. (1975). Experimental approaches to the study of catecholamines and emotion. In L. Levi (Ed.), *Emotions: Their Parameters and Measurement* (pp. 209–234). New York: Raven Press.

Fredrikson, M., Sundin, O., & Frankenhaeuser, M. (1985). Cortisol secretion during the defense reaction in humans. *Psychosomatic Medicine, 47,* 313–319.

Freedman, D.G. (1964). Smiling in blind infants and the issue of innate versus acquired. *Journal of Child Psychology and Psychiatry, 5,* 174–184.

Freedman, D.G. (1974). *Human Infancy: An Evolutionary Perspective.* Hillsdale, NJ: Lawrence Erlbaum Associates.

Freedman, D.G. (1979). *Human Sociobiology: A Holistic Approach.* New York: Free Press.

Freud, S. (1905). *Jokes and Their Relation to the Unconscious.* Pelican Freud Library, London: Penguin.

Freud, S. (1915). Instincts and their vicissitudes (translated by J. Riviere, 1949). In *Collected Papers of Sigmund Freud* (Vol. 4, pp. 60–83). London: Hogarth.

Freud, S. (1924). *Beyond the Pleasure Principle.* New York: Boni and Liveright.

Freud, S. (1977). *Introductory Lectures on Psychoanalysis,* (J. Strachey, Ed. and Trans.). New York: Liveright.

Freund, K., Langevin, R., Cibiri, S., & Zajac, Y. (1973). Heterosexual aversion in homosexual males. *British Journal of Psychiatry, 122,* 163–169.

Friedman, M., & Rosenman, R.H. (1974). *Type A Behavior and Your Heart.* New York: Knopf.

Frodi, A. (1985). When empathy fails: Aversive infant crying and child abuse. In B.M. Lester & C.F. Boukydis (Eds.), *Infant Crying: Theoretical and Research Perspectives* (pp. 263–277). New York, Plenum Press.

Fuller, J.L., & Thompson, W.R. (1960). *Behavior Genetics*. New York: John Wiley.

Funkenstein, D.H. (1955). The physiology of fear and anger. *Scientific American, 192*, 74–80.

Galef, B.G., Jr. (1977). Mechanisms for the transmission of acquired patterns of feeding from adult to weanling rats. In J.M. Weiffenbach (Ed.), *Taste and Development: The Genesis of Sweet Preference* (pp. 217–234). Bethesda, MD: U.S. Department of Health, Education, and Welfare.

Galef, B.G., Jr. (1985). Direct and indirect behavioral pathways to the social transmission of food avoidance. *Annals of the New York Academy of Sciences, 443*, 203–215.

Galef, B.G., Jr. (1996). Food selection: Problems in understanding how we choose foods to eat. *Neuroscience and Biobehavioral Reviews, 20*, 67–73.

Galton, F. (1865). Heredity, talent, and character. *Macmillan's Magazine, 12*, 157–166, 318–327.

Galton, F. (1889). *Natural Inheritance*. New York: Macmillan.

Gandelman, R. (1983). Hormones and infanticide. In B.B. Svare (Ed.), *Hormones and Aggressive Behavior* (pp. 105–118). New York: Plenum Press.

Ganong, W.F. (1973). *Review of Medical Physiology* (6th ed.). Los Altos, CA: Lange Medical Publications.

Garcia, J., Kimmeldorf, D.J., & Koelling, R.A. (1955). Conditioned aversion to saccharin resulting from exposure to gamma radiation. *Science, 122*, 157–158.

Garcia, J., Ervin, F.R., & Koelling, R.A. (1966). Learning with prolonged delay of reinforcement. *Psychonomic Science, 5*, 121–122.

Geary, N. (1990). Pancreatic glucagon signals postprandial satiety. *Neuroscience and Biobehavioral Reviews, 14*, 323–328.

Gessa, G.L., & Tagliamonte, A. (1975). Role of brain serotonin and dopamine in male sexual behavior. In M. Sandler & G.L. Gessa (Eds.), *Sexual Behavior: Pharmacology and Biochemistry* (pp. 117–128). New York: Raven Press.

Gibson, E.J., & Walk, R.D. (1960). The "visual cliff." *Scientific American, 202*, 64–71.

Gilman, A. (1937). The relation between blood osmotic pressure, fluid distribution and voluntary water intake. *American Journal of Physiology, 120*, 323–328.

Glass, D.C. (1977). *Behavior Patterns, Stress, and Coronary Disease*. New York: John Wiley.

Glass, J.D., & Lynch, G.R. (1981). Melatonin: Identification of sites of antigonadal action in mouse brain. *Science, 214*, 821–823.

Goldberg, L., & Gara, M.A. (1990). A typology of psychiatric reactions to motor vehicle accidents. *Psychopathology, 23*, 15–20.

Goodall, J. (1965). Chimpanzees of the Gombe Stream Reserve. In I. DeVore (Ed.), *Primate Behavior: Field Studies of Monkeys and Apes* (pp. 425–473). New York: Holt, Rinehart and Winston.

Goodall, J. (1968). The behavior of free-living chimpanzees in the Gombe Stream Reserve. *Animal Behavior Monographs, 1*, 165–311.

Goodwin, F.K., & Bunney, W.E., Jr. (1971). Depressions following reserpine: A reevaluation. *Seminars in Psychiatry, 3*, 435–446.

Gorski, R.A., Gordon, J.H., Shryne, J.E., & Southam, A.M. (1978). Evidence for a morphological sex difference within the medial preoptic area of the rat brain. *Brain Research, 148*, 333–346.

Gorzalka, B., & Mogenson, G.J. (1977). Sexual behavior. In G.J. Mogenson, *The Neurobiology of Behavior: An Introduction* (pp. 151–186). Hillsdale, NJ: Lawrence Erlbaum Associates.

Gotlib, I.H., & Asarnow, R.F. (1979). Interpersonal and impersonal problem-solving skills in mildly and clinically depressed university students. *Journal of Counselling and Clinical Psychology, 47*, 86–95.

Gottesman, I.I., & Shields, J. (1982). *Schizophrenia: The Epigenetic Puzzle*. Cambridge, UK: Cambridge University Press.

Graham, S., Doubleday, C., & Guarino, P.A. (1984). The development of relations between perceived controllability and the emotions of pity, anger, and guilt. *Child Development, 55*, 561–565.

Gray, J.A. (1979). Emotionality in male and female rodents. A reply to Archer. *British Journal of Psychology, 70*, 425–440.

Gray, J.A. (1982). Precis of "The Neuropsychology of Anxiety: An Enquiry into the Functions of the Septal-Hippocampal System." *The Behavioral and Brain Sciences, 5*, 469–534.

Gray, J.A. (1987). *The Psychology of Fear and Stress* (2nd ed.). Cambridge, UK: Cambridge University Press.

Green, B.L., Grace, M., Lindy, J., Gleser, G., Leonard, A., & Kramer, T. (1990). Buffalo Creek survivors in the second decade: Comparison with unexposed and nonlitigant groups. *Journal of Applied Social Psychology, 20*, 1033–1050.

Green, B.L., & Soloman, S.D. (1995). The mental health impact of natural and technological disasters. In J.R. Freedy & S.E. Hobfoll (Eds.), *Traumatic Stress: From Theory to Practice* (pp. 163–180). New York: Plenum Press.

Green, J.D., Clemente, C.D., & DeGroot, J. (1957). Rhinencephalic lesions and behavior in cats: An analysis of the Kluver-Bucy syndrome with particular reference to normal and abnormal sexual behavior. *Journal of Comparative Neurology, 108*, 505–545.

Greenwald, H.B., Bonica, J.J., & Bergner, M. (1987). The prevalence of pain in four cancers. *Cancer, 60*, 2563–2569.

Grossman, S.P. (1990). *Thirst and Sodium Appetite: Physiological Basis*. San Diego, CA: Academic Press.

Grossman, S.P., & Rechtschaffen, A. (1967). Variation in brain temperature in relation to food intake. *Physiology and Behavior, 2*, 379–383.

Gustavson, A.R., Dawson, M.E., & Bonett, D.G. (1987). Androstenol, a putative human pheromone, affects human (*Homo sapiens*) male choice performance. *Journal of Comparative Psychology, 101*, 210–212.

Hadaway, P.F., Alexander, B.K., Coambs, R.B., & Beyerstein, B.L. (1979). The effect of housing and gender on preference for morphine-sucrose solutions in rats. *Psychopharmacology, 66*, 87–91.

Hall, K.R.L., & DeVore, I. (1965). Baboon social behavior. In I. DeVore (Ed.), *Primate Behavior: Field Studies of Monkeys and Apes* (pp. 53–110). New York: Holt, Rinehart and Winston.

Hamer, D.H., Hu, S., Magnuson, V.L., Hu, N., & Pattatucci, A.M.L. (1993). A linkage between DNA markers on the X chromosome and male sexual orientation. *Science, 261*, 321–327.

Hamilton, W.D. (1964). The genetical theory of social behaviour (I and II). *Journal of Theoretical Biology, 7*, 1–52.

Hamilton, W.D. (1966). The moulding of senescence by natural selection. *Journal of Theoretical Biology, 12*, 12–45.

Hammen, C.L., & Cochran, S.D. (1981). Cognitive correlates of life stress and depression in college students. *Journal of Abnormal Psychology, 90*, 23–27.

Hanson, R.F., Kilpatrick, D.G., Falsetti, S.A., & Resnick, H.S. (1995). Violent crime and mental health. In J.R. Freedy & S.E. Hobfoll (Eds.), *Traumatic Stress: From Theory to Practice* (pp. 129–161). New York: Plenum Press.

Hapidou, E.G., & deCatanzaro, D. (1988). Sensitivity to cold pressor pain in dysmenorrheic and non-dysmenorrheic women as a function of menstrual cycle phase. *Pain, 34*, 277–283.

Hapidou, E.G., & deCatanzaro, D. (1992). Responsiveness to laboratory pain in women as a function of age and childbirth pain experience. *Pain, 48*, 177–181.

Hare, R.D. (1970). *Psychopathy: Theory and Research.* New York: John Wiley & Sons, Inc.

Harlow, H.F. (1958). The nature of love. *American Psychologist, 13*, 673–685.

Harlow, H.F. (1965). Total social isolation: Effects on Macacque monkey behavior. *Science, 148*, 666.

Harlow, H.F. (1971). *Learning to Love.* San Francisco, CA: Albion.

Harlow, H.F. (1974). Induction and alleviation of depressive states in monkeys. In N.F. White (Ed.), *Ethology and Psychiatry* (pp. 197–208). Toronto: University of Toronto Press.

Harlow, H.F., & Harlow, M.K. (1969). Effects of various mother-infant relationships on rhesus monkey behaviors. In B.M. Foss (Ed.), *Determinants of Infant Behavior, Vol. 4* (pp. 15–40). New York: Barnes & Noble.

Harlow, H.F., & Mears, C.E. (1983). Emotional sequences and consequences. In R. Plutchik & H. Kellerman (Eds.), *Emotion: Theory, Research, and Experience: Vol. 2: Emotions in Early Development* (pp. 171–197). New York: Academic Press.

Hart, B.L. (1967). Sexual reflexes and mating behavior in the male dog. *Journal of Comparative and Physiological Psychology, 64*, 388–399.

Harvey, J.A., & Hunt, H.F. (1965). Effects of septal lesions on thirst in the rat as indicated by water consumption and operant responding for water reward. *Journal of Comparative and Physiological Psychology, 59*, 49–56.

Hatfield, E., & Rapson, R.L. (1987). Passionate love/sexual desire: Can the same paradigm explain both? *Archives of Sexual Behavior, 16*, 259–278.

Hatfield, E., & Sprecher, S. (1986). Measuring passionate love in intimate relations. *Journal of Adolescence, 9*, 383–410.

Hatton, G.I. (1976). Nucleus circularis: Is it an osmoreceptor in the brain? *Brain Research Bulletin, 1*, 123–131.

Hebb, D.O. (1955). Drives and the C.N.S.—conceptual nervous system. *Psychological Review, 62*, 245–254.

Hefez, A., Metz, L., & Lavie, P. (1987). Long-term effects of extreme situational stress on sleep and dreaming. *American Journal of Psychiatry, 144*, 344–347.

Heim, N., & Hursch, C.J. (1979). Castration for sex offenders: Treatment or punishment? A review and critique of recent European literature. *Archives of Sexual Behavior, 8*, 281–304.

Helleday, J., Edman, G., Ritzen, E.M., & Siwers, B. (1993). Personality characteristics and platelet MAO activity in women with congenital adrenal hyperplasia (CAH). *Psychoneuroendocrinology, 18*, 343–354.

Helsing, K.J., Szklo, M., & Comstock, G.W. (1981). Factors associated with mortality after widowhood. *American Journal of Public Health, 71*, 802–809.

Helsing, K.J., Comstock, G.W., & Szklo, M. (1982). Causes of death in a widowed population. *American Journal of Epidemiology, 116*, 524–532.

Henderson, N.D. (1982). Human behavior genetics. *Annual Review of Psychology,* *33,* 403–440.

Hendry, D.P. (1969). *Conditioned Reinforcement.* Dorsey Press.

Heron, W. (1957). The pathology of boredom. *Scientific American, 196,* 52–56.

Hertsgaard, L., Gunnar, M., Erickson, M.F., & Nachmias, M. (1995). Adrenocortical response to the strange situation in infants with disorganized/disoriented attachment relationships. *Child Development, 66,* 1100–1106.

Hess, W.R. (1954). *Diencephalon: Autonomic and Extrapyramidal Function.* New York: Grune & Stratton.

Hetherington, A.W., & Ranson, S.W. (1942). The spontaneous activity and food intake of rats with hypothalamic lesions. *American Journal of Physiology, 136,* 457–474.

Hetherington, E.M. (1989). Coping with family transitions: Winners, losers, and survivors. *Child Development, 60,* 1–14.

Hinde, R.A., & Stevenson-Hinde, J. (1973). *Constraints on Learning: Limitations and Predispositions.* New York: Academic Press.

Hines, M., & Kaufman, F.R. (1994). Androgen and the development of human sex-typical behavior: Rough-and-tumble play and sex of preferred playmates in children of congenital adrenal hyperplasia (CAH). *Child Development, 65,* 1042–1053.

Hinkle, L. (1977). The concept of stress in the biological and social sciences. In Z. Lipowski (Ed.), *Psychosomatic Medicine: Current Trends and Clinical Applications* (pp. 27–49). New York: Oxford University Press.

Hoebel, B.G., & Teitelbaum, P. (1966). Weight regulation in normal and hypothalamic hyperphagic rats. *Journal of Comparative and Physiological Psychology, 61,* 189–193.

Hofer, M.A. (1981). *The Roots of Human Behavior.* San Francisco: W.H. Freeman.

Hofer, M.A. (1983). On the relationship between attachment and separation processes in infancy. In R. Plutchik & H. Kellerman (Eds.), *Emotion: Theory, Research, and Experience: Volume 2: Emotions in Early Development* (pp. 199–219). New York: Academic Press.

Hofer, M.A., & Shair, H. (1978). Ultrasonic vocalization during social interaction and isolation in 2 week old rats. *Developmental Psychobiology, 11,* 495–504.

House, J.S., Robbins, C., & Metzner, H.L. (1982). The association of social relationships and activities with mortality: Prospective evidence from the Tecumseh Community Health Study. *American Journal of Epidemiology, 116,* 123–140.

Huber, E. (1931). *Evolution of Facial Musculature and Facial Expression.* Baltimore: Johns Hopkins University Press.

Hubert, W., & deJong-Meyer, R. (1991). Autonomic, neuroendocrine, and subjective responses to emotion-inducing film stimuli. *International Journal of Psychophysiology, 11,* 131–140.

Huesmann, L.R., Eron, L.D., Lefkowitz, M.M., & Walder, L.G. (1984). Stability of aggression over time and generations. *Developmental Psychology, 20,* 1120–1134.

Hughes, C.W., & Lynch, J.J. (1978). A reconsideration of the psychological precursors of sudden death in infrahuman animals. *American Psychologist, 33,* 419–429.

Hull, C.L. (1951). *Essentials of Behavior.* New Haven, CT: Yale University Press.

Hull, E.M., Bitran, D., Pehek, E.A., Warner, R.K., Band, L.C., & Holmes, G.M. (1986). Dopaminergic control of male sexual behavior in rats: Effects of an intracerebrally infused agonist. *Brain Research, 370,* 73–81.

Hunt, H.F., & Brady, J.V. (1955). Some effects of punishment and intercurrent "anxiety" on a simple operant. *Journal of Comparative and Physiological Psychology, 48,* 305–310.

Hupka, R.B., & Bank, A.L. (1996). Sex differences in jealousy: Evolution or social construction? *Cross-Cultural Research*, *30*, 24–59.

Istvan, J. (1986). Stress, anxiety, and birth outcomes: A critical review of the evidence. *Psychological Bulletin*, *100*, 331–348.

Izard, C.E. (1971). *The Face of Emotion*. New York: Appleton.

Izard, C.E. (1977). *Human Emotion*. New York: Plenum Press.

Izard, C.E. (1991). *The Psychology of Emotions*. New York: Plenum Press.

Izard, C.E. (1994). Innate and universal facial expressions: Evidence from developmental and cross-cultural research. *Psychological Bulletin*, *115*, 288–299.

James, W. (1890). *Principles of Psychology*. New York: Holt.

Janowitz, H.D., & Grossman, M.I. (1949). Some factors affecting the food intake of normal dogs and dogs with esophagostomy and gastric fistula. *American Journal of Physiology*, *159*, 143–148.

Jauchem, J.R. (1992). Epidemiological studies of electric and magnetic fields and cancer: A case study of distortions by the media. *Journal of Clinical Epidemiology*, *45*, 1137–1142.

Jerome, N.J. (1977). Taste experience and the development of a dietary preference for sweet in humans: Ethnic and cultural variations in early taste experience. In J.M. Weiffenbach (Ed.), *Taste and Development: The Genesis of Sweet Preference* (pp. 233–248). Bethesda, MD: U.S. Department of Health, Education, and Welfare.

Jersild, A.T., & Holmes, F.B. (1935). Children's fears. *Child Development Monograph*, *20*.

Jessell, T.M., & Kelly, D.D. (1991). Pain and analgesia. In E.R. Kandel, J.H. Schwartz, & T.M. Jessell (Eds.), *Principles of Neural Science* (3rd ed., pp. 385–399). Norwalk, CT: Appleton & Lange.

Johnson, A.K., & Buggy, J. (1978). Periventricular preoptic-hypothalamus is vital for thirst and normal water economy. *American Journal of Physiology*, *234*, R122–127.

Johnson, A.K., & Cunningham, J.T. (1987). Brain mechanisms and drinking: The role of lamina terminalis-associated systems in extracellular thirst. *Kidney International*, *32* [Suppl. 21], S35–S42.

Jones, R.B., & Nowell, N.W. (1974). The urinary aversive pheromone of mice: Species, strain and grouping effects. *Animal Behaviour*, *22*, 187–191.

Kachhawaha, O.P. (1992). *History of Famines in Rajasthan (1900AD to 1990AD)*. Jodhpur, India: Research Publishers.

Kagan, J. (1971). *Change and Continuity in Infancy*. New York: Wiley.

Kagan, J., Henker, B.A., Hen-Tov, A., Levine, J., & Lewis, M. (1966). Infants' differential reactions to familiar and distorted faces. *Child Development*, *37*, 519–532.

Kalat, J.W. (1995). *Biological Psychology* (5th ed.). Pacific Grove, CA: Brooks/Cole.

Kalimi, M., Shafagoj, Y, Loria, R., Padgett, D., & Regelson, W. (1994). Anti-glucocorticoid effects of dehydroepiandrosterone (DHEA). *Molecular and Clinical Biochemistry*, *131*, 99–104.

Kandel, E.R. (1991a). Nerve cells and behavior. In E.R. Kandel, J.H. Schwartz, & T.M. Jessell (Eds.), *Principles of Neural Science* (3rd ed.) (pp. 18–33). Norwalk, CT: Appleton & Lange.

Kandel, E.R. (1991b). Transmitter release. In E.R. Kandel, J.H. Schwartz, & T.M. Jessell (Eds.), *Principles of Neural Science* (3rd ed.) (pp. 194–212). Norwalk, CT: Appleton & Lange.

Kandel, E.R. (1991c). Disorders of mood: Depression, mania, and anxiety disorders. In E.R. Kandel, J.H. Schwartz, & T.M. Jessell (Eds.), *Principles of Neural Science* (3rd ed.) (pp. 867–883). Norwalk, CT: Appleton & Lange.

Kandel, E.R., Siegelbaum, S.A., & Schwartz, J.H. (1991). Synaptic transmission. In E.R. Kandel, J.H. Schwartz, & T.M. Jessell (Eds.), *Principles of Neural Science (3rd ed.)* (pp. 123–134). Norwalk, CT: Appleton & Lange.

Kaplan, B.H., Cassel, J.C., & Gore, S. (1977). Social support and health. *Medical Care, 15*, 47–58.

Kappas, A., Hess, U., & Scherer, K.R. (1991). Voice and emotion. In R.S. Feldman & B. Rimé (Eds.), *Fundamentals of Nonverbal Behavior* (pp. 200–238). Cambridge, UK: Cambridge University Press.

Kardiner, A. (1941). *The Traumatic Neuroses of War*. New York: Paul B. Hoebner, Inc.

Kaufman, I.C., & Rosenblum, L.A. (1969). Effects of separation from mother on the emotional behavior of infant monkeys. *Annals of the New York Academy of Sciences, 159*, 681–695.

Keesey, R.E., & Powley, T.L. (1975). Hypothalamic regulation of body weight. *American Scientist, 63*, 558–565.

Kellerman, H. (1983). An epigenetic theory of emotions in early development. In R. Plutchik & H. Kellerman (Eds.), *Emotion: Theory, Research, and Experience– Volume 2: Emotions in Early Development* (pp. 315–34). New York: Academic Press.

Kelley, D.B., & Pfaff, D.W. (1978). Generalizations from comparative studies on neuroanatomical and endocrine mechanisms of sexual behaviour. In J. Hutchison (Ed.), *Biological Determinants of Sexual Behavior* (pp. 225–254). Chichester, UK: Wiley.

Kelly, D.D. (1991). Sexual differentiation of the nervous system. In E.R. Kandel, J.H. Schwartz, & T.M. Jessell (Eds.), *Principles of Neural Science (3rd ed.)* (pp. 959–973). Norwalk, CT: Appleton & Lange.

Kelly, J.P., & Dodd, J. (1991). Functional anatomy of the nervous system. In E.R. Kandel, J.H. Schwartz, & T.M. Jessell (Eds.), *Principles of Neural Science (3rd ed.)* (pp. 273–282). Norwalk, CT: Appleton & Lange.

Keltner, D., & Buswell, B.N. (1996). Evidence for the distinctness of embarrassment, shame, and guilt: A study of recalled antecedents and facial expressions of emotion. *Cognition and Emotion, 10*, 155–171.

Kendler, K.S. (1996). Parenting: A genetic-epidemiological perspective. *American Journal of Psychiatry, 153*, 11–20.

Kent, S., Bret-Dibat, J.L., Kelley, K.W., & Dantzer, R. (1996). Mechanisms of sickness-induced decreases in food-motivated behavior. *Neuroscience and Biobehavioral Reviews, 20*, 171–175.

Kestenbaum, R., Farber, E.A., & Stroufe, L.A. (1989). Individual differences in empathy among preschoolers: Relation to attachment history. In N. Eisenberg (Ed.), *Empathy and Related Emotional Responses* (pp. 51–64). San Francisco: Jossey-Bass Inc.

Kety, S.S. (1976). Studies based on a total sample of adopted individuals and their relatives: Why they were necessary, what they demonstrated and failed to demonstrate. *Schizophrenia Bulletin, 2*, 413–428.

Kety, S.S. (1987). The significance of genetic factors in the etiology of schizophrenia: Results from the national study of adoptees in Denmark. *Journal of Psychiatric Research, 6*, 345–362.

King, M.-C., & Wilson, A.C. (1975). Evolution at two levels in humans and chimpanzees. *Science, 188*, 107–116.

King, N.J., Ollier, K., Iacuone, R., Schuster, S., Bays, K., Gullone, E., & Ollendick, T.H. (1989). Fears of children and adolescents: A cross-sectional Australian study using the Revised-Fear Survey Schedule for Children. *Journal of Child Psychology and Psychiatry, 30*, 775–784.

Kirschbaum, C., & Hellhammer, D.H. (1989). Salivary cortisol in psychobiological research. *Neuropsychobiology, 22*, 150–169.

Kissileff, H.R. (1973). Nonhomeostatic controls of drinking. In A.M. Epstein, H.R. Kissileff, and E. Stellar (Eds.) *The Neuropsychology of Thirst* (pp. 163–198). New York: Wiley and Sons.

Klaus, H.M., & Kennell, J.H. (1976). *Maternal-Infant Bonding*. St. Louis: Mosby.

Kling, A. (1972). Effects of amygdalectomy on social-affective behavior in non-human primates. In B.E. Eleftheriou (Ed.), *The Neurobiology of the Amygdala* (pp. 511–536). New York: Plenum.

Klüver, H., & Bucy, P.C. (1937). "Psychic blindness" and other symptoms following bilateral temporal lobectomy in Rhesus monkeys. *American Journal of Physiology, 119*, 352–353.

Knapp, M.L. (1980). *Essentials of Non-Verbal Communication*. New York: Holt, Rinehart and Winston.

Komisaruk, B.R., & Steinman, J.L. (1986). Genital stimulation as a trigger for neuroendocrine and behavioral control of reproduction. *Annals of the New York Academy of Sciences, 474*, 64–75.

Krebs, J.R., & Davies, N.B. (Eds.) (1991). *Behavioural Ecology: An Evolutionary Approach* (3rd ed.). Oxford: Blackwell Scientific Publications.

Kreitman, N. (1977). *Parasuicide*. New York: John Wiley & Sons.

Kreuz, L.E., Rose, R.M., & Jennings, J.R. (1972). Suppression of plasma testosterone levels and psychological stress. *Archives of General Psychiatry, 26*, 479–482.

Krieckhaus, E.E., & Wolf, G. (1968). Acquisition of sodium by rats: Interaction of innate mechanisms and latent learning. *Journal of Comparative and Physiological Psychology, 65*, 197–201.

Kuhme, W. (1963). Erganzende beobachtungen an afrikaischen Elefanten im Freigehege. *Zeitschrift für Tierpsychologie, 20*, 66–79.

Kuhnle, U., Bullinger, M., Schwarz, H.P., & Knorr, D. (1993). Partnership and sexuality in adult female patients with congenital adrenal hyperplasia. First results of a cross-sectional quality-of-life evaluation. *Journal of Steroid Biochemistry and Molecular Biology, 45*, 123–126.

Kupfermann, I. (1991a). Hypothalamus and limbic system: Peptidergic neurons, homeostasis, and emotional behavior. In E.R. Kandel, J.H. Schwartz, & T.M. Jessell (Eds.), *Principles of Neural Science (3rd ed.)* (pp. 735–749). Norwalk, CT: Appleton & Lange.

Kupfermann, I. (1991b). Hypothalamus and limbic system: Motivation. In E.R. Kandel, J.H. Schwartz, & T.M. Jessell (Eds.), *Principles of Neural Science (3rd ed.)* (pp. 750–760). Norwalk, CT: Appleton & Lange.

Labott, S.M., Ahleman, S., Wolever, M.E., & Martin, R.B. (1990). The physiological and psychological effects of the expression and inhibition of emotion. *Behavioral Medicine, 16*, 182–189.

Labov, J. (1980). Factors influencing infanticidal behavior in wild male house mice. *Behavioral Ecology and Sociobiology, 6*, 297–303.

Lack, D. (1968). *Ecological Adaptations for Breeding in Birds*. London: Methuen.

Lagerspetz, K. (1964). *Studies on the Aggressive Behaviour of House Mice*. Helsinki: Suomaleinen Tiedeakatemia.

Lam, D.A., & Miron, J.A. (1994). Global patterns of seasonal variation in human fertility. *Annals of the New York Academy of Sciences, 709*, 9–28.

Lamb, M.E. (1977). Father-infant and mother-infant interaction in the first year of life. *Child Development, 48*, 167–181.

Lang, R.E., Heil, W.E., Ganten, D., Hermann, K., Unger, T., & Rascher, W. (1983). Oxytocin unlike vasopressin is a stress hormone in the rat. *Neuroendocrinology, 37,* 314–316.

Langhans, W. (1996). Role of the liver in the metabolic control of eating: What we know—and what we do not know. *Neuroscience and Biobehavioral Reviews, 20,* 145–153.

Langness, L.L. (1981). Child abuse and cultural values: The case of New Guinea. In J.E. Korbine (Ed.), *Child Abuse and Neglect* (pp. 13–34). Berkeley: University of California Press.

Lapouse, R., & Monk, M.A. (1959). Fears and worries in a representative sample of children. *American Journal of Orthopsychiatry, 29,* 803–818.

Lautenbacher, S., Roscher, S., Strain, D., Fassbender, K., Krumrey, K., & Krieg, J.C. (1994). Pain perception in depression: Relationships to symptomatology and naloxone-sensitive mechanisms. *Psychosomatic Medicine, 56,* 345–352.

Layne, C. (1983). Painful truths about depressives' cognitions. *Journal of Clinical Psychology, 39,* 848–853.

Leary, M.R., & Meadows, S. (1991). Predictors, elicitors, and concomitants of social blushing. *Journal of Personality and Social Psychology, 60,* 254–262.

LeBoeuf, B.J. (1974). Male-male competition and reproductive success in elephant seals. *American Zoologist, 14,* 163–176.

Lee, Y., Schulkin, J., & Davis, M. (1994). Effect of corticosterone on the enhancement of the acoustic startle reflex by corticotropin releasing factor (CRF). *Brain Research, 666,* 93–98.

Leedy, M.G., & Wilson, M.S. (1985). Testosterone and cortisol levels in crewmen of U.S. Air Force fighter and cargo planes. *Psychosomatic Medicine, 47,* 333–338.

Leighton, A.H., & Hughes, C.C. (1955). Notes on Eskimo patterns of suicide. *Southwestern Journal of Anthropology, 11,* 327–338.

LeMagnen, J., & Tallon, S. (1966). La periodicité spontanée de la prise d'aliments ad libitum du rat blanc. *Journal of Physiology (Paris), 58,* 323–349.

Lenz, H.J., Raedler, A., Greten, H., & Brown, M.R. (1987). CRF initiates biological reactions within the brain that are observed in response to stress. *American Journal of Physiology, 252,* R34–R39.

Leshner, A.I. (1983). The hormonal responses to competition and their behavioral significance. In B.B. Svare (Ed.), *Hormones and Aggressive Behavior* (pp. 393–404). New York: Plenum Press.

Lester, B.M. (1985). Introduction: There's more to crying than meets the ear. In B.M. Lester & C.F. Boukydis (Eds.), *Infant Crying: Theoretical and Research Perspectives* (pp.1–27). New York, Plenum Press.

Lester, D. (1986). Genetics, twin studies, and suicide. *Suicide & Life-Threatening Behavior, 16,* 274–285.

Leung, A.K.D., & Robson, W.L.M. (1991). Sibling rivalry. *Clinical Pediatrics, 30,* 314–317.

LeVay, S. (1991). A difference in hypothalamic structure between heterosexual and homosexual men. *Science, 253,* 1034–1037.

Levenson, R.W., & Ruef, A.M. (1992). Empathy: A physiological substrate. *Journal of Personality and Social Psychology, 63,* 234–246.

Levin, J.S., & DeFrank, R.S. (1988). Maternal stress and pregnancy outcomes: A review of the psychosocial literature. *Journal of Psychosomatic Obstetrics and Gynecology, 9,* 3–16.

Levine, R.J. (1994). Male factors contributing to the seasonality of human reproduction. *Annals of the New York Academy of Sciences, 709,* 29–45.

Levy, S., Herberman, R., Lippman, M., & d'Angelo, T. (1987). Correlation of stress factors with sustained depression of natural killer cell activity and predicted prognosis in patients with breast cancer. *Journal of Clinical Oncology, 5,* 348–353.

Lewinsohn, P.M. (1974). A behavioral approach to depression. In R.J. Friedman & M.M. Katz (Eds.), *The Psychology of Depression: Contemporary Theory and Research* (pp. 157–185). Washington, D.C.: Winston-Wiley.

Lewis, C.E. (1991). Neurochemical mechanisms of chronic antisocial behavior (Psychopathy). *Journal of Nervous and Mental Disease, 179,* 720–727.

Lewis, M., Alessandri, S.M., & Sullivan, M.W. (1992). Differences in shame and pride as a function of children's gender and task difficulty. *Child Development, 63,* 630–638.

Lewis, M., Stranger, C., Sullivan, M.W., & Barone, P. (1991). Changes in embarrassment as a function of age, sex, and situation. *British Journal of Experimental Psychology, 9,* 485–492.

Leyhausen, P. (1956). Verhaltensstudien an Katzen. *Zeitschrift für Tierpsychologie* Beiheft, 2.

Liebowitz, M.R. (1983). *The Chemistry of Love.* Boston: Little, Brown.

Lincoln, G.A. (1981). Seasonal aspects of testicular function. In H. Burger & D. deKretser (Eds.), *The Testis* (pp. 255–302). New York: Raven Press.

Lindemann, E. (1944). Symptomatology and management of acute grief. *American Journal of Psychiatry, 101,* 141–149.

Lindsley, D.B. (1957). Psychophysiology and motivation. In M.R. Jones (Ed.), *Nebraska Symposium on Motivation* (Vol. 5., pp. 44–105). Lincoln, NE: University of Nebraska Press.

Lindzey, G., Loehlin, J., Manosevitz, M., & Thiessen, O. (1971). Behavioral genetics. *Annual Review of Psychology, 22,* 39–94.

Llewellyn-Jones, D. (1974). *Human Reproduction and Society.* London: Faber and Faber.

Lorenz, K. (1950). The comparative method in the study of innate behavior patterns. *Symposia of the Society for Experimental Biology, 4,* 221–268.

Lorenz, K. (1963). *On Aggression.* New York: Bantam.

Louis-Sylvestre, J., & LeMagnen, J. (1980). A fall in blood glucose level precedes meal onset in freefeeding rats. *Neuroscience and Biobehavioral Reviews, 4,* 13–15.

Lucas, A., Morley, R., Cole, T.J., Lister, G., & Leeson-Payne, C. (1992). Breast milk and subsequent intelligence quotient in children born preterm. *The Lancet, 339,* 261–264.

Lumsden, C., & Wilson, E.O. (1981). *Genes, Mind, and Culture.* Cambridge, MA: Harvard University Press.

Lykken, D.T. (1982). Research with twins: The concept of emergenesis. *Psychophysiology, 19,* 361–373.

MacArthur, R.H., & Wilson, E.O. (1967). *The Theory of Island Biogeography.* Princeton, NJ: Princeton University Press.

MacKay, E.M., Callaway, J.W., & Barnes, R.H. (1940). Hyperalimentation in normal animals produced by protamine insulin. *Journal of Nutrition, 20,* 59–66.

MacRae, J., Scoles, M., & Siegel, S. (1987). The contribution of conditioning to drug tolerance and dependence. *British Journal of Addiction, 82,* 371–380.

Maddison, S., Rolls, B.J., Rolls, E.T., & Wood, R.J. (1977). Analysis of drinking in the chronically canulated monkey. *Journal of Physiology, 272,* 4–5.

Maddison, S., Rolls, B.J., Rolls, E.T., & Wood, R.J. (1980). The role of gastric factors in drinking termination in the monkey. *Journal of Physiology, 305,* 55–56.

Malmo, R.B., & Mundl, W.J. (1975). Osmosensitive neurons in the rat's preoptic area: Medial-lateral comparison. *Journal of Comparative and Physiological Psychology, 88,* 161–175.

Malsbury, C.W. (1971). Facilitation of male copulatory behavior by electrical stimulation of the medial preoptic area. *Physiology and Behavior, 7,* 797–805.

Mandler, G. (1975). *Mind and Emotion.* New York: Wiley.

Manning, A. (1961). Effects of artificial selection for mating speed in *Drosophila melanogaster. Animal Behaviour, 9,* 82–92.

Mariam, M.W. (1986). *Rural Vulnerability to Famine in Ethiopia—1958–1977.* London: Intermediate Technology Publications.

Maris, R.W. (1981). *Pathways to suicide: A survey of self-destructive behaviors.* Baltimore: Johns Hopkins University Press.

Marlatt, G.A., & Donovan, D.A. (1981). Alcoholism and drug dependence: Cognitive social-learning factors in addictive behaviors. In W.E. Craighead, A.E. Kazdin, & M.J. Mahoney (Eds.), *Behavior Modification: Principles, Issues, and Applications.* (2nd ed., pp. 264–285). Boston: Houghton Mifflin.

Marler, P. (1965). Communication in monkeys and apes. In I. DeVore (Ed.), *Primate Behavior: Field Studies of Monkeys and Apes* (pp. 544–584). New York: Holt, Rinehart and Winston.

Marler, P., & Tamura, M. (1964). Culturally transmitted patterns of vocal behavior in sparrows. *Science, 146,* 1483–1486.

Marquis, J.N. (1970). Orgasmic reconditioning: Changing the sexual object through controlling masturbation fantasies. *Journal of Behavior Therapy and Experimental Psychiatry, 1,* 263–271.

Marshall, W.L. (1974). The classical conditioning of sexual attractiveness: A report of four therapeutic failures. *Behavior Therapy, 5,* 298–299.

Masciuch, S., & Kienapple, K. (1993). The emergence of jealousy in children 4 months to 7 years of age. *Journal of Social and Personal Relationships, 10,* 421–435.

Maslow, A.H. (1968). *Toward a Psychology of Being* (2nd ed.). New York: Van Nostrand.

Mason, W.A. (1965). The social development of monkeys and apes. In I. DeVore (Ed.), *Primate Behavior: Field Studies of Monkeys and Apes* (pp. 514–543). New York: Holt, Rinehart and Winston.

Masters, W.H., & Johnson, V.E. (1966). *Human Sexual Response.* Boston: Little, Brown.

Masters, W.H., & Johnson, V.E. (1970). *Human Sexual Inadequacy.* Boston: Little, Brown.

Matussek, P. (1975). *Internment in Concentration Camps and Its Consequences.* New York: Springer-Verlag.

Maxson, S.C., Shrenker, P., & Vigue, L.C. (1983). Genetics, hormones, and aggression. In B.B. Svare (Ed.), *Hormones and Aggressive Behavior* (pp. 179–196). New York: Plenum Press.

Mayer, J. (1953). Glucostatic mechanisms in the regulation of food intake. *New England Journal of Medicine, 249,* 13–16.

Mazur, A. (1983). Hormones, aggression, and dominance in humans. In B.B. Svare (Ed.), *Hormones and Aggressive Behavior* (pp. 563–576). New York: Plenum Press.

Mazur, A., & Lamb, T. (1980). Testosterone, status, and mood in human males. *Hormones and Behavior, 14,* 236–246.

McClintock, M.K. (1971). Menstrual synchrony and suppression. *Nature, 229,* 244–245.

McClintock, M.K. (1983). Pheromonal regulation of the ovarian cycle: Enhancement, suppression, and synchrony. In J.G. Vandenbergh (Ed.), *Pheromones and Reproduction in Mammals* (pp. 113–150). New York: Academic Press.

McClintock, M.K. (1984). Group mating in the domestic rat as a context for sexual selection: Consequences for the analysis of sexual behavior and neuroendocrine responses. *Advances in the Study of Behavior, 14,* 1–50.

McCormick, C.M., & Witelson, S.F. (1991). A cognitive profile of homosexual men compared to heterosexual men and women. *Psychoneuroendocrinology, 16,* 459–473.

McDougall, W. (1911). *Body and Mind: A History and a Defense of Animism.* London: Methuen.

McDowell, R.J.S., & Wells, H.M. (1927). The physiology of monotony. *British Medical Journal, 1,* 414.

McGuire, R.J., Carlisle, J.M., & Young, B.G. (1965). Sexual deviations as conditioned behavior. *Behaviour Research and Therapy, 2,* 185–190.

McIntosh, E.G., & Tate, D.T. (1992). Characteristics of the rival and the experience of jealousy. *Perceptual and Motor Skills, 74,* 369–370.

McNeilly, A.S., Tay, C.C.K., & Glasier, A. (1994). Physiological mechanisms underlying lactational amenorrhea. *Annals of the New York Academy of Sciences, 709,* 145–155.

Medawar, P. B. (1957). *The Uniqueness of the Individual.* London: Methuen.

Meer, F. (1976). *Race and suicide in South Africa.* London: Routledge & Kegan Paul.

Mellinger, G.D. (1978). Use of licit drugs and other coping alternatives: Some personal observations on the hazards of living. In D.J. Lettieri (Ed.) *Drugs and Suicide.* London: Sage Publications.

Melzack, R., & Wall, P.D. (1965). Pain mechanisms: A new theory. *Science, 150,* 971–979.

Mendel, G.J. (1866). Versuche über Pflanzenhybriden. *Verhandungen des Naturforschunden Vereines in Bruenn, 4,* 3–47.

Menzel, E.W. (1973). Chimpanzee spatial memory organization. *Science, 182,* 943–945.

Mesquita, B., & Frijda, N.H. (1992). Cultural variation in emotions: A review. *Psychological Bulletin, 112,* 179–204.

Meyer-Bahlburg, H.F.L., Ehrhardt, A.A., Rosen, L.R., Gruen, R.S., Veridiano, N.P., Vann, F.H., & Neuwalder, H.F. (1995). Prenatal estrogen and the development of homosexual orientation. *Developmental Psychology, 3,* 12–21.

Millar, W.J. (1995). Accidents in Canada, 1988 and 1993. *Health Reports* (Statistics Canada), *7(2),* 7–16.

Miller, N.E. (1959). Liberalization of basic S-R concepts: Extensions to conflict behavior, motivation, and social learning. In S. Koch (Ed.), *Psychology: A Study of a Science* (vol. 2, pp. 196–293). New York: McGraw-Hill.

Miller, P.A., Eisenberg, N., Fabes, R.A., Shell, R., & Gular, S. (1989). Mothers' emotional arousal as a moderator in the socialization of children's empathy. In N. Eisenberg (Ed.), *Empathy and Related Emotional Responses* (pp. 65–83). San Francisco: Jossey-Bass.

Miller, R.S., & Tangney, J.P. (1994). Differentiating embarrassment and shame. *Journal of Social and Clinical Psychology, 13,* 273–287.

Miller, T.W. (1988). Advances in understanding the impact of stressful life events on health. *Hospital and Community Psychiatry, 39,* 615–622.

Mineka, S., & Cook, M. (1986). Immunization against the observational conditioning of snake fear in rhesus monkeys. *Journal of Abnormal Psychology, 95,* 307–318.

Mineka, S., Davidson, M., Cook, M., & Keir, R. (1984). Observational conditioning of snake fear in Rhesus monkeys. *Journal of Abnormal Psychology, 93,* 355–372.

Mischel, W., Shoda, Y., & Rodriguez, M.L. (1989). Delay of gratification in children. *Science, 244,* 933–938.

Modigh, K. (1973). Effects of isolation and fighting in mice on the rate of synthesis of noradrenaline, dopamine and 5-hydroxytryptamine in the brain. *Psychopharmacologia, 33,* 1–17.

Mogenson, G.J. (1977). *The Neurobiology of Behavior: An Introduction.* Hillsdale, NJ: Lawrence Erlbaum Associates.

Mogenson, G.J., Gentil, C.G., & Stevenson, J.A.F. (1971). Feeding and drinking elicited by low and high frequencies of hypothalamic stimulation. *Brain Research, 33*, 127–133.

Moltz, H. (1965). Contemporary instinct theory and the fixed action pattern. *Psychological Review, 72*, 27–47.

Money, J. (1961). Sex hormones and other variables in human eroticism. In W.C. Young (Ed.), *Sex and Internal Secretions* (3rd ed., vol. II, pp. 1383–1400). Baltimore: Williams & Wilkins.

Money, J., & Ehrhardt, A.A. (1972). *Man and Woman, Boy and Girl*. Baltimore: Johns Hopkins University Press.

Mook, D.G. (1987). *Motivation: The Organization of Action*. New York: Norton.

Mook, D.G., Culberson, R., Gelbert, R.J., & McDonald, K. (1983). Oropharyngeal control of ingestion in rats: Acquisition of sham-drinking patterns. *Behavioral Neuroscience, 97*, 574–584.

Morris, J.S., Frith, C.D., Perrett, D.I., Rowland, D., Young, A.W., Calder, A.J., & Dolan, R.J. (1996). A differential neural response in the human amygdala to fearful and happy facial expressions. *Nature, 383*, 812–815.

Morse, J.M., & Morse, R.M. (1988). Cultural variation in the inference of pain. *Journal of Cross-Cultural Psychology, 19*, 232–242.

Motto, J.A. (1986). Clinical considerations of biological correlates of suicide. *Suicide and Life-Threatening Behavior, 16*, 83–102.

Mousa, S., Miller, C.H., & Couri, D. (1981). Corticosteroid modulation and stress-induced analgesia in rats. *Neuroendocrinology, 33*, 317–319.

Moyer, K.E. (1968). Kinds of aggression and their physiological basis. *Communications in Behavioral Biology, 2*, 68–87.

Murdock, P.M. (1967). *Ethnographic Atlas*. Pittsburgh: University of Pittsburgh Press.

Nachman, M. (1962). Taste preference for sodium salts by adrenalectomized rats. *Journal of Comparative and Physiological Psychology, 55*, 1124–1129.

Nance, D.M., Shryne, J., & Gorski, R.A. (1975). Effects of septal lesions on behavioral sensitivity of female rats to gonadal hormones. *Hormones and Behavior, 6*, 59–64.

Neiss, R. (1988). Reconceptualizing arousal: Psychobiological states in motor-performance. *Psychological Bulletin, 103*, 345–366.

Nesse, R.M., Curtis, G.C., Thyer, B.A., McCann, D.S., Huber-Smith, M.J., & Knopf, R.F. (1985). Endocrine and cardiovascular responses during phobic anxiety. *Psychosomatic Medicine, 47*, 320–332.

Nevin, J.A., & Reynolds, G.S. (1973). *The Study of Behavior*. Glenview, IL: Scott, Foresman.

Newman, J.D. (1985). The infant cry of primates: An evolutionary perspective. In B.M. Lester & C.F. Boukydis (Eds.), *Infant Crying: Theoretical and Research Perspectives* (pp. 307–323). New York: Plenum Press.

Niijima, A. (1969). Afferent impulse discharges from glucoreceptors in the liver of the guinea pig. *Annals of the New York Academy of Sciences, 157*, 690–700.

Nisbett, R.E. (1972). Hunger, obesity, and the ventromedial hypothalamus. *Psychological Review, 79*, 433–453.

Nurnberger, J.L., & Gershon, E.S. (1981). Genetics of affective disorders. In E. Friedman (Ed.), *Depression and Antidepressants: Implications for Courses and Treatment* (pp. 23–39). New York: Raven Press.

O'Connell, S.M. (1995). Empathy in chimpanzees: Evidence for theory of mind. *Primates, 36*, 397–410.

O'Connor, L.H., & Feder, H.H. (1983). Effect of serotonin agonists on lordosis, myoclonus, and cytoplasmic progestin receptors in the guinea pig. *Hormones and Behavior, 17,* 183–196.

O'Hara, M.W. (1987). Post-partum "blues," depression, and psychosis: A review. *Journal of Psychosomatic Obstetrics and Gynecology, 7,* 205–227.

Olds, J., & Fobes, J.L. (1981). The central basis of motivation: Intracranial self-stimulation studies. *Annual Review of Psychology, 32,* 523–574.

Olds, J., & Milner, P. (1954). Positive reinforcement produced by electrical stimulation of septal area and other regions of the rat brain. *Journal of Comparative and Physiological Psychology, 47,* 419–427.

Ollendick, T.H., King, N.J., & Frary, R.B. (1989). Fears in children and adolescents: Reliability and generalization across gender, age and nationality. *Behaviour Research and Therapy, 27,* 19–26.

Oomura, Y., Yoshimatsu, H., & Aou, S. (1983). Medial preoptic and hypothalamic neuronal activity during sexual behavior of the male monkey. *Brain Research, 266,* 340–343.

Orians, G.H. (1969). On the evolution of mating systems in birds and mammals. *American Naturalist, 103,* 589–603.

Orpen, B.G., & Fleming, A.S. (1987). Experience with pups sustains maternal responding in postpartum rats. *Physiology and Behavior, 40,* 47–54.

Owens, M.J., & Nemeroff, C.B. (1994). Role of serotonin in the pathophysiology of depression: Focus on the serotonin transporter. *Clinical Chemistry, 40,* 288–296.

Palinkas, L.A., & Browner, D. (1995). Effects of prolonged isolation in extreme environments on stress, coping, and depression. *Journal of Applied Social Psychology, 25,* 557–576.

Panksepp, J. (1971). Aggression elicited by electrical stimulation of the hypothalamus in albino rats. *Physiology and Behavior, 6,* 317–320.

Panksepp, J. (1982). Toward a general psychobiological theory of emotions. *The Behavioral and Brain Sciences, 5,* 407–467.

Papez, J.W. (1937). A proposed mechanism of emotion. *Archives of Neurology and Psychiatry, 38,* 725–743.

Parkes, C.M., Benjamin, B., & Fitzgerald, R.G. (1969). Broken heart: A statistical study of increased mortality among widowers. *British Medical Journal, 1,* 740–743.

Parkes, C.M. (1972). *Bereavement.* New York: International Universities Press.

Parkin, D., & Stengel, E. (1965). Incidence of suicidal attempts in an urban community. *British Medical Journal, 2,* 133–137.

Parrott, W.G., & Smith, R.H. (1993). Distinguishing the experiences of envy and jealousy. *Journal of Personality and Social Psychology, 64,* 906–920.

Parvez, H., & Parvez, S. (1973). The regulation of monoamine oxidase activity by adrenal cortical steroids. *Acta Endocrinologica, 73,* 509–517.

Patrick, C.P., Bradley, M.M., & Lang, P.J. (1993). Emotion in the criminal psychopath: Startle reflex modulation. *Journal of Abnormal Psychology, 102,* 82–92.

Patrick, C.P., Cuthbert, B.N., & Lang, P.J. (1994). Emotion in the criminal psychopath: Fear image processing. *Journal of Abnormal Psychology, 103,* 523–534.

Patterson, G.R., DeBaryshe, B.D., & Ramsey, E. (1989). A developmental perspective on antisocial behavior. *American Psychologist, 44,* 329–335.

Paul, G.L., & Bernstein, D.A. (1973). *Anxiety and Clinical Problems: Systematic Desensitization and Related Techniques.* Morristown, NJ: General Learning Press.

Pavlov, I.P. (1927). *Conditioned Reflexes.* G.V. Anrep (Trans.) Oxford: Clarendon Press.

Pederson, A.M., Awad, G.A., & Kindler, A.R. (1973). Epidemiological differences between white and non-white suicide attempters. *American Journal of Psychiatry, 130,* 1071–1076.

Pederson, N.L., Plomin, R., McClearn, G.E., & Friberg, L. (1988). Neuroticism, extraversion and related traits in adult twins reared apart and reared together. *Journal of Personality and Social Psychology, 55,* 950–957.

Peele, S. (1985). *The Meaning of Addiction: Compulsive Experience and Its Interpretation.* Lexington, MA: Lexington Books.

Pfaff, D.W. (1980). *Estrogens and Brain Function.* New York: Springer-Verlag.

Pfaffmann, C. (1977). Biological and behavioral substrates of the sweet tooth. In J.M. Weiffenbach (Ed.), *Taste and Development: The Genesis of Sweet Preference* (pp. 3–24). Bethesda, MD: U.S. Department of Health, Education, and Welfare.

Phillips, D.P. (1974). The influence of suggestion on suicide: Substantive and theoretical implications of the Werther effect. *American Sociological Review, 39,* 340–354.

Phillips, D.P., & King, E.W. (1988). Death takes a holiday: Mortality surrounding major social occasions. *The Lancet, 2,* 728–732.

Phillips, D.P., & Smith, D.G. (1990). Postponement of death until symbolically meaningful occasions. *Journal of the American Medical Association, 263,* 1947–1951.

Phoenix, C. (1974). Effects of dihydrotestosterone on sexual behavior of castrated male Rhesus monkeys. *Physiology and Behavior, 12,* 1045–1055.

Pinel, J.P.J. (1997). *Biopsychology* (3rd ed.). Boston: Allyn & Bacon.

Pinel, J.P.J., Gorzalka, B.B., & Ladak, F. (1981). Cadaverine and putrescine initiate the burial of dead conspecifics by rats. *Physiology and Behavior, 27,* 819–824.

Pinel, J.P.J., & Treit, D. (1978). Burying as a defensive response in rats. *Journal of Comparative and Physiological Psychology, 92,* 708–712.

Pintrich, P.R., & Schunk, D.H. (1996). *Motivation in Education: Theory, Research, and Applications.* Upper Saddle River, NJ: Prentice Hall.

Plomin, R., DeFries, J.C., & McClearn, G.E. (1990). *Behavioral Genetics: A Primer* (2nd Ed.). New York: W.H. Freeman.

Plutchik, R. (1983). Emotions in early development: A psychoevolutionary approach. In R. Plutchik & H. Kellerman (Eds.), *Emotion: Theory, Research, and Experience—Volume 2: Emotions in Early Development* (pp. 221–257). New York: Academic Press.

Plutchik, R. (1994). *The Psychology and Biology of Emotion.* New York: HarperCollins.

Povinelli, D.J., Nelson, K.E., & Boysen, S.T. (1992a). Comprehension of role reversal in chimpanzees. *Animal Behaviour, 43,* 633–640.

Povinelli, D.J., Parks, K.A., & Novak, M.A. (1992b). Role reversal by rhesus monkeys, but no evidence of empathy. *Animal Behaviour, 43,* 269–281.

Powley, T.L., & Opsahl, C.A. (1974). Ventromedial hypothalamic obesity abolished by subdiaphragmatic vagotomy. *American Journal of Physiology, 226,* 25–33.

Poyatos, F. (1988). *Cross-Cultural Perspectives in Nonverbal Communication.* Toronto: C. J. Hogrefe Inc.

Premack, D. (1959). Toward empirical behavior laws: I. Positive reinforcement. *Psychological Review, 66,* 219–233.

Provine, R.R. (1986). Yawning as a stereotyped action pattern and releasing stimulus. *Ethology, 72,* 109–122.

Quadagno, D.M., Briscoe, R., & Quadagno, J.S. (1977). Effects of perinatal gonadal hormones on selected nonsexual behavior patterns: A critical assessment of the non-human and human literatures. *Psychological Bulletin, 84,* 62–80.

Rabedeau, R.G., & Whalen, R.E. (1959). Effects of copulatory experience on mating behavior in the male rat. *Journal of Comparative and Physiological Psychology, 52*, 482–484.

Rachman, S.J. (1978). *Fear and Courage.* San Francisco: W.H. Freeman and Company.

Rachman, S.J., & Seligman, M.E.P. (1976). Unprepared phobias: "Be prepared." *Behavior Research and Therapy, 14*, 333–338.

Ramcharan, S., Love, E.J., Fick, G.H., & Goldfien, A. (1992). The epidemiology of premenstrual symptoms in a population-based sample of 2650 urban women: Attributable risk and risk factors. *Journal of Clinical Epidemiology, 45*, 377–392.

Rastogi, R.B., & Singhal, R.L. (1978). Evidence for the role of adrenocortical hormones in the regulation of noradrenaline and dopamine metabolism in central brain areas. *British Journal of Pharmacology, 62*, 131–136.

Redd, W.H., Porterfield, A.L., & Anderson, B.L. (1979). *Behavior Modification: Behavioral Approaches to Human Problems.* New York: Random House.

Redelmeier, D.A., Rozin, P., & Kahneman, D. (1993). Understanding patient's decisions: Cognitive and emotional perspectives. *Journal of the American Medical Association, 270*, 72–76.

Reid, M., & Hetherington, M. (1997). Relative effects of carbohydrates and protein on satiety—a review of methodology. *Neuroscience and Biobehavioral Reviews, 21*, 295–308.

Reinberg, A., Lagouguey, M., Chauffournier, J.M., & Cesselin, F. (1975). Rythmes annuels et circadiens de la testosterone plasmatique chez cinq parisiens jeunes, adultes et sains. *Annales d'Endocrinologie, 36*, 44–45.

Reiter, R.J. (1983). The pineal gland: An intermediary between the environment and the endocrine system. *Psychoneuroendocrinology, 8*, 31–40.

Resnick, H.S., Kilpatrick, D.G., Dansky, B.S., Saunders, B.E., & Best, C. (1993). Prevalence of civilian trauma and post-traumatic stress disorder in a representative national sample of women. *Journal of Consulting and Clinical Psychology, 61*, 984–991.

Revelle, W., Humphreys, M.S., Simon, L., & Gilliland, K. (1980). The interactive effect of personality, time of day and caffeine: A test of the arousal model. *Journal of Experimental Psychology: General, 109*, 1–31.

Reynolds, V., & Reynolds, F. (1965). Chimpanzees of the Budongo Forest. In I. DeVore (Ed.), *Primate Behavior: Field Studies of Monkeys and Apes* (pp. 368–424). New York: Holt, Rinehart and Winston.

Rice, J.P., Reich, T., Andreasen, N.C., Endicott, J., Van Eerdewegh, M., Fishman, A., Hirschfeld, R.M.A., & Klerman, G.L. (1987). The familial transmission of bipolar illness. *Archives of General Psychiatry, 41*, 441–447.

Richter, C.P. (1957). On the phenomenon of sudden death in man and animals. *Psychosomatic Medicine, 19*, 191–197.

Rimé, B., & Schiaratura, L. (1991). Gesture and speech. In R.S. Feldman & B. Rimé (Eds.), *Fundamentals of Nonverbal Behavior* (pp. 239–281). Cambridge, UK: Cambridge University Press.

Rodin, J. (1981). Current status of the internal-external hypothesis for obesity: What went wrong? *American Psychologist, 36*, 361–372.

Rohner-Jeanrenaud, F., Cusin, I., Sainsbury, A., Zakrzewska, K.E., & Jeanrenaud, B. (1996). The loop system between neuropeptide Y and leptin in normal and obese rodents. *Hormone and Metabolic Research, 28*, 642–648.

Role, L.W., & Kelly, J.P. (1991). The brain stem: Cranial nerve nuclei and the monoaminergic systems. In E.R. Kandel, J.H. Schwartz, & T.M. Jessell (Eds.), *Principles of Neural Science* (3rd ed.) (pp. 683–700). Norwalk, Connecticut: Appleton & Lange.

Rollman, G.B. (1979). Signal detection theory pain measures: Empirical validation studies and adaptation-level effects. *Pain, 6*, 9–21.

Rolls, B.J., Wood, R.J., & Rolls, E.T. (1980). Thirst: The initiation, maintenance, and termination of drinking. In J.M. Sprague & A.N. Epstein (Eds.), *Progress in Psychobiology and Physiological Psychology* (Vol. 9) (pp. 263–321). New York: Academic Press.

Roper, M.K. (1969). A survey of the evidence for intrahuman killing in the Pleistocene. *Current Anthropology, 10,* 427–459.

Rosen, G. (1971). History in the study of suicide. *Psychological Medicine, 1,* 267–285.

Rosenstein, D., & Oster, H. (1988). Differential facial response to four basic tastes in newborns. *Child Development, 59,* 1555–1568.

Rosenthal, D. (1970). *Genetic Theory and Abnormal Behavior.* New York: McGraw-Hill.

Rosenzweig, M.R., Leiman, A.L., & Breedlove, S.M. (1996). *Biological Psychology.* Sunderland, MA: Sinauer Associates.

Rossi, A.S., & Rossi, P.E. (1980). Body time and social time: Mood patterns by menstrual cycle phase and day of week. In J.E. Parsons (Ed.), *The Psychobiology of Sex Differences and Sex Roles* (pp. 269–304). New York: McGraw-Hill.

Roth, W.E. (1970). *Animism and Folk-Lore of the Guiana Indians.* New York: Johnson Reprint Corporation. (Original work published in 1915.)

Rothblum, E.D. (1990). Psychological factors in the Antarctic. *The Journal of Psychology, 124,* 253–273.

Rowell, T. (1963). Behavior and female reproductive cycles of Rhesus macaques. *Journal of Reproduction and Fertility, 6,* 193–203.

Roy, A. (1992). Genetics, biology, and suicide in the family. In R.W. Maris, A.L. Berman, J.T. Maltsberger, & R.I. Yufit (Eds.), *Assessment and Prediction of Suicide.* New York: Guilford.

Rozin, P. (1968). Specific aversions and neophobia as a consequence of vitamin deficiency and/or poisoning in half-wild and domestic rats. *Journal of Comparative and Physiological Psychology, 66,* 82–88.

Rozin, P. (1989). The role of learning in the acquisition of food preferences by humans. In R. Shepherd (Ed.), *Handbook of the Psychophysiology of Human Eating* (pp. 205–227). Chichester UK: John Wiley & Sons Ltd.

Rozin, P., & Kalat, J.W. (1971). Specific hungers and poison avoidance as adaptive specializations of learning. *Psychological Review, 78,* 459–486.

Russek, M. (1963). Participation of hepatic glucoreceptors in the control of intake of food. Nature *197,* 79–80.

Russell, J.A. (1994). Is there universal recognition of emotion from facial expression? A review of the cross-cultural studies. *Psychological Bulletin 115,* 102–141.

Sackett, G.P. (1966). Monkeys reared in isolation with pictures as visual input: Evidence for an innate releasing mechanism. *Science, 154,* 1468–1473.

Sandner, G., Oberling, P., Silveira, M.C., Di Scala, G., Rocha, B., Bagri, A., & Depoortere, R. (1993). What brain structures are active during emotions? Effects of brain stimulation elicited aversion on *c-fos* immunoreactivity and behavior. *Behavioural Brain Research, 58,* 9–18.

Sarbin, T.R. (1968). Ontology recapitulates philology: The mythic nature of anxiety. *American Psychologist, 23,* 411–418.

Sarles, H., Dani, R., Prezlin, G., Souville, C., & Figarella, C. (1968). Cephalic phase of pancreatic secretion in man. *Gut, 9,* 214–221.

Sarrieau, A., Dussaillant, M., Agid, F., Philibert, D., Agid, Y., & Rostene, W. (1986). Autoradiographic localization of glucocorticoid and progesterone binding sites in the human post-mortem brain. *Journal of Steroid Biochemistry, 25,* 717–721.

Savins-Williams, R.C. (1987). An ethological perspective on homosexuality during adolescence. *Journal of Adolescent Research, 2,* 283–302.

Schachter, S. (1971). Some extraordinary facts about obese humans and rats. *American Psychologist, 26,* 129–144.

Schachter, S., & Singer, J.E. (1962). Cognitive, social, and physiological determinants of emotional state. *Psychological Review, 69,* 379–399.

Schaller, G.B. (1965). The behavior of the mountain gorilla. In I. DeVore (Ed.), *Primate Behavior: Field Studies of Monkeys and Apes* (pp. 324–367). New York: Holt, Rinehart and Winston.

Schaller, G.B. (1972). *The Serengeti Lion: A Study of Predator-Prey Relations.* Chicago: University of Chicago Press.

Scherer, K.R. (1986). Vocal affect expression: A review and a model for future research. *Psychological Bulletin, 99,* 143–165.

Schleidt, W. (1965). Gaussian interval distributions in spontaneously occurring innate behaviour. *Nature, 206,* 1061–1062.

Schmidt, L.A., Fox, N.A., Rubin, K.H., Sternberg, E.M., Gold, P.W., Smith, C.C., & Schulkin, J. (1997). Behavioral and neuroendocrine responses in shy children. *Developmental Psychobiology, 30,* 127–140.

Schmitt, M. (1973). Influences of hepatic portal receptors on hypothalamic feeding and satiety centers. *American Journal of Physiology, 225,* 1089–1095.

Schneller, R. (1988). The Israeli experience of cross-cultural misunderstanding: Insights and lessons. In F. Poyatos (Ed.), *Cross-Cultural Perspectives in Nonverbal Communication* (pp. 153–171). Toronto: C. J. Hogrefe Inc.

Schulkin, J., McEwen, B.S., & Gold, P.W. (1994). Allostasis, amygdala, and anticipatory angst. *Neuroscience and Biobehavioral Reviews, 18,* 385–396.

Schulsinger, F., Kety, S., Rosenthal, D., & Wender, P. (1979). A family study of suicide. In M. Schou & E. Stromgren (Eds.), *Origin, Prevention and Treatment of Affective Disorders* (pp. 277–287). London: Academic Press.

Schwartz, G.J., & Moran, T.H. (1996). Sub-diaphragmatic vagal afferent integration of meal-related gastrointestinal signals. *Neuroscience and Biobehavioral Reviews, 20,* 47–56.

Schwartz, J.H. (1991). Chemical messengers: Small molecules and peptides. In E.R. Kandel, J.H. Schwartz, & T.M. Jessell, (Eds.), *Principles of Neural Science (3rd ed.)* (pp. 213–224). Norwalk, CT: Appleton & Lange.

Sclafani, A. (1976). Appetite and hunger in experimental obesity syndromes. In D. Novin, W. Warwicka, & G.A. Bray, (Eds.), *Hunger: Basic Mechanisms and Clinical Implications* (pp. 281–295). New York: Raven Press.

Scott, J.P. (1962). Critical periods in behavioral development. *Science, 138,* 949–958.

Scott, J.P., & Fuller, J.L. (1965). *Genetics and the Social Behavior of the Dog.* Chicago: University of Chicago Press.

Scotti, J.R., Beach, B.K., Northrop, L.M.E., Rode, C.A., & Forsyth, J.P. (1995). The psychological impact of accidental injury. In J.R. Freedy, & S.E. Hobfoll (Eds.), *Traumatic Stress: From Theory to Practice* (pp. 181–212). New York: Plenum Press.

Seaford, H.W., Jr. (1978). Maximizing replicability in describing facial behavior. *Semiotica, 24,* 1–32.

Seay, B., Hansen, E.W., & Harlow, H.F. (1962). Mother-infant separation in monkeys. *Child Psychology and Psychiatry, 3,* 123–132.

Seckl, J.R., Dickson, K.L., Yates, C., & Fink, G. (1991). Distribution of glucocorticoid and mineralocorticoid receptor messenger RNA expression in human postmortem hippocampus. *Brain Research, 561,* 332–337.

Seiden, R.H. (1966). Campus tragedy: A story of student suicide. *Journal of Abnormal and Social Psychology, 71*, 389–399.

Seitz, P.F.D. (1959). Infantile experience and adult behavior in animal subjects. II: Age of separation from the mother and adult behavior in the cat. *Psychosomatic Medicine, 21*, 353–378.

Seligman, M.E.P. (1971). Phobias and preparedness. *Behavior Therapy, 2*, 307–320.

Seligman, M.E.P. (1975). *Helplessness*. San Francisco: W.H. Freeman.

Seligman, M.E.P., & Hager, J.L. (1972). *Biological Boundaries of Learning*. New York: Appleton-Century-Crofts.

Seligman, R., Gleser, G., Rauh, J., & Harris, L. (1974). The effect of earlier parental loss in adolescence. *Archives of General Psychiatry, 31*, 475–479.

Selye, H. (1936). A syndrome produced by diverse nocuous agents. *Nature, 138*, 32.

Selye, H. (1956). *The Stress of Life*. New York: McGraw-Hill.

Selye, H. (1973). The evolution of the stress concept. *American Scientist, 61*, 692–699.

Shafir, E., Simonson, I., & Tversky, A. (1993). Reason-based choice. *Cognition, 49*, 11–36.

Shearn, D., Bergman, E., Hill, K., Abel, A., & Hinds, L. (1990). *Facial coloration and temperature responses in blushing. Psychophysiology, 27*, 687–693.

Shettleworth, S. (1973). Food reinforcement and the organization of behaviour in Golden Hamsters. In R.A. Hinde, & J. Stevenson-Hinde (Eds.), *Constraints on Learning: Limitations and Predispositions* (pp. 243–263). New York: Academic Press.

Shneidman, E.S. (1968). Classifications of suicidal phenomena. *Bulletin of Suicidology, 2*, 1–9.

Shore, J., Tatum, E., & Vollmer, W. (1986). Psychiatric reactions to disaster: The Mount St. Helen's experience. *American Journal of Psychiatry, 143*, 590–595.

Short, R.V. (1994). Human reproduction in an evolutionary context. *Annals of the New York Academy of Sciences, 709*, 416–425.

Shughrue, P.J., Stumpf, W.E., Elger, W., Schulze, P.-E., & Sar, M. (1991). Progestin receptor cells in mouse cerebral cortex during early postnatal development: A comparison of preoptic area and central hypothalamus using autoradiography with [^{125}I]progestin. *Developmental Brain Research, 59*, 143–155.

Shukla, A., Forsyth, H.A., Anderson, C.M., & Marwah, S.M. (1972). Infantile overnutrition in the first year of life: A field study in Dudley, Worcestershire. *British Medical Journal, 4*, 507–515.

Siegel, H.I. (1986). Hormonal basis of maternal behavior in the rat. *Annals of the New York Academy of Sciences, 474*, 202–215.

Siegel, P. (1972). Genetic analysis of male mating behaviour in chickens, 1. Artificial selection. *Animal Behaviour, 20*, 564–570.

Siegel, S., Krank, M.D., & Hinson, R.E. (1987). Anticipation of pharmacological and nonpharmacological events: Classical conditioning and addictive behavior. *Journal of Drug Issues, 17*, 83–110.

Sierles, F.S., Chen, J.J., McFarland, R.E., & Taylor, M.A. (1983). Post traumatic stress disorder and concurrent psychiatric illness: a preliminary report. *American Journal of Psychiatry, 140*, 1177–1179.

Simerly, R.B., Chang, C., Muramatsu, M., & Swanson, L.W. (1990). Distribution of androgen and estrogen receptor mRNA-containing cells in the rat brain: An in situ hybridization study. *Journal of Comparative Neurology, 294*, 76–95.

Skinner, B.F. (1938). *The Behavior of Organisms*. New York: Appleton-Century-Crofts.

Skinner, B.F. (1953). *Science and Human Behavior*. New York: Macmillan.

Sklar, L.S., & Anisman, H. (1980). Social stress influences tumor growth. *Psychosomatic Medicine, 42,* 347–365.

Slater, E., & Shields, J. (1969). Genetic aspects of anxiety. In M.H. Lader (Ed.), *Studies of Anxiety* (pp. 62–71). Ashford, England: Headley Brothers.

Slater, P.J.B., & Halliday, T.R. (Eds.) (1994). *Behaviour and Evolution*. Cambridge, UK: Cambridge University Press.

Smith, G.P. (1996). The direct and indirect controls of meal size. *Neuroscience and Biobehavioral Reviews, 20,* 41–46.

Smith, G.P., & Epstein, A.N. (1969). Increased feeding in response to decreased glucose utilization in the rat and monkey. *American Journal of Physiology, 217,* 1083–1087.

Smith, G.P., & Gibbs, J. (1994). Satiating effect of cholecystokinin. *Annals of the New York Academy of Sciences, 713,* 236–241.

Smith, P.K. (1982). Does play matter? Functional and evolutionary aspects of animal and human play. *The Behavioral and Brain Sciences, 5,* 139–184.

Smith, R.P. (1981). Boredom: A review. *Human Factors, 23,* 329–340.

Snyder, S.H., Taylor, K.M., Coyle, J.T., & Meyerhoff, J.L. (1972). The role of brain dopamine in behavioral regulation and the actions of psychotropic drugs. In E.H. Ellinwood & S. Cohen (Eds.), *Current Concepts of Amphetamine Abuse.* (DHEW Publication No. HSM 72-9085). Washington, D.C.: U.S. Government Printing Office.

Solomon, G.F. (1987). Psychoneuroimmunology: Interactions between central nervous system and immune system. *Journal of Neuroscience Research, 18,* 1–9.

Solomon, G.F., & Amkraut, A.A. (1983). Emotions, immunity, and disease. In L. Temoshok, C. Van Dyke, & L.S. Zegans (Eds.), *Emotions in Health and Illness: Theoretical and Research Foundations* (pp. 167–186). New York: Grune & Stratton.

Soulairac, M.-L., & Soulairac, A. (1975). Monoaminergic and cholinergic control of sexual behavior in the male rat. In M. Sandler & G.L. Gessa (Eds.), *Sexual Behavior: Pharmacology and Biochemistry* (pp. 99–116). New York: Raven Press.

Spangler, G., & Grossmann, K.E. (1993). Biobehavioral organization in securely and insecurely attached infants. *Child Development, 64,* 1439–1450.

Sparhawk, C.M. (1981). Contrastive-identification feature of Persian gesture. In T.A. Sebeok, J. Umiker-Sebeok, & A. Kendon (Eds.), *Nonverbal Communication, Interaction, and Gesture* (pp. 421–458). The Hague: Mouton Publishers.

Spitz, R.A. (1946). Anaclitic depression. In *The Psychoanalytic Study of the Child* (Vol. 2). New York: International Universities Press.

Stanley, M., Stanley, B., Traskman-Bendz, L., Mann, J.J., & Meyendorff, E. (1986). Neurochemical findings in suicide completers and suicide attempters. *Suicide & Life-Threatening Behavior, 16,* 286–300.

Stassinopoulos, A., & Beny, R. (1983). *The Gods of Greece.* Toronto: McClelland and Stewart.

Steffens, A.B. (1975). Influence of reversible obesity on eating behavior, blood glucose, and insulin in the rat. *American Journal of Physiology, 228,* 1738–1744.

Steiner, J. (1973). The gustofacial response: Observation on normal and anencephalic newborn infants. In J. Bosma (Ed.), *Fourth Symposium on Oral Sensation and Perception* (pp. 254–278). Bethesda, MD: U.S. Department of Health, Education and Welfare.

Steiner, J. (1977). Facial expression of the neonate infant indicating the hedonics of food-related chemical stimuli. In J.M. Weiffenbach (Ed.), *Taste and Development: The Genesis of Sweet Preference* (pp. 173–189). Bethesda, MD: U.S. Department of Health, Education, and Welfare.

Steinmetz, S.R. (1894). Suicide among primitive peoples. *American Anthropologist, 7*, 53–60.

Stengel, E. (1973). *Suicide and Attempted Suicide.* Harmondsworth, England: Penguin Books.

Stipek, D.J. (1993). *Motivation to Learn: From Theory to Practice* (2nd ed.). Boston: Allyn & Bacon.

Stürup, G.K. (1968). Treatment of sexual offenders in Herstedvester, Denmark: The rapists. *Acta Psychiatrica Scandinavica, 44,* Suppl. 204.

Suarez, S.D., & Gallup, G.G. (1985). Depression as a response to reproductive failure. *Journal of Social and Biological Structures, 8,* 279–287.

Sundberg, N.D., Latkin, C.A., Farmer, R.F., & Saoud, J. (1991). Boredom in young adults: Gender and cultural comparisons. *Journal of Cross-Cultural Psychology, 22,* 209–223.

Surbey, M.K., deCatanzaro, D., & Smith, M.S. (1986). Seasonality of conception in Hutterite colonies of Europe and North America. *Journal of Biosocial Science, 18,* 337–345.

Svare, B.B., & Mann, M.A. (1983). Hormonal influences on maternal aggression. In B.B. Svare (Ed.), *Hormones and Aggressive Behavior* (pp. 91–104). New York: Plenum Press.

Sveback, S. (1975). Respiratory patterns: A predictor of laughter. *Psychophysiology, 12,* 62–65.

Swaab, D.F., & Fliers, E. (1985). A sexually dimorphic nucleus in the human brain. *Science, 228,* 1112–1114.

Symons, D. (1978). *Play and Aggression: A Study of Rhesus Monkeys.* New York: Columbia University Press.

Symons, D. (1979). *The Evolution of Human Sexuality.* Oxford: Oxford University Press.

Tabachnick, N. (1973). *Accident or suicide? Destruction by an automobile,* Springfield, IL: Charles C Thomas.

Tallman, J.F., & Gallagher, D.W. (1985). The GABA-ergic system: A locus of benzodiazepine action. *Annual Review of Neuroscience, 8,* 21.

Tefft, B.M., Pederson, A.M., & Babigian, H.M. (1977). Patterns of death among suicide attempters, a psychiatric population, and a general population. *Archives of General Psychiatry, 34,* 1155–1161.

Tellegen, A., Lykken, D.T., Bouchard, T.J., Wilcox, K., Segal, N., & Rich, S. (1988). Personality similarity in twins reared apart and together. *Journal of Personality and Social Psychology, 54,* 1031–1039.

Terrace, H.S. (1973). Classical conditioning. In J.A. Nevin & G.S. Reynolds (Eds.), *The Study of Behavior* (pp. 71–112). Glenview, IL.: Scott, Foresman.

Terzian, H., & Ore, G.D. (1955). Syndrome of Kluver and Bucy reproduced in man by bilateral removal of the temporal lobes. *Neurology 5,* 373–380.

Thomas, A., & Chess, S. (1977). *Temperament and Development.* New York: Brunner/Mazel.

Thomas, A., & Chess, S. (1982). Temperament and follow-up to adulthood. In Ciba Foundation Symposium 89, *Temperamental Differences in Infants and Young Children.* London: Pitman, pp.168–175.

Thorndike, E.L. (1911). *Animal Intelligence.* New York: Macmillan.

Thornhill, R., & Thornhill, N.W. (1989). The evolution of psychological pain. In R. Bell (Ed.), *Sociobiology and the Social Sciences* (pp.73–103). Lubbock, TX: Texas Technical University Press.

Tinbergen, N. (1951). *The Study of Instinct.* Oxford: Clarendon Press.

Tomaszuk, A., Simpson, C., & Williams, G. (1996). Neuropeptide Y, the hypothalamus and the regulation of energy homeostasis. *Hormone Research, 46,* 53–58.

Towbin, E.J. (1949). Gastric distention as a factor in the satiation of thirst in esophagostomized dogs. *American Journal of Physiology, 159,* 533–541.

Trentini, G.P., Mess, B., De Gaetani, C.F., & Ruzsas, C. (1979). Pineal-brain relationship. *Progress in Brain Research, 52,* 341–367.

Trivers, R. (1971). The evolution by reciprocal altruism. *The Quarterly Review of Biology, 46,* 35–47.

Trivers, R. (1972). Parental investment and sexual selection. In B. Campbell (Ed.), *Sexual Selection and the Descent of Man* (pp. 136–179). Chicago: Aldine.

Tversky, A., & Shafir, E. (1992). Choice under conflict: The dynamics of deferred decision. *Psychological Science, 3,* 358–361.

Tylor, E.B. (1871). *Primitive Culture.* London: Murray.

Udry, J.R., & Morris, N.M. (1968). Distribution of coitus in the menstrual cycle. *Nature, 220,* 593–596.

United Nations (1995). *Demographic Yearbook—1993.* New York: United Nations.

Urca, G., Segev, S., & Sarne, Y. (1985). Stress-induced analgesia: Its opioid nature depends on the strain of rat but not on the mode of induction. *Brain Research, 343,* 216–222.

Ursin, H., & Kaada, B.R. (1960). Functional localization within the amygdaloid complex in the cat. *Electroencephalography and Clinical Neurology, 12,* 1–20.

Valenstein, E.S. (1973). *Brain Control.* New York: Wiley.

Valentine, C.W. (1930). The innate basis of fear. *Journal of Genetic Psychology, 37,* 394–419.

Valunjkar, T.M. (1966). *Social Organization, Migration and Change in a Village Community.* Ph.D. Dissertation from Deccan College, Poona, India.

van Abeelen, J.H.F., & van der Kroon, P.H.W. (1967). *Nijmegen waltzer:* A new neurological mutant in the mouse. *Genetical Research, 10,* 117–118.

Vandenbergh, J.G. (1967). Effect of the presence of a male on the social maturation of female mice. *Endocrinology, 81,* 345–359.

Vandenbergh, J.G. (1988). Pheromones and mammalian reproduction. In E. Knobil & J. Neill (Eds.), *The Physiology of Reproduction* (pp. 1679–1696). New York: Raven Press.

Vandenheede, M., & Bouissou, M.F. (1993). Effect of androgen treatment on fear reactions in ewes. *Hormones and Behavior, 27,* 435–448.

Van Dyke, C., & Kaufman, I.C. (1983). Psychobiology of bereavement. In L. Temoshok, C. Van Dyke, & L.S. Zegans (Eds.), *Emotions in Health and Illness: Theoretical and Research Foundations* (pp. 37–49). New York: Grune & Stratton.

Van Goozen, S.H.M., Cohen-Kettenis, P.T., Gooren, L.J.G., Frijda, N.H., & Van de Poll, N.E. (1995). Gender differences in behaviour: Activating effects of cross-sex hormones. *Psychoneuroendocrinology, 20,* 343–363.

Van Goozen, S.H.M., Frijda, N.H., Wiegant, V.M., Endert, E., & Van de Poll, N.E. (1996). The premenstrual phase and reactions to aversive events. *Psychoneuroendocrinology, 21,* 479–497.

van Velzen, W.J. (1975). Autoplexy or self-destruction in mental retardation. In D.A.A. Primrose, (Ed.), *Proceedings of the Third Congress of the International Association for the Scientific Study of Mental Deficiency.* Warsaw: Polish Medical Publishers.

Vayda, A.P. (1974). Warfare in ecological perspective. *Annual Review of Ecology and Systematics, 5,* 183–193.

Veith, J.L., Buck, M., Getzlaf, S., Van Dalfsen, P., & Slade, S. (1983). Exposure to men influences the occurrence of ovulation in women. *Physiology and Behavior, 31,* 313–315.

Virkkunen, M. (1988). Cerebrospinal fluid: Monoamines among habitually violent and impulsive offenders. In T.E. Moffitt & S.A. Mednick (Eds.), *Biological Contributions to Crime Causation* (pp. 147–157). Boston: Martinus Nijhoff.

Vodanovich, S.J., & Kass, S.J. (1990). Age and gender differences in boredom proneness. *Journal of Social Behavior and Personality, 5,* 297–307.

vom Saal, F.S., & Bronson, F.H. (1980). Sexual characteristics of adult female mice are correlated with their blood testosterone levels during prenatal development. *Science, 208,* 597–599.

Wadhera, S., & Millar, W.J. (1996). Pregnancy outcomes. *Health Reports* (Statistics Canada), *8*(1), 7–15.

Wagatsuma, H. (1981). Child abandonment and infanticide: A Japanese case. In J.E. Korbine (Ed.), *Child Abuse and Neglect* (pp. 120–138). Berkeley: University of California Press.

Wall, P.D. (1979). On the relationship of injury to pain. *Pain, 6,* 253–264.

Wall, P.D., Melzack, R., & Bonica, J.J. (1994). *Textbook of Pain* (3rd ed.). Edinburgh: Churchill-Livingstone.

Wallerstein, J.S. (1991). The long-term effects of divorce on children: A review. *Journal of the American Academy of Child and Adolescent Psychiatry, 30,* 349–360.

Ward, I.L. (1972). Prenatal stress feminizes and demasculinizes the behavior of males. *Science, 175,* 82–84.

Warwick, Z.S. (1996). Probing the causes of high-fat diet hyperphagia: a mechanistic and behavioral dissection. *Neuroscience and Biobehavioral Reviews, 20,* 155–161.

Washburn, S.L., & Hamburg, D.A. (1965). The study of primate behavior. In I. DeVore (Ed.), *Primate Behavior: Field Studies of Monkeys and Apes* (pp. 1–13). New York: Holt, Rinehart and Winston.

Watson, J.B. (1930). *Behaviorism.* Chicago: University of Chicago Press.

Watt, J.D., & Vodanovich, S.J. (1992). Relationship between boredom proneness and impulsivity. *Psychological Reports, 70,* 688–690.

Waxenberg, S.E., Drellich, M.G., & Sutherland, A.M. (1959). The role of hormones in human behavior. I. Changes in female sexuality after adrenalectomy. *Journal of Clinical Endocrinology, 19,* 193–202.

Weathers, F.W., Litz, B.T., & Keane, T.M. (1995). Military trauma. In J.R. Freedy & S.E. Hobfoll (Eds.), *Traumatic Stress: From Theory to Practice* (pp. 103–128). New York: Plenum Press.

Weiderman, M.W., & Allgeier, E.R. (1992). Gender differences in sexual jealousy: Adaptationist or social learning explanation? *Ethology and Sociobiology, 14,* 115–140.

Weingarten, H.P. (1996). Cytokines and food intake: The relevance of the immune system to the student of ingestive behavior. *Neuroscience and Biobehavioral Reviews, 20,* 163–170.

Weingarten, H.P., & Kulikovsky, O.T. (1989). Taste-to-postingestive consequence conditioning: Is the rise in sham feeding with repeated experience a learning phenomenon? *Physiology and Behavior, 45,* 471–476.

Weinrich, J.D. (1987). A new sociobiological theory of homosexuality applicable to societies with universal marriage. *Ethology and Sociobiology, 8,* 37–47.

Weisfeld, G.E. (1993). The adaptive value of humor and laughter. *Ethology and Sociobiology, 14,* 141–169.

Weisfeld, G.E., & Berger, J.M. (1983). Some features of human adolescence viewed in evolutionary perspective. *Human Development, 26,* 121–133.

Weiss, J.M. (1971). Effects of coping behavior with and without a feedback signal on stress pathology in rats. *Journal of Comparative and Physiological Psychology*, *77*, 22–30.

Weisz, J., & Ward, I.L. (1980). Plasma testosterone and progesterone titers of pregnant rats, their male and female fetuses and neonatal offspring. *Endocrinology*, *106*, 306–316.

Welch, A.S., & Welch, B.L. (1971). Isolation, reactivity, and aggression: Evidence for involvement of brain catecholamines and serotonin. In B.E. Eleftheriou & J.P. Scott (Eds.), *The Physiology of Aggression and Defeat* (pp. 91–142). New York: Plenum Press.

Welch, B.L., & Welch, A.S. (1969). Fighting: Preferential lowering of norepinephrine and dopamine in the brainstem, concomitant with a depletion of epinephrine from the adrenal medulla. *Communications in Behavioral Biology*, *3*, 125–130.

West, M. (1974). Social play in the domestic cat. *American Zoologist*, *14*, 427–436.

Whalen, R.E., Beach, F.A., & Kuehn, R.E. (1961). Effects of exogenous androgen on sexually responsive and unresponsive male rats. *Endocrinology*, *69*, 373–380.

Whalen, R.E., Luttge, W.G., & Gorzalka, B.B. (1971). Neonatal androgenization and the development of estrogen responsivity in male and female rats. *Hormones and Behavior*, *2*, 83–90.

White, B.W., & Martin, R.J. (1997). Evidence for a central mechanism of obesity in the Zucker rat: Role of neuropeptide Y and leptin. *Proceedings of the Society for Experimental Biology and Medicine*, *214*, 222–232.

Whitten, W.K. (1956). Modification of the oestrous cycle of the mouse by external stimuli associated with the male. *Journal of Endocrinology*, *13*, 399–404.

Wicks-Nelson, R., & Israel, A.C. (1997). *Behavior Disorders of Childhood* (3rd ed.). Upper Saddle River, NJ: Prentice Hall.

Wilcott, R.C. (1966). Adaptive value of arousal sweating and the epidermal mechanism related to skin potential and skin resistance. *Psychophysiology*, *2*, 249–262.

Wilkie, D.M., MacLennan, A.J., & Pinel, J.P.J. (1979). Rat defensive behavior: Burying noxious food. *Journal of the Experimental Analysis of Behavior*, *31*, 299–306.

Wilkins, K. (1995). Causes of death: How the sexes differ. *Health Reports* (Statistics Canada), *7*, 33–43.

Willard, F.H. (1993). *Medical Neuroanatomy*. Philadelphia: J.B. Lippincott Company.

Williams, G.C. (1957). Pleiotropy, natural selection, and the evolution of senescence. *Evolution*, *11*, 398–411.

Wilson, E.O. (1971). *The Insect Societies*. Cambridge, MA: Harvard University Press.

Wilson, E.O. (1975). *Sociobiology*. Cambridge, MA: Harvard University Press.

Wilson, E.O. (1978). *On Human Nature*. Cambridge, MA.: Harvard University Press.

Wilson, T.D., & Schooler, J.W. (1991). Thinking too much: Introspection can reduce the quality of preferences and decisions. *Journal of Personality and Social Psychology*, *60*, 181–192.

Winchel, R.M., & Stanley, M. (1991). Self-injurious behavior: A review of the behavior and biology of self-mutilation. *American Journal of Psychiatry*, *148*, 306–317.

Wittling, W., & Pflüger, M. (1990). Neuroendocrine hemisphere asymmetries: Salivary cortisol during lateralized viewing of emotion-related and neutral films. *Brain and Cognition*, *14*, 243–265.

Wolpe, J. (1958). *Psychotherapy by Reciprocal Inhibition*. Stanford, CA: Stanford University Press.

Woods, S.C., Chavez, M., Park, C.R., Riedy, C., Kaiyala, K., Richardson, R.D., Figlewicz, D.P., Schwartz, M.W., Porte, D., Jr., & Seeley, R.J. (1996). The evaluation of insulin as a metabolic signal influencing behavior via the brain. *Neuroscience and Biobehavioral Reviews, 20,* 139–144.

World Health Organization (1995). *World Health Statistics Annual—1994.* Geneva: World Health Organization.

Wrangham, R.W. (1993). The evolution of sexuality in chimpanzees and bonobos. *Human Nature, 4,* 47–79.

Wright, S. (1922). Coefficients of interbreeding and relationship. *American Naturalist, 56,* 330–339.

Wyrwicka, W. (1988). *Brain and Feeding Behavior.* Springfield, IL: Charles C Thomas.

Zajonc, B. (1980). Preferences without inferences. *American Psychologist, 35,* 151–175.

Zeskind, P.S. (1985). A developmental perspective of infant crying. In B.M. Lester & C.F. Boukydis (Eds.), *Infant Crying: Theoretical and Research Perspectives* (pp. 159–185). New York, Plenum Press.

Zeskind, P.S., & Iacino, R. (1984). Effects of maternal visitation to preterm infants in the neonatal intensive care unit. *Child Development, 55,* 1887–1893.

Zuckerman, M. (1984). Sensation seeking: A comparative approach to a human trait. *The Behavioral and Brain Sciences, 7,* 413–471.

Zuckerman, M.K., Kolin, E.A., Price, L., & Zoob, I. (1964). Development of a sensation seeking scale. *Journal of Consulting Psychology, 28,* 477–482.

Author Index

Subject Index